.NET Programming

A Practical Guide Using C#

ISBN 0-13-066945-8

9 790130 669451

Hewlett-Packard® Professional Books

OPERATING SYSTEMS

Diercks	MPE/iX System Administration Handbook
Fernandez	Configuring CDE: The Common Desktop Environment
Lund	Integrating UNIX and PC Network Operating Systems
Madell	Disk and File Management Tasks on HP-UX
Mosberger, Eranian	IA-64 Linux Kernel: Design and Implementation
Poniatowski	HP-UX Virtual Partitions
Poniatowski	HP-UX 11i System Administration Handbook and Toolkit
Poniatowski	HP-UX 11.x System Administration Handbook and Toolkit
Poniatowski	HP-UX 11.x System Administration "How To" Book
Poniatowski	HP-UX System Administration Handbook and Toolkit
Poniatowski	Learning the HP-UX Operating System
Poniatowski	UNIX User's Handbook, Second Edition
Rehman	HP Certified, HP-UX System Administration
Roberts	UNIX and Windows 2000 Interoperability Guide
Sauers, Weygant	HP-UX Tuning and Performance
Stone, Symons	UNIX Fault Management
Weygant	Clusters for High Availability: A Primer of HP Solutions, Second Edition
Wong	HP-UX 11i Security

ONLINE/INTERNET

Amor	The E-business (R)evolution: Living and Working in an Interconnected World, Second Edition
Caldwell	Fast Track to Profit: An Insider's Guide to Exploiting the World's Best Internet Technologies
Greenberg, Lakeland	A Methodology for Developing and Deploying Internet and Intranet Solutions
Greenberg, Lakeland	Building Professional Web Sites with the Right Tools
Klein	Building Enhanced HTML Help with DHTML and CSS
Werry, Mowbray	Online Communities: Commerce, Community Action, and the Virtual University

NETWORKING/COMMUNICATIONS

Blommers	OpenView Network Node Manager: Designing and Implementing an Enterprise Solution
Blommers	Practical Planning for Network Growth
Bruce, Dempsey	Security in Distributed Computing: Did You Lock the Door?
Lucke	Designing and Implementing Computer Workgroups

.NET Programming

A Practical Guide Using C#

Pradeep Tapadiya

Hewlett-Packard Company

www.hp.com/hpbooks

Prentice Hall PTR
Upper Saddle River, New Jersey 07458
www.phptr.com

Library of Congress Cataloging-in-Publication Data

A CIP catalog record for this book can be obtained from the Library of Congress.

Editorial/production supervision: *MetroVoice Publishing Services*
Cover design director: *Jerry Votta*
Cover design: *Talar Boorujy*
Buyer: *Maura Zaldivar*
Executive editor: *Jill Harry*
Editorial assistant: *Jeanie Joe*
Marketing manager: *Dan DePasquale*
Full-service production manager: *Anne R. Garcia*

Publisher, Hewlett-Packard Books: *Patricia Pekary*

© 2002 by Hewlett-Packard Company

Published by Pearson Education Inc.
Publishing as Prentice Hall PTR
Upper Saddle River, New Jersey 07458

Prentice Hall books are widely used by corporations and government agencies for training, marketing, and resale. For information regarding corporate and government bulk discounts please contact: Corporate and Government Sales (800) 382-3419 or corpsales@pearsontechgroup.com

Printed in the United States of America

10   9   8   7   6   5   4   3   2   1

ISBN 0-13-066945-8

Pearson Education Ltd.
Pearson Education Australia PTY Ltd.
Pearson Education Singapore, Pte. Ltd.
Pearson Education North Asia Ltd.
Pearson Education Canada, Ltd.
Pearson Educación de Mexico, S.A. de C.V.
Pearson Education—Japan
Pearson Education Malaysia, Pte. Ltd.

Contents

4 Essentials of the .NET Framework   111

5 Programming with the Base Class Library   163

8 Concurrency   319

9 Security   355

Introduction

Computing lifestyles and development needs change with time. Over the years, a number of paradigms and programming methodologies have been offered to support the needs of the developers and software vendors.

In the mid 1990s we saw monolithic applications being broken into smaller applications that communicated with each other. To facilitate code reusability and application communication across compiler boundaries and programming language boundaries, Microsoft introduced a framework called Component Object Model (COM). To further facilitate the communication across machine boundaries, Microsoft extended the model to Distributed COM (DCOM).

The late 1990s witnessed an incredible explosion of the Internet that caused a revolution in the way information was made available to the users. In developing enterprise systems, the traditional client/server model was replaced by a three-tier programming model, enhanced for Internet applications. Developing such enterprise systems was a time- and resource-consuming affair, as the systems had to meet extra enterprise-level requirements such as scalability, robustness, security, transaction support, and so on. To help developers meet these challenges, Microsoft introduced COM+, an advanced runtime environment that ran on Microsoft Windows 2000. Developers could now leverage the services provided by COM+ instead of building the services themselves.

In the new millennium, the Internet is evolving from a collection of isolated Web sites and applications into a general "communication bus" for distributed applications that can run on various hardware and operation system (OS) platforms.

Microsoft's .NET platform is based around this vision.

As part of the .NET initiative, Microsoft has provided a framework and some tools that developers can use to build applications targeting .NET platform.

Although .NET achieves many of the same goals that COM does, make no mistake—.NET is a radically new platform. The programming model has been an evolution over COM, but the framework implementation is completely different. However, the enterprise system needs (e.g., scalability, transaction support, etc.) haven't changed much. Therefore, many COM+ services have found their way into .NET.

This book focuses on understanding .NET architecture from a developer's perspective and building .NET applications primarily using C#, a new programming language that offers the flexibility of C++ and the simplicity of Visual Basic.

ABOUT THIS BOOK

The purpose of writing this book is twofold:

1. To help you understand .NET architecture in detail.
2. To explore the services provided by the .NET Framework in building enterprise-level applications.

To achieve the first goal, a hands-on approach is employed in this book. As we progress through unfolding .NET technology, I present a key concept, accompanied by code samples as necessary.

The second goal is to use .NET productively in building enterprise-level applications. Enterprise-level requirements include security, transaction support, scalability, dealing with concurrency, distributed three-tier computing, dealing with legacy code, and so on. This book seeks to do the following:

- Provide an in-depth analysis of all aspects of .NET technologies related to enterprise-level application development.
- Provide ideas to develop robust .NET applications.
- Provide programming code to achieve common .NET programming tasks.
- Provide concise, complete sample programs to illustrate the concepts presented.

I have tried to present the material such that it makes interesting reading for developers. Not only can developers gain an in-depth knowledge of .NET platform, but they can also get familiar with programming in other related technologies such as SOAP, XML, ADO.NET, and ASP.NET.

The book starts with an overview of .NET platform from a nontechnical perspective. Then I progress through unfolding the .NET architecture and services. Wherever applicable, code samples are provided to illustrate and explain the concepts. This book provides enough sample code to enable readers to be more productive and to carry out further research.

Throughout the book, I have identified important points and tips for effective .NET programming. The pad-and-pencil icon marks important notes:

 An Important Note

The light bulb icon flags tips:

 A Tip

INTENDED AUDIENCE

The intended audience includes the following groups:

- Software developers and engineers who are involved in developing software products for the Windows platform and typically use C++ or Visual Basic as their programming language.
- Managers who actively supervise a software product.
- Computer science students. Today, more and more companies expect job candidates to understand COM and COM+ technologies. Senior students and graduate students are becoming more aware of COM technology as a software engineering discipline. The next logical step for them would be to start programming in .NET.

CHOICE OF PROGRAMMING LANGUAGE

A vast majority of the .NET programming community will be using C# for developing .NET applications. As a matter of fact, a large part of the .NET

Framework has been developed in C#. Hence, I chose C# to present samples in most cases. However, in some instances I have used Visual Basic.NET or another language that is appropriate for the given situation.

PREREQUISITES

The most important prerequisite for this book is a willingness to learn.

The book is written for intermediate to advanced developers. It is assumed that readers have a working knowledge of the following:

- C++ or Java programming languages.
- Windows 2000 operating system.

Note that knowledge of C# is helpful but not mandatory, as long as you are familiar with C++ or Java. As we go through developing sample code, I am confident readers will automatically pick up adequate information about the language.

SAMPLE CODE

All the examples provided in the book are concise and complete. For brevity, I sometimes show only the relevant code sample in the book. However, complete source code is available on the companion Web site. All the examples and tools have been compiled with Microsoft Visual C# 1.0 and the .NET Framework Software Development Kit (SDK), and have been tested on Windows 2000 SP2 and Windows XP.

The samples are organized by chapters. Each sample is built as a separate project. A project can be compiled either from Visual Studio .NET or from the command-line makefile. The makefile can be found in the bin directory under each project, except for Chapter 2. In order to illustrate some key compiler concepts, Chapter 2 contains the makefile in the same directory as the project.

Note that Visual Studio .NET requires that a project belongs to a solution. The project file has an extension .csproj and the solution file has an extension .sln.

In order to build the projects from the command line, you need to set up proper paths in the environment. If you have installed Visual Studio .NET, then you can use the command-line link that is provides called the "Visual Studio .NET Command Prompt." This link initializes the environment for the command window such that the .NET Framework SDK tools can be accessed from the command line.

REFERENCES

This book frequently refers to other books, Microsoft's Knowledge Base articles, articles from various journals, and Microsoft's Developers Network (MSDN) Library. All the references for a particular chapter are listed at the end of that chapter. Each reference entry is indexed by a keyword that uses a combination of author's last name and year the reference was published. For example, Don Box's book *Essential COM*, which was published in 1998, is indexed as [Box-98]. In the book, each time I cite a reference, I use the relevant keyword.

CHAPTER ORGANIZATION

The book is divided into two parts. The first part, Chapters 1–5, focuses on the fundamentals of .NET Programming Model and shows how to develop .NET-based applications.

The second part, Chapters 6–10, focuses on the services provided by .NET. Each chapter focuses on a specific aspect of .NET. These chapters are largely independent of each other.

Chapter 1: What is .NET?

.NET is Microsoft's new initiative for building applications regardless of the platforms or languages in use. The .NET label applies to three distinct but related items: a vision for how information technology (IT) will evolve, a software platform to build .NET applications, and an application-hosting business designed to support the vision and market the platform. In this chapter, we inspect each of these items from a fairly nontechnical perspective. By the end of the chapter, the readers will have a good idea of where Microsoft is going with the .NET initiative and will understand the terminology, features, and services offered by the .NET Framework, the software platform for .NET applications.

Chapter 2: From C++ to C#

This chapter focuses on various stages of building .NET applications—from development to debugging and deploying. You will write simple C# programs to explore common programming paradigms under the .NET Framework. In the process, you will learn the differences and similarities between C++ and C#. By the end of the chapter, readers will understand many key concepts of the .NET Framework and will be fairly comfortable developing simple .NET applications using C#.

Chapter 3: Assemblies

Under .NET, assemblies form the fundamental building block of program components. In defining the format for the assembly, .NET had many goals. These goals included interoperability among different programming languages, side-by-side execution of multiple versions of the same assembly, performance enhancements, and so on. In this chapter, we take an in-depth look at the assemblies and examine how these goals were achieved. By the end of the chapter, you will have a good knowledge of the assembly internals and the packaging and deployment model under .NET.

Chapter 4: Essentials of the .NET Framework

In this chapter, we examine the facilities that the .NET Framework provides to load and execute the code and provide services to the executing code. We start with an overview of various components that constitute the .NET Framework. Then we look at the overall process of managed code execution. We will see how .NET applications can be administratively controlled using external configuration files and how the configuration mechanism can be extended to store custom settings. We then look at the type system used by the common language runtime and examine the memory and performance considerations of using reference types versus value types. We examine how the CLS provides for cross-language interoperability. We look at how the execution engine validates the metadata, verifies the MSIL code for type-safety, and performs JIT compilation on the MSIL code. Finally, we look at the automatic memory management features of the runtime and how it simplifies or complicates programming under .NET. By the end of the chapter, you will have a good understanding of .NET architecture and how it helps in producing robust applications that can potentially be reused by any programming language under .NET. You will also learn the strategies of generating efficient code.

Chapter 5: Programming with the Base Class Library

The .NET BCL includes hundreds of classes that provide a number of useful services to help developers boost their productivity. In this chapter, we look at how to solve many common programming tasks using these classes. By the end of the chapter, you will become familiar with many important classes under the .NET Framework.

Chapter 6: Distributed Computing

In this chapter, we look at how to develop distributed applications under .NET that can communicate within intranets as well as over the Internet. We will see how .NET remoting offers seamless remote activation and remote method calls, among other things. We examine how to develop intranet applications using this support. Over the Internet, Web services have become the building blocks for distributed Web-based applications. We will look at the support offered by ASP.NET to create and deploy Web services. By the end of this chapter, readers will be comfortable developing applications using the common language runtime object-remoting and will be fairly conversant with ASP.NET Web services development.

Chapter 7: Interoperability

The .NET Framework provides support for managed code to interoperate with unmanaged code. The unmanaged code could either be COM-based or be in native DLLs. The .NET Framework has been designed to provide smooth interoperability. In this chapter, we examine the support for interoperability provided by the .NET Framework. By the end of the chapter, readers will be comfortable making calls from managed code into unmanaged code and vice versa.

Chapter 8: Concurrency

Under Windows, and most other modern OSs, a process can execute multiple threads concurrently, each of which carry out a specific task. The .NET Framework supports developing multithreaded applications in two ways—by supporting the creation and use of threads and by providing a mechanism to make asynchronous calls. In this chapter, we examine both these techniques in detail. We also look at various issues involved with multithread programming and the support provided by the .NET Framework in developing classes that are safe from concurrent access.

Chapter 9: Security

The .NET Framework offers two security mechanisms—code access security and role-based security. Both security mechanisms are built on top of the security provided by the underlying OS. Code access security keeps track of where the assemblies come from and what security permissions should be granted to them. Role-based security enables the code to make security decisions based on the role of the user executing the code.

In this chapter, we look at the concepts underlying code access security and role-based security. We also examine the classes and services provided by the .NET Framework to facilitate the use of these security mechanisms.

Security is also an important consideration for ASP.NET applications. ASP.NET applications need to authenticate clients and provide restricted access to any sensitive data, based on the client credentials. In addition, the ASP.NET applications may also have to act on behalf of the client in some cases to access OS secured resources such as NTFS files. In this chapter, we also examine various security features that ASP.NET provides to deal with authentication, authorization, and impersonation..

Chapter 10: Enterprise Services

Enterprise system development has historically been a very time- and resource-consuming process. The development complexity arises from the extra enterprise-level requirements such as scalability, robustness, security, automatic transaction processing, and so on.

The .NET Framework provides many infrastructural services to meet the needs of enterprise systems. This allows businesses to focus on their core competencies instead of building the plumbing themselves.

In this chapter, we examine in detail some important requirements for enterprise systems and the services provided by .NET to meet these requirements.

COMPANION WEB SITE

The companion Web site (*www.phptr.com/tapadiya/dotnet/*) contains the source code for all the examples in the book, arranged by chapters. For the most up-to-date information, see the read-me file at the Web site.

AUTHOR BIOGRAPHY

Pradeep Tapadiya is a lead software architect at the OpenView R&D Division of Hewlett-Packard in Roseville, CA, and has been working with Microsoft enterprise development technologies since 1996. He holds a doctoral degree in Computer Science from Texas A&M University. Tapadiya is also the author *of COM+ Programming—A Practical Guide Using Visual C++ and ATL.* Tapadiya can be reached at pradeep@tapadiya.net.

Acknowledgments

First of all, I'd like to thank Kent Sharkey, Microsoft Technical Evangelist for the .NET Framework, who provided me with valuable feedback by critically reviewing the technical contents of the book.

There were many people who helped me review my manuscript over the course of writing the book. I'd especially like to thank Mihir Dalal and Sanjay Mehta (my colleagues at Hewlett-Packard), and Terrance Simkin (Professor, Computer Engineering Technology, New Hampshire Technical Institute) who offered me valuable suggestions on presenting my thoughts and ideas.

A round of gratitude is also due for the following folks for helping me with technology-specific questions—Stacey Giard and Connie Sullivan (Managers, Microsoft .NET Authors Web Community), Paddy Srinivasan (Microsoft), Ranjeeth Ramakrishnan (Microsoft), Ron Jacobs (Microsoft), Shajan Dasan (Microsoft), Kit George (Microsoft), Steven Pratschner (Microsoft), Brad Adams (Microsoft), Jim Hogg (Microsoft), Michael Day (Microsoft), Paul Harrington (Microsoft) and Juval Lowy (Author).

I'd like to thank David Wilkie, my direct manager at Hewlett Packard, and Russ Daniels (Hewlett Packard) for providing support and encouragement to write the book.

I'd also like to thank the editorial team at Prentice Hall PTR and Hewltt-Packard Press—Jill Harry (Executive Editor), Anne Garcia (Production Editor), Jim Markham (Developmental Editor), Pat Pekary (Publisher and Manager, HP Books), and Scott Suckling (MetroVoice Publishing Services).

Finally, and most important of all, I'd like to thank my wife Vrushali and my 3-year old son Jay, both of whom patiently stood by me despite the fact that I broke my promise of spending more time with them.

PART I

What Is .NET?

$\mathbf{N}$ET is Microsoft's new initiative for building applications regardless of the platforms or languages in use. The .NET label applies to three distinct but related items: a vision for how information technology (IT) will evolve, a software platform to build .NET applications, and an application-hosting business designed to support the vision and market the platform. In this chapter, we inspect each of these items from a fairly nontechnical perspective. By the end of the chapter, the readers will have a good idea of where Microsoft is going with the .NET initiative and will understand the terminology, features, and services offered by the .NET Framework, the software platform for .NET applications.

INTRODUCTION

In June 2000, Microsoft announced the .NET initiative—a major shift in the technical direction for Microsoft and a major shift for those engaged in developing software based on Microsoft tools and technologies.

The label .NET has been applied to three distinct entities. They are:

1. A vision of how software will evolve to take advantage of the Internet and encompass the increasing variety of computing devices that are joining the PC in customers' offices, pockets, and homes.

2. A software platform to help developers build such applications and also to address some long-time shortcomings of Windows.

3. An application-hosting business that will deliver applications as services over the Internet.

In the rest of the chapter, we examine these three ideas in detail.

THE VISION

The Web has evolved a long way from browsing static Hypertext Markup Language (HTML) pages. Today, users can download music, participate in auctions, buy items online, and even talk to their family face-to-face over the Internet. Even businesses are not behind. They have been implementing business-to-business (B2B) and business-to-consumer (B2C) applications that communicate over the Internet.

Microsoft believes that the Internet will evolve from a collection of isolated Web sites and applications into a general "communication bus" for distributed applications. Individual parts of the distributed application could be running on different hardware and software platforms. The computing devices include your desktop systems as well as mobile devices such as cellular phones, Pocket PCs, personal digital assistants (PDAs), and so on. Even household appliances such as microwaves and dishwashers will participate in this communication over the Internet.

Web Services

To be fair, this vision of anytime, anywhere, any-device computing is also shared by many other software companies, such as IBM and Hewlett-Packard, and many respected computer scientists around the world. A key technology enabler for this distributed computing model is Web services. A *Web service* can be defined as a service that can be accessed programmatically over the Web. Companies can make their business applications available as Web services. These Web services, for example, can be used to integrate applications within various divisions of the same company. The Web services can also be used to automate communication over the Internet between two companies.

To be able to develop distributed applications that transcend geographical, hardware, and OS boundaries, Web services need to be based on universally accepted standards. Table 1.1 lays out the foundation elements of Web services.

TABLE 1.1.   Web Services Foundation

Standard	Purpose
Internet	Ubiquitous communication
Extensible Markup Language (XML)	Universal data format
Simple Object Access Protocol (SOAP)	Communication protocol
Web Services Description Language (WSDL)	Describe the semantics of the methods available on a Web service
Universal Description, Discovery, and Integration (UDDI)	Publish and find Web services

In the "anywhere computing" vision, clients that wish to access Web services can be geographically distant from the servers. As the Internet has a broad geographical reach, it makes sense to deliver the services over the Internet.

To develop distributed client–server applications that transcend hardware and OS boundaries, Extensible Markup Language (XML) has been accepted as the universal language for defining data formats. XML provides a common data format that does not require business partners or customers to use a particular programming language, application, OS, or hardware.

XML by itself is not enough to achieve the client–server communication. To access a Web service, a client has to make a procedural call to the server, pass in the needed parameters, and get back the return value. A protocol has to be defined for such an exchange of information. To this effect, the W3C[1] has defined a protocol called Simple Object Access Protocol (SOAP). SOAP is a lightweight protocol for exchange of information in a decentralized, distributed environment. It specifies how a remote procedure call can be expressed in XML format. It is an XML-based protocol that consists of three parts:

1. An envelope that defines a framework for describing what is in a message and how to process it.

2. A set of encoding rules for expressing instances of application-defined data types.

3. A convention for representing remote procedure calls and responses.

Although the SOAP specification is independent of the underlying transport protocol, Hypertext Transport Protocol (HTTP) has been the sweet spot for the industry. Most companies let HTTP traffic pass through the firewall. Contrast this to other distributed object technologies such as Distributed Component Object Model (DCOM) and Common Object Request Broker Architecture (CORBA) that require opening ports on the firewall, thus compromising security.

Also note that although the client and the server can communicate with each other using raw SOAP packets, helper utilities are available on most platforms to hide the grunge work of creating SOAP packets:

1. The client makes a method call passing in the required parameters.

---

1. The World Wide Web Consortium (W3C) is a standards body that develops specifications to promote the evolution of the Web. More information on W3C can be found at *www.w3.org*.

2. A helper utility on the client side packages the method call and its parameters into a SOAP-compliant XML format and sends the SOAP packet to
   the remote server over a network protocol, preferably HTTP.

3. A helper utility on the server side unpackages the SOAP packet and calls
   the actual method, passing in the method parameters. On returning from
   the method, the utility repackages the return value into a SOAP packet
   and sends it back to the client.

4. The client-side utility unpackages the SOAP packet and returns the value
   to the client.

From a programming perspective, using the SOAP helper utilities makes
calling a method to a remote system as simple as making a local method call.

Why is SOAP important? Because it provides the foundational invocation mechanism for application-to-application computing, irrespective of the
underlying hardware or operating system platforms.

The SOAP specification is a work in progress. The current draft of the
specification can be found at W3C's Web site [W3C-01].

Now we know how to make method calls on a Web service programmatically. However, we still don't know what methods are available as part
of the Web service. We need a mechanism that describes the programmatic
"interface" of the Web service; that is, the methods available on the Web
service, the parameters for each method, and the return value of each
method. A popular choice is to define this interface in Web Services
Description Language (WSDL), an XML-based language that lets you
express the functions and formats supported at any endpoint of the service.
This programmatic interface is referred to as the *contract* of the Web service.

At this point, we know how to obtain method information on a Web service and how to make the method call. The remaining problem is to identify
the server running the Web service.

It is likely that in some cases the server is known to the client. However,
it is possible that the client is not particularly happy with the quality of the
service or the cost of accessing the service, and may wish to use a different
server. The beauty of the Web services programming model is that it doesn't
matter which server provides the service, as long as the server adheres to the
Web service contract. Coding-wise, all that is needed is to point to the right
server. There is no change required to the rest of the code.

An industry-wide effort is underway to promote e-commerce among
businesses. This project, called Universal Description, Discovery, and Inte-

gration (UDDI[2]), is an initiative to create an open framework for describing Web services, discovering businesses, and integrating business services over the Internet. UDDI enables business applications to do the following:

1. Discover each other.
2. Define how they interact over the Internet.
3. Share information in a global registry that will more rapidly accelerate the global adoption of B2B e-commerce.

Essentially, UDDI provides the "yellow pages" on the Internet for the industry. UDDI has also embraced SOAP and WSDL, making it convenient to obtain information from its repository programmatically.

Note that standards such as XML, SOAP, WSDL, UDDI, and so on, are not proprietary to Microsoft, although Microsoft has been a major contributor in driving these standards.

Microsoft's .NET initiative is built around XML, SOAP, and WSDL. The .NET technology and tools make it easy for companies to develop Web services and to consume other Web services.

Heterogeneous Environment

It is possible that Web services and other future applications may run on a variety of computing devices, not just PCs or mainframes. These devices need not run the same operating system. Microsoft Windows is not the only choice for the OS. Therefore, jointly with Intel and Hewlett-Packard, Microsoft has submitted the core .NET Framework specifications to European Computer Manufacturer's Association (ECMA[3]).This ECMA specification is referred to as the Common Language Infrastructure (CLI). The CLI specifications are not wedded to any OS. The .NET runtime is Microsoft's implementation of the CLI for Windows OS. However, Microsoft has also made available the source code to a working implementation of ECMA CLI that builds and runs on FreeBSD, a variation of the UNIX OS. Currently, there are various other initiatives underway to implement CLI on other variations of UNIX such as Linux.

Among other things, the CLI also specifies that a CLI-compliant application must run on different platforms without being rewritten for each specific

---

2. Complete information on UDDI can be found at *www.uddi.org.*
3. ECMA is an international standards organization. Their purpose is to standardize information and communication systems. More information on ECMA can be found at *www.ecma.ch.*

platform. A .NET application, for example, can run on many processors and platforms (currently, only x86 compatible CPUs are supported) as long as no OS-specific calls are made. So, if things go as expected by various implementers of CLI, you will be able to take a .NET executable that is built on one OS and run it on many other Windows and non-Windows OSs.

Smart Devices

In the not so distant future, Microsoft expects that PCs will be joined by many new kinds of smart devices such as data-enabled wireless phones, handheld computers, tablet PCs, home appliances, and so on. If an application has to run on all these devices, the application will have to automatically adapt its user interface to the capabilities of the device it runs on. This not only means adapting to each device's display and input capabilities, but also supporting new modes of communication such as spoken language and hand-written text.

To support software development for the smart devices, Microsoft has announced to release a subset of the .NET Framework called the .NET Compact Framework.

Compelling User Experience

Microsoft believes that, in this new distributed computing world, the experience should be very simple and compelling for the end users. To provide such experience, Microsoft intends to host a set of foundation services or building-block services. These building-block services will act as a central repository of data for users, allowing them to store e-mail, calendar information, contacts, and other important data, and present this data as needed to other Web sites.

THE PLATFORM

Figure 1.1 shows an overview of the .NET platform.

The central component of the .NET platform is the .NET Framework. This consists of a runtime environment called the common language runtime and a set of supporting libraries. The runtime environment controls the installation, loading, and execution of .NET applications. The libraries provide code for common programming tasks, thus increasing developer productivity. The libraries also provide a layer over many OS APIs, providing an isolation from OS dependencies.

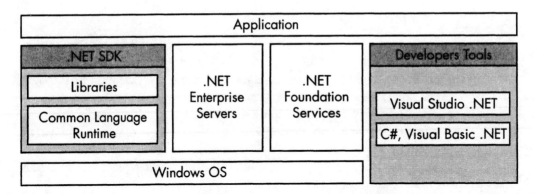

FIGURE 1.1 The .NET Platform.

Most enterprise applications and Web services require back-end servers to perform operations such as storing data, exchanging messages via e-mail, and so on. Microsoft's family of .NET servers such as SQL Server, Exchange Server, and so on, can be used to obtain such functionality. The family also includes some special servers that provide a higher level of integration and aggregation of Web services. BizTalk Server and Commerce Server, application frameworks for e-commerce, fall under this category.

The .NET platform also includes a set of developer tools such as Visual Studio .NET and programming languages such Visual Basic .NET and C# (pronounced *C sharp*).

In developing applications, developers can also take advantage of the foundation services offered by Microsoft or other software vendors. We take a look at a few important foundation services in a later section of this chapter.

Finally, the Windows operating system is at the base of the .NET platform. Operating systems such as Windows NT, Windows 2000, and Windows XP do not come preinstalled with the .NET Framework. However, one can install the framework separately by downloading it from Microsoft's Web site. Windows .NET and the newer releases of the Windows operating system are expected to ship with elements of the .NET vision.

THE .NET FRAMEWORK

The .NET Framework is a high-productivity, standards-based, multilanguage application execution environment. It consists of a runtime environment called the common language runtime and a set of libraries to boost programmers' productivity.

Common Language Runtime

The common language runtime, or just the runtime, is Microsoft's implementation of the ECMA CLI specification. When a .NET application is run, the common language runtime manages the loading and execution of the code and provides many runtime services to the application.

If you have been developing your code under COM, you will be surprised by the simplicity the .NET model offers. Forget dealing with GUIDs, CLSIDs, PROGIDs, IDL, type-libraries, apartments, server registration, `AddRef()`, `Release()`, and so on. They all have been replaced by a simpler model of programming.

It would not be fair to say that COM is dead. The basic tenet of COM, the ability for applications to communicate across hardware and programming language boundaries, is still present in .NET. In particular, the first release of the .NET Framework still depends on COM+ to provide enterprise services such as transaction and queuing. However, the COM infrastructure has certainly been replaced under .NET.

Besides providing a simpler model of communication, the .NET runtime provides many other services to simplify programming and to develop robust and secure applications. Any code that targets the .NET runtime is called the *managed code*—it can take advantage of the services offered by the .NET runtime. All other code, including existing legacy code, is called the *unmanaged code*. Although, the common language runtime can execute the unmanaged code, the code cannot avail the services provided by the common language runtime.

Let's examine some services provided by the common language runtime.

Simplified Deployment

In the simplest case, the directory hierarchy of an application can be copied to a machine and the application can be executed. There is no need to modify any registry entry. This is referred to as *XCOPY deployment*.

The framework also solves the "DLL hell" problem. A common problem with Windows is that upgrading a dynamic-link library (DLL) routinely breaks an already installed application. Under .NET, two versions of an application can execute side-by-side without breaking any application.

Hardware Independence

When a .NET application is built, the code is stored in a language called Microsoft Intermediate Language (MSIL). When the application is executed, the runtime performs a just-in-time (JIT) compilation to convert the MSIL code to machine instructions. This makes a .NET application run on any CPU type, as long as a JIT compiler is available for the CPU. Moreover, the JIT compiler can perform hardware-specific optimizations, boosting execution performance.

Automatic Memory Management

When writing managed code, developers need not worry about memory deallocation issues. The runtime automatically frees any unused memory using a mechanism called *garbage collection*. Not only does this simplify programming, but it also makes the application more robust; as programmers sometimes simply forget to free previously allocated memory.

Cross-Language Integration

The .NET Framework defines a specification called the Common Language Specification (CLS). Among other things, the CLS defines a set of data types that is intended to work across all .NET-compliant programming languages. If these data types are used, the runtime provides seamless integration between applications developed in different programming languages. The integration is so seamless that a type defined in one language can be inherited in another language. Even exceptions can be thrown from one language and caught in another language.

Metadata Driven

An application developed for .NET contains complete information about the types it implements, the methods each type defines, the parameters for each method, and so on. The presence of such metadata eliminates the need for COM-style IDL and type libraries. This also makes it possible to keep the Windows registry clean.

Enhanced Security

.NET defines a permission-based security model that offers fine-grained control over which assembly can access what resource on the local machine. The security becomes especially important when users access code over the Internet. The runtime prevents the executions of any unauthorized code.

Interoperability

The runtime provides the functionality to integrate with legacy COM servers. The runtime also provides the ability to invoke any unmanaged code or Windows APIs (although such an application may not be portable to other platforms).

Class Libraries

The .NET Framework also provides hundreds of types (classes, interfaces, structures, etc.) that not only enable programmatic access to the features of the common language runtime, but also provide a number of useful high-level services to help developers boost their productivity. These types are collectively referred to as the .NET Framework Class Library.

The .NET Framework Class Library can roughly be broken down into four groups—the Base Class Library (BCL), ADO.NET and XML, Windows Forms, and ASP.NET.

The BCL implements the set of functionality that is shared by all the applications targeting the .NET Framework. It defines and implements all the core data types (e.g., string, integer, float, etc.) used by every application.

ADO.NET is the successor to an earlier data access technology called Active Data Object (ADO). ADO.NET provides a set of classes to access and manipulate data. The data is typically obtained from a database and can be converted to XML for better remote manipulation.

Windows Forms (often called WinForms) provide features for developing standard Windows desktop applications. They provide a rich, unified set of controls and drawing functions for all languages, effectively wrapping Windows user interface (UI) APIs in such a way that developers rarely would need to access the Windows APIs directly.

ASP.NET is the successor to a Web-request processing technology called Active Server Pages (ASP). ASP.NET adds two significant enhancements to ASP:

1. It simplifies the process of developing Web services.

2. It provides a model of developing a Web browser-based UI called Web Forms. Controls on the Web Forms run on the server but the UI is displayed on the client browser. This takes lots of coordination and behind-the-scenes activity. However, the end result is Web interfaces that look and behave very much like WinForms interfaces. Moreover, the Web interfaces can deal with a broad range of browsers such as Microsoft Internet Explorer as well as less capable browsers such as the ones found on wireless palmtop devices. WebForms will render themselves appropriately on the target device.

DEVELOPMENT TOOLS

A productive set of tools is critical to developer success on a new platform like .NET. Microsoft offers many development tools to build Web services as well as traditional Windows applications.

Programming Languages

.NET offers an improved ball game for programmers. Features such as automatic memory management make it unnecessary for programmers to deal with these issues. The .NET programming model encourages object-oriented programming.

To simplify programming under .NET and to exploit the capability of the .NET Framework to its fullest extent, Microsoft has introduced a new programming language called C#, which offers the simplicity of Visual Basic and the flexibility of C++. C# borrows most of its constructs directly from C++, making C++ and Java programmers feel right at home. More information about the origins of C# can be found in an interview with Anders Hejlsberg [Osb-00], the chief architect for C#.

Microsoft has also introduced Visual Basic .NET, an upgrade to its popular Visual Basic programming language. Visual Basic .NET adds object-oriented features as well as provides full access to .NET platform features. The new feature list of Visual Basic.NET can be found in [Pat-01a] and [Pat-01b].

Microsoft has also extended C++ to develop code for .NET. This extension is referred to as Managed Extension for C++.

Finally, .NET provides an open standard for developing language compilers that target .NET. Many independent software vendors are providing their own programming language support for .NET.

The .NET Framework SDK

The .NET Framework SDK contains documentation, tools, C# and Visual Basic .NET compilers, and samples for developers to write, build, test, and deploy .NET applications. The SDK also includes the .NET Framework as a redistributable package.

The SDK can be downloaded free of charge from Microsoft's Web site. Remember to read the licensing agreement when you download the SDK.

Visual Studio .NET

Visual Studio .NET is the next generation of Microsoft's popular multilanguage development tool, built especially for .NET. Visual Studio .NET helps
you build as well as consume Web services and .NET applications quickly. It
supports C#, Visual Basic .NET, and C++. Any other .NET programming language can be easily integrated into Visual Studio .NET. The Integrated Development Editor (IDE) contains many features, such as IntelliSense, to boost
programmers' productivity. Visual Studio .NET will likely remain the most
popular choice for developing .NET applications.

FOUNDATION SERVICES

Microsoft also envisions that providing a compelling user experience to consumers is important for the success of Internet as a communication bus. To
this effect, Microsoft plans to release some foundation or building block Web
services. Software vendors can leverage against these foundation services.
With time, Microsoft intends to release more such foundation services.

The first set of foundation services are being released as a product called
Microsoft .NET My Services. Table 1.2 lists these services.

TABLE 1.2.   Microsoft .NET My Services

Name	Description
.NET Address	Billing, shipping, and other addresses
.NET Profile	Name, picture, and so on
.NET Contacts	Electronic address book
.NET Location	Electronic and geographical locations
.NET Alerts	Send and/or electronic notifications
.NET Inbox	E-mail and voice-mail storage
.NET Calendar	Appointment management
.NET Documents	Users can store, share, and back up important files
.NET ApplicationSettings	Application settings
.NET Favorite WebSites	List of favorite Web sites
.NET Wallet	Credit card information, coupons, receipts, and so on
.NET Devices	Settings for various personal devices
.NET Services	List of services provided
.NET Usage	Usage report for the preceding services

A common theme behind Microsoft's foundation services is that the user information is stored at a central place and can be retrieved anytime, anywhere. These foundation services open the door for developing innovative software applications. For example, using .NET Calendar, a scheduling application at your doctor's Web site might be able to access your Web-hosted calendar to see when you are available, schedule an appointment at an appropriate time, and remind you using .NET Alerts (on your PC, pager, or any other notification device) when the appointment is approaching. As a Web service is based on open standards, the scheduling application can be developed for Windows, UNIX, or any other OS.

The foundation services are built around user identity. Microsoft provides a user authentication service called Microsoft Passport that deserves special attention.

User Authentication Service

Consumers do their Internet shopping on many Web sites. A common problem that they face today is that they are asked to enter account information, such as user name and password, on each Web site they visit because each Web site maintains its own database of customers.

Microsoft Passport promises a solution to this dilemma. Rather than signing up for an account on every Web site, the user signs up for a Passport account, either through *www.passport.com* or through related services like Hotmail (every Hotmail user automatically has a Passport account). The user can choose how much information to store in the MS Passport account—from a simple user name and password to a complete wallet with credit card information, shipping and billing addresses, and more.

Using Microsoft's single sign-in (SSI) service, a Passport member can use one sign-in name and password at all participating Web sites. Passport sign-in names are tied to individuals and not computers, members can access Passport sites from a wide range of devices.

What Does It All Mean?

Microsoft's .NET initiative impacts consumers, businesses, software vendors, and developers.

Consumers will be the biggest beneficiaries of .NET and the foundation services. As the data is stored on the Web, they will be able to access documents and other personal information anytime, anywhere, from any smart device.

For businesses, implementing applications using Web services solves many of today's B2B and B2C integration challenges.

By making their business applications available as Web services, or by providing innovative Web services, software vendors may be able to find newer modes of revenue. Microsoft itself is gravitating toward providing a subscription-based model for its services, thereby ensuring a monthly source of revenue.

The .NET Framework helps developers write robust, secure, Internet-enabled code in a language of their choice. The rich set of class libraries provided by the .NET Framework, as well as new features in Visual Studio .NET will boost developer productivity.

REFERENCES

[W3C-01]   Gudgin, Martin, et al., "SOAP Version 1.2," W3C Working Draft, July 2001.
             www.w3.org/TR/2001/WD-soap12-20010709/

[Osb-00]   Osborn, John, "Deep Inside C#: An Interview with Microsoft Chief Architect Anders Hejlsberg," July 2000.
             windows.oreilly.com/news/hejlsberg_0800.html

[Pat-01a]   Pattison, Ted, "Basic Instincts: New Features in Visual Basic .NET," *MSDN Magazine*, May 2001.
             msdn.microsoft.com/msdnmag/issues/01/05/instincts/instincts0105.asp

[Pat-01b]   Pattison, Ted, "Basic Instincts: Exploiting New Language Features in Visual Basic .NET, Part 2," *MSDN Magazine*, August 2001.
             msdn.microsoft.com/msdnmag/issues/01/08/Instincts/Instincts0108.asp

From C++ to C#

This chapter focuses on various stages of building .NET applications—from development to debugging and deploying. You will write simple C# programs to explore common programming paradigms under the .NET Framework. In the process, you will learn the differences and similarities between C++ and C#. By the end of the chapter, readers will understand many key concepts of the .NET Framework and will be fairly comfortable developing simple .NET applications using C#.

A SIMPLE "HELLO USER" PROGRAM

Let's get right down to business. The following program displays a greeting to the console:

```
// Project HelloUser

class MyApp
{
    public static void Main() {
        System.String userName = "Jay";
        System.Console.WriteLine("Hello " + userName);
    }
}
```

This simple application defines a class called MyApp that has a single static public method called Main. Under .NET, methods must generally be members of a class or a struct. A class or a struct form the basic unit of organization under .NET and are generally referred to as *types*. We explore the differences between a `class` and a `struct` in detail in Chapter 4.

Static method `Main` is considered the entry point for the program. When the program is run, the .NET runtime starts executing the code in `Main`.

Inside method `Main` is a reference to two other types called `System.Console` and `System.String`. These two types are defined in the BCL, a library provided by the .NET Framework, and are implemented in `MSCorLib.dll` file. Among other methods, `System.Console` provides a method `WriteLine` to write a string to the console.

This code prefixes a greeting to the specified user name and displays the resultant string to the console.

How are we able to call a method such as `Writeline` from the `System.Console` class without even creating an instance of the class? This is possible because this method is marked as `static`. As with C++, for any .NET language, calling a static method on a class does not require the class to be instantiated.

`System.Console` actually is the fully qualified name of class `Console` belonging to the namespace `System`. A namespace provides scope to your data types, thus reducing naming conflicts in large projects. Within a single namespace, no two types can have the same name. However, two types from two different namespaces can have the same name, but by qualifying the type with its namespace, each type can be uniquely identified.

Obviously, typing fully qualified class names each time you refer to a class can quickly become unbearable. Fortunately, C# allows a way to declare the namespaces to be used up front. This is done with the `using` keyword. Using this keyword, our "hello user" code can be rewritten as follows:

```
// Project HelloUser

using System;

class MyApp
{
    public static void Main() {
        String userName = "Jay";
        Console.WriteLine("Hello " + userName);
    }
}
```

When processing the source file, the compiler searches for an identifier in the current namespace. If the identifier cannot be resolved in the current namespace, the compiler then searches each of the namespaces specified in the `using` statements. For our application, the compiler automatically resolves references to types `Console` and `String` from the namespace `System`.

You may be wondering what the current namespace for class `MyApp` is. The code doesn't seem to scope the class under any namespace. It just so happens that scoping a C# class within a namespace is optional. If not explicitly scoped, a class automatically gets scoped under an unnamed namespace, also called the *global namespace*.

Let's build our application. The SDK provides a command-line tool, `csc.exe`, to compile C# programs. Assuming the code is defined in file `HelloUser.cs`, the following command line, when executed, generates our executable:

```
csc.exe -t:exe -out:HelloUser.exe -r:MSCorLib.dll HelloUser.cs
```

Command-line switch `-t:exe` tells the compiler to generate a console user interface (CUI) executable as target. Other possible targets are Windows user interface (WUI) executables (switch `-t:winexe`) and library executables (switch `-t:library`).

Switch `-out` can be used to specify the filename for the generated executable, `HelloUser.exe` in our case.

Switch `-r` requires some explanation.

The .NET Framework provides a number of library files that implement a variety of classes, such as the one introduced earlier, `MSCorLib.dll`. These library files are actually referred to as *assemblies*. We cover assemblies in detail in the next chapter. For now, it is sufficient to know that an assembly stores a collection of types (`class`, `struct`, etc.). Think of an assembly as a logical EXE or DLL file. Even `HelloUser.exe` is an example of an assembly.

While processing `HelloUser.cs`, the compiler needs to know which assembly to use to resolve reference to external types `System.Console` and `System.String`. The specified compiler option, `-r:MSCorLib.dll`, tells the compiler to look for external types in `MSCorLib.dll` assembly.

Compiler Response File

There is yet another way to specify the command-line parameters to the compiler. You can specify some or all of the parameters in a text file and ask the compiler to process this file using the `@<file>` command-line option. This file is referred to as the response file. For example, you can create a response file `HelloUser.rsp` that contains the following text:

```
-t:exe
```

```
-out:HelloUser.exe
-r:MSCorLib.dll
```

To generate the executable, you can now use the following command:

```
csc.exe @HelloUser.rsp HelloUser.cs
```

If you just name the file csc.rsp, the compiler will always automatically read it. The .NET Framework supplies a csc.rsp response file that is located in the same directory as csc.exe. The compiler always reads this file first, followed by a csc.rsp file from the current directory, if present.

You can turn off reading csc.rsp files by specifying the -noconfig option to the compiler.

Note that MSCorLib.dll is a special file in the sense that it contains all the core types such as integers, characters, strings, and so on. As these types are used so frequently, the C# compiler automatically references MSCorLib.dll. This makes our command-line option, -r:MSCorLib.dll, redundant.

Besides MSCorLib.dll, there are many other assemblies in the framework that also get used frequently. These assemblies are all listed in the framework-supplied csc.rsp file.

The C# compiler generates a console executable by default (i.e., if no target type is specified) and, if the output filename is not specified, it is named as the first source filename with the extension replaced as .exe. Thus, our previous command line can actually be reduced to the following and still would produce the same result:

```
csc.exe HelloUser.cs
```

Let's run our application, HelloUser.exe. The following is the output:

```
Hello Jay
```

Congratulations! You just completed your first .NET program.

Behind the Scenes

HelloUser.exe is a standard Win32 portable executable (PE) file, that is, the Windows OS should be able to load this file and, if required, execute the instructions stored in the file. However, unlike normal PE files, HelloUser.exe does not contain native machine language instructions. Instead, it contains code in MSIL. MSIL code resembles assembly language instructions.

So how does `HelloUser.exe` run and produce the desired output? After all, a machine can execute only the native code.

The .NET Framework provides the common language runtime environment to manage the execution of MSIL code. Any code that targets the common language runtime is called *managed code*; it benefits from many features offered by the common language runtime. One such feature is on the fly conversion (also referred to as JIT conversion) of MSIL code to native machine language instructions.

Why not just produce the native code in the first place? Recall from the previous chapter that Microsoft envisions making .NET available on a wide range of devices. As machine language instructions are tied to a specific processor type, the same executable may not be able to run on a device with a different processor type. By compiling program logic into a processor-independent intermediate language, .NET makes it possible to achieve platform independence. Plus, the generated native code can take advantage of hardware-specific optimizations.

What Is Managed Code?

For the common language runtime to manage the execution of the code and to provide features to the code, the *managed* code contains extra information about the code, such as the methods available in a class, the parameters and return value for each method, and so on. This extra information is called the *metadata* (data about data). MSIL code is always managed code.

Unlike managed code, unmanaged code does not contain any .NET style metadata. Examples of unmanaged code are COM applications and any legacy software. Although unmanaged code can execute under the common language runtime, it cannot benefit from its features.

We will look at common language runtime and its features in detail in Chapter 4.

At this point, we have already covered quite a few important terms used under .NET. Here is a small quiz for you. Can you define the terms MSIL, the common language runtime, type, assembly, namespace, and BCL? For your convenience, I have defined them once again in Table 2.1.

TABLE 2.1   .NET Terminology

Name	Description
MSIL	Microsoft Intermediate Language. It resembles assembly language instructions.
Common language runtime	The heart of .NET. It provides the runtime environment for executing .NET applications. Also referred to as the .NET runtime or simply runtime.
Type	Basic unit of encapsulating data with a set of behaviors. Classes and structures are examples of types.
Assembly	A logical DLL or EXE file that contains type definitions and their implementation.
Namespace	A logical scoping of types. By qualifying a type with a namespace, naming conflicts between types can be reduced.
BCL	Base Class Library. A library that contains core types such as `System.String`. The BCL is spread over a couple of assemblies. `MSCorLib.dll` is one such assembly.

Please review Table 2.1. It is very important that you get accustomed to these terms, as we use them quite frequently throughout the book.

C# FOR C++ PROGRAMMERS

C# offers many features that make a C++ or Java programmer feel right at home. The curly braces and the statements ending with semicolons all made their way into the language. However, C# also introduces many new features. Some features will make a Java programmer more at home. Let's take a brief look at a few of these features. In many respects, we really are examining the programming language support provided by the .NET Framework.

Before we proceed further, it is worth discussing the coding conventions that has been adopted by the .NET community. The Visual Studio .NET documentation includes an article on coding techniques and programming practices for improving the quality of the source code. Search for "Coding Techniques" under the documentation. Some important ones regarding naming conventions that I wish to mention are as follows:

* Since most names are constructed by concatenating several words, use mixed-case formatting to simplify reading them.
* Use Pascal casing for methods, properties, and events (the latter two covered shortly). Here, the first letter of each word is capitalized. An example of a method name is `GetDirectoryName` and a property is `UserName`.

- Use camel casing for member fields, local variables, and method parameters. In this case, the first letter of each word except the first is capitalized. Some examples are `dirName` and `documentType`.

- Avoid Hungarian notation if possible. Many languages under .NET (e.g., Visual Basic .NET) do not have this notion. The only exception I have is that I prefer member fields to be prefixed with m_. This helps me differentiate between member fields and local variables.

Primitive Data Types

Like any other typed programming languages, C# provides its own primitive datatypes. However, C# primitive types are nothing more than a mapping to the base datatypes supported by the common language runtime. For example, C# primitive data type `string` is an alias of `System.String`, a class that we have already come across. As a matter of fact, the following two lines of code generate identical compiler output:

```
string = "Jay";
System.String = "Jay";
```

This begs the following question: Should you use `string` or `String` in your code? This is really a matter of personal preference.

The base types supported by the common language runtime are all defined in the BCL. Table 2.2 shows a list of C# primitive datatypes and their corresponding BCL counterparts.

TABLE 2.2 C# Primitive Datatypes

C# Type	Description	BCL Type
bool	32-bit true/false value	System.Boolean
sbyte	8-bit signed integer	System.SByte
byte	8-bit unsigned integer	System.Byte
char	16-bit Unicode character	System.Char
short	16-bit signed integer	System.Int16
ushort	16-bit unsigned integer	System.UInt16
int	32-bit signed integer	System.Int32
uint	32-bit unsigned integer	System.UInt32
long	64-bit signed integer	System.Int64
ulong	64-bit unsigned integer	System.UInt64
float	IEEE 32-bit float	System.Single

TABLE 2.2   C# Primitive Datatypes (Continued)

C# Type	Description	BCL Type
double	IEEE 64-bit float	System.Double
decimal	96-bit monetary type (used in financial calculations)	System.Decimal
string	String of Unicode characters	System.String
object	Root system class	System.Object

Take note of the datatype System.Object. This type is the root class; all other types get derived from System.Object, either directly or indirectly (through another type that ultimately gets derived from System.Object). We examine System.Object in detail in Chapter 4 when we discuss the .NET infrastructure.

Member Accessibility

Under C#, the accessibility level of a type, and each member of the type (method, member field, etc.), can be individually controlled by means of specifying an access modifier on the member. Table 2.3 shows the list of possible access modifiers.

TABLE 2.3   Access Modifiers under C#

Modifier	Description
public	Access is not restricted. Any method from any type can access this member.
private	Access is limited to the containing type.
protected	Access is limited to the containing type and any of its derived types.
internal	Same as public except access is limited to the current assembly. External assemblies have no access.
protected internal	Full access within the current assembly. For external assemblies, access is limited to types that are derived from the containing type.
sealed	When applied to a class, the class cannot be inherited. When applied to a overridden method, the method cannot be overridden in a derived class. Structs are implicitly sealed.

The following code excerpt demonstrates how access modifiers can be applied to a type and its members:

```
// Project AccessModifiers

public class Foo
{
    public int x;
    internal int y;
    protected internal int z;
    private void Test1() {}
    public void Test2() {}
}
```

Note that specifying access modifiers is not mandatory. If not specified, the member defaults to private for a `class` or a `struct` and public for an `interface` or an `enum`.

Also note that a top-level type, such as class `Foo` in our example, can itself be qualified with a `public` access modifier. This makes the class accessible from external assemblies. If not explicitly specified, a top-level type defaults to the `internal` accessibility level.

Field Initialization

Consider the following code excerpt:

```
// Project FieldInit

class Foo {
    private int x;
    private String y;
    private Baz z;
    public Foo() {
        x = 10;
        y = "Hello";
        z = new Baz();
    }
    // Other methods
}
```

Initializing a class' member fields in the class' instance constructor is a common programming technique. C# offers a shorthand mechanism to achieve this task. The fields can be initialized at the time of their declaration, as shown here:

```
class Bar {
    private int x = 10;
    private String y = "Hello";
```

```
    private Baz z = new Baz();

    // Other methods
}
```

Note that you can still define a constructor and initialize the fields. If a field is initialized in the declaration statement as well as in the instance constructor, the runtime initializes the field twice, first from the declaration and then from the instance constructor.

Type Constructors

You are already familiar with instance constructors, which are responsible for setting an object instance to its initial state. In addition to instance constructors, C# (and the .NET Framework) supports type constructors (also known as static constructors or class constructors). A type constructor lets you perform any initialization required before any members declared within the type are accessed. The common language runtime guarantees that the type constructor gets executed before any instance of the type is created or before any static field or any method is referenced.

To understand type constructors, consider the following C# code:

```
class Foo {
    static public int x = 10;
}
```

When this code is compiled, the compiler automatically generates a type constructor for Foo. This constructor is responsible for initializing the value of static member variable x to 10.

In C#, you can also implement the type constructor yourself. You just need to define a constructor on the type and qualify it with static keyword, as illustrated here:

```
// Project TypeConstructor

class Foo {
    static public int x;
    static Foo() {
      x = 10;
    }
}
```

Note that a type constructor does not accept any parameters and it can access only the static members of the type. Its usual purpose is to initialize static fields.

Reference and Value Types

Under C#, some datatypes can be instantiated only on the stack, whereas other datatypes can be instantiated only on the heap. Simple datatypes (int, long, double, etc.) and structs are always instantiated on the stack. These types are called *value types*. Types that are created on the heap are called *reference types*. C# classes belong to the reference type; that is, an instance of a class is always created on the heap.

There is one exception to the rule—if a value type is contained within a reference type, then the value type is created on the heap (at the time the reference type is being instantiated).

A datatype can be instantiated using the new keyword, as shown here:

```
class Foo
{
    ...
}


    ...
    Foo a = new Foo();
```

Note that when instantiating an object on the heap, there is no need to use C++ style pointer declaration. As a matter of fact, the C# compiler prevents you from specifying a pointer unless you mark your code as unsafe. Unsafe mode is primarily used for interoperability with C-style APIs, which we discuss in a later chapter.

It is possible to instantiate a value type without using new. In this case, however, the instance has to be initialized before it is used. Otherwise, the compiler generates an error. The following code excerpt illustrates this:

```
public void sub()
{
    int a = new int(); // Legal
    int b;
    int c = b; // Illegal. b has to be initialized first
    int d = 5;
    int e = d; // Legal
    ...
}
```

It is worth noting the dissimilarity between C# and C++ when treating the value type. Under C++, you can create a value type either on the stack or on the heap. For example, the following C++ line of code creates an instance of int type on the heap:

```
int* p = new int();
```

The following line under C#, however, creates the instance on the stack.

```
int p = new int();
```

From a programming perspective, there is an important distinction between the reference type and the value type. When a reference type variable is assigned to another, the memory location for the underlying object is shared. In contrast, value type variables hold a separate copy of the object. The following code excerpt demonstrates the behavior for the reference type:

```
// Project ReferenceType

public class Foo
{
    public int x;

    public static void Test(Foo a, Foo b) {
        a.x = 5;
        b.x = 10;
        b = a;
        Console.WriteLine(b.x); // will display "5"
        a.x = 20;
        Console.WriteLine(b.x); // will display "20"
    }
};
```

Note that if one reference type variable is assigned to another, changing a member field's value via one variable causes the value for the corresponding member field in the other variable to change.

Finally, the common language runtime provides for automatic conversion between a value type and a reference type wherever possible. Conversion of a value type to a reference type is called *boxing* and the conversion from a reference type to a value type is called *unboxing*. We look at boxing and unboxing and its performance impact when we discuss the internals of the common language runtime in Chapter 4.

Arrays

The notion of an array is similar to that in C and C++: An array contains elements that can be accessed through indexes. All the elements in an array should be of the same type. The length of the array is the number of elements it can contain and the rank of an array is the number of dimensions in the array.

The following code shows how to create an array of four elements of type `int`:

```
int[] arr = new int[4];
```

The following code shows how to create an array and initialize it with values:

```
int[] arr = new int[] {20, 10, 40, 30};
```

Note that the length of the array need not be explicitly specified. The compiler automatically computes the proper length based on the number of elements.

Here is the traditional C way of accessing the elements in an array:

```
// Project Arrays

for(int i=0;i<arr.Length;i++) {
    Console.WriteLine(arr[i]);
}
```

C# also defined a keyword `foreach` to repeat a group of statements for each element in an array, as shown in the following code excerpt:

```
// Project Arrays

foreach(int elem in arr) {
    Console.WriteLine(elem);
}
```

Behind the scenes, an array gets derived from `System.Array` class. This class provides methods for creating, manipulating, searching, and sorting arrays. For example, the following code sorts our array in ascending order:

```
Array.Sort(arr);
```

The following code searches for an element of value 50 in the sorted array using the binary search algorithm:

```
int index = Array.BinarySearch(arr, 50);
Console.WriteLine (( index < 0) ? "Not found" : "Found");
```

The returned value contains the index of the element if a match is found. Otherwise, it returns a negative number that is a bitwise complement of the index of the first element that is larger than the specified value.

Arrays and Binary Search

Always ensure that the array to be binary-searched has been sorted. Performing a binary search on an unsorted array results in unpredictable behavior.

Also, note that if a match is not found, the return value could be any negative number and not necessarily –1. Do not specifically check for –1 in your code.

Once allocated, the size of an array cannot be changed. If you need an array that can grow dynamically, take a look at `ArrayList`, a smarter cousin of `Array`.

Properties

Under the common language runtime, a property is a controlled way of exposing a class's member fields to the client code. Instead of exposing the member field directly to the client, using a property provides a smart way to validate the input value or to restrict access to the data member.

A property can have a get accessor (code responsible for reading a member field's value), a set accessor (code responsible for setting a member field's value), or both. A property without a get accessor is write-only and a property without a set accessor is read-only.

The following code excerpt demonstrates how to define a property under C#:

```
// Project Properties

class Foo {

  private String m_userName;
  ...

  public String UserName {
    set {
      m_userName = value;
    }
    get {
```

```
                    return m_userName;
              }
          }
      }
```

Under C#, keyword `get` is used to implement the get accessor and keyword `set` is used to implement the set accessor. For the set accessor, the input value is stored in an implicit parameter named `value`. The preceding code shows how the member variable `m_userName` can be exposed via property `UserName`.

The following C# code excerpt shows how to set or get a property:

```
Foo x = new Foo();
...
x.UserName = "Jay"; // calls the set accessor on UserName
String y = x.UserName; // calls the get accessor on UserName
```

Indexers

Much like C/C++, C# provides indexed access to an element of an array. Under C#, however, indexed access is not just limited to array types. A type such as a `class` or a `struct` can also be accessed using an index. This is done by defining an indexer on the type. An *indexer* is a special property named `this` that takes an index as parameter.

The following code excerpt shows how to define an indexer. Here, class `Foo` is just a wrapper for a string array:

```
// Project Indexer

class Foo {
    public Foo(int val)
    {
      m_arr = new String[val];
    }

    public String this[int index]
    {
      get {
        return m_arr[index];
      }
      set {
        m_arr[index] = value;
      }
    }

    private String[] m_arr;
};
```

As can be seen, defining an indexer is similar to defining a property. As with properties, you can drop either one of the accessors.

The following code excerpt illustrates how to get indexed access to `Foo`:

```
public static void Main() {
    Foo f = new Foo(5);
    f[0] = "Jay";
    Console.WriteLine(f[0]);
}
```

Remember that all the code used in this book is available on the companion Web site.

Delegates and Events

A delegate is roughly equivalent to a function pointer in C; it encapsulates a method with a specific signature. Unlike a function pointer, however, a delegate is type-safe; the prototype of the function assigned to the delegate has to strictly match the delegate definition.

The following code shows an example of defining a delegate:

```
public delegate void MyDelegate();
```

In this code, type `MyDelegate` encapsulates a function that takes an empty parameter list and has a `void` return type.

The following code excerpt shows how to declare a variable of `MyDelegate` type. The intention is to simulate clicking a Windows button.

```
public class MyButton {
    public MyDelegate Click;
};
```

Even though a member variable can be exposed to the public directly, it is a good practice to expose it as a property. The revised code is shown here:

```
// Project Delegates

public class MyButton {
    private MyDelegate m_Click;
    public MyDelegate Click {
      get {
        return m_Click;
      }
      set {
        m_Click = value;
```

```
        }
      }
  }
```

A delegate can store either a static method or an instance method as a callback element, as shown in the following code:

```
public class MyApp {
    public void X() {
      Console.WriteLine("Instance method called");
    }

    static public void Y() {
      Console.WriteLine("Static method called");
    }

    static void Main() {
      // create a button
      MyButton btn = new MyButton();

      // Case 1: Adding a static method to the delegate
      btn.Click += new MyDelegate(MyApp.Y);

      // Case 2: Add an instance method to the delegate
      MyApp a = new MyApp();
      btn.Click += new MyDelegate(a.X);

      // Simulate button click (invoke the delegate)
      btn.Click();
    }
}
```

The last statement in the preceding code invokes the delegate (this is equivalent to simulating a button click in our example). When the delegate is invoked, it results in calling each element on the invocation list. Here is the output from the program:

```
Static method called
Instance method called
```

Note that the code uses += syntax for specifying the callback elements. Under C, you are used to assigning a single callback function to a function pointer. This functionality is still supported under .NET—you can assign a single callback element to a delegate using the = operator. However, delegates under .NET also support multicast functionality; that is, a single delegate can have a callback list of more than one element. C# uses += syntax to specify additional callback elements on a delegate.

Although delegates can be used as a notification mechanism, the .NET Framework introduces a formal notion of event for this purpose. Keyword event can be applied to a delegate field or a delegate property to convert it to an event, as shown in the following code:

```
// Project Events

public class MyButton {
    private event MyDelegate m_Click;
    public event MyDelegate Click {
      add {
        m_Click += value;
      }
      remove {
        m_Click -= value;
      }
    }
}
```

Note that an event property differs from a normal property in the sense that the accessors are defined using add and remove keywords. Also, unlike a normal property where defining just one accessor is permitted, an event property requires both the accessors to be defined.

The callbacks can be added to the event similar to that for delegates. However, the preferred term for the callbacks in this case is *event handlers*.

Events introduce a few subtle changes to the way a delegate works. One important change is that only the class that defines the event can raise the event. The following line of code taken from class MyApp of our previous example on delegates will not work any more:

```
btn.Click();
```

A work-around is to add a method to the event holder class to raise the event, as highlighted in the following code:

```
public class MyButton {
    private event MyDelegate m_Click;
    public event MyDelegate Click {
      add {
        m_Click += value;
      }
      remove {
        m_Click -= value;
```

```
      }
    }

    public void RaiseEvent() {
      if (null != m_Click) {
        m_Click();
      }
    }
};
```

Now the users of class `MyButton` can call `RaiseEvent` to raise the event.

Note that the event variable holds a `null` reference until an event handler gets added. Therefore, it is a good idea to check for `null` before invoking the delegate.

Invoking a Delegate

Always check for null before invoking a delegate.

Programming sample `Events` also defines a Visual Basic .NET project `MyVBApp` that demonstrates how events can be used across languages. Interested readers may wish to look at the source code which can be found in the file `MyVBApp.vb`.

Method Parameters

Under C#, when a method is defined, each argument can be marked as either an input to the method, an output from the method, or an input as well as an output.

Specifying an input parameter is similar to pass-by-value semantics in C++. Here is an example:

```
void MyMethod(int val1, String val2);
```

As in C++, the parameters are passed on the stack; that is, `MyMethod` gets a local copy of the parameters. Any change made to these parameters within the function does not get reflected in the caller's space. Obviously, if a parameter is of reference type, it is pointing to the memory in the heap. Therefore, any change made to its contents is also reflected in the caller's space.

If the parameter is intended to be used purely as an output type, then it can be attributed with the `out` keyword, as shown in the following code:

```
// Project Parameters

// Method declaration
void MyMethod(out Int32 val1, out String val2);

// Caller code
Int32 count;
String name;
MyMethod(out count, out name);
```

Note that the caller need not initialize the `out` type arguments.

As the `out` type arguments are meant only for updates within the method, any attempt to read the parameter within the method is flagged as an error by the compiler.

To indicate that a parameter will be used both as an input to the method and an output from the method, the parameter must be qualified with the `ref` keyword.

If a `ref` keyword is specified, the parameters must be initialized (assigned a value) before the method can be called, as demonstrated in the following code excerpt:

```
// Method declaration
void MyMethod(ref Int32 val1, ref String val2);

// Caller code
Int32 count = 5;
String name = "Pradeep";
MyMethod(ref count, ref name);
```

Implementation Inheritance

C# lets one class inherit implementation from another class, much like C++. The following C# code excerpt demonstrates the syntax for implementation inheritance:

```
class DerivedClass : SomeBaseClass {
    ...
}
```

Unlike C++, however, C# restricts the implementation inheritance to a single parent; that is, a child class cannot have more than one class as its parent.

Note that this restriction is actually placed by the common language runtime; C# just enforces it. Later in the chapter, we look at another kind of inheritance called *interface inheritance* that somewhat offsets for this restriction.

If a class is not explicitly inherited from another class, as in our previous examples, then C# implicitly inherits it from System.Object. Recall that System.Object is the root class for any type defined under .NET.

Often, a base class needs to be initialized with some value during the construction of the derived class. C# provides a keyword base for this purpose. The following code excerpt demonstrates the use of this keyword:

```
// Project Inheritance

class MyBaseClass {
    public MyBaseClass(String a) {
       ...
    }
    ...
}

class MyDerivedClass : MyBaseClass {
    public MyDerivedClass(String b) : base(b) {
       ...
    }
    ...
}
```

In this sample, MyBaseClass requires a String parameter in its constructor. When MyDerivedClass is instantiated in the code, the constructor argument passed to MyDerivedClass (which is a String type) gets passed to its base class, MyBaseClass.

Keyword base can also be used from any method in the derived class to explicitly indicate that the method or the field being accessed is that of the base class, as illustrated in the following code excerpt:

```
// Project Inheritance

class MyBaseClass {
    ...
    public String MyMethod1() {
      return m_val;
    }
}

class MyDerivedClass : MyBaseClass {
    ...
    public String MyMethod2() {
      return "Hello " + base.MyMethod1();
    }
}
```

Error Handling

Windows C++ programmers have to deal with myriad (and inconsistent) ways of obtaining error information. For example, Win32 APIs return DWORD error code. COM APIs return HRESULT. Visual C++ built-in support for COM throws _com_error exceptions.

Under the .NET Framework, there is only one way of indicating an error—by throwing an exception. Moreover, exception handling is uniform across all the languages. For example, an exception thrown from C# can be handled by Visual Basic .NET.

All exceptions under .NET are ultimately derived from System.Exception, a class defined in the BCL. The following line of code shows how to throw an exception containing an error string:

```
// Project ErrorHandling

void MyMethod() {
    ...
    throw new Exception("Houston, we have a problem");
}
```

Although one can throw exceptions using System.Exception, it is intended to be used only by the common language runtime and the .NET Framework classes. For application developers, the preferred way is to use another exception class, System.ApplicationException, to return application-specific errors. System.ApplicationException extends System.Exception but does not add any new functionality.

An exception that is thrown by a method can be caught by any of the callers in the call chain using a try-catch block, as illustrated in the following code excerpt:

```
public void Test() {
    try {
      MyMethod();
    }catch(Exception e) {
      Console.Error.WriteLine(e.Message);
      Console.Error.WriteLine(e.StackTrace);
      Console.Error.WriteLine(e.Source);
    }
}
```

System.Exception provides a number of helpful properties such as Message (contains the error message), StackTrace (the trace of call sequence), Source (the name of the application), and so on.

If the caller wishes to provide some cleanup code, a `try-finally` block can be used, as shown in the following code excerpt:

```
public void Test() {
    try {
      MyMethod();
    }finally {
      Console.WriteLine("My cleanup");
    }
}
```

Note that the code in the `finally` block is called *irrespective* of whether or not an exception occurs. If an exception does occur, it gets propagated to the next `try-catch` block in the call stack.

To catch an exception and provide the cleanup code, a `try-catch-finally` block can be used, as shown here:

```
public void Test() {
    try {
      MyMethod();
    }catch(Exception e) {
      Console.Error.WriteLine(e.Message);
    }finally {
      Console.WriteLine("My cleanup");
    }
}
```

The language also provides the mechanism to throw the same exception that was caught, as shown in the following code excerpt:

```
public void Test() {
    try {
      MyMethod();
    }catch(Exception e) {
      Console.Error.WriteLine(e.Message);
      throw;
    }
}
```

Even though `System.Exception` (or `System.ApplicationException`) provides a mechanism to return an error string, sometimes it is desirable to obtain extra error information. This can be done by extending the `ApplicationException` class. The following code excerpt shows an exception class that also returns an integer error code:

```
public class MyException : ApplicationException
{
    private int m_errorCode;
    public MyException(String sMsg, int eCode)
      : base(sMsg) { // pass error string to the base class
      m_errorCode = eCode;
    }
    public int ErrorCode {
      get {
        return m_errorCode;
      }
    }
};
```

The caller can catch this specific exception type, if interested, as demonstrated in the following code:

```
public void Test() {
    try {
      MyMethod();
    }catch(MyException e) {
      Console.WriteLine(e.Message);
      Console.WriteLine(e.ErrorCode);
    }catch(Exception e) {
      Console.Error.WriteLine(e.Message);
    }
}
```

Finally, when the caller catches an exception, it can rethrow a new type of exception while still preserving the information from the caught exception. The Exception class provides a property called InnerException that can be used to store the caught exception. This in effect provides a mechanism to cascade all the exceptions in the call stack. The following code excerpt shows a class that preserves the old exception while providing for its own error information:

```
public class MyExceptionEx : ApplicationException
{
    private int m_errorCode;

    public MyExceptionEx(String sMsg, int eCode, Exception e)
        : base(sMsg, e)
    {
      m_errorCode = eCode;
    }
```

```
    public int ErrorCode {
      get {return m_errorCode;}
    }
};
```

The following code excerpt demonstrates displaying error messages from a cascaded exception:

```
void DumpExceptionInfo(Exception e) {
    Console.Error.WriteLine(e.Message);
    Exception innerE = e.InnerException;
    while(null != innerE) {
        Console.Error.WriteLine(innerE.Message);
        innerE = innerE.InnerException;
    }
}
```

Garbage Collection

C++ programmers will detect the noticeable absence of the delete keyword in C#. We know that under traditional C++, an instance of a class created (with keyword new) if not deleted (with keyword delete) results in a resource leak. Things are different for code that targets the common language runtime. Recall that any code that targets the common language runtime is called managed code; it benefits from many features offered by the common language runtime. One such feature is memory management—the common language runtime automatically detects if an allocated memory resource is no longer in use and frees it for us. This mechanism is called *garbage collection*. Because the garbage collector knows when to delete an object, there is no need to explicitly delete the object.

Note that, as in C++, you can define destructors on your C# classes. However, the destruction of your object is not deterministic under .NET. You cannot rely on the destructor to be called, for example, at the time a variable goes out of scope. The destructor may be called later, at the time of the garbage collection.

To help cope with this lack of deterministic finalization, .NET proposes an alternate technique. We look at this technique in Chapter 4 when we examine the mechanics of garbage collection.

At this stage, I think we have covered enough basics of C# language. As we go through the rest of this chapter and the following chapters, we will discover many other features of the language. Meanwhile, those who wish to get more familiar with C# may wish to read Joshua Trupin's MSDN article [Tru-00] or can pick up a copy of Eric Gunnerson's book, *A Programmer's Intro-*

duction to C# [Gun-00]. Some C# traps awaiting the unwary programmer can be found in [Lib-01]. C# has also been submitted to the ECMA, an international standards organization. The draft specifications of the language can be picked up from [Misc-00].

For now, I am anxious to do some coding.

COMMON PROGRAMMING PARADIGMS

In this section, we explore some common programming paradigms under .NET

Client–Server Programming

Software engineering, to a large extent, is about writing software such that generic code can be reused in multiple applications. Let's rewrite the very first program we wrote. This time we factor out the logic for greeting the user. The intent is to provide the ability to reuse this greeting code in any other application.

We first develop a console-based application.

Console-Based Greeting

Here is our new class that implements the greeting logic:

```csharp
// Project ReusableCode, File ConsoleGreeting.cs

using System;

namespace MyGreeting {
    class ConsoleGreeting {

        private String m_userName;

        public void Greet() {
            Console.WriteLine("Hello " + m_userName);
        }

        public String UserName {
            set {
                m_userName = value;
            }
            get {
                return m_userName;
            }
        }
    }
}
```

This class defines a method, Greet, which displays a greeting to the console. To make things slightly more interesting, I have scoped this class into a namespace, MyGreeting.

Here is our new implementation of MyApp class, revised to use the ConsoleGreeting class. The changes have been highlighted.

```
//Project ReusableCode, File HelloUser.cs
using System;
using MyGreeting;

class MyApp
{
    public static void Main() {
        ConsoleGreeting obj = new ConsoleGreeting();
        obj.UserName = "Jay";
        obj.Greet();
    }
}
```

First we create an instance of class ConsoleGreeting. Once an object is obtained, we set the user name on the object and invoke the method Greet on the object.

Let's build the application. Assuming the greeting code has been saved in ConsoleGreeting.cs, here is the command line to build the application:

```
csc.exe HelloUser.cs ConsoleGreeting.cs
```

Compile and run the program. The results should be the same as the one from our previous run (Project HelloUser), only now we have some reusable code in the form of file ConsoleGreeting.cs. This file can potentially be used with any other application being developed. As a software vendor, you can even sell this source code to other companies that can use it to build their own applications. Admittedly, there is not much meat in our code to be a sellable product, but it does illustrate the point.

Reusing a piece of software logic at the source code level, however, has one major problem. Let's say a bug is found in the reusable code after all the applications using this code have been shipped. Once you fix the bug, there is no way to field-replace just the fix. Your only choice is to build all the dependent applications once again and ship them to the customers.

The crux of the problem is that the reusable code has been linked and absorbed in the final executable during the compilation process. Once the executable has been created, any change in the reusable code does not get reflected in the already generated executable.

We need to get away from such static linking of reusable code. If we could package the reusable code as a separate library that can be linked to the application during runtime, then field-replacing such a library would be relatively easy. Obviously, the runtime has to support such "dynamic" linking of a library when the application is executed.

Fortunately, the common language runtime provides a mechanism to load a library dynamically as and when an application needs to use it. As you may have guessed, such a library is called an assembly. Even the very first program that we wrote used such an assembly—MSCorLib.Dll. If a bug is found in, for example, Console.WriteLine, all that Microsoft has to do is fix the bug and field-replace MSCorLib.Dll, with no need for us to rebuild our application(s).

An assembly that provides the software logic that can be used by other applications is loosely referred to as a *server*. An application using such a service is called a *client*.

Let's use our MyGreeting class to build a library assembly. Here is the modified code excerpt for the class:

```
// Project ClientServer

using System;

namespace MyGreeting {
    public class ConsoleGreeting {
       private String m_userName;

       public void Greet() {
          Console.WriteLine("Hello " + m_userName);
       }


       ...

    }
}
```

Note that we had to specify keyword public on the class. Without this access modifier on the class, the client application will not be able to access any methods from the class, even if the methods themselves are marked as public.

Here is the command line to build the library assembly:

```
csc.exe -t:library ConsoleGreeting.cs
```

Option −t:library tells the compiler to build a library assembly. The generated output file is named ConsoleGreeting.dll.

The client code requires no changes. The only change is in the command-line parameters; we need to let the compiler know that our client code references `ConsoleGreeting.dll`, as shown here:

```
csc.exe -t:exe -r:ConsoleGreeting.dll HelloUser.cs
```

Build and run the client application. For now, make sure that `Hello-User.exe` and `ConsoleGreeting.dll` are both in the same directory. In a later chapter, we look at how an assembly can be placed in a location such that multiple applications can access it.

By breaking a monolithic application into client and server assemblies, we achieved our goal of field-replacing just the broken assembly without requiring a change to any other assemblies.

There is yet another problem that we solved inadvertently—the problem of reusing software logic across programming language boundaries. Take a look at `ConsoleGreeting.cs`—the code is written in C#. If you wish to reuse this code in another programming language, such as Visual Basic .NET, it is practically impossible. The Visual Basic .NET compiler cannot possibly compile C# source code and link it with Visual Basic .NET code. Thanks to the common language runtime, however, it is easy to reuse assemblies written in one language to be reused from assemblies written in another language. The following Visual Basic .NET code, for example, shows how to reuse the code from `ConsoleGreeting.dll`:

```
Imports MyGreeting

Module MyVBApp

    Sub Main()
      Dim obj As New ConsoleGreeting()
      obj.UserName = "Jay"
      obj.Greet()
    End Sub

End Module
```

The .NET SDK ships with a command-line tool, `vbc.exe`, to build Visual Basic .NET applications. Assuming this code is saved in `MyVBApp.vb`, the following command line shows how to compile `MyVBApp.vb` to build `MyVBApp.exe`, our client application:

```
vbc.exe -t:exe -r:ConsoleGreeting.dll MyVBApp.vb
```

The reason this cross-language operability is possible under .NET is because all the .NET compilers generate output in the same intermediate form, MSIL. In this respect, any programming language under .NET is a first-class language. The choice of a programming language is more of a preference issue.

Let's now develop a server that displays a greeting using the graphical user interface (GUI).

Windows-Based Greeting

The .NET Framework provides a class, MessageBox, under the namespace System.Windows.Forms that provides a static method Show to display a message box to the user. Using this method, the code for our new server can be written as follows:

```
using System;
using System.Windows.Forms;

namespace MyGreeting {
    public class WindowsGreeting {
      public void Greet() {
        MessageBox.Show("Hello " + m_userName);
      }
      ...
    }
}
```

Displaying the greeting using MessageBox isn't much of a challenge. Let's write code to create our own window.

The goal of our exercise is to create a dialog box with a greeting label and a "Close" button, as shown in Figure 2.1.

The .NET Framework provides a class, Form (namespace System.Windows.Forms) to represent a window displayed in an application. This class can be used to create non-modal as well as modal windows (e.g., a dialog

FIGURE 2.1 A simple dialog box.

box). The class provides many properties and methods to control various aspects of the window such as appearance, size, and so on.

Typically, you extend the Form class to customize it for your needs, so let's define a new class that inherits from Form class. The code excerpt is shown here:

```
// Project WindowsGreeting

using System.Windows.Forms;

public class WindowsGreeting : Form {
    ...
}
```

The .NET Framework provides the label control in the form of the Label class and the button control in the form of the Button class. Both these classes are defined under the namespace System.Windows.Forms. We would need to create an instance of each of these classes. The code excerpt is shown here:

```
public class WindowsGreeting : Form {
    private Label m_label;
    private Button m_btnClose;

    // Initialization in the constructor
    public WindowsGreeting() {
      m_label = new Label();
      ...

      m_btnClose = new Button();
      ...

    }
}
```

The controls need to be positioned and sized properly. The framework provides a class Point to specify a location and a class Size to specify a size. These classes are defined under the namespace System.Drawing. The following code excerpt uses these classes to control the appearance of our controls:

```
        m_label.Location = new Point(16, 16);
        m_label.Size = new Size(136, 24);
        ...

        m_btnClose.Location = new Point(48, 50);
        m_btnClose.Size = new Size(56, 24);
        ...
```

The text for the button control needs to be set:

```
m_btnClose.Text = "Close";
```

We now need to add the logic to close the form when the user clicks the button control.

The button control exposes an event `Click` (you probably expected that) with a delegate of type `EventHandler`. Here is its definition:

```
public delegate void EventHandler(Object sender, EventArgs e);
```

Flexible Event Handler

The `EventHandler` delegate takes two parameters. The first parameter specifies the sender of the event. The second parameter can be used to pack any event-specific arguments. This makes `EventHandler` so flexible that all the standard events in the .NET class library use it. In theory, one can write a generic event handler that can accept virtually any event raised by the class library.

Let's ignore the parameters for the moment as they are of no current interest to us. Here is our code to handle the button click, based on the `EventHandler` definition:

```
void CloseButton_Click(Object sender, EventArgs e) {
    this.Close(); // close the form
}
```

Let's associate this method with the button click event:

```
m_btnClose.Click += new EventHandler(CloseButton_Click);
```

The controls have to be added to the form before they can be displayed. `Form` class exposes a property called `Controls` that can be used to add the controls, as shown here:

```
this.Controls.Add(m_label);
this.Controls.Add(m_btnOK);
...
```

We now need to set the dialog box window to a reasonable size:

```
this.ClientSize = new Size(150, 90);
```

Finally, although not needed for our demonstration, we will add a small enhancement to our dialog box. We will let the users press the Esc key to close the dialog box.[1] The Form class provides a property, CancelButton, that can be set to a specific button, as shown here:

```
this.CancelButton = m_btnClose;
```

With this change, when the user presses Esc, CloseButton_Click gets invoked and the form closes.

We are done with the dialog box initialization code. Here is the initialization code in its entirety:

```
public WindowsGreeting() {
    // Create the label control and specify settings
    m_label = new Label();
    m_label.Location = new Point(16, 16);
    m_label.Size = new Size(136, 24);
    m_label.Text = "";

    // Create the button control and specify settings
    m_btnClose = new Button();
    m_btnClose.Location = new Point(48, 50);
    m_btnClose.Size = new Size(56, 24);
    m_btnClose.Text = "Close";
    m_btnClose.Click += new EventHandler(CloseButton_Click);

    // Add the controls to the dialog
    this.Controls.Add(m_label);
    this.Controls.Add(m_btnClose);

    // Dialog settings
    this.ClientSize = new Size(150, 90);

    // set ESC to work as cancel button
    this.CancelButton = m_btnClose;
}
```

There is just one more piece of business to be taken care of; we need a way to specify the user name for the greeting to be displayed. Let's define a property on the class called UserName. All we need is a set accessor on this property. The code excerpt is shown here:

```
public class WindowsGreeting : Form {
    ...
    public String UserName {
        set {
```

---

1. Those of us who prefer using the keyboard over the mouse appreciate this.

```
            m_label.Text = "Hello " + value;
        }
    }
    . . .
}
```

We are done. Compile and build the assembly. Call it `WindowsGreeting.dll`. Here is the command line:

```
csc.exe -t:library \
    -r:System.Windows.Forms.dll WindowsGreeting.cs
```

Let's now write a client to use this class. Here is our new code for the client:

```
using System;
using MyGreeting;

class MyApp
{
    public static void Main() {
        WindowsGreeting dlg = new WindowsGreeting();
        dlg.UserName = "Jay";
        dlg.ShowDialog();
    }
}
```

Build this application using the following command line:

```
csc.exe -t:winexe -r:WindowsGreeting.dll HelloUser.cs
```

Option `-t:winexe` tells the compiler to build a GUI application.

Run this program. It should bring up a form similar to one shown in Figure 2.1. Click the `Close` button (or press `Esc`), and the form should disappear.

Interface-Based Programming

In the previous section, we developed a console-based server and a corresponding client. We then developed a Windows-based server and a corresponding client. Why can't we write just one client that can pick up a specified server implementation during runtime? Well, we can. Let's see how.

For our experiment, we see if there is any command-line parameter passed to our client program during execution. If there is any parameter present, we assume that the user intends to display a console greeting. If no parameters are detected, we display a Windows greeting.

So far in our examples, the entry point of the program, Main, did not have any arguments. The common language runtime accepts many overloaded method definitions for Main, which we examine in Chapter 4. There is one overloaded definition of Main that takes a single argument. If this overloaded method is used instead, then the common language runtime packages all the command-line parameters as an array of strings and passes it to the function.

Here is the new implementation of Main for the client program:

```
// Project MultipleServers

public static void Main(String[] args) {
    String userName = "Jay";

    bool bConsole = (args.Length >= 1);
    if (bConsole) {
      // console dialog
      ConsoleGreeting obj = new ConsoleGreeting();
      obj.UserName = userName;
      obj.Greet();
    }else {
      WindowsGreeting dlg = new WindowsGreeting();
      dlg.UserName = userName;
      dlg.ShowDialog();
    }
}
```

Looking at the code, there is a philosophical issue we need to address. Both ConsoleGreeting and WindowsGreeting have the same purpose—to display a greeting. However, one thing that stands out from the code is that there is no consistency in the way they are used. For example, ConsoleGreeting requires method Greet to be called, whereas WindowsGreeting requires method ShowDialog to be called. If in the future you define another class that implements a newer greeting mechanism, it probably will define a different method signature[2] to display the greeting.

It would be nice to somehow formalize the behavior so that each class can implement this behavior in its own way but the client gets to treat all the

---

2. The signature of a method is the combination of the name of the method, the parameters it has, and its return type.

classes in the same fashion. Fortunately, the common language runtime provides support for formalizing behavior in an abstraction called an *interface*.

Interfaces

An interface is simply a special type that consists of a set of methods. Unlike normal types, however, the methods are all pure virtual; that is, they do not have any implementation. Any other class that wishes to expose the behavior described by the interface can inherit from the interface and provide its own implementation. As a matter of fact, a class can inherit from as many interfaces as it desires. This support by the common language runtime for *multiple interface inheritance* more or less compensates for the *single implementation inheritance* restriction on a class.

Note that an interface can also define properties and indexers (after all, they all map to methods anyway). Also, an interface itself can inherit from one or more interfaces.

In C#, the keyword `interface` is used to define an interface. Using this keyword, the interface to greet a user can be defined as follows:

```
// Project Interfaces

// File Greeting.cs

using System;

namespace MyGreeting {
    public interface IGreeting {
        String UserName { set; }
        void Greet();
    }
}
```

Note that the interface name is prefixed with an `I`. This is a convention that the programming community has adopted to differentiate it from classes and other types.

As with classes, scoping an interface within a namespace is optional. If not explicitly scoped, the interface belongs to the global namespace.

Note that an interface can specify the type of accessor required on a property. Interface `IGreeting` mandates that a `set` accessor be implemented on property `UserName`.

Based on this interface, our `ConsoleGreeting` class can be modified as follows:

```
public class ConsoleGreeting : IGreeting {
    private String m_userName;

    public String UserName {
      set {
        m_userName = value;
      }
    }

    public void Greet() {
      Console.WriteLine("Hello " + m_userName);
    }
}
```

Interfaces versus Abstract Classes

The common language runtime (and therefore C#) also defines the notion of abstract methods and abstract classes. An abstract method is equivalent to pure virtual method in C++; that is, it does not have an implementation. An abstract class is a class that cannot be instantiated. An abstract class contains one or more abstract methods.

At first glance, an abstract class looks very similar to an interface. However, there are subtle differences between the two that you need to be aware of. First, although you can derive your class from more than one interface, you cannot derive it from more than one abstract class. Second, an abstract class may implement some functionality, whereas interfaces do not implement any functionality. Interfaces make you think in terms of interfaces—pure protocols to enforce black box communication between independent parties.

When designing your application, use interfaces to define interaction between different components and use abstract classes to define hierarchical relationships.

Similarly, our `WindowsGreeting` class can be redefined as follows:

```
public class WindowsGreeting : Form, IGreeting {
    ...
    public String UserName {
      set {
        m_label.Text = "Hello " + value;
      }
    }

    public void Greet() {
      this.ShowDialog();
    }
}
```

The following client-side code excerpt shows how to obtain an interface from a specific implementation:

```
public static IGreeting GetGreeting(bool bConsole) {
    Object obj;
    if (bConsole) {
      obj = new ConsoleGreeting();
    }else {
      obj = new WindowsGreeting();
    }
    return (IGreeting) obj;
}
```

As can be seen from the code, obtaining the desired interface from an object is as simple as typecasting the object to the interface.

What if the object doesn't support the requested interface? In this case, the common language runtime raises an exception of type InvalidCastException.

Remember that for more information on .NET defined types (e.g., InvalidCastException), you can look up the SDK documentation.

Test an Object's Type

Under C#, there are two more methods of checking if an object supports an interface. The first method is by using the keyword as, as shown here:

```
IGreeting greet = obj as IGreeting
```

If variable greet is not null, it implies that the object supports interface IGreeting:

```
if (greet != null) {
   // do something with greet
}
```

The second method is by using the keyword is, as shown here:

```
if (obj is IGreeting) {
   // do something with obj
}
```

Note that the keywords as and is are not just limited to interfaces; they can be used to check if an object can be converted to any other type. This is different than casting in that there is no exception thrown if the object is not compatible with the specified type.

The client-side main code can be rewritten as follows:

```
public static void Main(String[] args) {
    String userName = "Jay";
    bool bConsole = (args.Length >= 1);
    IGreeting greetObj = GetGreeting(bConsole);
    greetObj.UserName = userName;
    greetObj.Greet();
}
```

As can be seen, once a specific implementation has been selected, the client can use it in the same consistent manner.

Interface-based programming drives down the separation of behavior from implementation and is an important programming paradigm. It forces the clients to think in terms of interaction and not implementation. Get familiar with this paradigm. The .NET class library defines many interfaces that we use during the course of the book.

Using Interfaces or Classes?

Those who have programmed in COM know that there is no way for a client to talk to a server other than using the interfaces. .NET, however, offers class-based communication as well as interface-based communication. This raises an interesting question: What should the client use? A class or an interface? Or, what should a server expose? Classes or interfaces?

Interfaces are good paradigms for exposing generic functionality that can potentially have multiple implementations. If you think various implementations can be expressed in terms of some generic functionality, then interfaces make sense. For example, most collection classes (e.g., Array, ArrayList, etc.) under .NET provide a mechanism to iterate through each item in the collection. This functionality is nicely expressed through an interface called IEnumerator. As we will see later in the book, .NET defines quite a few interfaces, each of which express a different functionality.

Exposing a class makes sense if a single implementation can be reused. A good example is the System.Windows.Forms class that we saw earlier. It captures most of the Windows GUI functionality in just one implementation. Developers can customize their user-interface behavior by just extending this class.

DEPLOYMENT

Windows users are aware that installing an application on Windows can be complicated. For example, an installation program may copy files to various subdirectories and may update various registry settings. Backing up such an application or moving it to a different machine is not easy, as you have to hunt down all the files (spread over various directories) as well as the relevant registry entries. Moreover, uninstalling the applications may leave some files or registry entries behind, making your machine very messy.

One of the goals of .NET deployment is to simplify installation.

In the simplest case, a stand-alone .NET executable, when copied to a machine on which the .NET Framework is already installed, can simply be executed. No registry entries are changed. Moreover, simply deleting the file removes the application.

If an application consists of more than one assembly, simply copying all the assemblies to a single directory is enough to make the application run. No modifications are needed to the registry. To uninstall the application, just delete the files. This kind of deployment is often referred to as XCOPY deployment.

Of course, a real application most likely will be packaged using other mechanisms such as .cab files (used in Internet downloads) or .msi files (used by the Windows Installer service). However, there is still no need to modify registry entries just to make the application run. Creating shortcut links on users' desktop or the Start menu may require changes to some registry entries, but this is more of a Windows issue and not specific to .NET deployment.

Assemblies that are deployed to the same directory as the application are called *private assemblies,* as the assembly files are not shared with any other application (unless the other application is also copied in the same directory, but this is rare). Private assemblies are a big win for trouble-free installation. When the application is run, the common language runtime checks the local directory first to load the required assembly. This means that the common language runtime will not load a different assembly that just happens to have the same name, thus preventing administrative problems.

Private assemblies need not always be installed in the same directory as the application. For better organization, they can be installed in any subdirectory under the directory that contains the application. In this case, however, .NET requires that a configuration file be supplied to indicate the path to pick the assemblies from.

The configuration file is an XML file with a name that is the filename of the application executable with .Config at the end. For example, if the application executable were HelloUser.exe, the configuration filename would be HelloUser.exe.Config. The file must be installed in the same directory as the application.

The configuration file provides a simple administrative control. As we will see in later chapters, there are many settings, such as those related to versioning and remoting, that are best decided by the user or administrator of the application. Such settings can be specified in this file.

The setting that we are concerned with here is called the PrivatePath setting. The following configuration shows how the common language runtime can be asked to look for private assemblies in a subdirectory called MyBin (Project Interfaces):

```
<?xml version="1.0"?>
<configuration>
   <runtime>
     <assemblyBinding xmlns="urn:schemas-microsoft-com:asm.v1">
         <probing privatePath="MyBin"/>
     </assemblyBinding>
   </runtime>
</configuration>
```

Private assemblies should be used whenever possible. However, there are times when an assembly has to be installed such that it is shared with multiple applications. Things start getting a bit complicated in this case. In a later chapter, we will look at how shared assemblies are installed, locally, as well as when downloaded from the Internet.

DIAGNOSTICS AND SUPPORT

So far we have looked at developing and deploying .NET applications. Part of software development is also to specify what the code is expected to do (by means of documentation) and to debug and verify that the code is working the way you expect. The .NET SDK provides many useful tools and mechanisms for these purposes. Let's take a look at some of them.

Tracing

The simplest way to check the behavior of the code is to add some trace statements into the code. The .NET Framework provides a class Debug (namespace System.Diagnostics) that provides many useful static methods to instrument your code. For example, Debug.Write can be used to output a string, as shown in the following code excerpt:

```
// Project Tracing

public static void Main() {
    Debug.Write("Debug: I am in main");
    ...
}
```

`Debug.Write` is a conditional statement; it is included in the source code only if a symbol `DEBUG` is defined. With the C# compiler, this can be done by specifying `–d:DEBUG` as a command-line parameter, as shown here:

```
csc.exe -t:exe -d:DEBUG -out:MyAppDebug.exe MyApp.cs
```

The output of the Debug statement is captured by a BCL-defined static collection object, `Debug.Listeners`. By default, this collection object contains just one listener, `DefaultTraceListener`. This default trace listener outputs to the Windows system debugger (using `OutputDebugString` Windows API). Most standard debuggers such as the one that comes with Visual Studio .NET can catch this output. When a debug executable is run from Visual Studio .NET, the trace messages can be seen in the Output window in Visual Studio .NET.

You can also catch the output from `OutputDebugString` using the Debug Monitor (`DbMon.exe`), a tool that comes with the Windows Platform SDK. The source code (`DbMon.c`) can be downloaded from [MS-90].

Besides `Write`, class `Debug` provides many other useful routines such as `WriteLine`, `Assert`, `WriteLineIf`, and so on. Look into the SDK documentation for more details.

Symbol `DEBUG` is used only for debug builds and should never be used with builds that will be shipped to the customers. What if you wish to trace execution in a shipping product? The .NET Framework defines yet another class `Trace` just for this purpose. `Trace` is identical to `Debug` in most respects, except that it gets enabled when a symbol `TRACE` is defined during compilation.

Debug Build Settings

For debug builds, it is a good idea to define both DEBUG and TRACE symbols.

No matter which tracing class you use, you are not limited to use just the default trace listener. You can always create your own `TraceListener` derived class and add it to `Debug.Listeners` or `Trace.Listeners`. As a matter of fact, the framework defines two such classes, `TextWriter-TraceListener` and `EventLogTraceListener`, that you can use to customize tracing within your application. The former class can be used to redirect tracing to a stream class (such as a file) and the second one can be used to redirect tracing to the Windows event log.

You can also control the amount of tracing information by means of some switches. The SDK documentation explains this in detail.

Using the Debugger

The .NET SDK supplies a console-based tool (CorDbg.exe) and a Windows-based tool (DbgClr.exe) to debug an application. However, the Visual Studio .NET debugger is much more powerful than either of these debuggers and probably would remain the most popular choice of debugger.

No matter which debugger is used, the application being debugged has to be compiled such that it contains debugging information (unless you are good at debugging in hex numbers). This can be done by using the -debug command-line option on the compiler, as shown in the following example (Project Debugging):

```
csc.exe -t:exe -debug -out:MyAppDebug.exe MyApp.cs
```

Option -debug does two things:

1. It creates a programmer's database (PDB) file that maps MSIL instructions to source code lines.

2. Creating just the PDB file is not enough. We also need a mapping between the MSIL instructions and the native code. Recall that the native code is generated on the fly. The JIT compiler has to be instructed to create the mapping between native code and MSIL. Option -debug causes this to happen by setting an assembly-level attribute called JITTracking.

Note that the JITTracking attribute gets set automatically if you run the program from within the debugger. However, if you attach to an already running process, and if this attribute was not set during compilation, then there is no mapping back to MSIL instructions and therefore to the source code. In this case, the only code that you can see from the debugger is the native language instructions.

To run a program using CorDbg.exe, you can specify the executable name as a command-line parameter, as shown here:

```
CorDbg.exe MyAppDebug.exe
```

Once you are in the debugger, you can set breakpoints, examine variables, execute the code to the next breakpoint, and so on, pretty much what you would expect from a standard debugger.

As a bonus, the source code for CorDbg is supplied as an SDK sample. It is a good reference sample to get more insight into how the common language runtime executes a program.

DbgClr.exe is based on work that was being done for the Visual Studio .NET debugger. Although not as powerful as Visual Studio .NET debugger, it is still a decent GUI-based debugger.

Documentation

We all agree that documenting code is as important as developing code, although it is a tedious job.[3] Fortunately, C# provides a simple mechanism for the developers to document their code using XML. Structures, classes, interfaces, methods, events, properties, and so on, can all be documented using the /// commenting style followed by a predefined XML tag. The following code excerpt demonstrates the use of some common tags to document classes and methods (Project Documentation):

```
/// <summary>This is my main application class</summary>
/// <remarks>
///  This is where a longer comment for my class goes.
/// </remarks>
class MyApp
{
    /// <summary>
    ///  This function greets the specified user
    /// </summary>
    /// <param name="user">The name of the user</param>
    /// <returns>Doesn't return any value</returns>
    public static void Greet(String user) {
      Console.WriteLine("Hello " + user);
    }

    /// <summary>The main entry point</summary>
    public static void Main()
    {
      MyApp.Greet("Jay");
    }
}
```

---

3. Most developers I have worked with do not seem to like documenting code.

Any valid XML tag can be used for documentation. However, some commonly used tags are documented in the SDK under C# Language Features.

The compiler can be directed, using –doc option, to process this source file and produce an XML documentation file. The following command line results in producing MyDoc.xml as the documentation file.

```
csc.exe -out:MyApp.exe MyApp.cs -doc:MyDoc.xml
```

The generated XML file can be run through a transformation mechanism that produces the output in the desired format.

SUMMARY

C# provides the flexibility of C++ and the simplicity of Visual Basic. It has many features that have a close tie to the .NET Framework. It also provides productivity features such as automated documentation.

The heart of the .NET Framework is the common language runtime, the runtime environment that manages the execution of MSIL code. Any code that targets the common language runtime is called managed code; it benefits from many features offered by the common language runtime, such as automatic garbage collection, JIT compilation of MSIL to native code, and cross-language operability. The common language runtime also provides a uniform mechanism for error handling by way of exceptions.

The .NET Framework defines many base datatypes such as System.String, System.Int32, and so on. These types are implemented in the BCL, a framework-supplied library. The BCL is a set of assemblies, MSCorLib.dll being one example.

Under .NET, all types get derived from System.Object, either directly or indirectly.

The common language runtime supports the class-based as well as the interface-based client–server programming model.

An assembly is a unit of deployment. It can be thought of as a logical DLL or EXE file that exposes types.

There are three types of assemblies—library assembly, console-based assembly, and Windows-based (GUI) assembly.

The .NET Framework provides many classes to simplify developing console-based as well as GUI applications. It also provides classes and tools to help diagnose problems.

By this time, readers should be reasonably familiar with C#, the common programming paradigms under .NET, and many key aspects of the .NET Framework. The framework, and therefore C#, offers many other features such as attribute-based programming and interoperability with COM+ components and Win32 APIs. In the coming chapters, we unfold many such features.

REFERENCES

[Tru-00]   Trupin, Joshua, "C# Offers the Power of C++ and Simplicity of Visual Basic," *MSDN Magazine*, September 2000.
msdn.microsoft.com/msdnmag/issues/0900/csharp/csharp.asp

[MS-90]   Microsoft, "DBMON: Implements a Debug Monitor," Microsoft SDK samples, 1990.
msdn.microsoft.com/library/devprods/vs6/visualc/vcsample/vcsmpdbmon.htm

[Gun-00]   Gunnerson, Eric, *A Programmer's Introduction to C#*, Associate Press, September 2000.

[Lib-01]   Liberty, Jesse, "What You Need to Know to Move From C++ to C#," *MSDN Magazine*, July 2001.
msdn.microsoft.com/msdnmag/issues/01/07/ctocsharp/ctocsharp.asp

[Misc-00]   Hewlett-Packard, Intel Corporation and Microsoft, "ECMA Standardization," October 2000.
msdn.microsoft.com/net/ecma

Assemblies

In the previous chapter, we learned that the executables generated by the
.NET compilers are called assemblies. Under .NET, assemblies form the fundamental building block of program components. In defining the format for
the assembly, .NET had many goals. These goals included interoperability
among different programming languages, side-by-side execution of multiple
versions of the same assembly, performance enhancements, and so on. In this
chapter, we take an in-depth look at the assemblies and examine how these
goals were achieved. By the end of the chapter, you will have a good knowledge of the assembly internals and the packaging and deployment model
under .NET.

ASSEMBLIES

Assemblies are the building blocks of .NET Framework applications. They
form the smallest unit of code distribution in the .NET Framework.

An assembly consists of one or more Win32 Portable Executable (PE)
files. A Win32 PE file is built in a file format for executables that is common
across all flavors of Windows. More information about PE file format (and
the newer enhancements to it for 64-bit Windows) can be found in [Pie-02].
Each PE file within the assembly is referred to as a *module*.

An assembly can also contain auxiliary files such as HTML files, read-
me files, and so on. Although an assembly may consist of multiple modules
and auxiliary files, the assembly is named, versioned, and deployed as an
atomic unit. For our current discussion, it is easier to view an assembly as a
single executable file. This by far is the most common case for assemblies.

The .NET compilers can build an assembly either as a library file (with a typical filename extension `.dll`) or a stand-alone executable (extension `.exe`) file. Table 3.1 shows the compiler switches available with C# compiler (and most other .NET compilers) to build different types of assemblies.

TABLE 3.1   Assembly Type Compiler Switches

Switch	Assembly Type
`-t:library`	Library
`-t:exe`	Console user interface (CUI) executable
`-t:winexe`	GUI executable

An EXE-based assembly can be executed just as a standard stand-alone Win32 executable, for example, by entering the filename from a console window or by double-clicking the filename from Windows Explorer. A DLL-based assembly, on the other hand, is required to be loaded dynamically, either implicitly by the common language runtime or explicitly in your code.

To emulate the behavior of a stand-alone Win32 executable, an EXE-based assembly contains two additional pieces of information:

1. It contains a small piece of bootstrapping code that points to `CorExe-Main`, an API exported by the common language runtime. This function contains the logic to host the common language runtime. So, when the application is executed, the control is transferred to `CorExeMain`, which in turn loads the common language runtime into the process and transfers control over to it.

2. It defines an entry point that the common language runtime can start executing code from. When we write code in a higher level language such as C#, the compiler automatically assumes that the entry point is a static method named `Main`.

Other than these two differences, both types of assemblies are treated similarly by the runtime. For example, an EXE-based assembly can just as easily be loaded dynamically, as illustrated in the following code excerpt:

```
// Project LoadAssembly

   public static void Main(String[] args) {
      Assembly a = Assembly.LoadFrom("ConsoleGreeting.exe");
      Console.WriteLine(a.FullName);
   }
```

The .NET Framework defines a class `Assembly` (namespace `System.Reflection`) to encapsulate an assembly. This class defines a static method, `LoadFrom`, to load an assembly given its filename. The preceding code loads an assembly named `ConsoleGreeting.exe` and outputs the display name of the assembly (property `FullName`). The display name of an assembly is the string representation of the identity of the assembly. The output from the program is shown here:

```
ConsoleGreeting, Version=1.2.3.4, Culture=neutral, PublicKeyToken=null
```

Let's see how we can interpret this identity of the assembly.

ASSEMBLY IDENTIFICATION

An assembly is uniquely identified by four parts—its name, version, culture, and public key. The assembly resolver, a part of the common language runtime that is responsible for locating assemblies, uses this four-part information to locate the correct assembly.

Name

The `Name` part of the assembly name typically corresponds to the underlying filename (without the extension) of the assembly.

Strictly speaking, the `Name` of the assembly need not match the underlying filename. However, keeping the two names in sync makes the job of the assembly resolver (and humans) easier.

Version

Each assembly has a four-part version number of the form `Major.Minor.Build.Revision`. This version number is set at build time using an assembly-level attribute (attributes provide extra information on parts of your code) called `AssemblyVersionAttribute` (namespace `System.Reflection`), as illustrated here:

```
// File ConsoleGreeting.cs
[assembly: AssemblyVersionAttribute("1.2.3.4")]
```

If the version number is not explicitly set on an assembly, the default value is 0.0.0.0.

When specifying the version number, only the `Major` field is mandatory. Any other missing fields are assumed to be zero. For example, specifying a version string of 1.2 results in an actual version value of 1.2.0.0.

Using Visual Studio .NET IDE

If you create your .NET project using the Visual Studio .NET Integrated Development Environment (IDE), the IDE automatically generates `AssemblyVersion-Attribute`, and other related attributes, stores them in a file named `AssemblyInfo.cs`, and adds the file to the project.

It is also possible to let the compiler generate the build and the revision number. This is done by replacing the build and the revision field by a single asterick, as in `1.2.*`. In this case, the compiler generates the build number as the number of days that have elapsed since January 1, 2000 and the revision number as half the number of seconds since midnight.

You can also use `*` just for the revision number, but not for the build number. For example, `1.2.3.*` is legal but `1.2.*.3` is illegal.

Culture

A culture, in simple terms, identifies a specific language and optionally a sublanguage (e.g., Australian English). Associated with the language (and the sublanguage) also are some culture-specific operations such as currency, number, and date formatting.

Each culture is identified by a name. The naming scheme is based on Request for Comments (RFC) 1766 [Alv-95]. For example, U.S. English is "en-US" and Spanish from Spain is "es-ES."

Culture settings are typically used to build resource-only assemblies, commonly known as *satellite assemblies*. The main idea behind building satellite assemblies is that an application can load a resource from the appropriate satellite assembly, based on the current culture setting of the application.

The culture setting is assigned to a satellite assembly at the time of building the assembly.

We will look into building satellite assemblies in a later section. For now, it is important to note that the assemblies containing the code are marked as culture-neutral—such an assembly can contain resources that can run under any culture settings.

Public Key

The .NET Framework provides a mechanism to guarantee that an assembly has not been tampered with, perhaps by a malicious hacker, once the assembly has been created. This is done by using standard public-key cryptographic techniques—the assembly is signed with a cryptographic public–private key pair. Such an assembly is called *strong-named assembly*. Assemblies that are not strong-named are referred to as *simple assemblies*.

Strong-named assemblies are also useful to ensure correct binding between an application and its referenced assemblies. For each strong-named assembly that the application references (or loads dynamically), the common language runtime tries to bind the assembly that has the exact name, version, culture, and public key. The importance of this will become evident when we discuss the "DLL hell" problem later in the chapter.

A Restriction on Strong-Named Assemblies

When you use a strong-named assembly, you get certain benefits such as versioning and integrity check. If a strong-named assembly in turn references a simple-named assembly, these benefits are lost. Therefore, the framework prohibits a strong-named assembly from referencing simple-named assemblies.

To build a strong-named assembly, you must first obtain a public–private key pair. The framework provides a utility called the Strong Name tool (sn.exe) that can be used to generate the key pair. The following command line, for example, generates a key pair and stores it in MyKey.snk:

```
sn.exe -k MyKey.snk
```

Switch -k is used to generate a key pair and store it in the specified file (.snk is the typical extension for such files). The public key is made of a 128-byte blob with 32 bytes of header information. The private key is made of a 436-byte blob. This brings the size of the generated public–private key pair file to 596 bytes.

An assembly can be signed with the strong-named key file by using an attribute, AssemblyKeyFileAttribute (namespace System.Reflection), in any one of the source files. The following source line, for example, specifies that the assembly be signed using MyKey.snk:

```
[assembly: AssemblyKeyFileAttribute("MyKey.snk")]
```

When this attribute is specified, the compiler takes care of signing the resulting assembly with the specified filename.

Project `SharedAssembly` on the companion Web site demonstrates building shared assemblies.

Note that there are also some other ways to sign an assembly. For example, the .NET Framework provides a tool called the Assembly Linker (`al.exe`) that can be used to sign the assembly. The tool uses a command-line switch `-keyfile` for this purpose.

Building from VS .NET and Command Line

If a complete path to the key file is not specified to `AssemblyKeyFile` attribute, the build process expects the file to be in a directory relative to the directory from which the build was initiated. Almost all the projects on the companion Web site that create strong-named assemblies have the key file in the output directory (`\Bin`). This directory also contains the makefile for command line builds. In order to be able to build the assemblies from VS .NET as well as from the command line makefile, the source code defines the key file attribute as follows:

```
#if CMDLINE
[assembly: AssemblyKeyFile("MyKey.snk")]
#else
[assembly: AssemblyKeyFile(@".\Bin\MyKey.snk")]
#endif
```

The makefile defines the symbol CMDLINE, as shown in the following example:

```
csc.exe -define:CMDLINE ...
```

Using a conditional directive in the source code for the key file attribute to achieve builds from VS .NET as well as from the command line is a common programming technique under .NET. You will see this technique being used in many .NET SDK samples.

Public keys are represented by a large number of bytes (a 128-byte blob with 32 bytes of header information). To conserve storage space, the framework hashes the public key and takes the last 8 bytes of the hashed value. This reduced public key value, also known as the *public key token*, has been determined to be statistically unique.

Obtaining the Public Key Token

To get the public key token from a strong-named assembly, run `sn.exe` in a command window with the `-T` command-line switch, as shown here:

```
sn.exe -T ConsoleGreeting.dll
```

Using `sn.exe -T` is also a good way to check if an assembly is strong-named. Note that the command-line switch specified is uppercase T. Do not make the mistake of using -t (lowercase). It results in displaying a bogus public key token. This switch is meant to be specified on a file that contains only the public key (as opposed to the public–private key pair).

The combination of the name, version, and culture, along with the public key (or its token) creates a unique identity for an assembly. Assemblies with the same strong name are expected to be identical. It is impossible for a hacker to create a new assembly with exactly the same name and the same public key as your assembly. A strong name also ensures that no one else can produce a subsequent version of your assembly (as long as the cryptographic key file is not leaked out).

Note that an assembly that is not cryptographically signed has a public key token value of null, as we saw in the output of the last example that we ran.

The common language runtime defines a standard format to represent the four parts as a string. This string representation is called the display name of the assembly. Its format is shown here:

```
Name <,Version=value> <,Culture=value> <,PublicKeyToken=value>
```

Although an assembly can be loaded by using its filename, as we saw earlier, a more common technique is to load the assembly by means of its display name. This is done using a static method Assembly.Load, as illustrated in the following code:

```
// Project LoadAssembly

    public static void Main(String[] args) {
        ...
        String name =
        "ConsoleGreeting, Version=1.2.3.4, Culture=neutral,
            PublicKeyToken=null";
        Assembly b = Assembly.Load(name);
        ...
    }
```

Method Assembly.Load causes the resolver to look into the application directory (and some other subdirectories of the application). Only the Name property of the assembly name is mandatory. All other parts are optional. Here are some examples of identifying an assembly:

```
ConsoleGreeting,Version=1.2.3.4,Culture="",
    PublicKeyToken=4028b28a1c16b46e
ConsoleGreeting,Version=1.2.3.4,Culture=""
```

```
ConsoleGreeting,Version=1.2.3.4
ConsoleGreeting
ConsoleGreeting, PublicKeyToken=4028b28a1c16b46e
```

Note that there is a difference between Culture=neutral and Culture="" or omitting the Culture keyword altogether. In the first case, the assembly resolver looks for a culture-neutral assembly. In the second case, the resolver matches any Culture settings.

A similar difference exists between PublicKeyToken=null and no PublicKeyToken keyword. The first case indicates that an assembly to be loaded does not have any public key. In the second case, the resolver matches any PublicKeyToken setting.

Here is an example of loading an assembly by using just the Name field:

```
// Project LoadAssembly

    public static void Main(String[] args) {
        ...
        String name = "ConsoleGreeting";
        Assembly c = Assembly.Load(name);
        ...
    }
```

Note that the Name of the assembly does not contain any extension. The assembly resolver automatically appends an extension to the name. In the preceding case, the resolver first tries to load ConsoleGreeting.dll, failing which it tries to load ConsoleGreeting.exe.

If the resolver cannot locate an assembly, it throws a standard exception of type System.IO.FileNotFoundException.

ANATOMY OF AN ASSEMBLY

Figure 3.1 shows the major parts of an assembly.

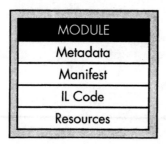

FIGURE 3.1 Parts of an assembly.

Let's look at each of these parts in detail.

Modules

Technically, an assembly is not limited to just one PE file; it may contain more than one PE file, each referred to as a *module*.

A module is uniquely identified by a GUID called the module version ID (MVID). This extra level of indirection makes it possible to change the module filename while keeping a record of the original filename. The MVID is automatically generated by the compiler.

It should be noted that the most common case for an assembly is to contain just a single module. In this case, the module and the assembly are one and the same.

Building multimodule assemblies is covered under advanced topics later in the chapter.

Metadata

Consider the following simple Hello User application, taken from the previous chapter:

```
// Project HelloUser

class MyApp
{
    public static void Main() {
        System.String userName = "Jay";
        System.Console.WriteLine("Hello " + userName);
    }
}
```

When this code is compiled, how does the compiler know that there exist classes called System.String and System.Console, and that System.Console provides a static method called WriteLine that takes a System.String type parameter?

Recall from the previous chapter that we had to reference assembly MSCorLib.dll while compiling this application. For your convenience, the command line is shown here once again:

```
csc.exe -t:exe -out:HelloUser.exe -r:MSCorLib.dll HelloUser.cs
```

As you might have guessed, the information on the available classes and methods is coming from MSCorLib.dll.

When a .NET compiler processes the source code and generates the module, not only does it generate the MSIL code, but it also generates the information about every type the source code contains. This information is referred to as the metadata (data about data). The metadata is necessary for the common language runtime to provide managed services to the code while it executes.

The metadata is stored in a binary form within the module. All .NET-compliant compilers are required to generate full metadata information about every class type in the compiled source code file. Among other things, this metadata contains a declaration for each type, the base class and the interfaces the type inherits from, the name and type (methods, properties, events, and fields) of all its members, and the signature of each of the methods.

Armed with the metadata information, the compiler can now verify if a class being accessed in the source code is present in the referenced assemblies and whether or not the parameters being passed to a method match the signature of the method.

Metadata versus Type Libraries

Readers who are familiar with COM may notice the conceptual similarity between the metadata and COM technologies such as type-libraries and IDL files. The important thing to note is that the metadata is far more complete and is always embedded in the same executable as the code. A type library, for example, need not always be embedded with the executable.

The fact that the metadata is embedded in the assembly makes for another interesting possibility: A client can explicitly load an assembly during runtime, instantiate a class stored in the assembly, and invoke a method on the instance. Such late-bound method invocation capability is provided by a .NET Framework subsystem called Reflection. We will see some examples of Reflection under advanced topics later in the chapter. Java language users may be aware that Java provides a similar functionality.

Viewing the Metadata

The .NET Framework provides a tool called the IL Disassembler (ildasm.exe) to disassemble a .NET module. This disassembler not only shows the MSIL code in the module but also lets you examine the embedded metadata.

Checking if a File Is a .NET Assembly

Here is a quick way to check if an EXE or DLL file is an assembly. Run
ildasm.exe on the file. If the file is not a valid assembly file, ildasm.exe displays an error message.

Let's run the IL Disassembler on HelloUser.exe. Here is the command line:

```
ildasm.exe HelloUser.exe
```

Here is the partial output from ildasm.exe:

```
.assembly extern mscorlib
{
  .publickeytoken = (B7 7A 5C 56 19 34 E0 89 )
  .ver 1:0:3300:0
}

.module HelloUser.exe
// MVID: {90A8865C-4C5F-477D-A8CA-4D45A1CE9B65}

.class private auto ansi beforefieldinit MyApp
       extends [mscorlib]System.Object
{
  .method public hidebysig static void  Main() cil managed
  {
    . . .
  } // end of method MyApp::Main

  .method public hidebysig specialname rtspecialname
          instance void   .ctor() cil managed
  {
    . . .
  } // end of method MyApp::.ctor
} // end of class MyApp
```

As can be seen, HelloUser.exe implements MyApp, a private class that is inherited from System.Object, a class defined in the BCL. Recall from the previous chapter that every type under .NET is ultimately derived from System.Object (we cover System.Object in more detail in the next chapter). Furthermore, MyApp defines a public method Main and a public class constructor (ctor). The signature of the method Main indicates that it takes no parameters and has a void return type.

Class MyApp is marked with attributes such as auto, ansi, beforefiel-dinit, and so on. The SDK documentation explains these attributes under TypeAttributes enumeration. Likewise, method attributes such as hide-bysig, specialname, and so on, can be found under MethodAttributes enumeration in the SDK documentation. It is not important to fully understand these attributes. We discuss them only on a need-to-know basis.

You may be wondering where the constructor code came from, even though MyApp doesn't define one. It just so happens that the C# compiler generates a default constructor if one is not explicitly defined. You can easily guess that the default constructor simply invokes the constructor for the base class, System.Object.

You can also see from the output that HelloUser.exe references an assembly named mscorlib version 1.0.3300.0. As an exercise, you can run ildasm on MsCorLib.dll to verify that there exist classes called System.String and System.Console, and that System.Console provides a static method called WriteLine that takes a System.String type parameter.

Disassembler for Advanced Users

The IL Disassembler provides an undocumented command-line switch -adv that makes it run in an advanced mode. In this mode, the Disassembler provides some additional metadata information about the disassembled file. For more information, type ildasm.exe -adv -? on the command line.

At this point, is worth mentioning that a type is implicitly identified by the assembly it is defined in. For example, if you define a public class Foo in two different assemblies, they are treated as two different types, even though they share the same name. Hopefully, by scoping them in a different namespace, you can avoid any naming conflicts.

A namespace, on the other hand, can span multiple assemblies. However, it is important to keep in mind that if two assemblies define a type with the same name and the same namespace, the runtime still treats them as two different types. A type is always scoped within the assembly it is defined in.

Extending the Metadata—Attributes

An important aspect of the metadata under .NET is that it is fully extensible. Developers can add extra information on various parts of the code using *attributes*. Attributes can be applied to classes, structs, events, delegates, member fields, constructors, methods, method parameters, return values, and even assemblies. Unlike comments, which get stripped off when the code is compiled, compilers store the attributes as part of the metadata. They can later be examined either by the common language runtime or whoever else is interested, using Reflection API.

Attributes provide a flexible way to extend the behavior of a program entity. Earlier, we saw how attributes can be used to specify the version number on an assembly. As we go through the rest of the book, you will see that attribute-based programming is quite pervasive under the .NET Framework. The usefulness of attributes is limited only by your imagination.

Manifest

The manifest is a part of the assembly that stores some record-keeping information pertaining to the module. This information includes, among other things, the MVID and the list of referenced assemblies.

Assembly Paths

Note that the manifest does not store the file path of the referenced assemblies, just their display names. It is the responsibility of the assembly resolver to locate the referenced assemblies when the application is run.

Technically, the manifest is a part of the metadata. However, metadata generally is used to refer to type metadata, not to manifest metadata.

It is relevant to understand the distinction between the assembly manifest and the module manifest. Each module within an assembly contains the manifest. However, there is one module within the assembly with a manifest that contains some extra information pertaining to the assembly as a whole. The extra information includes, among other things, the identity of the assembly and the list of files that constitute the assembly. The module is called the prime module and the manifest it stores is referred to as the assembly manifest. In general, unless explicitly stated, a manifest refers to the assembly manifest.

Resources

Generally, it is not a good idea to hard-code strings in the source code. Storing strings in a separate file makes it easy to modify the strings without modifying the source code.

The .NET Framework makes it possible to embed resources such as strings and images stored in external files into an assembly. The resources can then be loaded programmatically using a BCL class `ResourceManager` (namespace `System.Resources`).

It should be noted that when dealing with localized resources (i.e., resources dealing with a specific culture), it is better to store them in a satellite assembly. We look at storing resources in an assembly as well as creating satellite assemblies later in the chapter.

SHARED ASSEMBLIES

Assemblies frequently reference other assemblies. Recall from the previous chapter that the references can be specified either by using `-r` switch on the C# compiler or by using a response file.

An assembly can execute only if the assembly resolver is able to locate the referenced assemblies. One way to ensure this is to deploy all the referenced assemblies in the same directory as that of the main application or a subdirectory under the application's directory, as we saw in the previous chapter. In this case, the referenced assemblies are called private assemblies as they are "private" to the application using them.

Private assemblies are good if there is only one application consuming them, and they are preferred. There are times, however, when you wish to share an assembly with multiple applications. A good example of such a shared assembly is `MsCorLib.dll`; it is used by multiple applications. Shared assemblies are typically created by one company and used by other companies.

Obviously, a shared assembly has to be installed in a common place such that it is accessible to other applications. Under .NET, this shared area is called the Global Assembly Cache (GAC).

The GAC is present on each machine that has the .NET Framework installed and acts as a machine-wide code cache. It is located in the `<windir>\assembly` subdirectory where `<windir>` is the Windows directory (e.g., `C:\Windows`).

A region of the GAC is used to store assemblies downloaded over the Internet or intranet. This region is called the download cache. There is one download cache per user.

To add an assembly to the GAC, the .NET Framework provides a utility called the GAC tool (`gacutil.exe`). To add `ConsoleGreeting.dll` from our previous chapter to the GAC, for example, the following command line can be used:

```
gacutil.exe -i ConsoleGreeting.dll
```

Switch -i indicates that the specified assembly should be added to the GAC. For a multifile assembly, the prime module (the module containing the assembly's manifest) must be specified as the parameter.

Note that you need administrative privileges to install an assembly in the GAC.

Choose Your Installer Wisely

XCOPY installation works very well for simple applications that use just the private assemblies. However, the mechanism is not suitable if you wish to install assemblies into the GAC or perform some special operations, such as running an assembly as a service.

On a customer's machine, the preferred way of installing assemblies in the GAC is by using an installer that is designed to work with the GAC. Windows Installer 2.0 is one such installer.

Table 3.2 lists important switches on the GAC tool. Check the SDK documentation for a complete list.

TABLE 3.2   GAC Tool Switches

Switch	Description
-l	List assemblies in the GAC
-u	Uninstall an assembly from the GAC
-ldl	List assemblies in the download cache for the current user
-cdl	Clear the download cache for the current user

There is one more way to view and manipulate the contents of the GAC, using the Windows Explorer. The .NET Framework provides a Windows shell extension called the Assembly Cache Viewer (shfusion.dll) for this purpose. For example, to view the contents of the GAC, you just have to navigate to the <windir>\assembly subdirectory from Windows Explorer. A snapshot of the GAC from the viewer is shown in Figure 3.2.

To add an assembly to the GAC, you can just drag and drop the assembly file to this directory. To delete an assembly, select its name in the Explorer and press delete.

Note that the download cache for the current user can be found under <windir>\assembly\Download subdirectory.

Global Assembly Name	Type	Version	Culture	Public Key Token
mscorlib	Native Images	1.0.3300.0		b77a5c561934e089
MSDATASRC		7.0.3300.0		b03f5f7f11d50a3a
MSDDSLMP		7.0.3300.0		b03f5f7f11d50a3a
MSDDSP		7.0.3300.0		b03f5f7f11d50a3a
Office		7.0.3300.0		b03f5f7f11d50a3a
Regcode		1.0.3300.0		b03f5f7f11d50a3a
SoapSudsCode		1.0.3300.0		b03f5f7f11d50a3a
stdole		7.0.3300.0		b03f5f7f11d50a3a
System	Native Images	1.0.3300.0		b77a5c561934e089
System		1.0.3300.0		b77a5c561934e089
System.Configuration.Install		1.0.3300.0		b03f5f7f11d50a3a
System.Data		1.0.3300.0		b77a5c561934e089
System.Design	Native Images	1.0.3300.0		b03f5f7f11d50a3a

FIGURE 3.2 Global Assembly Cache.

Viewing Raw GAC

When the assembly is installed in the GAC, a unique subdirectory is created and all the files of the assembly are copied into the subdirectory. You cannot see this subdirectory from Windows Explorer (because of the Window shell extension). However, you can open a console window and navigate to the GAC directory to see its contents in raw form.

There is an important security issue to be considered when installing shared assemblies. As a shared assembly can potentially be used by many applications, it is important to ensure that the assembly is not tampered with after it is created. By maliciously tampering the assembly, a hacker can cause substantial damage, especially if the assembly gets executed in a privileged account. Therefore, .NET mandates that only strong-named assemblies can be installed in the GAC.

Earlier, I mentioned that to load an assembly programmatically, only the filename field of its identity is a must, the other fields are optional. However, the preferred way to load an assembly from the GAC is to provide a full reference (e.g., the complete identity string), as illustrated in the following code. Here, we are trying to load a runtime installed assembly, System.Windows.Forms, from the GAC:

```
// Project LoadAssembly

name = @"System.Windows.Forms, Version=1.0.3300.0,
   Culture=neutral, PublicKeyToken=b77a5c561934e089";
Assembly e = Assembly.Load(name);
Console.WriteLine(e.FullName);
```

For partial references, method `Assembly.Load` does not even bother to look into the GAC. The only exception to this is the assembly `MsCor-Lib.dll`, which does not require a full reference. The assembly resolver gives special treatment to this assembly and lets you locate it with just the name field of the identification.

If you wish the assembly resolver to consider looking into the GAC as well as application-specific directories, then you can use another method, `Assembly.LoadWithPartialName`, as shown in the following example:

```
// Load with partial reference from the GAC
name = @"System.Windows.Forms";
Assembly a6 = Assembly.LoadWithPartialName(name);
Console.WriteLine(a6.FullName);
```

The End of DLL Hell

Windows users have probably experienced the problem of installing a new application that suddenly breaks some other previously installed application(s) on the machine. This usually happens when the applications share a DLL and the newer version of the DLL is not compatible with previously installed applications. This problem is referred to as DLL hell.

.NET eliminates this DLL hell problem once and for all. The crux of the DLL hell problem is that the newer version of the DLL replaced the existing version of the DLL, but this newer version is not fully compatible with previously installed applications, thus breaking those applications.

.NET makes it possible for multiple versions of a shared assembly to coexist on the same machine. To install a newer version of an assembly, just add it to the GAC. The GAC will store the older and newer versions. From GAC's point of view, these are two different assemblies, as their strong names do not match (because of the version number). As a matter of fact, as the GAC indexes an assembly by the strong name, it is entirely possible to have two assemblies with the same name, public key, and version, but different culture settings.

We already know that when an application is executed, for each strong-named assembly the application references, the assembly resolver tries to bind with the exact version of the assembly that the application was built with. As a result, if a newer version of a shared assembly is installed on the machine, the previous installed application can continue to use the older version of the assembly, effectively eliminating the DLL hell problem.

Although the default behavior of the runtime is to find an exact match on the version number of the strong-named assemblies, it is possible to customize this behavior by means of configuration files. This gives the administrators a chance to use the older applications with the newer version of the shared assemblies and, if things don't work as expected, revert back to the older version.

Let's see how the assembly binding behavior can be customized using the configuration files.

CONFIGURATION FILES

Assembly binding behavior can be configured based on three XML-based files: the application configuration file, the publisher policy configuration file, and the machine configuration file. These files follow the same syntax and provide information such as binding redirects and the location of the code.

Using a file-based configuration mechanism gives tremendous flexibility in terms of customizing an application's or assembly's behavior.

Let's take a look at each of the configuration files.

Application Configuration File

An application configuration file contains settings specific to an application. The name and location of the application configuration file depends on the application's host.

- *Executable-hosted application*: These applications generally have an `.exe` filename extension and can be run, for example, by double-clicking them in the Explorer window. For such an application, the name of the configuration file is the name of the application with a `.config` extension. For example, the configuration file for `MyApp.exe` must be named `MyApp.exe.config` (the name is case-insensitive). The configuration file should stay in the same directory as that of the application.

- *ASP.NET-hosted application*: These files are named `Web.config`. These files can be stored in either the application's root directory or any of its subdirectories. Configuration files in ASP.NET inherit the settings of configuration files in the Uniform Resource Locator (URL) path. For example, if the application is located at *www.mycompany.com/abc*, then the ASP.NET pages at *www.mycompany.com/abc/def/* looks at the configuration settings of `abc` as well as `abc/def` directories.

The configuration information is stored in text files as XML files. The root element of the configuration file is `<configuration>`. At the next level, configuration settings are grouped by their purpose. For example, configuration settings related to the common language runtime are stored under the `<runtime>` element, as illustrated in the following code:

```
<?xml version="1.0"?>
<configuration>
  <runtime>
    <assemblyBinding xmlns="urn:schemas-microsoft-com:asm.v1">
        <probing privatePath="MyBin"/>
    </assemblyBinding>
  </runtime>
</configuration>
```

We came across this example in Chapter 2. The `privatePath` entry here informs the common language runtime to include `MyBin` in the search path for locating assemblies for the application. Here, I show you its usage for two frequently used tasks:

1. Redirect the runtime to use a different assembly version.

2. Ask the runtime to download an assembly over the network.

Binding Redirection

In our earlier `HelloUser` example, `HelloUser.exe` references assembly `ConsoleGreeting.dll` version 1.2.3.4. Let's say `ConsoleGreeting.dll` was subsequently upgraded to version 1.2.3.5 (and the old version removed from the system). If `HelloUser.exe` is executed, an exception of type `File-LoadException` (namespace `System.IO`) occurs; the runtime could not find a match for `ConsoleGreeting.dll` version 1.2.3.4. However, using the `bindingRedirect` XML tag in `HelloUser.exe.config`, as shown here, the runtime can be redirected to use the newer version of `ConsoleGreeting.dll`:

```
<?xml version="1.0"?>
<configuration>
  <runtime>
    <assemblyBinding xmlns="urn:schemas-microsoft-com:asm.v1">
      <dependentAssembly>
        <assemblyIdentity name="ConsoleGreeting"
            publicKeyToken="6083A74B29858FF1" />
        <bindingRedirect oldVersion="1.2.3.4"
            newVersion="1.2.3.5" />
      </dependentAssembly>
```

```
      </assemblyBinding>
   </runtime>
</configuration>
```

This sample can be found on the companion Web site under `Project AppConfiguration`.

Using such binding redirections, administrators can force an older application to use the newer versions of the referenced assemblies. If the application shows any incompatible behavior, administrators can revert back to the old settings.

Note that binding redirections require the public key token of the assembly. In general, the assembly resolver does not take into account the version number of a referenced assembly unless it is strong-named.

.NET Admin Tool

Although the configuration files can be created manually, the runtime provides a Microsoft Management Console (MMC) snap-in called the .NET Admin Tool (`MsCorCfg.msc`) that can be used to generate configuration files. Besides managing the assemblies, the tool can also configure assemblies in the GAC. It also serves some other purposes that we will come across in later chapters.

Network Downloading

Using the configuration file, it is also possible to instruct the common language runtime to download an assembly over the network. This is done using the `codeBase` tag in the configuration file. The following configuration example, downloads `ConsoleGreeting.dll` version 1.2.3.4 from an HTTP site (Project `CodebaseConfiguration`).

```
<?xml version="1.0"?>
<configuration>
   <runtime>
      <assemblyBinding xmlns="urn:schemas-microsoft-com:asm.v1">
         <dependentAssembly>
            <assemblyIdentity name="ConsoleGreeting"
              publicKeyToken="6083A74B29858FF1" />
            <codeBase version="1.2.3.4"
        href="http://mycompany.com/MyTest/ConsoleGreeting.dll"/>
         </dependentAssembly>
      </assemblyBinding>
   </runtime>
</configuration>
```

When the application is run, assembly `ConsoleGreeting.dll` is downloaded and installed in the download cache. Recall that you can view the download cache either from the Windows Explorer or by running the command `gacutil.exe -ldl`.

You may also wish to clear the download cache if need be (using the command `gacutil.exe -cdl`). As long as the `codeBase` entry for a referenced assembly is present in the configuration file, the assembly automatically gets downloaded again whenever the corresponding application tries to use it.

For other possibilities with the configuration files and for the XML format specification for the configuration file, consult the SDK documentation.

Programmatic Download

It is also possible to download an assembly programmatically. The trick is to use the method `Assembly.LoadFrom` and to specify the URL path as the argument. This is illustrated in the following code excerpt:

```
// Project CodebaseConfiguration

class MyApp{
    static void Main(string[] args){
        Assembly a = Assembly.LoadFrom(
          "http://localhost/MyTest/ConsoleGreeting.dll");
        Console.WriteLine(a.FullName);
    }
}
```

Publisher Policy Configuration File

Publisher policy files are typically distributed by assembly's publishers (vendors). It is the way the vendor of a shared assembly makes a compatibility statement about a particular version of assembly he or she is releasing. The configuration specified in the publisher policy affects all applications that use the shared assembly.

The publisher policy is most commonly used when a vendor ships a maintenance release; that is, a newer revision of the shared assembly that contains individual bug fixes.

The publisher policy file is an XML-based file with a format similar to that of the application configuration file. As a matter of fact, the application configuration file that we used earlier for redirecting version 1.2.3.4 of `ConsoleGreeting.dll` to version 1.2.3.5 can be used as a publisher policy file.

Although the policy can be defined in an XML format, the policy file itself cannot be consumed directly for publishing the policy. The vendor has to create an assembly that links the policy file using the Assembly Linker (al.exe) tool. The name of the assembly is required to begin with Policy.<major version>.<minor version> where <major version> and <minor version> correspond to the major and minor version of the shared assembly this policy assembly will be applied to. For example, the following command line creates a policy assembly Policy.1.2.ConsoleGreeting.dll that can be applied to the shared assembly ConsoleGreeting.dll version 1.2.x.x. Here, the policy file is assumed to be ConsoleGreeting.cfg:

```
al.exe -link:ConsoleGreeting.cfg
-out:Policy.1.2.ConsoleGreeting.dll -keyfile:MyKey.snk
```

Note that the assembly needs to be signed with a strong-named key pair (MyKey.snk). The .NET Framework requires that the policy assembly be signed with the same strong-named key pair as the original assembly. This ensures that the policy assembly comes from the same vendor that shipped the original assembly.

To apply this publisher policy to a machine, the policy assembly has to be registered in the GAC using our familiar tool, gacutil.exe, as shown here:

```
gacutil.exe -i Policy.1.2.ConsoleGreeting.dll
```

The sample code for publisher policy can be found on the companion Web site (project PublisherPolicy).

You may be wondering why the policy assemblies are tied to the major and minor versions of the main assembly. This certainly looks like a restriction as you will need to define a new policy assembly by major and minor version. Deciding on the version number granularity was a challenge for Microsoft. At one extreme, you could require a policy assembly for every assembly version. This would become unmanageable, as the number of policy assemblies would be horrendous. At the other extreme, you could have just one policy assembly for all versions of an assembly, but then expressing compatibility rules for all versions in just one file would get unwieldy. Microsoft decided to go with the middle ground. Moreover, this strategy fits well in the real world. Vendors typically do not change the major and minor versions of an assembly when shipping a maintenance release of an assembly.

Safe Mode

It is possible for an application to run into problems (e.g., DLL hell) because of a publisher policy being in use. To turn the publisher policy off for the specific application, you can set the `apply` attribute to `no` for the `publisher-Policy` XML element in the application configuration file, as shown here:

```xml
<?xml version="1.0"?>
<configuration>
  <runtime>
    <assemblyBinding xmlns="urn:schemas-microsoft-com:asm.v1">
      <publisherPolicy apply="no"/>
    </assemblyBinding>
  </runtime>
</configuration>
```

Turning the publisher policy off using the application configuration file is referred to as the safe mode operation.

It is also possible to finely control the safety level for each individual dependent assembly. You can set the `apply` tag (on the `publisherPolicy` element) to either `yes` or `no` for each individual dependent assembly, as shown in the following example:

```xml
<?xml version="1.0"?>
<configuration>
  <runtime>
    <assemblyBinding xmlns="urn:schemas-microsoft-com:asm.v1">
      <dependentAssembly>
        <assemblyIdentity name="ConsoleGreeting"
            publicKeyToken="6083A74B29858FF1" />
        <publisherPolicy apply="no" />
      </dependentAssembly>
    </assemblyBinding>
  </runtime>
</configuration>
```

Machine Configuration File

The machine configuration file contains settings that apply to all the applications on the machine. This file, named `Machine.Config`, resides in the `Config` subdirectory of the common language runtime's root directory. The format of this file is similar to that of the application configuration file.

When executing an application, the common language runtime first reads the machine configuration file and then reads the application-specific configuration file. This makes it possible to override machine-wide settings for a specific application.

Although the machine configuration file can be edited manually, the preferred way is to use the .NET Admin Tool (`MsCorCfg.msc`). Figure 3.3

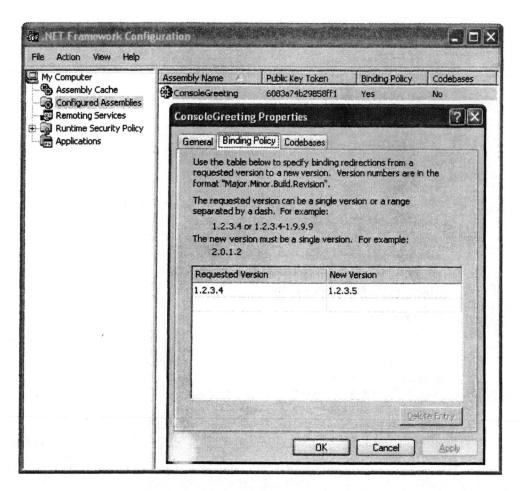

FIGURE 3.3   NET Admin Tool.

shows a snapshot of the .NET Admin Tool being used to redirect version 1.2.3.4 of `ConsoleGreeting.dll` to version 1.2.3.5.

ASSEMBLY BINDING

So far we have learned that assembly bindings can be redirected using either the application configuration file, the machine configuration file, or the publisher policy. In addition, a referenced assembly can be located in either the GAC, the application local directory, or any of its subdirectories as dictated by the `privatePath` entry in the configuration file. This complexity makes you wonder if there is any order that the assembly resolver follows to bind to an assembly. Adding to this complexity is the fact that an assembly can automatically be downloaded and installed based on the `codeBase` entry in the configuration file. Fortunately, there is a method to the madness.

Let's first recap how an assembly gets loaded in an application. There are two ways:

1. When the application tries to access a type defined in a referenced assembly, and the assembly has not already been loaded. These references are called *static references*. Recall that static references are recorded in the application's manifest.

2. When the application explicitly loads an assembly using methods such as `Assembly.Load`, `Assembly.LoadFrom`, or `Assembly.LoadWithPartialName`. Such references are called *dynamic references*.

Deferred Loading of Assemblies

Under .NET, a referenced assembly does not get loaded until the application tries to access a type defined in the assembly. It is entirely possible, for example, to run an application even though a referenced assembly is missing. As long as the current execution path does not access a type from the missing assembly, the application runs as expected.

Contrast this to linking with import libraries in the case of non-.NET applications. If a linked DLL cannot be found when the application is started, the execution aborts in the start-up phase itself.

Irrespective of the way an assembly is loaded, the assembly resolver uses the same algorithm for binding to the assembly. Note that the assembly name to be loaded need not always be fully specified; in this case it is referred to as a partial reference.

The assembly resolver initiates a bind in the following order:

1. The assembly resolver determines from the input the name and culture (if any) of the assembly to load. In addition, for loading strong-named assemblies, the resolver determines the correct assembly version to load by examining the publisher policy (if any), the machine configuration file, and the application configuration file (if any). The settings in the publisher policy are overridden by the settings in the machine configuration file. The settings in the machine configuration file are overridden by the settings in the application configuration file. If the specified assembly is not strong-named, the version number is ignored.

2. If the requested assembly has already been loaded (as a result of a previous request), the resolver binds to the assembly that is already loaded.

3. For strong-named full references (non-null public key token) or if `Assembly.LoadWithPartialName` is called, the resolver checks the GAC. If the assembly is found, the resolver binds to this assembly.

4. For strong-named references (full or partial), the resolver probes the `codeBase` entry in the configuration files. If the entry is found, the resolver downloads the assembly and binds to it. If the download fails for some reason, the resolver determines that the binding request has failed. No further probing occurs.

5. Finally, the runtime probes the application's base directory, followed by other subdirectories specified in the `privatePath` entry of the configuration file(s). If the reference contains culture information, the runtime also looks into the subdirectory that matches the culture string.

If the assembly bind is unsuccessful, the runtime throws the familiar `FileLoadException`.

Assembly Binding Log Viewer

If the assembly bind is unsuccessful, the runtime writes the information to a log file. The framework provides a tool called the Assembly Binding Log Viewer (`Fuslogvw.exe`) that can be used to examine the log file and obtain details about a specific failure. This is an important tool that can save hours of frustration.

Let's pause for a moment and briefly recap what we have learned so far. An assembly is a basic unit of versioning and deployment. It consists of MSIL code, type metadata, the manifest, and resources. An assembly can either be private to an application or can be installed in the GAC. When loading an assembly, the assembly resolver goes through a series of steps to locate and bind to the assembly.

An important feature of the type metadata under .NET is that it is extensible. Using attributes, you can add extra information to any element of your code in a nonprogrammatic way. The attribute information gets saved in the assembly, thus making the assembly completely self-describing. Attribute-based programming is so pervasive under .NET that it deserves special attention. Let's take a look at this style of programming.

ATTRIBUTE-BASED PROGRAMMING

It is often desirable to expose certain aspects of the code such as architectural constraints, behaviors, features, and so forth, in a nonprocedural way. You are already familiar with C++ and C# keywords such as `public` and `private`. These keywords further define the behavior of the class members by describing their accessibility to other classes. .NET lets you define additional aspects of a programming element, such as types and fields, by means of annotating the entity with attributes. The following code excerpt illustrates this idea:

```
// Project Attributes

[ObsoleteAttribute("Please don't use this method")]
public static int Add(int x, int y) {
   return x + y;
}

public static void Main() {
   int z = Add(10,20);
}
```

In this code, method `Add` is marked with an attribute named `Obsolete-Attribute`. If any other part of the code tries to call this method, the compiler generates a warning such as follows (note that this is just a warning, and not error, so the code still works):

```
main.cs(16,11): warning CS0618: 'MyApp.Add(int, int)'
     is obsolete: 'Please don't use this method'
```

The C# compiler has hard-coded logic to specifically deal with some attributes such as `ObsoleteAttribute`. In general, attributes are meant to provide meaningful information to whoever is interested in such information. For example, consider the following declaration for a class:

```
[SerializableAttribute]
class Foo {
   ...
}
```

Annotating a class with `[SerializableAttribute]` informs the runtime that it is okay to serialize the instances of this class. We will look at the serialization process in a later chapter.

To make attribute information available to the runtime (or any other interested party), attributes are stored in the type metadata when the assembly is built. Contrast this to source code comments that get stripped off in the compiled output.

Note that many .NET compilers, including the one for C#, allow you to drop the `Attribute` suffix for convenience. For example, [Serializable-Attribute] can also be represented as [Serializable]. The compiler takes care of expanding it to the proper form while saving the information in the metadata.

Custom Attributes

The beauty of attributes is that they provide a mechanism to extend the metadata. Extra information can be added to the code either by using the standard attributes defined by the .NET Framework or by creating your own custom attributes. The kind of information that you can add (and inspect later) is limited only by your imagination.

Under .NET, an attribute is implemented as a class. The .NET Framework requires that the attribute class be inherited from `System.Attribute`. Here is an example of a custom attribute, `DeveloperAttribute`, that stores the name of the developer working on a piece of the code.

```
// Project Attributes

[AttributeUsage(
    AttributeTargets.Assembly |
    AttributeTargets.Module |
    AttributeTargets.Delegate |
    AttributeTargets.Event |
    AttributeTargets.Enum |
    AttributeTargets.Interface |
    AttributeTargets.Struct |
    AttributeTargets.Class |
    AttributeTargets.Field |
    AttributeTargets.Property |
    AttributeTargets.Constructor |
    AttributeTargets.Method |
    AttributeTargets.Parameter |
    AttributeTargets.ReturnValue,
    AllowMultiple=true)]
public class DeveloperAttribute : System.Attribute {
    private String m_Name;
    public DeveloperAttribute(String name) {
      m_Name = name;
    }
}
```

.NET requires that an attribute class itself be annotated with an attribute called `AttributeUsage`. It takes a parameter of enumeration type `AttributeTargets` to indicate the element of the code the attribute can be applied on. As can be seen in the preceding example, the enumeration list for `AttributeTargets` is quite extensive; it includes classes, structs, interfaces, methods, method parameters, and so on.

Attribute That Is Valid on Any Target

If your attribute is designed to work with any target, you can simply use an enumeration value `AttributeTargets.All` instead of listing each target individually.

The following example shows how `DeveloperAttribute` can be used to annotate various parts of the code:

```
[Developer("Jay")]
public class MyTest {

    [Developer("Pradeep")]
    public void MyMethod() {}
}
```

Class `AttributeUsage` also defines a `boolean` property `AllowMultiple` that can be used to control whether the attribute can be applied multiple times on the same code element. For our class `DeveloperAttribute`, this value is set to true, indicating that multiple developers can be assigned to the same part of the code, as illustrated here:

```
[Developer("Jay")]
[Developer("Pradeep")]
public class MyTest {
    . . .
}
```

Besides the `AllowMultiple` property, `AttributeUsage` defines some other properties. Check the SDK documentation for more information.

It is also possible to define properties for custom attributes. The following code excerpt defines a property `Team` (to indicate the team the developer belongs to) on the class `DeveloperAttribute`.

```
public enum CompanyTeam {Development, QA, Support, Unknown};

. . .

public class DeveloperAttribute : System.Attribute {
```

```
    . . .
    private CompanyTeam m_Team = CompanyTeam.Unknown;
    public CompanyTeam Team {
      get {return m_Team;}
      set {m_Team = value;}
    }
}
```

Using this property, developers can optionally specify the team they belong to, as illustrated here:

```
public class MyTest {
    [Developer("Pradeep")]
    public void MyMethod() {}

    [Developer("Jay", Team = CompanyTeam.Development)]
    public void AnotherMethod() {}
}
```

When the code is compiled, the attribute information is saved in the assembly. One way to inspect this information is to run the assembly through the IL Disassembler. A better way under .NET is to write a program using the Reflection APIs to obtain the needed information. We will see how to do this later in this chapter.

ADVANCED TOPICS

This section contains some advanced topics. You can skip this section if you wish and visit it later. The topics include the following:

- Building assemblies that contain multiple modules as well as other files such as HTML files.

- Loading resources such as strings and images programmatically and localizing resources by means of satellite assemblies.

- The internals of manifest and digital signing of strong-named assemblies.

- Using Reflection to inspect metadata and to invoke methods programmatically.

Multifile Assemblies

So far, all the assemblies we have built consisted of a single module. Although this is the most common case for an assembly, it is also possible to build assemblies containing multiple modules.

From the assembly consumer's perspective (the external view), an assembly contains MSIL code, metadata, manifest, and resources. From the assembly developer's perspective (the internal view), an assembly consists of one or more modules, each of which contains metadata and manifest and may additionally contain MSIL code and resources.

Why do we need a multimodule assembly? There are two cases in which creating a multimodule assembly makes sense:

1. To mix code from multiple programming languages. The respective language compiler can produce modules that can all be combined into a single assembly.

2. A more compelling reason is that a module is loaded into memory only if a type from the module is accessed. This allows you to lazy load a module. This is quite useful over a slow link. For example, if an assembly is being accessed over the Internet, the runtime downloads a module only if needed. You could put the frequently used types in one module and less frequently used types in another. If the client doesn't access the less frequently used types, the corresponding module is never downloaded, thereby improving performance.

Adding Modules

Let's see how we can develop a multimodule assembly. We can take ConsoleGreeting.cs and WindowsGreeting.cs from our previous chapter and build a module for each of the source files. We then create an assembly using these two modules.

The C# compiler provides a command-line switch, -t:module, to generate a module file. Using this option, the modules ConsoleGreeting.mod and WindowGreeting.mod can be generated as follows (Project MultiModule-Assembly):

```
csc.exe -t:module -out:ConsoleGreeting.mod ConsoleGreeting.cs
csc.exe -t:module -out:WindowsGreeting.mod WindowsGreeting.cs
```

Note that in this example, one module is built per source file. In general, a module can be based on any number of source files. The first release of Visual Studio .NET does not have any support for building modules.

To create an assembly from the modules, the C# compiler provides another command switch, `-addmodule`. Using this switch, any number of modules can be added to an assembly, as shown in the following code (Project `MultiModuleAssembly`):

```
csc.exe -t:library -out:Greeting.dll \
    -addmodule:ConsoleGreeting.mod \
    -addmodule:WindowsGreeting.mod
```

The generated assembly technically consists of three modules. The file `Greeting.dll` is the prime module. Recall that a prime module stores the assembly manifest.

Note that module `Greeting.dll` does not contain any MSIL code. It is not necessary for a module to contain any code.

Although `csc.exe` can be used to build a multimodule assembly, you can also use the Assembly Linker (`al.exe`) for this purpose. Using this tool, our assembly could have been created as follows:

```
al.exe -t:library -out:Greeting.dll \
    ConsoleGreeting.mod WindowsGreeting.mod
```

Adding Non-PE Files

An assembly is not just limited to module files. It can also contain non-PE files such as bitmap files or HTML files. The assembly linker provides a switch, `-link`, to link external files to the assembly. The following command line, for example, adds `ReadMe.htm` as an external file to the assembly:

```
al.exe -t:library -out:Greeting.dll -link:ReadMe.htm \
    ConsoleGreeting.mod WindowsGreeting.mod
```

Resources

Consider the following sample code that displays a greeting to the console:

```
using System;
class MyApp
{
    public static void Main() {
        String greeting = "Hello everyone!";
        Console.WriteLine(greeting);
    }
}
```

In this code string, "Hello everyone!" is hard-coded. However, the .NET Framework also provides a way to define the string in an external file. That external file can then be embedded into the assembly. The application can subsequently load the resource programmatically.

What's the big deal about moving strings to an external file? For one, it simplifies localization, the process of customizing application for multiple human languages. The team responsible for translating the strings (and images, if need be) to various languages won't have to deal with the code; they just deal with text-based files. A second reason, and a more important one, is that resources for a specific culture can be embedded into a resource-only assembly and a proper resource can be loaded based on the current culture setting of the application. Such resource-only assemblies are referred to as satellite assemblies.

Embedding Resources

Embedding a resource in an assembly is a multistep process. In the first step, the resources have to be defined in an XML format referred to as the ResX format. A `.ResX` file can hold strings as well as binary images. The necessary XML schema is documented in the SDK under the `ResourceSchema` property of `ResXResourceWriter` class.

 ## Utilities to Manipulate Resources

ResX files are text based. To store a binary image file (such as a `.jpg` or a `.bmp` file) into the `.ResX` file, the binary data has to be converted into ASCII format using Base64 encoding. The SDK samples include a tool, `ResXGen`, that takes a binary image file as input and converts it to XML-formatted `.ResX` output file. The source code for `ResXGen` is also provided.

Some other useful utilities in the SDK samples include `ResDump`, a tool to enumerate the resources in a `.resources` file, and `ResEditor`, a GUI tool to add string and image resources to a `.ResX` or a `.resources` file.

If you are dealing with just the string resources, as in our case, then .NET provides an alternative to using `.ResX` files. Name–value pairs can be defined in a text file (typically with extension `.txt`) where the name is a string that describes the resource and the value is the resource string itself. The following excerpt shows the content of our text-based resource file:

```
Greeting = Hello everyone!
```

In the second step, the `.txt` or the `.ResX` file has to be converted to a binary resource file (`.resources`). The framework provides a tool called the

Resource File Generator (`ResGen.exe`) that can be used to generate such a file. `ResGen.exe` expects an input filename and an optional output filename as a parameter. If an output filename is not specified, it creates a binary resource file that has the same name as the input file but has a `.resources` extension. It is not important to know the format of this file.

Assuming our text-based resource file is named `MyStrings.txt`, the following command line generates a `.resources` binary resource file:

```
resgen.exe MyStrings.txt MyStrings.resources
```

Converting between Resource File Formats

`Resgen.exe` is capable of converting any resource file (`.txt`, `.resx`, or `.resources`) to any other resource file. The conversion is done based on the extension of the input and the output filenames. Just remember that text files can only contain string resources. If a `.resx` file or a `.resources` file contains any images, converting it to a `.txt` file will lose the image information.

The last step is to embed the binary resource file into an assembly. Assuming our new code, revised for loading a string dynamically, is stored in `HelloAll.cs`, the following command line creates an assembly `HelloAll.exe` that has `MyStrings.resources` embedded in it:

```
csc.exe -t:exe -out:HelloAll.exe \
    -res:MyStrings.resources HelloAll.cs
```

So how does the revised code in `HelloAll.cs` look? Here it is with the changes highlighted:

```
// Project EmbeddedResources

using System;
using System.Resources;

class MyApp
{
    public static void Main() {
        ResourceManager rm = new
          ResourceManager("MyStrings", typeof(MyApp).Assembly);
        String greeting = rm.GetString("Greeting");
        Console.WriteLine(greeting);
    }
}
```

The framework provides a class `ResourceManager` (namespace `System.Resources`) that can be used to load resources dynamically. `ResourceManager` defines many overloaded constructors. The one that we are using requires two parameters. The first parameter is the root name of the resource file. For the `MyStrings.resources` file, the root name is `MyStrings`. The second parameter is the assembly where this resource can be found. As we know that the resource is in the same assembly as `MyApp` is, we can ask the runtime to locate the assembly that contains the definition of type `MyApp`, as shown in the code.

Once the `ResourceManager` object has been created, we can load the string by calling the `GetString` method on the object. This method takes the resource identifier as a parameter.

Note that `ResourceManager` also provides a more generic method, `GetObject`, that can be used to load any type of resource (text or image). For example, we could also use the following line of code to load our string:

```
String greeting2 = (String) rm.GetObject("Greeting");
```

Loading an image is equally simple, as shown in the following line of code:

```
Image img = (Image) rm.GetObject("MyImage");
```

It is left as an exercise for you to extend the sample program to deal with embedded images.

Satellite Assemblies

Let's build a multilanguage application. We will extend our earlier example to deal with U.S. English and Spanish.

Recall that the common language runtime supports the notion of culture-neutral assemblies that do not have any culture-specific settings; it contains resources that can run under any culture.

Typically, the main assembly is built to be culture neutral. The idea is that if a requested resource for a particular culture is not found in the satellite assembly, the runtime can fall back to the main assembly to load the resource.

For our example, we will build the satellite assembly with Spanish culture. The main assembly will embed an English language resource string, but will be built culture-neutral.

Let's create two subdirectories, `en-US` and `es-ES`. The importance of the directory names will become evident when we examine how the runtime locates satellite assemblies. I have also created a file `MyStrings.txt` under both the subdirectories, one with English strings and the other with Spanish strings.

The first step is to generate `.resources` files for both the languages. The command lines are shown here:

```
resgen.exe en-US\MyStrings.txt en-US\MyStrings.en-US.resources
resgen.exe es-ES\MyStrings.txt es-ES\MyStrings.es-ES.resources
```

Notice the filenames for the output files. The standard convention is to specify a resource filename as `<root-file-name>.<culture-name>.resources`.

The next step is to build the Spanish satellite assembly, as shown in the following command line:

```
al.exe -out:es-ES\HelloAll.Resources.dll -c:es-ES \
    -embed:es-ES\MyStrings.es-ES.resources
```

The assembly linker supports a switch, `-c:<culture-name>`, to specify the culture for the assembly, as shown in the command line.

For proper lookup during runtime, the root filename of the satellite assembly should be the same as that of the main assembly and the extension should be marked `.Resources.dll`. For example, the satellite assembly for `HelloAll.exe` would be `HelloAll.Resources.dll`. The filename is not case sensitive.

A culture string can also be assigned in the source code using the `AssemblyCultureAttribute` (namespace `System.Reflection`) assembly-level attribute (attributes are covered in the next chapter). Here is an example:

```
// Set assembly's culture to U.S. English
[assembly: AssemblyCulture("en-US")]
```

The main assembly is typically culture neutral and hence should not be assigned any culture string.

To build the main assembly, the following command can be used:

```
csc -res:en-US\MyStrings.en-US.resources,MyStrings.resources \
    HelloAll.cs
```

Note the comma-separated syntax for the resource being embedded; the first part is the actual filename of the resource and the second part is the name given to the resource when stored in the assembly. This is because of the way the resource manager looks up a resource.

To understand the lookup algorithm, it would help us to make the following assumptions:

1. The name of the main assembly is `HelloAll.exe`.

2. The root name of the resource file is `MyStrings`. In the code, this is the first parameter to the resource manager's constructor.

3. The current culture is `es-ES`.

4. The identifier for the string to be loaded is `Greeting`.

Here is how the resource manager performs the lookup:

1. Try to locate culture-specific `HelloAll.Resources.Dll` in the GAC.

2. Try to locate `HelloAll.Resources.Dll` in the `es-ES` subdirectory.

3. Verify whether the culture of the assembly is `es-ES`.

4. Try to locate the resource file `MyStrings.es-ES.resources` from the satellite assembly.

5. Try to load the named resource, `Greeting`, from `MyStrings.es-ES.resources`.

6. If any of these steps fail, try to locate the culture-neutral resource file `MyStrings.resources` from the main assembly.

7. If Step 5 fails, throw an exception of type `MissingManifestResourceException`.

8. Otherwise, try to load the named resource, `Greeting`. If the resource is not found, return a null reference.

In this algorithm, the filenames and directory names are all case-insensitive.

There are ways to customize this behavior. For example, there is an overloaded method `GetString` that can be used to load a string from a specific culture, irrespective of the current cultural settings. As a matter of fact, even the current culture can be changed, as shown in the following code excerpt, taken from `HelloAll.cs`:

```
// Project SatelliteAssemblies

class MyApp
{
    public static void Main(String[] args) {
        if (args.Length == 1) {
            String sCulture = args[0];
            CultureInfo culture = new CultureInfo(sCulture);
            Thread.CurrentThread.CurrentUICulture = culture;
        }

        ...

    }
}
```

.NET classifies the properties of a culture into two groups—Current-Culture and CurrentUICulture. The first one is used for sorting and formatting purposes and the second one is used for user-interface purposes. This distinction was created, for example, to support large enterprises that want their employees to be able to use the local language for the user interface but always have currencies and dates formatted the same way. The resources are loaded (by ResourceManager) using the CurrentUICulture setting (unless a specific culture setting is explicitly requested in the call). Each thread within an application can have a different culture. The preceding code sets the culture of the current thread based on the command-line arguments passed. Run the program as follows to display the greeting in Spanish:

```
HelloAll.exe es-ES
```

Manifest Tables

Internally, the metadata is organized as a block of binary data that consists of several tables. These tables can be broadly classified into two groups—type metadata tables and manifest metadata (or simply manifest) tables. The type metadata contains information on each type within the module. The manifest metadata contains some record-keeping information.

Each module in the assembly stores type metadata tables as well as manifest tables. Recall that there is one module within the assembly with a manifest that contains some extra information pertaining to the assembly as a whole. The module is called the prime module and the manifest it stores is referred to as the assembly manifest.

When dealing with assemblies, it is not really that important to know the manifest of each module in the assembly. What is important is to know the contents of the assembly manifest. Table 3.3 describes some important tables in the assembly manifest, which is valuable information.

In general, unless explicitly stated, a manifest refers to the assembly manifest.

TABLE 3.3   Assembly Manifest Tables

Table Name	Description
AssemblyDef	Contains a single entry containing the assembly's name, version, culture, and so on.
FileDef	Contains one entry for each module and resource file that is part of the assembly.

TABLE 3.3 Assembly Manifest Tables (Continued)

Table Name	Description
ManifestResourceDef	Contains information on each resource that is part of the assembly.
ExportedTypeDef	Contains one entry for each public type exported from all the modules in the assembly.
AssemblyRef	Contains one entry for each assembly referenced by the module. Note that each module individually defines the list of referenced assemblies.
ModuleRef	Contains one entry identifying the module. It includes the module's filename and its MVID.

All the assembly manifest tables listed in Table 3.3, except `ExportedTypeDef`, can also be found in the manifest for other (nonprime) modules in the assembly. For a nonprime module, the `AssemblyDef` table does not contain any entries.

Storing Assembly References

When an application is built, the compiler stores the name, the version number, the culture, and the public key token (if any) of the referenced assemblies in the `AssemblyRef` table of the manifest.

It is interesting to note that the `AssemblyRef` table stores the public key token (instead of the public key) for each referenced assembly. This is done to conserve file space.

It is interesting to learn the internals of building a strong-named assembly.

The `FileDef` metadata table of the assembly's manifest contains the list of files that make up the assembly. As each file is added to the manifest, the file's content is hashed and stored along with the file name. The default hash algorithm is SHA-1 but can be changed in two ways: using the `AssemblyAlgIDAttribute` (namespace `System.Reflection`) attribute or with `al.exe`'s `–algid` switch.

Once the PE file containing the assembly manifest (the prime module) has been built, the PE file's entire content is hashed. The hash algorithm used here is always SHA-1 and cannot be changed (although this may change in later releases). This hash value (typically around 160 bytes in size) is signed with the specified private key and the resulting Rivest-Shamir-Adleman (RSA) digital signature is stored in a reserved section (not included in the hash) within the PE file. Another section of the PE file, called the .NET runtime header, is updated to reflect the location where the digital signature is embedded within the file.

The specified public key is also embedded in the manifest. The public–private key mechanism guarantees that no other company can produce an assembly with the same public key, as long as your company does not share the key pair with others. Those interested in learning more about the public–private key and the RSA digital signature can see the MSDN documentation on cryptographic APIs (CryptoAPI).

The bottom line of this whole process is that it provides the common language runtime a foolproof way to ensure that a shared assembly has not been tampered with. When the assembly is being installed into the GAC, the system hashes the PE file's contents and compares the hash value with the RSA digital signature embedded in the file (after it is unsigned with the public key). If the values are identical, then the file's content has not been tampered with. This is a very fast check. Similar strategies have been used for signing e-mails.

In the case of a multimodule assembly, the integrity check is performed only on the module that contains the manifest. For all other modules, the check is performed when the module gets loaded at runtime.

Note that only a strong-named assembly can be installed into the GAC. Attempts to install any other assembly result in an error.

It should be noted that the strong-named mechanism only guarantees that an assembly, once created, has not been tampered with. It doesn't tell you who the publisher of the assembly is. If the publisher wants to associate its identity with the assembly, then the publisher must use Microsoft's Authenticode technology. Covering Authenticode is beyond the scope of this book

Delayed Signing

Once a public–private key pair is generated, the private key should never be compromised. Many companies prefer that the private key be accessed only by a few privileged people in the company. The public key can be freely distributed.

Inability to access the private key could be a huge burden during developing and testing the assembly. Fortunately, the framework provides a mechanism to develop an assembly without using a private key at all; just the public key is sufficient. This mechanism is called *delayed signing*.

The Strong Name tool (sn.exe) provides switch -p to extract the public key from a strong-named file (the file containing the public–private key pair). The following command, for example, extracts the public key from MyKey.snk and stores it in MyKey.public:

```
sn.exe -p MyKey.snk MyKey.public
```

`MyKey.snk` can now be stored away in a safe place and the public key file is distributed to the developers.

The next step is to embed the public key information (using the familiar `AssemblyKeyFile` attribute) and indicate to the compiler that the signing of the assembly is being delayed. This is done by means of the assembly-level attribute `AssemblyDelaySign`. Relevant code is shown here (Project `DelayedSigning`):

```
[assembly: AssemblyKeyFile("MyKey.public")]
[assembly: AssemblyDelaySign(true)]
```

Obtaining Public Key Token

Here is a quick way to obtain the public key token from a strong-named file; that is, the file containing the key pair. First extract the public key from the key pair using sn.exe and save it in a file. For example, the following command extracts the public key from `MyKey.snk` and saves it in `MyKey.public`:

```
sn.exe -p MyKey.snk MyKey.public
```

Next, run sn.exe -t on the public key file, as shown here:

```
sn.exe -t MyKey.public
```

The command displays the public key token in the console window.

Note that running the command on the original file that contains both the public and the private key also generates a public key token. However, this value is bogus because the file does not store any extra information to indicate that it contains something besides the public key. As a result, sn.exe cannot determine if the file contains extra information. It simply runs through the bits and returns a result.

When the source is compiled, the compiler embeds the public key information (in the `AssemblyDef` table) so that other assemblies that reference this assembly can generate and use the public key token. In addition, the compiler leaves enough space in the resulting PE file for the RSA digital signature (the compiler can determine how much space is needed).

Note that, instead of using the assembly-level attributes, delayed signing can also be accomplished by using `al.exe`'s `-keyfile` and `-delaysign` switches.

At this point, the resulting assembly does not have a valid signature. If we try to install this assembly in the GAC, the .NET Framework assumes that the assembly has been tampered with and fails to load. To force the runtime to accept the assembly, you must tell it to skip the verification of this assembly. This is accomplished using `sn.exe` with `-Vr` switch, as shown here:

```
sn.exe -Vr ConsoleGreeting.dll
```

A bit of a warning is in order. You should never do something like this with an assembly you don't know about.

The assembly can now be installed in the GAC:

```
gacutil.exe -i ConsoleGreeting.dll
```

At this point, you can go ahead and test your application as normal.

Note that the `-Vr` switch does not actually modify the assembly. Instead, it adds the specified assembly's strong name to a list of assemblies for which verification should be skipped on the local machine. The list is stored as a set of subkeys under the registry key `HKLM\Software\Microsoft\Strong-Name\Verification`. If you plan to install the assembly on a different machine, you need to run `sn.exe -Vr` on the file once again on the new machine.

Once you are ready to ship the assembly, you can be signed with the original private key, as shown here:

```
sn.exe -R ConsoleGreeting.dll MyKey.snk
```

Reflection

All .NET-compliant compilers are required to generate full metadata information about every class type in the compiled source code file. Among other things, this metadata contains a list of modules in the assembly, a declaration for each type in the assembly, the base class and the interfaces the type inherits from, the name and type (methods, properties, events, and fields) of all its members, and the signature of each of the methods. Figure 3.4 shows a simplified layout of the information contained in the type metadata.

The type metadata is organized in a hierarchical fashion:

- An assembly contains a list of modules.
- A module contains a list of types and global methods. Note that C# does not allow defining global methods. A method, even if defined as static, still needs to be defined as part of a type.
- A type contains a list of methods, a list of fields, a list of properties, and a list of events.
- A method contains a list of parameters and a return type.

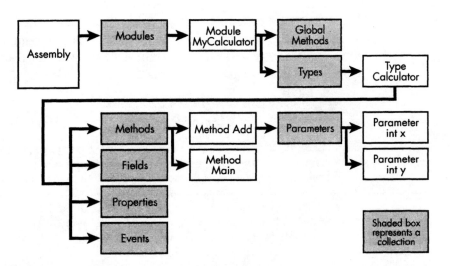

FIGURE 3.4 Metadata hierarchy within an assembly.

Not shown in Figure 3.4 is that all the elements of the code including assembly, module, type, method, and so on, also contain a list of associated attributes.

Here is the sample code that corresponds to the type Calculator used in Figure 3.4. The code is compiled into an assembly named MyCalculator.exe:

```
// Project Reflection/MyCalculator

using System;

namespace MyCompany
{
    public class Calculator
    {
      public int Add(int x, int y) {
        return (x+y);
      }

      public static void Main() {
        Calculator calc = new Calculator();
        int sum = calc.Add(10, 20);
        Console.WriteLine(sum);
      }
    }
}
```

The .NET Framework provides a set of classes under the namespace System.Reflection to inspect the metadata. The following code excerpt illustrates how you can load an assembly and obtain information on modules, types, and methods contained in the assembly:

```
// Project Reflection/MetadataViewer
// Note: Code has been modified slightly for easy reading

public static void DumpAssembly(String assemblyName) {
    Assembly assembly = Assembly.Load(assemblyName);
    Console.WriteLine("Assembly={0}", assembly.FullName);

    // Get the list of modules in the assembly
    Module[] moduleList = assembly.GetModules();
    foreach(Module mod in moduleList) {
      Console.WriteLine("Module={0}", mod.Name);

      // Get a list of types in the module
      Type[] typeList = mod.GetTypes();
      foreach(Type type in typeList) {
        Console.WriteLine(" Type={0}", type.Name);

        // Get a list of methods in the type
        MethodInfo[] methodList = type.GetMethods();
        foreach(MethodInfo method in methodList) {
          Console.Write("  Method= {0} {1}(",
            method.ReturnType, method.Name);
          ParameterInfo[] pL = method.GetParameters();
          for(int i=0;i<pL.Length;i++) {
            Console.Write("{0} {1}",
              pL[i].ParameterType, pL[i].Name);
          } // for each param
        } // for each method
      } // for each type
    } // for each module
}
```

Information on classes Assembly, Module, Type, MethodInfo, ParameterInfo can be obtained from the SDK documentation. Each of these classes encapsulate a specific element of the code.

Here is the output when the program is run against MyCalculator.exe:

```
Assembly=MyCalculator, Version=0.0.0.0, Culture=neutral, \
    PublicKeyToken=null
Module=mycalculator.exe
  Type=Calculator
```

```
Method= System.Int32 GetHashCode()
Method= System.Boolean Equals(System.Object obj)
Method= System.String ToString()
Method= System.Int32 Add(System.Int32 x, System.Int32 y)
Method= System.Void Main()
Method= System.Type GetType()
```

As can be seen, assembly MyCalculatore.exe contains one module. This module contains type Calculator, which defines methods Add and Main, as expected.

You may be wondering where the other four methods on Calculator came from. These methods are defined by class System.Object. Recall that every type under .NET directly or indirectly inherits from System.Object.

Using Reflection, it is also possible to invoke a method programmatically. In the following code excerpt, method Add on an instance of Calculator is invoked dynamically:

```
// Project Reflection-MetadataViewer

public static void MethodInvokeDemo() {
    Type t =
        Type.GetType("MyCompany.Calculator, MyCalculator");
    object calc = Activator.CreateInstance(t);

    MethodInfo mi = t.GetMethod("Add");
    object[] pL = new object[] { 10 /*x*/, 20 /*y*/};
    int sum = (int) mi.Invoke(calc, pL);
    Console.WriteLine("Sum={0}", sum);
}
```

Under .NET, just as an assembly can be represented by a display name, a type can also be represented by a display name. The syntax for the display name for a type is:

```
Namespace.TypeName <,assembly name>
```

Given the display name of a type, the type can be loaded by calling a static method Type.GetType and an instance of the type (Calculator in our case) by calling a static method System.Activator.CreateInstance. The rest of the code obtains the method information that we are interested in invoking, packs the method parameters in an array, and invokes the method on the Calculator instance.

This concludes our basic introduction to Reflection under .NET. For other possibilities with Reflection and metadata inspection, check the SDK documentation as well as the SDK samples. You may also wish to check out the `System.Reflection.Emit` namespace; it contains classes to allow generating metadata and MSIL instructions programmatically and optionally generate a PE file on the disk.

SUMMARY

An assembly is the basic unit of versioning, culture, and deployment. Your source code is ultimately assimilated into an assembly that becomes available for distribution.

From the assembly consumer's perspective (the external view), an assembly contains the following:

- Type metadata (describing the properties, methods, and fields of each type defined in the assembly).
- MSIL code (the implementation of each type defined in the assembly).
- Assembly manifest (describing overall information about the assembly).
- Resources (e.g., strings and bitmaps).

From the assembly developer's perspective (the internal view), an assembly consists of one or more executables (PE files) called modules, each of which contains type metadata (optional), manifest, resources (optional), and MSIL code (optional). One module is designated as the holder of the assembly's manifest.

The assembly's manifest contains information such as name of the assembly, its version and culture settings, the list of files in the assembly, its public key (if any), the list of referenced assemblies, and so on.

The assembly's type metadata contains complete information on types that are present in the assembly. This type metadata can be obtained programmatically using Reflection APIs.

In case of a single-module assembly, the module itself designates the assembly. This is by far the most common case for an assembly.

An assembly can also embed resources (e.g., strings or images) or can have links to external files such as HTML pages. Assemblies storing just the resources for a specific culture are called satellite assemblies.

Assemblies can either be private to an application or can be shared by multiple applications.

A shared assembly has to be installed in the GAC. To ensure that a shared assembly has not been tampered with, it has to be signed using a public–private key pair mechanism. Such a signed assembly is referred to as a strong-named assembly.

A strong-named assembly contains a digital signature based on the public–private key pair. The common language runtime can verify this digital signature using just the public key. This guarantees that an assembly has not been tampered with after it has been shipped.

The .NET Framework has gone to great lengths to ensure that assembles are not subject to the traditional software deployment problems such as DLL hell.

The assembly resolver undergoes a series of steps to locate and bind any assembly that needs to be loaded. If an assembly could not be located for some reason, the resolver writes the failure information in a log file that can be viewed through the assembly binding log viewer.

The runtime's assembly binding behavior can be customized by means of configuration files. The configuration files can be either created for a specific application, or the vendor of a shared assembly can specify its configuration using publisher policies. Yet another option is to administratively define a configuration at the machine level.

It is also possible to turn off publisher policies for a specific application using the application's configuration file. This mode of operation is referred to as safe mode operation.

REFERENCES

[Pie-02]   Pietrek, Matt, "An In-Depth Look into the Win32 Portable Executable File Format," *MSDN Magazine*, February 2002.
msdn.microsoft.com/msdnmag/issues/02/02/PE/PE.asp

[Alv-95]   Alvestrand, H., "Tags for the Identification of Languages," RFC 1766, The Internet Engineering Task Force, March 1995.
www.ietf.org/rfc/rfc1766.txt

bib. xml.

```
<? xml ver >
<bib
    <book isbn = "   .   ">
        <title>  ____  </title>
        <author>  ___  <ent >
    </book>
</bib>
```

Essentials of the
.NET Framework

In the previous chapter, we looked at how to write, compile, and execute code that targets .NET. In this chapter, we examine the facilities that the .NET Framework provides to load and execute the code and provide services to the executing code. We start with an overview of various components that constitute the .NET Framework. Then we look at the overall process of managed code execution. We will see how .NET applications can be administratively controlled using external configuration files and how the configuration mechanism can be extended to store custom settings. We then look at the type system used by the common language runtime and examine the memory and performance considerations of using reference types versus value types. We examine how the CLS provides for cross-language interoperability. We look at how the execution engine validates the metadata, verifies the MSIL code for type-safety, and performs JIT compilation on the MSIL code. Finally, we look at the automatic memory management features of the runtime and how it simplifies or complicates programming under .NET. By the end of the chapter, you will have a good understanding of .NET architecture and how it helps in producing robust applications that can potentially be reused by any programming language under .NET. You will also learn the strategies of generating efficient code.

.NET FRAMEWORK OVERVIEW

The Internet is evolving from a collection of isolated Web sites into a general communication bus for distributed applications. Not only could the applications be geographically separate, but they also could be running on different hardware and OS platforms. Yet, they can communicate with each other over the Internet. The key that makes this communication possible is *Web services*, a mechanism to exchange messages between distributed applications using industry standards such as XML and HTTP.

The .NET Framework was designed from the ground up around this vision. Support for XML and Web services is built into the framework. Any application developed for .NET has the potential to run on a variety of hardware and OS platforms.

The .NET Framework, however, had many other design goals as well. The following are some of the important ones that the .NET Framework addresses:

- *Reduced plumbing*: To provide a rich set of classes so that developers can write less code and reuse more.

- *Simpler development*: To provide a code execution environment that reduces software issues. For example, developers need not write code to free previously allocated memory; the framework provides a memory-management mechanism that frees any unused memory automatically.

- *Simpler deployment*: To make installing applications as easy as using a simple XCOPY command; also to support running multiple versions of the same component side by side.

- *Unified programming model*: To define a standard, consistent way of programming and facilitate cross-language programming.

- *Scalability*: To provide features that help developing scalable applications.

- *Security*: To support developing secure applications. Security is an important consideration for applications, especially if they are communicating over the Internet. The framework must guarantee that the code is safe to execute. Furthermore, the security system is granular—rather than a simple on–off switch, enabling the programmer or the administrator to control what can run depending on the user and the source of the program.

- *Cross-platform integration*: To build communication on industry standards such as SOAP so that .NET-based code can communicate with any other code.

- *Interoperability*: To support integrating .NET applications with native Win32 APIs and COM+ components.

Even if you do not intend to develop applications targeting the Internet, you can still use the .NET Framework to develop applications that are robust, secure, and reliable. Moreover, by leveraging the rich set of classes provided by the framework, you can achieve greater productivity.

Anatomy of the Framework

Figure 4.1 shows the major components of the .NET Framework.

The heart of the .NET Framework is the common language runtime, which is responsible for executing the managed code. During execution, the common language runtime provides features to the code such as automatic memory management, security, and so on. It sits on top of the Windows OS and, in the first version, uses COM+ services internally for some of its functionality.

The .NET Framework also provides more than 2,000 types (classes, interfaces, structures, etc.) that not only enable programmatic access to the features of the common language runtime, but also provide a number of useful high-level services to help developers boost productivity. These types are collectively referred to as the .NET Framework Class Library.

The .NET Framework Class Library can be broken down roughly into four groups:

1. BCL

2. ADO.NET and XML

3. Windows Forms

4. ASP.NET

The BCL implements the set of functionality that is shared by all the applications targeting the .NET Framework. It defines and implements all the

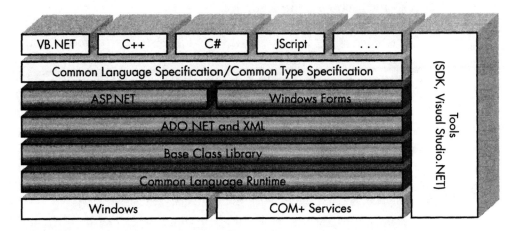

FIGURE 4.1   .NET Framework components.

core types such as `System.String`, `System.Int32`, and so on, that we have seen in the previous chapter, used by every application.

ADO.NET is the successor to an earlier data access technology called Active Data Object (ADO). ADO.NET provides a set of classes to access and manipulate data. The data is typically obtained from a database and can be converted to XML for better remote manipulation.

Windows Forms (often called WinForms) provides features for developing standard Windows desktop applications. It provides a rich, unified set of controls and drawing functions for all languages. It effectively wraps Windows user interface APIs in such a way that developers rarely need to access the Windows APIs directly.

ASP.NET is the successor to a Web request processing technology from Microsoft called Active Server Pages (ASP). ASP.NET adds two significant enhancements to ASP:

1. It simplifies the process of developing Web services.

2. It provides a model of developing a Web browser-based user interface called Web forms. Controls on the Web forms run on the server but the user interface is displayed on the client browser. ASP.NET takes care of all the coordination and behind-the-scenes activities. The result is Web interfaces that look and behave very much like WinForms interfaces. Moreover, the Web interfaces can deal with a broad range of browsers such as Internet Explorer, as well as less capable browsers such as the ones found on wireless palmtop devices. Web forms render themselves appropriately on the target device.

It is worth noting that the term *ASP.NET* is used in two different contexts. As a class library, it provides a rich set of classes to develop applications such as Web services and Web forms. ASP.NET also refers to a runtime infrastructure that runs under Internet Information Services (IIS) and services ASP.NET applications.

The Common Type Specification (CTS) defines rules so that compiler vendors can implement a programming language of their choice on .NET. Microsoft itself has implemented .NET compilers for many languages including C#, Visual Basic.NET, J#, JScript, and so on. Even existing C++ code can be compiled for .NET under what Microsoft calls It Just Works (IJW).

The CLS makes it possible for applications developed in different languages such as C# and Visual Basic.NET to communicate with the class library as well as with each other.

To develop applications, Microsoft also provides tools such as the .NET Framework SDK and Visual Studio .NET IDE. The SDK provides useful documentation, samples, programmer's tools, and so on. The IDE provides a number of features to boost developers' productivity.

A detailed coverage of ADO.NET and Windows forms is beyond the scope of this book, but we touch on them as necessary. As for ASP.NET, our focus is on the core aspects such as developing Web services. User interface-related topics are not covered.

Installing the Framework

To install the .NET Framework, Microsoft provides a stand-alone program (dotnetredist.exe) that can be downloaded from Microsoft's Web site. This file contains a file, dotnetfx.exe, that can be extracted by executing dotnetredist.exe. Running dotnetfx.exe installs the framework in the %windir%\Microsoft.Net\Framework\v<version> directory where %windir% points to the Windows directory and <version> is the version number of the framework. On my system, this directory is C:\WinNT\Microsoft.NET\Framework\v1.0.3705.[1]

Note that installing the Framework SDK or Visual Studio.NET automatically installs the .NET Framework.

Redistributing the Framework

You can download the Microsoft .NET Redistributable Package (dotnetredist.exe) from Microsoft's Web site, extract dotnetfx.exe, and use it for redistribution. From your setup program, you need to execute dotnetfx.exe before installing any of your .NET executables.

Dotnetfx.exe can also be found on the Windows Component Upgrade CD of Visual Studio. NET install CDs.

Check the article ".NET Framework Deployment Guide" [MS-02] for complete information and the End-User License Agreement on redistributing the .NET Framework.

Managed Code Execution Overview

Figure 4.2 presents the overall picture of how the source code gets compiled, loaded, executed, and serviced by the .NET Framework.

---

1. The version number for the first release of the .NET Framework is 1.0.3705.

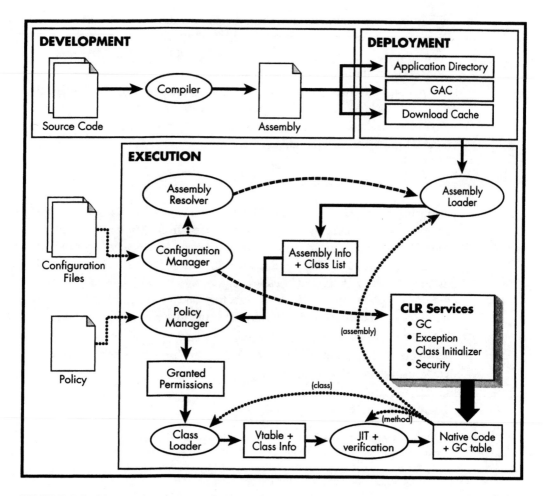

FIGURE 4.2   Managed code execution.

A .NET-compliant compiler takes one or more source files as input and generates an assembly file (Chapter 3) as output.

A traditional compiler processes the source code and stores native machine language instructions in the output. A .NET-compliant compiler, however, does not generate machine language instructions. Instead, the instructions are stored in the assembly in a format called MSIL. As we will see shortly, when the assembly is executed, the runtime converts the MSIL instructions to native machine language instructions on the fly.

An assembly can be built either as a library (DLL) or as a stand-alone executable (EXE). From the runtime's perspective, there is no difference between these two types except that an EXE-based assembly is required to have an entry point of execution. The entry point method must be declared `static` and must be named `Main`. The method can optionally take command-line parameters as input and can optionally return an integer value. The following are possible method signatures for `Main` in C#:

```
static void Main();
static void Main(System.String[] argv);
static int Main();
static int Main(System.String[] argv);
```

Once built, the assembly can be copied to an application's local directory or subdirectory on the user's machine. An assembly can also be installed into the GAC (Chapter 3), if it is desired that the assembly be shared by many applications.

An application can also specify that an assembly be downloaded over the Internet. In this case, the runtime stores the assembly in an area called the download cache. Assemblies downloaded over the Internet run under lesser security privileges, thus safeguarding the machine from malicious intentions.

The part of the common language runtime that is responsible for loading and executing an assembly is called the execution engine (EE). The EE is composed of many units, each of which is responsible for executing a specific task or tasks:

- The *assembly resolver* locates an assembly using some heuristics and externally specified configuration information.
- The *assembly loader* loads an assembly and stores in memory information about the assembly such as the name and version of the assembly and the available list of classes.
- The *policy manager* grants certain security permissions to an assembly based on externally specified security policy and the source of the assembly.
- The *class loader* loads a class and constructs an in-memory representation of the class such as its virtual table (vtable).

- The *JIT compiler* coverts the MSIL code to the native code. In the process, it checks the metadata for consistency (this is called validation) and verifies whether the code is safe to execute.

- The *configuration manager* makes externally specified configuration information available to any entity within the EE that needs it.

When an assembly's code is to be executed, the assembly resolver locates the assembly based on the name of the assembly and certain other characteristics, such as its version number and the external configuration. If need be, the assembly is downloaded over the network. The assembly is then loaded into the EE. The loader stores the information about the assembly and the list of classes it exposes in an internal table.

Before any code from the assembly can be executed, the EE consults the policy manager for granting certain security permissions for the code. In granting permissions, the policy manager checks the externally specified policy against certain characteristics of the assembly. For example, an assembly that has been downloaded over the Internet is granted a lesser degree of permissions such as being unable to read or write to the hard drive.

The class loader then loads the class containing the code to be executed and stores information about the class in an internal table.

Recall that the code is typically stored in MSIL form in the assembly. Before executing a class method, the MSIL code has to be converted into the native code. This on-the-fly conversion is referred to as JIT conversion. The part of EE that is responsible for this conversion is called the JITter. Besides compiling the MSIL code, the JITter also performs some additional checks on the code, such as verifying the code for type safety.

As the code is executing, the EE provides certain services to the code, such as the following:

- Automatic memory management
- Code access security
- Debugging and profiling services
- Interoperability with unmanaged code

We have already learned about managed code and unmanaged code in the previous chapter, but here is a refresher. For the EE to provide services to the executing code, the code must meet certain requirements of the common language runtime and must supply certain necessary metadata to the EE. Such code is called managed code. All code based on MSIL executes as managed code. However, one can always develop code without regard for the convention and requirements of the common language runtime. There is plenty of existing code written this way. Such code is referred to as unmanaged code. Although the EE can execute unmanaged code, the code cannot avail the services provided by the EE. For example, the EE cannot provide automatic memory management or code safety for unmanaged code.

As the code executes, it may call additional methods. If the method being called has not yet been compiled, the EE interrupts the code to JIT the method. In the process, a new assembly may get loaded (e.g., if the method being called belongs to a different assembly) or additional classes may get loaded.

The execution continues until the program comes to a logical ending (returns from Main). The execution also stops if the program gets aborted. This may happen, for example, if an exception is thrown, either by the program or by the runtime, and the program fails to catch the exception.

In the rest of the chapter, we examine each of the major steps of the managed-code execution process. The idea is to get a good understanding of the development, deployment, and execution processes under .NET. Some other aspects, such as interoperability, security, distributed computing, and so on, are covered in later chapters.

Before we proceed further, there is one thing worth mentioning. The .NET Framework provides a decent set of performance counters that you may wish to look at. It will give you a good insight into the managed execution process and help you track the performance of your application.

.NET Performance Counters

Track your application's performance by monitoring .NET performance counters. These counters can be viewed, for example, by using an OS-supplied tool, perfmon.exe.

CONFIGURATION

The .NET Framework provides a file-based configuration mechanism that gives administrators control over the way .NET applications run, without any need for recompiling the applications. For example, administrators can control:

- which protected resources an application can access
- which version of an assembly an application can use (binding redirection)
- which version of the common language runtime an application should use
- where the common language runtime should search for an assembly

- which channel (TCP, HTTP, etc.) and ports an application should use
- which machine, channel, and port a remote object can be obtained from
- custom application configuration settings
- security permissions that should be granted to an assembly

Based on their usage, the configuration under .NET can be classified as a general-purpose configuration or a security configuration.

General-Purpose Configuration

In Chapter 3, we learned that there are two types of general-purpose configuration files that are available under .NET: One is at the machine level and the other is at the application level. We also learned how some of the tasks mentioned earlier, such as binding redirections, can be performed using these configuration files. We will be covering many aspects of the configuration in the chapters to come. In this section, we look at how the application configuration file can be used to provide custom configuration settings.

Custom Configuration Settings

Application configuration files are good candidates to store custom application settings. The .NET Framework provides a predefined configuration section called appSettings that developers can use to store key–value pairs, as shown in the following example:

```
<configuration>
  <appSettings>
    <add key="License" value="abracadabra"/>
  </appSettings>
</configuration>
```

To programmatically access configuration settings, the .NET Framework provides a set of classes and interface under the namespace System.Configuration. Of interest to us is a class, ConfigurationSettings, that lets us read the configuration sections. This class provides a property, AppSettings, that can be used to read the values from the appSettings section, as illustrated in the following code:

```
// Project CustomSettings

public static void DemoSimpleSettings() {
    String s = ConfigurationSettings.AppSettings["License"];
    if (s != "abracadabra") {
      Console.WriteLine(
```

```
        "Please contact your software vendor!");
      return;
   }
   Console.WriteLine("Proceeding...");
}
```

The predefined section appSettings is useful for storing key–value pairs. If your needs require more than just key–value pairs, then it is possible to define your own sections and the handler code for the sections. For example, you might wish to define an XML tag <owner> that stores the first name and the last name of the product's owner as attributes. An example is shown here:

```
<owner FirstName="Pradeep" LastName="Tapadiya" />
```

To be able to process this information, you need to define a configuration section handler class. A configuration section handler class implements a standard interface IConfigurationSectionHandler. Here is the definition for this interface:

```
interface IConfigurationSectionHandler {
    object Create(object parent, object context, XmlNode node);
}
```

While reading the configuration, the configuration system calls method Create on the handler associated with a configuration section. This method is required to read the configuration section (passed in as parameter node) and return an object representing the configuration.

The first two parameters to the method Create are meaningful only under ASP.NET; otherwise the configuration system sets them to null. Parameter parent points to the object created by the section handler for the parent web.config if you have multiple web.config files in the hierarchy. Parameter context points to an HttpConfigurationContext object that provides the current ASP.NET context information such as the virtual path to the Web.config file.

Here is the implementation of our section handler:

```
// Project CustomSettings

public struct Person {
    public String FirstName;
    public String LastName;
}
```

```
public class PersonHandler : IConfigurationSectionHandler {
    public object Create(Object parent, object configContext,
        XmlNode section) {
      XmlAttributeCollection attribCol = section.Attributes;

      Person person = new Person();
      person.FirstName = attribCol["FirstName"].Value;
      person.LastName = attribCol["LastName"].Value;
      return person;
    }
}
```

Our implementation of the method `Create` simply reads the attributes from the supplied XML node and constructs and returns an object of type `Person`.

The next step is to let the configuration system know that the `<owner>` section in the configuration file should be handled by type `PersonHandler`. This is done by means of the `<section>` entry in the configuration file. This is illustrated in the following configuration settings:

```
<configuration>
  <configSections>
      <section name="owner" type="PersonHandler, MyApp" />
  </configSections>

  <owner FirstName="Pradeep" LastName="Tapadiya" />

</configuration>
```

This configuration indicates that the `<owner>` section and anything underneath it be handled by the type `PersonHandler` that is defined in assembly `MyApp`. Note that the configuration system requires that the `<section>` entries be grouped under a node `<configSections>`.

At this point, we are set to read the configuration. This is done by means of a static method, `Configuration.GetConfig`. The following code excerpt shows how we can read the `<owner>` section from the configuration file and obtain a `Person` object:

```
public static void DemoComplexSettings() {
    Person owner =
        (Person) ConfigurationSettings.GetConfig("owner");
    . . .
}
```

A final word: If XML attributes are what you are interested in reading, as was our case, then you can also use a .NET-defined class `SingleTagSectionHandler`. You can find a usage example on the companion Web site.

This concludes our introduction to reading custom configuration settings. Check the SDK documentation for more details on custom configuration.

Security Policies

Under .NET, security-related configuration settings are stored under a different file, the security policy file. This file includes security information such as permissions granted to an assembly. We will look at the security configuration settings in a later chapter on security.

COMMON LANGUAGE RUNTIME

The ECMA standards define an infrastructure in which a single application can be developed using multiple high-level languages. The standards also specify that the application should be capable of running on different system (hardware and OS) platforms without being rewritten for each specific platform. This ECMA specification is referred to as the CLI. The current specifications for the CLI can be downloaded from the ECMA's Web site (*www.ecma.ch*). It is worth mentioning that C# specifications have also been submitted to the ECMA.

Microsoft's implementation of the CLI is called the common language runtime. The common language runtime forces a unified programming model and provides features such as cross-language integration and type safety. It also manages the execution of the code and provides certain runtime services to the managed code. In this section, we examine some important aspects of the common language runtime.

Strictly speaking, the common language runtime implements more than what is specified in the CLI. For example, the common language runtime provides support for managed code to interoperate with COM components. This is not part of the CLI specification. The focus of the CLI is more toward what makes sense across different platforms.

Common Type System

At the center of the CLI is a single type system, the CTS. The CTS is a model that defines the rules CLI follows when declaring, using, and managing types.

The CTS establishes a framework that enables cross-language integration, type safety, and high-performance code execution.

The CTS also defines a base set of datatypes (e.g., int, string, etc.) and specifications for extending these types. The base datatypes are defined in the BCL. The complete list of base data types can be obtained from the ECMA specifications. We will look at a few important ones shortly.

Confusion over BCL

Note that the ECMA standards distinguish between the Runtime Infrastructure Library, Base Class Library, Network Library, Reflection Library, Floating-Point Library, and Extended Array Library. However, Microsoft lumps all these libraries into one and calls it the BCL.

The ECMA standards document is still a work in progress as of this writing. Hopefully, this discord will be addressed eventually.

The CTS is shared by the compilers, tools, and the runtime. Compiler vendors can write compilers and tools targeting the runtime. The runtime enforces the rules defined by CTS when managing types.

Under CTS, a type is defined as the unit that encapsulates a dataset and defines possible operations on the dataset. A type can have methods as well as other members such as fields, properties, and events. C# classes and structures are examples of types.

An important aspect of CTS is that all types are ultimately inherited from System.Object, a class defined in the BCL. This guarantees that every instance of every type supports the methods provided by CTS. Table 4.1 describes some of the important methods.

TABLE 4.1   Public Methods of System.Object

Method	Description
GetHashCode	Returns a hash value
Equals	Checks if two objects are the same
Finalize	Method called by the common language runtime when the object is about to be destroyed
GetType	Returns the type of the object
MemberwiseClone	Makes a shallow copy of the object
ToString	Returns a string representation of the object

Method `GetHashCode` returns a 32-bit integer that is suitable for use in data structures such as hash tables. The default implementation returns a value that is guaranteed to be the same for the same instance. However, it is not guaranteed that two different instances have different hash codes or two objects storing the same value have the same hash code. This implementation is not particularly useful for hashing. Therefore, derived classes that can be used in hash tables should override `GetHashCode` and provide a more suitable implementation. For example, class `System.String` overrides `GetHashCode` such that if two instances of the `System.String` class contain the same string, the returned hash code is the same.

Method `Equals` checks if two objects are the same. The default implementation of `Equals` checks objects by reference; that is, whether two references point to the same object. However, any derived class can override this method to specify its own equality condition. For example, the `Equals` method of `System.String` returns true for any two instances of a string that contain exactly the same characters in the same order.

If `Equals` deems two objects equal, then a good rule of thumb is that `GetHashCode` on the two objects be equal as well. Therefore, if you override `Equals` on a type, you should (although not required) also override `GetHashCode`. The C# compiler, for example, will generate a warning otherwise.

Method `Finalize` is automatically invoked by the common language runtime when the object is about to be destroyed. The default implementation of `Finalize` does nothing. However, a derived class can override this method if need be. This is typically done to free any resources the object is holding or to perform some other cleanup operations on the object.

Note that C# does not let you override the `Finalize` method directly. However, you can implement a destructor on your class to express your finalization needs, as shown here:

```
class Foo {
    ...
    ~Foo() {
      // implement your cleanup code here
    }
}
```

During compilation, the compiler converts this destructor to `Finalize` method. In the process, the compiler also guarantees that the `Finalize` method for the base class, if any, is invoked.

Method `GetType` returns an instance of the `System.Type` class, which can be used to obtain metadata information (e.g., list of methods in a class) about the object. This method cannot be overridden.

Method `MemberwiseClone` creates and returns a copy of the object it is called on. We revisit this method when we discuss deep versus shallow copy.

Finally, method `ToString` returns the string representation of the object. The default implementation returns the fully qualified name of the type the object belongs to. For example, if a class `Bar` is defined under a namespace `Foo`, then `ToString` on an instance of `Bar` returns `Foo.Bar` by default. However, any derived class can override `ToString` and construct a more sensible string.

Operator Overloading in C#

When you compare two objects using C#'s == operator, do not expect that `Object.Equals` will be invoked. There is no relationship between the two. However, C# specifies a way to overload operators similar to that of C++. The following code excerpt shows how to overload operator ==:

```
class Foo {
    ...
    private int m_Value;

    static public bool operator==(Foo left, Foo right) {
      return (left.m_Value == right.m_Value);
    }

    ...

}
```

With this change, when you compare two instances of class `Foo` as shown here, then the overloaded operator gets invoked:

```
Foo x = new Foo();
Foo y = new Foo();
if (x == y) {
    ...
}
```

Generally, when you overload the equals operator, it is a good practice to overload not equals (!=) as well.

Behind the scenes, the C# compiler expands the overloaded equals operator as `op_Equality`, a BCL-defined standard method name for comparing two values. The framework SDK defines all possible operator overloads, their equivalent BCL method names, and overloading usage guidelines. Table 4.2 shows some common overload operators.

TABLE 4.2　Some C# Overload Operators

Operation	C# Operator Symbol	BCL Method Name
Equals	==	op_Equality
Not equals	!=	op_Inequality
Bitwise (binary) And	&	op_BitwiseAnd
Logical And	&&	op_LogicalAnd
Bitwise (binary) Or	|	op_BitwiseOr
Logical Or	||	op_LogicalOr
Logical True	true	op_True
Logical False	false	op_False

Sample project `OperatorLoading` demonstrates the behavior for many overload operators.

Beware of Overloading & AND | Operators

Consider the following C# code excerpt:

```
If (x && y) { // logical and
  ...
}
```

Under .NET, the behavior of this logical and can be represented as follows:

```
T.op_False(x) ? T.op_True(x) : T.op_True(T.op_BitwiseAnd(x,y))
```

The operation first invokes `op_False` on x. If x is false, then y is simply ignored. If x is true, however, then the code calls `op_BitwiseAnd` on x and y and then calls `op_True` on the result of `op_BitwiseAnd`. What this means is that even if x and y are true when tested individually, it is possible that (x && y) may still return false. Likewise, if y is false, (x && y) may still return true. It all depends on how `op_BitwiseAnd` is defined.

Similarly, the behavior of the logical or operation can be represented as follows:

```
T.op_True(x) ? T.op_True(x) : T.op_True(T.op_BitwiseOr(x,y))
```

The bottom line is that you have to be especially careful when defining `op_BitwiseAnd` and `op_BitwiseOr` when creating a new type.

Common Language Specification

Although CTS provides the base types that all languages can use, not all base types are intended to be supported by all programming languages. For example, Visual Basic .NET does not support unsigned datatypes. Depending on the specifications of a programming language, the compiler vendor may support only the subset of CTS types needed by the language.

The CLS is an agreement between compiler vendors and .NET Framework designers. It defines the minimum set of features a .NET-compliant compiler should support. Among other things, the CLS dictates the subset of CTS datatypes that are intended to work across all .NET languages and a set of usage conventions. Whereas CTS is wide enough to allow many features so that languages can implement any feature they want, CLS is narrow enough to allow just those language features needed to support cross-language integration. Table 4.3 lists CTS-defined base datatypes along with their C# datatype and CLS compliance.

TABLE 4.3　C# Primitive Datatypes

BCL Type	Description	C# Type	CLS Compliant?
System.Boolean	A true/false value	bool	Yes
System.SByte	8-bit signed integer	sbyte	No
System.Byte	8-bit unsigned integer	byte	Yes
System.Char	16-bit Unicode character	char	Yes
System.Int16	16-bit signed integer	short	Yes
System.UInt16	16-bit unsigned integer	ushort	No
System.Int32	32-bit signed integer	int	Yes
System.UInt32	32-bit unsigned integer	uint	No
System.Int64	64-bit signed integer	long	Yes
System.UInt64	64-bit unsigned integer	ulong	No
System.Single	IEEE 32-bit float	float	Yes
System.Double	IEEE 64-bit float	double	Yes
System.Decimal	96-bit monetary type (used in financial calculations)	decimal	Yes
System.String	String of Unicode characters	string	Yes
System.Object	Root system class	object	Yes

Use CLS-Compliant Datatypes

Whenever possible, use CLS-compliant datatypes (unless cross-language interoperability is not important for your needs).

To ensure that your code is in compliance with CLS, add the following line to any of the source file used in building your assembly:

```
[assembly:System.CLSCompliant(true)]
```

With this change, the compiler flags an error if it finds code that is not compliant with CLS.

Note that CLS compliance is meant only for public and family members. As private members are never exposed to any other type, they need not be compliant.

Here is the code excerpt that shows how an assembly based on Visual Basic .NET can make a cross-language method call into a C#-based assembly.

```csharp
// Project CrossLanguage

// File ConsoleGreeting.cs
// Compile as: csc.exe -t:library ConsoleGreeting.cs
namespace MyGreeting {
    public class ConsoleGreeting {
        private String m_userName;

        public void Greet() {
            Console.WriteLine("Hello " + m_userName);
        }

        public String UserName {
            set {
                m_userName = value;
            }
            get {
                return m_userName;
            }
        }
    }
}
```

```vb
' File MyVBApp.vb
' Compile as: vbc.exe -t:exe -r:ConsoleGreeting.dll MyVBApp.vb

Imports MyGreeting
Module MyVBApp
    Sub Main()
```

```
    Dim obj As New ConsoleGreeting()
    obj.UserName = "Jay"
    obj.Greet()
  End Sub
End Module
```

Value Types and Reference Types

Another important aspect of the CTS is its classification of types. The CTS classifies types into two broad categories—value types and reference types. There are two major differences between these types:

1. *Storage*: A value type instance is created on the stack and a reference type instance is created on the heap (managed heap, more specifically).

2. *Assignment*: When a value type instance is assigned to another instance (of the same type), the second instance gets a duplicate copy of the first instance's data. In case of a reference type, both the instances share the same memory location.

Consider the following C# code excerpt:

```
System.Int32 a,b;
a = 5;
b = a;
```

Datatype `System.Int32` (int in C#) is of value type. Therefore, when variable a is assigned to variable b, b gets a copy of a. Thereafter, changing the value of a does not cause a change in the value of b.

Under C#, classes and interfaces are always that of a reference type. Consider the following C# class:

```
public class Foo
{
    public int x;
};
```

The following code excerpt demonstrates how the assignment operation works for a reference type:

```
        public static void Test(Foo a, Foo b) {
            a.x = 5;
            b.x = 10;
            b = a;
            Console.WriteLine(b.x); // will display "5"
            a.x = 20;
            Console.WriteLine(b.x); // will display "20"
```

```
    }
```

As can be observed from the test, once a is assigned to b, changing the contents of a automatically reflect in b. This is because the assignment operation just assigned the reference (the memory location) of a to b.

Under C#, a struct definition is always that of a value type. Here is an example:

```
// Project ValueType

struct Point {
    public int x;
    public int y;
};

public static void Main()
{
    Point a, b;

    // All the fields of a value type variable have to be
    // assigned a value before the variable can be used
    a.x = 10;
    a.y = 20;

    b = a;

    Console.WriteLine("Point b is ({0},{1})", b.x, b.y);
}
```

Note that, unlike reference type instances, it is not necessary to instantiate a value type using the new operator. However, if not instantiated using the new operator, the value type variable has to be assigned a value before it can be used. Otherwise, the compiler generates an error.

To identify a datatype as a value type, the CTS requires that the type be derived from System.ValueType. This class overrides the virtual methods Equals, GetHashCode, and ToString from its base class, System.Object, to provide more appropriate implementation for value types.

Note that System.ValueType internally uses Reflection when overriding the virtual methods. Using Reflection is performance intensive. Moreover, the default implementation of GetHashCode just returns the hash code of the first non-null field of the value type. Therefore, it is highly recommended that each value type definition provide its own implementation of these methods.

The following code excerpt illustrates this idea:

```
// Project ValueType

struct Point {
    public int x;
    public int y;

    public override bool Equals(Object obj) {
      if(!(obj is Point)) {
        return false;
      }

      Point p = (Point) obj;
      return ((this.x == p.x) && (this.y == p.y));
    }

    public override int GetHashCode() {
      return (this.x ^ this.y); // a simple scheme
    }

    public override string ToString() {
      string s = "(" + this.x + "," + this.y + ")";
      return s;
    }
};
```

Implementing Value Types

Whenever possible, define your own implementation of `Equals`, `GetHashCode`, and `ToString` for value type definitions.

Boxing and Unboxing

It is possible, and sometimes necessary, to convert between value types and reference types. The conversion of a value type to a reference type is called boxing and the conversion of a reference type to a value type is called unboxing. The following code excerpt illustrates this idea:

```
// Project BoxingUnboxing

public static void Main()
{
    int i = 10; // "int" (System.Int32) is value type
```

```
Object o;    //   "object" (System.Object) is reference type

o = (object) i; // Boxing "i"

int j = (int) o; // Unboxing "o" to integer

Console.WriteLine(j);
}
```

Boxing results in creating an object on the heap and copies the value from the value-type object onto the object. This makes it fairly performance intensive. It is a good idea to inspect your code and remove unnecessary boxing operations if possible. Read Gunnerson's article on MSDN [Gun-01a] to check how box-savvy you are. Also, read [Gun-01b] to learn the performance implications of boxing.

Unboxing first checks if the source object is a boxed value of the requested value type. If the source object is null or is a reference to an incompatible object, an `InvalidCastException` is thrown. Otherwise, the value from the source object is copied into the destination value type object.

Sometimes it is a good idea to perform the compatibility check yourself before unboxing an object. This is exactly what we did in our implementation of the `Point.Equals` method in the previous section.

Let's now see what happens when a managed application is executed.

MICROSOFT INTERMEDIATE LANGUAGE

The CLI also specifies an environment for executing the code targeting the CLI. The environment is called the Virtual Execution System (VES). Among other things, the VES defines a hypothetical machine with an associated machine model and instructions. The machine instructions are defined in a language called Common Intermediate Language (CIL). A detailed description of the CIL instruction set can be found in the ECMA specifications.

As you may have guessed, Microsoft's implementation of CIL is called Microsoft Intermediate Language (MSIL).

Consider the following C# code to multiply two numbers:

```
public static int Multiply(int i, int j) {
    int k = i * j;
    return k;
}
```

When this code is compiled, the compiler creates the following MSIL code in the generated assembly (recall that you can use the IL disassembler to view the contents of an assembly). I have added comments to each instruction for better readability.

```
.method public hidebysig
     static int32  Multiply(int32 i, int32 j) cil managed
 {
   .maxstack  2; maximum number of items this
             ; method will push on the stack
   .locals (int32 V_0) ; local variables this method needs
               ; V_0 is the first local variable
   ldarg.0    ; push the first argument onto the stack
   ldarg.1    ; push the second argument onto the stack
   mul        ; multiply the two arguments
   stloc.0    ; pop the result from the stack to V_0
   ldloc.0    ; push V_0 to the stack (return value)
   ret        ; return from the method
 } // end of method MyApp::Multiply
```

Note that while traditional machine language instruction sets use registers and stacks, the MSIL instruction set uses only the stack. In the above code, the two arguments are pushed onto the stack and the multiply instruction is called. This instruction pops the two values from the stack and pushes the result back onto the stack. The code then pops the value from the stack to the local variable. The local variable is pushed back to the stack as the stack is also used to place the return value of the method. Finally, the method returns to its caller.

Under MSIL, copying values from memory to the stack is referred to as loading and copying values from the stack to memory is referred to as storing.

More information on the IL instruction set can be found in the ECMA CLI documents at www.ecma.ch. A copy can also be found under the subdirectory "Tools Developers Guide" in the directory where the .NET Framework SDK is installed.

Protecting the Intellectual Property

Given that it is so easy to disassemble an assembly, it seems feasible for someone to reverse engineer the logic of your program. Is there any form of protection for your code?

Microsoft is currently working on a basic obfuscator that will mangle all non-public names in an assembly. Although not a fool-proof scheme, it will at least make disassembled programs harder to comprehend.

Hello World in IL

It is possible to write a program in MSIL although most programmers would prefer using a higher level language. The following MSIL code shows how to display "Hello World!" to the console:

```
/**************************************************
   Hello World program written in MSIL
   NOTE: Anything that starts with a period is
         a directive for the assembler
 *************************************************/

// This module is the holder of assembly manifest
.assembly hello {}

.method static public void MyMain() cil managed
{
    // Mark this method as the entry point
    .entrypoint

    // Push a string onto the stack
    ldstr "Hello World!"

    // Invoke System.Console.WriteLine
    call void [mscorlib]
      System.Console::WriteLine(class System.String)

    // return from the method
    ret
}
```

The `entrypoint` directive informs the IL assembler to mark the specified method as an entry point. When the execution engine loads the application, it starts executing code from the specified entry point. When we write code in a higher-level language such as C#, the compiler automatically assumes that the entry point is static method named `Main`.

Obviously, the entry point is needed only for an EXE-based assembly. For a DLL-based assembly, the application responsible for loading it dictates what method(s) to call.

The framework provides a tool called IL assembler (`ilasm.exe`) for assembling MSIL files. Assuming the above code is stored in a file `HelloWorld.il`, the following command line will generate an assembly named `HelloWorld.exe`.

```
ilasm.exe HelloWorld.il
```

This concludes our short introduction to MSIL. Let's now examine the process of executing managed code.

MANAGED CODE EXECUTION

To load and execute an assembly, the common language runtime has to be hosted within a process first. The .NET Framework provides APIs to let an application host the common language runtime. Some examples of such host applications are ASP.NET, SQL Server .NET, and so on.

An EXE-based assembly contains a small piece of bootstrapping code that points to a function exported by the .NET runtime, named `CorExeMain`. When such an assembly is executed, the OS creates a process and executes `CorExeMain`. This function in turn loads the common language runtime into the process and transfers control to it.

Using a standard PE file mechanism to bootstrap the common language runtime is a clever technique on the part of Microsoft. It ensures that many things "just work." For example, to run the application, you can double-click an application in the Explorer window or enter its name at the command line.

The function `CorExeMain` loads the EE, reads the assembly's manifest, and loads the module containing the entry point for the application. From this point, the common language runtime (the EE, more specifically) goes through the following general steps:

1. Metadata validation
2. Code verification
3. Compilation of MSIL code to native machine code
4. Execution of the compiled code

Figure 4.3 shows the overall process of how a method is compiled and executed.

As the code executes, it may make references to other types. The common language runtime loads the module containing the referenced type, if it has not been loaded already, as illustrated in Figure 4.3.

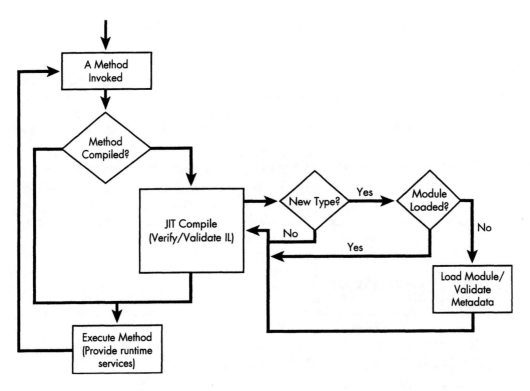

FIGURE 4.3 Method execution.

Once a module has been loaded and validated, and the reference to the type has been resolved, the runtime is ready to execute the type's method. However, before this is done, the runtime has to take care of a few things:

- The MSIL code for the method has to be validated. For example, the MSIL code should not contain any invalid opcodes.

- The MSIL code has to be checked for unsafe code. This is called code verification.

- Finally, the MSIL code for the method has to be converted to the native machine language instructions. This on-the-fly conversion is referred to as just-in-time (JIT) compilation.

We will cover these steps in more detail shortly.

After the MSIL instructions have been converted to native machine language instructions, the common language runtime steps aside and let the native machine code execute. While the code is executing, the common language provides any runtime service that is needed such as automatic memory management, enhanced security, interoperability with COM components and so on.

The process of loading a module when needed, metadata validation, verification, compilation, and then executing the native code is repeated until the execution is complete.

It is interesting to note that a module is loaded as a side effect of referencing a type contained in the module. If some types within an assembly are placed in a module such that a particular execution path never references any of the types in the module, then the runtime will not load the module. By bundling least used types in a separate module, you can improve execution performance, especially if the assembly needs to be downloaded over a slow link. If the module is not used, it will not be downloaded.

Metadata Validation

As each module is loaded, the common language runtime performs a set of tests on it to ensure that the file format and the metadata are self-consistent. This set of tests is referred to as *metadata validation*. The ECMA specifications define what constitutes valid metadata. As of this writing, the specification consists of about 500 rules.

Note that MSIL code is not validated when the module is loaded. This is done on a per-method basis—when the method is about to be executed. As a result, if a method is never executed, its MSIL code is never validated.

Code Validation and Verification

Once a module has been loaded and validated and the reference to the type has been resolved, the common language runtime is ready to execute the type's method. However, before this is done, the common language runtime has to validate and verify the MSIL code.

Validation checks if the MSIL code is consistent. For example, the code should not contain any invalid MSIL instruction. This can happen, for example, as a result of a bug in the front-end compiler. If the validation fails, the runtime throws an exception.

Verification examines the MSIL code and the metadata to ensure that the code accesses memory locations it is authorized to access and that the code calls methods only through properly defined types. Such type safety is necessary to ensure that objects do not cause any inadvertent or malicious corruption of memory or other important resources. Using pointers, for example, generates potentially unsafe code.

During the verification process, the code is examined against a well-defined set of type-safe rules. The code is deemed unsafe if it fails any of the rules.

Do not confuse unsafe code with unmanaged code. Only managed code is verified for type safety. If the code is unsafe, it still remains managed code. Unmanaged code, on the other hand, is the code that the runtime has no control over, such as native calls to the platform.

Verification ensures that each type is only asked to execute valid operations. It is not possible for verification to check runtime conditions such as array bounds violation. Such runtime conditions are handled by the runtime, not verification.

Verification Is Limited

It is quite possible that your code may fail the verification test even though it is perfectly safe to use. This is due to the limitations of the verification process. Moreover, some languages do not produce verifiably type-safe code, which causes the verification to fail.

Under C#, if you wish to write unsafe code, you need to explicitly scope the code using a keyword `unsafe`, as shown in the following example:

```
// Project UnsafeCode

public void GetValueByRef(ref int value) {
    int retValue = 0;
    unsafe {
      byte* p = (byte*) &retValue;
      p[0] = 10;
    }
    value = retValue;
}
```

Keyword `unsafe` can also be applied at the method level or the type level. Here are some examples:

```
// Project UnsafeCode

public class Foo {
    ...

    unsafe public void GetValueByPointer(int* value) {
      *value = 20;
```

```
    }
}

public unsafe class Bar {
    private int* m_Count = null;

    ...

}
```

The Microsoft C# compiler produces verifiable type-safe code by default. You need to explicitly instruct the compiler to generate unsafe code. This is done using the -unsafe switch, as shown in the following command line:

```
csc.exe -unsafe MyCode.cs
```

Recall that verification is performed on a method that is about to be executed. During verification, if any unsafe code is encountered, the runtime throws an exception of type VerificationException (namespace System.Security). The unsafe code is not executed.

The only way to run unsafe code is to force the runtime to skip verification on the assembly. The assembly has to request for a security permission called SkipVerification and the administrator has to set the security policy on the local machine such that the assembly is granted this permission. We will look at this in Chapter 9 on security.

By default, all the assemblies on the local machine are granted full trust (which includes the SkipVerification permission). Files downloaded over the network (Internet or intranet) have a reduced set of permissions.

Offline Verification

It is also possible to validate and verify your assembly without executing it. The framework provides a tool called *PEVerify* (peverify.exe) to check if the MSIL code and the metadata in the assembly meet the type-safety requirements. The following command line, for example, checks if Foo.dll is type-safe:

```
peverify.exe Foo.dll
```

Check the SDK documentation for the command line switches for this tool.

Note that out of all the metadata validation rules defined in the ECMA specifications, PEVerify checks only the important ones. Perhaps the next version of the .NET Framework will have a more elaborate coverage.

Also note that there is an important behavioral difference between PEVerify and the JIT compiler. The JIT compiler verifies only those methods that are executed whereas PEVerify verifies all the methods in the assembly. It is recommended that you test your assemblies with PEVerify before you ship it.

JIT Compilation

Once the method to be executed has been validated and verified, the MSIL code for the method has to be converted to the native machine language code; that is, code that is specific to the local machine's CPU architecture. This on-the-fly conversion is referred to as JIT compilation.

JIT compilation makes it possible to develop the code once but run it on different hardware platforms. All that is needed is the availability of a JIT compiler (or the JITter, as it is called) for the target CPU architecture. Of course, if your managed code makes native calls to the specific OS platform, then your code might not be able to run on another platform.

As the JIT compiler is written for a specific CPU architecture, it can potentially perform all the hardware-specific optimization, thus producing a performance-efficient native code.

Note that the JIT compiler compiles code only for the method that is about to be executed, not the type's module or the assembly. As a matter of fact, if a type's method is never called during the execution, the method's MSIL code is never compiled, saving both time and memory.

The scheme for activating JIT compilation is very simple and efficient. When a type is loaded by the common language runtime, the loader creates and attaches a stub to each of the type's methods. On the first call to the method, the stub passes control to the JIT compiler. The JIT compiler converts the MSIL code for that method into native code and patches the stub to point directly to the native code. As a result, subsequent calls to the JIT-compiled method proceed directly to the native code.

In some cases, the JIT compiler may also expand the method inline, that is, within the calling code. This reduces the overhead associated with making a call.

Native-Code Assemblies

The JIT compiler generates native code that stays in memory only for the specific process. The generated code is not retained to be used from one run to the next.

It is also possible to compile the MSIL code to native code before executing an assembly, perhaps during assembly installation. This pre-jitting results in reduced application startup time and improved runtime performance, as there is no need to create and attach stubs to each type's methods during run-time or to compile the methods dynamically.

The framework provides a tool called the Native Image Generator (ngen.exe) to compile an assembly. This tool not only creates a native image for the specified assembly but also installs the assembly into a special region of the runtime called the native image cache. The following command line, for example, compiles the assembly ConsoleGreeting.dll into a native image and adds the image to the native image cache:

```
ngen.exe ConsoleGreeting.dll
```

Note that even though the native image has been installed in the native image cache, the source assembly has to be present on the machine in the same location where it was originally compiled from. This is because the runtime checks whether the source assembly has been modified with respect to its native image. If so, then the runtime does not use the "stale" native image, but silently falls back to the JIT compilation.

The native image is considered stale if the source assembly has been re-created, if the common language runtime has been modified, if the assembly bindings have been changed by way of configuration, and so forth.

The .NET Framework installs a few assemblies as the native images. This can be observed from the GAC viewer. Another way to get a list of currently installed native images on a machine is to use -show switch on ngen.exe, as shown here:

```
ngen.exe -show
```

To remove an image from the native image cache, you can use ngen.exe with -delete switch. You can also use gacutil.exe with the switch -ungen, as shown in the following command line:

```
gactuil.exe –ungen ConsoleGreeting
```

Rebasing Executables

Under Windows, each executable stores a value that identifies the starting address where the executable should be loaded in a process' memory. However, to avoid any address overlaps, the OS may have to load the executable at a different location. This relocation results in increased load time for the executable. This relocation penalty can be avoided if each executable that will be loaded within a process is specified a base address that avoids any load-time address collisions.

Under .NET, base-address collision is not a problem for assemblies that contain IL code. Recall that the runtime "extracts" the MSIL code from the assembly and loads it into the execution engine.

Native-code assemblies, however, are loaded into the process' memory space. Therefore, it is a good idea to properly base such assemblies before compiling them into native code. The C# compiler creates executables with the base address of 0x00400000. However, this default behavior can be customized by using -baseaddress compiler switch.

Note that native-code images can be twice as large as the corresponding MSIL-code image. The exact factor depends on the content.

Also note that most of the .NET assemblies are loaded into 0x79000000 to 0x7D000000 range.

Needless to say, if your managed code interacts with any unmanaged code (DLLs and COM servers), these unmanaged executables should also be rebased properly.

Code Execution

After the MSIL instructions have been converted to native machine language instructions, the common language runtime steps aside and lets the native machine code execute. While the code is executing, the common language runtime provides any runtime service that is needed, such as automatic memory management, enhanced security, interoperability with COM components and unmanaged code, and so on.

In this chapter, we look at perhaps the most important service that the runtime provides—automatic memory management. Other services such as security, interoperability, and so forth, are covered in later chapters.

AUTOMATIC MEMORY MANAGEMENT

Every program stores instances of datatypes in memory. This per-instance memory can be allocated either in the data segment, the stack, or the heap. Typically, static variables in a program are stored in the data segment and local variables to a method are stored on the stack. The compiler inserts appropriate logic in the output code to deal with memory management of data-segment-bound and stack-based types. For heap-based types, a programmer has to explicitly deal with memory management issues. Here are the typical steps a programmer goes through to deal with heap-based types:

1. Allocate memory of proper size for the instance of the type. Under C++ and C#, for example, this can be done using the operator `new`.

2. Initialize the instance. Member fields of the type are assigned a value. Any system resources that the instance needs, such as opening a file or a network connection, are also acquired. Under C++ and C#, this can be done either in the constructor of the type or in a different method.

3. Use the instance (and the acquired resources).

4. Dispose of the resources; for example, close the file or the network connection opened previously.

5. Free the allocated memory. Under C++, this can be done using the operator `delete`.

Humans make mistakes. While programming, it is quite possible that someone will forget to call Step 4. C++ has a neat solution for this. When `delete` is called on an object, the compiler ensures that the class's destructor is invoked first before the memory is freed. If the disposing logic is moved in the destructor, Step 4 is automatically taken care of when Step 5 is called.

If you forget to call Step 5, not only will it result in a memory leak, but it might also cause the resources not to be disposed off.

This problem has plagued programmers forever. A plethora of tools came into existence to detect such memory leaks in the program. Many "smart pointer" [Ede-92] techniques were designed to ensure that Step 5 is automatically performed. A typical smart pointer implementation keeps count of the number of outstanding references on the object. When the last reference goes away (implying that the object is no longer in use), the object is deleted.

.NET addresses this problem in a different way. In Chapter 2, I touched on the noticeable absence of a `delete` operator in C#. There is no need to delete an object. The runtime automatically detects whether the object is no longer in use and deletes it. This mechanism is called garbage collection (GC). Let's see how it works.

It is worth mentioning that GC is not a new technique. There are many GC algorithms in use today, but our focus is on the GC algorithm used under .NET.

Also note that what I cover here are some important aspects of memory management. For more intricate details, please read Richter's articles [Ric-00a] and [Ric-00b] in *MSDN Magazine*.

Garbage Collection

When the common language runtime is initialized in a process, it reserves a contiguous region of memory space on the process's heap. This memory region is called the *managed heap*.

When an application creates an object using the `new` operator, the runtime assigns the required size on the managed heap to the object. As each new object is created, a contiguous memory location is assigned to the object.

This simple mechanism makes allocating an object on the managed heap very efficient. In fact, the operation is as fast as allocating memory on the stack.

Note that even though a big chunk of memory is reserved on the heap initially, it is the virtual memory of the process, not the actual storage. The storage is committed as necessary when objects are created at runtime. The implication is that the working set size of the process is relatively small during initialization but may grow as objects are created.

As objects are assigned memory on the managed heap, the heap starts filling up. What happens when a new object needs to be created but there is not enough space available in the managed heap?

This is where the GC kicks in. Here is what it does:

1. With the help of the runtime, the GC first constructs a list of objects that are in use. The rest of the objects are garbage and the memory occupied by them is available for reuse.

2. The collector then compacts the memory, effectively removing the "gaps" in the heap caused by the garbage objects. The nongarbage objects are shifted in memory as necessary. After the collection, all the used objects are placed contiguously at one end of the heap. The remaining space is available for reuse.

3. As the nongarbage objects have been shifted in the memory, all pointers to those objects have become invalid. The collector fixes these pointers to point to the new locations.

4. The `new` operation is tried again and the memory request is satisfied.

It is interesting to know how the list of nongarbage objects is created. Each application has a set of root objects, or objects that the GC can use as a starting point to detect other objects being used. For example, all the global and static objects in an application are considered root objects. Local variables and method arguments on a thread's stack also constitute as root objects. Finally, any CPU register containing pointers to objects in the managed heap is also considered part of the application's roots. The set of root objects may change as execution proceeds. With some help from the JIT compiler, the runtime maintains the list of active roots.

When the garbage collector starts running, it walks the active roots and builds a graph of all objects reachable from the root. These are the objects that are in use. The rest of the objects are garbage and hence can be collected.

Note that an object is a candidate for collection as soon as it is no longer used. For example, variables that go out of scope are all candidates for collection. Even within the scope, if the execution has passed the last use of a variable, such a variable is also a candidate for collection.

Debugger Changes the Behavior

When an application is being debugged, the runtime extends the lifetime of a variable even after it no longer is used within the scope. This gives you a chance to inspect the objects within the debugger.

Performance Considerations

Because of its nature, GC is a costly operation. Depending on the gaps left in the managed heap, shifting memory could be quite expensive. An even bigger impact is for multithreaded applications. As memory is being shifted around, the runtime has to suspend all other threads to ensure that objects do not point to invalid memory locations.

On the positive side, though, the GC algorithm uses a few different mechanisms to keep threads running as long as possible and to reduce overhead. These mechanisms include fully interrupting the code (on each thread), hijacking a thread, and letting the JIT compiler introduce additional GC-related code at some safe points within a method. The algorithm also employs some other techniques to take advantage of multiple processors, if available. A detailed description of these techniques can be found in [Ric-00b].

Note that all these mechanisms for performance improvement are transparent to your application.

GC Performance Counters

The runtime provides many performance counters that show the status of managed memory for a specific process. These counters are grouped under the .NET CLR memory performance object.

By default, the GC takes place when an object is being created and there is not enough space left in the managed heap. However, it is also possible to programmatically force a GC within the application. The framework provides a class, GC (namespace System), to deal with GC. The following line of code forces a GC:

```
GC.Collect();
```

Generally, it is best to let the garbage collector run on its own accord. However, as your application knows more about its behavior than the runtime, you could call this method at some strategic places in your code. For example, it would be a good time to force GC when your application is sitting idle, perhaps waiting for the user's input.

By default, the runtime creates a separate thread to run the GC concurrently. However, it is possible to specify the runtime to run the GC on the same thread as the application. This is done by means of configuration setting gcConcurrent, as shown here:

```
<configuration>
    <runtime>
        <gcConcurrent enabled="false"/>
    </runtime>
</configuration>
```

Running GC concurrently reduces performance. For applications based on a user interface, it makes sense to run GC concurrently so the application does not appear to pause. However, for a background application not dependent on the user interface, it is advisable to turn off concurrent GC.

Generations

The GC algorithm has many features to improve collection performance. One such feature is called *generations*, which based on the following assumptions:

- The newer an object is, the shorter its lifetime will be. For example, variables local to a method are created once the method is entered and are of no use once the method is exited.

- Newer objects tend to have a strong relationship with each other and are frequently accessed around the same time.

- Compacting a portion of the heap is faster than compacting the whole heap.

Many studies have demonstrated that these assumptions are valid for a large set of existing applications.

Under .NET, the managed heap is logically (not physically) grouped into zones called generations. The first release of .NET runtime contains three generations (numbered 0–2, inclusive) and most likely will stay the same for future releases.

When an object is created, it is stored in generation 0. Simply stated, objects in generation 0 are young objects and have not been touched by the garbage collector.

As more objects are created, they are placed in generation 0. When generation 0 fills up, a GC is performed. Those objects that survive the collection are considered older and are moved to generation 1. After the collection, generation 0 is empty.

When the next GC occurs, survivors from generation 1 move to generation 2 and survivors from generation 0 move to generation 1.

As generation 2 is currently the highest generation, when the next GC occurs, survivors from generation 2 simply stay there.

The GC class provides a `GetGeneration` method that can be used to examine the generation of an object. The following code excerpt demonstrates how an object moves up the generation ladder:

```
// Project GCGenerations

public static void Main() {
    Object o = new Object();
    Console.WriteLine(GC.GetGeneration(o)); // displays 0

    GC.Collect();
    Console.WriteLine(GC.GetGeneration(o)); // displays 1

    GC.Collect();
    Console.WriteLine(GC.GetGeneration(o)); // displays 2
}
```

How does generational GC improve performance? When the GC occurs, the garbage collector may choose to examine only the objects in generation 0 and ignore the objects in higher generations. After all, the newer an object is, the shorter its lifetime is expected to be. Collecting and compacting just generation 0 objects is likely to reclaim significant amount of space from the heap and be faster than examining all the objects in all generations.

Of course, if collecting generation 0 doesn't provide the necessary amount of storage, then objects in generation 1 can be collected. Failing this, objects in generation 2 can be collected.

Another performance benefit comes from the statistical likelihood that newer objects have a strong relationship with each other and are frequently accessed around the same time. As new objects are allocated contiguously in memory, you gain performance from locality of reference. It is highly likely that all the new objects can reside in the CPU's cache. Accessing the CPU's cache is much faster than accessing RAM. The application will be able to perform most of its manipulation without having cache misses (which forces RAM access).

It is also possible to programmatically force collection at a higher level. Class GC provides an overloaded version of Collect that takes the generation number as a parameter. The following line of code, for example, forces a GC at generation 2.

```
GC.Collect(2);
```

A collection at generation 2 automatically implies a collection at generations 1 and 0.

View Generation Status

.NET provides performance counters to view the number of times objects are collected at various generation levels.

Finalization

GC manages memory, but not any other resources. Read that line again. It's important to understand that the GC can release any unused memory but it cannot deal with any other resources. If you have resources such as file handles that are open, it is your responsibility to release such resources.

Consider the following code excerpt for example:

```
// Project Finalization

class MyFile {

    public MyFile(String fileName) {

        // Call native Win32 API to open a file
        m_handle = CreateFile(fileName,...);
    }
```

```
public String ReadLine() {
  ...
}

private IntPtr m_handle; // native Win32 file handle
}

class MyApp {
  public static void Main() {
    MyFile f = new MyFile("Readme.Txt");
    Console.WriteLine(f.ReadLine());
  }
}
```

Class MyFile opens a file handle in its constructor using the native Windows API called CreateFile. We will look at invoking platform specific calls in a later chapter on interoperability.

When a MyFile object is collected by the garbage collector, the file handle that was opened never gets closed. If you use such an object a few times, soon you start running short of file handles.

Fortunately, .NET provides a feature called *finalization* that allows an object to clean itself up when it is being collected. The root system object, System.Object, defines a method called Finalize that a derived class can override and provide its cleanup functionality. The following is its prototype:

```
protected virtual void Finalize();
```

So, all we need is to override this method in MyFile class and close the file handle, right? Well, not exactly! C# doesn't let you override Finalize. The compiler flags this as an error. Instead, you need to use the destructor semantics to implement your cleanup, as shown here:

```
class MyFile {
  ...
  ~MyFile() {
    CloseHandle(m_handle);
  }
}
```

Under the hood, the compiler converts the destructor code to the Finalize method. Here is how the generated code would look:

```
protected override void Finalize() {
  try {
    CloseHandle(m_handle);
```

```
    }finally {
      base.Finalize();
    }
}
```

Note that in the generated code, the compiler also inserts logic to invoke the base (parent class) type's `Finalize` method. The compiler does not let you call base type's `Finalize` method directly. Implementing a destructor is the only way to ensure that base type's `Finalize` is called.

The `finally` clause in C# ensures that irrespective of the outcome of the `try` block, the code in the `finally` block is always executed.

How does finalization work? When an object is being collected, the garbage collector sees that the type has a `Finalize` method and calls the method.

C# Destructor versus C++ Destructor

At first glance, a C# destructor looks very similar to a C++ destructor. However, they are two very different beasts.

The invocation of C++ destructors is deterministic. They are called when an object gets deleted or when a variable goes out of scope. Under C#, there is no such deterministic finalization. You have no idea at what point in your code the finalizer will be invoked.

Under C++, the thread that invokes the destructor is deterministic. Therefore, C++ destructors can use thread-specific features such as thread local storage. Under .NET, the finalizer is invoked by a special runtime thread. Therefore, C# destructors should never use thread-specific features.

Under C++, if you do not define a destructor, the compiler generates one for you. Under C#, the compiler does not generate the destructor for you. As we will see later, finalization under .NET is an expensive process and should be avoided if possible.

Under C++, the order of destructors is deterministic. For example, if a class contains member fields, the destructor for the class (the outer object) is invoked before the destructor of member fields (inner objects). In C#, the order of `Finalize` is not guaranteed. The inner objects might get finalized even before the outer object does. Therefore, the `Finalize` method must never try to access any inner objects.

Although finalization seems pretty simple on the surface, the internal workings of finalization are not that simple. Essentially, an object that has a `Finalize` method is placed in a separate data structure (called the Finalization queue) within the managed heap. When a GC occurs, the garbage objects from the Finalization queue are moved to a different queue called the Freachable queue. A special runtime thread is dedicated to calling `Finalize` on all the objects in the Freachable queue.

Finalization Gotchas

Because of a separate dedicated thread handling the finalization, there are some things that you should be aware of:

- You should not use any thread-specific feature in your finalizer. It is not your thread.
- Your finalization code should be as quick to execute as possible. There are other objects waiting in the queue behind you.
- You should avoid all actions that would block the `Finalize` method, including any thread-synchronization operations.

Richter's article [Ric-00b] is a good reference to understanding the internals of finalization. For now, it is important to know that invoking finalization on an object is performance intensive and therefore should be avoided when possible.

So now you completely understand that implementing `Finalize` (i.e., the C# destructor) should be avoided as much as possible, however, your original problem is still not solved. You cannot leave the file handles open. What possible choice do you have to force closing such opened resources?

Disposing Resources

A simple way to clean up the object is to provide an additional method that the consumer of your type can explicitly call. For types that "open" resources, a method name such as `Close` makes sense for closing the opened resources. The following code excerpt illustrates this:

```
// Project Dispose

    public void Close() {
      if (INVALID_HANDLE_VALUE != m_handle) {
        CloseHandle(m_handle);
        m_handle = INVALID_HANDLE_VALUE;
      }
    }
```

Although you can define a method such as `Close` in your class, and it is quite appropriate, the framework formalizes this notion of explicit cleanup of an object. A type that wishes to expose such functionality must implement a framework-defined interface, IDisposable. Here is its prototype:

```
interface IDisposable {
    void Dispose();
}
```

The following code excerpt illustrates how our class MyFile can be modified to support this interface:

```
// Project Dispose

class MyFile : IDisposable{
    ...

    public void Dispose() {
      if (INVALID_HANDLE_VALUE != m_handle) {
        CloseHandle(m_handle);
        m_handle = INVALID_HANDLE_VALUE;
      }
    }
}
```

The client code can now explicitly call Dispose to dispose of the resources.

Let's back up a little. The reason we are going through these extra steps is to avoid finalization. However, the finalizer code is still there. We haven't really fixed the actual problem. Let's take out the destructor that we defined. That should fix the problem, right?

Our problem is not really that we added a finalizer on the class. Our problem is that finalization is still being done on our object. If the client calls Dispose, it makes sense that the finalization be suppressed. This is why class GC defines a method, SuppressFinalize, to suppress finalization on an object. Using this method, we can modify our Dispose method as follows:

```
// Project Dispose

    public void Dispose() {
      if (INVALID_HANDLE_VALUE != m_handle) {
        CloseHandle(m_handle);
        m_handle = INVALID_HANDLE_VALUE;
      }
      GC.SuppressFinalize(this);
    }
```

Now we have covered all the bases. If the client calls `Dispose`, finalization is suppressed. If the client forgets to call `Dispose`, the GC invokes the finalizer as usual.

There is now a new issue we need to consider. We have three methods, `Close`, `Dispose`, and `Finalize`, that are doing pretty much the same thing. From a software engineering point of view, it makes sense that they all call the same method internally. This gives us a single point of maintenance. More lines of code also imply more chances of introducing bugs. For instance, look back at our implementation of `Close`. Even this method must call `SuppressFinalize`, which we didn't.

Before we do that, there is a subtle difference between `Dispose` and `Finalize` that you need to be aware of. Recall that when `Finalize` is invoked, its inner objects may have already been collected. The lifetime of these objects is managed by the garbage collector. Therefore, `Finalize` cannot touch these objects. However, the garbage collector has no control over the resources that it doesn't manage, such as the native file handle in `MyFile`. Therefore, `Finalize` should clean up only its unmanaged resources. As a matter of fact, if your class does not have any unmanaged resources, there is no need to implement `Finalize`.

Note that an unmanaged resource can be wrapped in a managed class, saving others from implementing finalizers. For example, for a class that either inherits from `MyFile` or uses the `MyFile` type as a member field, there is no need for the class to implement `Finalize` on account of `MyFile`.

Avoid `Finalize` if Possible

If your class does not have any unmanaged resources, do not implement `Finalize` on the class. Implementing `Finalize` for this case does not serve any real purpose. Moreover, you pay a performance penalty for doing so.

`Dispose`, on the other hand, can and should clean its inner objects and should call its base type's `Dispose` (or equivalent method), if available.

Based on this subtle difference, we can rewrite our methods as follows:

```
// Project ABetterDispose

class MyFile : IDisposable {
    ...
    // Common resource clean-up implementation
    protected virtual void Dispose(bool disposing) {
        if (disposing) {
            // ... dispose managed resources
```

```
    }
    // ... dispose unmanaged resources
    if (INVALID_HANDLE_VALUE != m_handle) {
      CloseHandle(m_handle);
      m_handle = INVALID_HANDLE_VALUE;
    }
  }

  public void Close() {
    Dispose();
  }

  public void Dispose() {
    Dispose(true);
    GC.SuppressFinalize(this);
  }

  ~MyFile() {
    Dispose(false);
  }
}
```

This pattern of using a helper Dispose method that can be used from IDisposable.Dispose implementation as well as from Finalize and any other method is generally referred to as the Dispose pattern.

You can use this code as a template for designing a class that needs the dispose and finalize semantics.

Implement Dispose **Along with** Finalize

Make it a habit to always implement Dispose on a class if you implement Finalize on the class. Do remember to call SuppressFinalize within your Dispose implementation.

There is a subtle problem if you implement Finalize without implementing Dispose. A class derived from such a class cannot dispose of the parent class from its Dispose method. There are only two ways to dispose of a class—either call Dispose or call Finalize. However, the parent class doesn't implement Dispose and the compiler won't let you call parent class's Finalize directly. The implication of this is that the child class should not call SuppressFinalize from its Dispose. Otherwise, the Finalize for the parent class will get suppressed, resulting in a resource leak.

Using IDisposable Objects

Once a class implements IDisposable, the users of the class can call Dispose when done with the object. This is illustrated in the following code excerpt:

```
public static void Main() {
  MyFile f = new MyFile("Readme.Txt");
  Console.WriteLine(f.ReadLine());
  f.Dispose();
}
```

Although this code works, there is a slight programming issue here. Programmers have to remember to call Dispose on an object, even in the face of an exception. For a method with many return paths, it is easy to forget calling Dispose on one of the return paths.

Now you have a new problem. You are relying on your clients to call Dispose on you. What if they forget to do so?

C# offers a better syntactic flavor for dealing with objects that implement IDisposable. An object can be created within the using scope as follows:

```
// Project ABetterDispose

public static void Main() {
  using (MyFile f = new MyFile("Readme.Txt")) {
    Console.WriteLine(f.ReadLine());
  }
}
```

The compiler expands this to something like:

```
public static void Main() {
  {
    MyFile f = new MyFile("Readme.Txt");
    try {
      Console.WriteLine(f.ReadLine());
    }finally {
      if (null != f) {
        ((IDisposable) f).Dispose();
      }
    }
  }
}
```

All the code within the using scope is moved into the try block. Once this code is executed, the code in the finally block is executed, ensuring that Dispose is called on an IDisposable object that was successfully constructed.

Note that the using clause can be nested, making it possible to create multiple IDisposable objects.

Verifying If Dispose() Is Called

If you have implemented Dispose as well as Finalize on your class, but you are expecting that users of the class call Dispose on the object, you can add a Debug.Write in your Finalize method. If you see a trace output during testing, you can check the user code to see why Dispose was not called.

A final note on calling Dispose: It is important to understand that calling Dispose on an object implies strong ownership of the object. If an object is being referenced by many other objects, and the ownership of the object is not clear, then Dispose should not be called on the object. Otherwise, some other object may end up using an already disposed object, which would result in an unpredictable behavior. By the same logic, Dispose should not be called multiple times. These are general considerations. If your specific needs require that Dispose is callable multiple times or from multiple threads, you must add appropriate safety to your implementation of Dispose.

HOSTING THE RUNTIME

This section includes information for readers who are interested in hosting the common language runtime within their own application. If this does not interest you, you may wish to skip this section and revisit it later.

The common language runtime manages running code and provides services such as automatic memory management, interoperability, security, etc. In order to use these services, the common language runtime has to be loaded into a process first. In the future, the support for common language runtime will hopefully be built into the operating system. Today, however, an application targeting the common language runtime requires a piece of code to get the runtime up and running. This piece of code is referred to as a runtime host.

The common language runtime comes with a DLL called MsCorEE.dll that can be found in <WinDir>\System32 directory. This DLL exports an API called CorExeMain that implements the logic to host the common language runtime.

Recall that an EXE-based assembly is built as a standard PE file. This PE file contains a small piece of bootstrapping code that points to CorExeMain. As a result, when the application is executed, the control is transferred to CorExeMain.

Let's take a look at the intricacies of hosting the common language runtime.

Side-by-Side Execution

The concept of shipping a separate runtime is not new to .NET. Other runtimes that have been shipped in the past include Visual Basic runtime, the Java virtual machine, MTS, etc.

A problem with requiring a separate runtime is that the administrators are forced to upgrade to a newer version of the runtime even if only one application requires it. This may break one or more of the already installed applications (that were dependent on the previous version of the runtime) because of some possible incompatibilities.

To address this problem, the .NET Framework has been designed such that multiple versions of the common language runtime can run fully side-by-side. Now you know why the directory path for the runtime contains the version number of the runtime. Each version of the runtime is installed under <windir>\Microsoft.Net\Framework\v<version> directory.

Essentially, not only two versions of an assembly can run side-by-side (Chapter 3), but also two versions of the common language runtime can run side-by-side.

Loading the Runtime

While the flexibility of side-by-side execution of common language runtime is great for administrators, it makes the job of hosting the runtime more difficult. For starters, the host has to decide which version of the runtime to load into a given process (there can be only one version of the runtime in a particular process).

To solve this problem, the .NET Framework provides a startup shim. A shim is a thin piece of code that accepts a version number and other startup parameters from the host and starts the common language runtime. This shim is implemented in MsCorEE.dll. Only one version of the shim can exist on a machine. The shim is kept as small and simple as possible to ensure its compatibility with future versions of the common language runtime.

The shim exports an API called `CorBindToRuntimeEx` that a host can call to load the runtime into the process. Here is its prototype:

```
STDAPI CorBindToRuntimeEx(LPCWSTR pwszVersion,
    LPCWSTR pwszBuildFlavor, DWORD startupFlags,
    REFCLSID rclsid, REFIID riid, LPVOID FAR *ppv);
```

Parameter `pwszVersion` specifies the version of the runtime to load. If `null` is specified, the latest version of the common language runtime is loaded.

Parameter `pwszBuildFlavor` can be used to specify which build of the runtime to use. The .NET Framework ships with two builds of the runtime: a workstation build (in `MsCorWks.dll`) and a server build (in `MsCorSvr.dll`). The server build is designed to take advantage of multiple processors. The workstation build outperforms the server build on a single processor machine.

To load the workstation build, either `null` or `wks` can be specified as `pwszBuildFlavor` parameter. To load the server build, the parameter should be `svr`. On a single-processor machine, however, it is the workstation build that is always loaded, even if the host requests for the server build.

Where is the Execution Engine Implemented?

Note that `MsCorEE.dll` contains just the shim. The bulk of the execution engine is implemented in `MsCorWks.dll` and `MsCorSvr.dll`.

Parameter `startupFlags` is used to specify loader optimization settings such as:

- If the garbage collection is to be done on background threads or the threads that run the user code.
- If assemblies should be loaded in a domain-neutral manner; that is, the assembly code and read-only data structures be shared among all application domains in the process. We will learn more about domain-neutral assemblies in Chapter 6.

Parameter `rclsid` specify the CLSID of the runtime to load to. The CLSID for the common language runtime is `CLSID_CorRuntimeHost`.

The next two parameters are used by the host to request an interface from the common language runtime. For example, the host can request an interface named `ICorRuntimeHost`. This interface allows the host to begin creating application domains, running user code, and to control numerous additional control parameters.

By now it should be obvious that `CorExeMain` ends up calling `CorBind-ToRuntimeEx`. The former method reads the common language runtime version from the executing assembly's PE file and passes it on to `CorBind-ToRuntimeEx`.

To host the common language runtime, you can call `CorBindToRun-timeEx`. Read Steven Pratschner's article in MSDN [Pra-01] to learn more on designing your host architecture. I have included a simple custom host program on the companion Web site.

It should be noted that the common language runtime is not allowed to be loaded more than once within a process. A second call to `CorBindToRun-TimeEx` within the same process will just return without loading a new copy of the runtime.

SUMMARY

In designing the .NET Framework, Microsoft had many goals, including simpler development and deployment, cross-language interoperability, performance efficiency, security, interoperability with native platform, and so on.

The .NET Framework lets administrators control the way .NET applications run by means of configuration files. There are two types of configuration files—general-purpose and security related. There are two types of general-purpose configuration files—`machine.config` (to store system-wide settings) and application-specific.

The .NET Framework provides a mechanism to store and retrieve custom configuration settings from the configuration files.

The CTS defines a set of base datatypes and specifies rules for defining and extending datatypes. When managing types, the common language runtime enforces the rules defined by the CTS.

There are two important aspects of the CTS:

1. All types are ultimately derived from `System.Object`.
2. Types are classified as reference types and value types.

Reference type objects are created on the heap and value type objects are created on the stack. The framework provides a mechanism for conversion between value types and reference types. Conversion from value type to reference type is called boxing. Conversion from reference type to value type is called unboxing.

The CLS defines features that are intended to work across all .NET languages. Among other things, it defines a subset of CTS datatypes that can be used by any .NET language. CLS-compliant code in one .NET language can be reused in another .NET language.

The heart of the .NET Framework is the common language runtime. It enforces the rules of the CTS, loads the assemblies, manages execution of the code and provides runtime services to the applications.

The .NET Framework comes with two hosts for the common language runtime—a host `CorExeMain` that is bootstrapped in any EXE-based assembly and ASP.NET. The .NET Framework also provides APIs to host the common language runtime within your application.

Before executing a method, the JIT compiler of the runtime compiles the MSIL code of the method to native machine language code. In the process, the MSIL code is also validated (checked for invalid code) and verified for type safety. Code that is invalid can never be executed. Code that can be validated and verified is safe. Code that can be validated and not verified is unsafe.

The security mechanism of the runtime will not let any unsafe code be executed, unless the assembly containing the unsafe code is permitted to do so.

While the code is being executed, the runtime provides many services to the application. One such service is automatic memory management. The GC mechanism provided by the framework automatically collects objects that are no longer in use.

GC deals with managed objects. It is the responsibility of the implementer to clean up unmanaged resources, if any, in the class. This cleanup logic can be implemented in the destructor of the class. The compiler automatically converts the destructor to `Finalize` method.

Implementing `Finalize` is resource intensive. An alternative is to implement `Dispose` on the class.

There are three possible cases of how a class handles resources:

1. A class holds both managed and unmanaged resources.
2. A class holds only unmanaged resources.
3. A class holds only managed resources.

`Dispose` is typically implemented in all three cases. `Finalize` should be implemented for the first two cases.

Besides automatic memory management, the runtime provides many other services. In later chapters, we will look at some of the important services such as interoperability, security, remoting, and so on.

REFERENCES

[MS-02]   ".NET Framework Deployment Guide," Microsoft Corporation, January 2002.
               msdn.microsoft.com/library/en-us/dnnetdep/html/dotnetframedepguid.asp

[Gun-01a]   Gunnerson, Eric, "Nice Box. What's in It?," *MSDN Library*, February 2001.
               msdn.microsoft.com/library/en-us/dncscol/html/csharp02152001.asp

[Gun-01b]   Gunnerson, Eric, "Open the Box! Quick," *MSDN* Library, March 2001.
               msdn.microsoft.com/library/en-us/dncscol/html/csharp03152001.asp

[Pra-01]   Pratschner, Steven, "Implement a Custom Common Language Runtime Host for Your
               Managed App," *MSDN Magazine*, March 2001.
               msdn.microsoft.com/library/en-us/dnmag01/html/clr.asp

[Ede-92]   Edelson, D. R., "Smart Pointers: They're Smart, but They're Not Pointers," *Proceedings
               of the 1992 USENIX C++ Conference*, Portland, OR, August 1992.

[Ric-00a]   Richter, Jeffrey, "Automatic Memory Management in the Microsoft .NET Framework,"
               MSDN Magazine, November 2000.
               msdn.microsoft.com/msdnmag/issues/1100/GCI/GCI.asp

[Ric-00b]   Richter, Jeffrey, "Part 2: Automatic Memory Management in the Microsoft .NET Frame-
               work," *MSDN Magazine*, December 2000.
               msdn.microsoft.com/msdnmag/issues/1200/GCI2/GCI2.asp

Programming with the Base Class Library

The .NET BCL includes hundreds of classes that provide a number of useful services to help developers boost their productivity. In this chapter, we look at how to solve many common programming tasks using these classes. By the end of the chapter, you will become familiar with many important classes under the .NET Framework.

ENUMERATION

A common programming task is to iterate over a collection of elements. For example, a GUI application may be required to iterate over all the open documents to close them on exit or a database reader application may wish to iterate over the set of records obtained as a result of an SQL query to the database.

In Chapter 2, we saw that in C# one can iterate over an array using the `foreach` keyword. However, there are forms of collections that cannot always be represented as arrays. Wouldn't it be nice if you could use `foreach` on your own collection type that is not an array?

Under .NET this capability is achieved using enumeration. *Enumeration* is defined as a mechanism for providing a simple iteration over a set of elements. Any datatype that supports enumeration is essentially saying that it contains some sort of collection that can be iterated over. This iteration can be achieved, for example, using the `foreach` keyword in C#. As you may have guessed, arrays support enumeration. Many classes in `System.Data` and

System.XML also implement enumeration. As we will see in the next section, all of the collection types under .NET implement enumeration.

To support enumeration, a type must implement a standard (meaning framework-defined) interface, IEnumerable. Here is its prototype:

```
interface IEnumerable {
    IEnumerator GetEnumerator();
}
```

Interface IEnumerable defines just one method, GetEnumerator. The intention of this method is to return a separate object with the sole purpose of granting access to individual elements in the set. This object is called the enumerator. The enumerator must implement a standard interface IEnumerator. Here is its prototype:

```
interface IEnumerator {
    Boolean MoveNext();
    Object Current { get; }
    void Reset();
}
```

Here is a simple example that demonstrates how to use IEnumerator to enumerate over a set.

```
// Project Enumeration

public static void Main() {
    ArrayList a = new ArrayList();
    a.Add("Hello");
    a.Add("World!");

    IEnumerator  e = a.GetEnumerator();
    while(e.MoveNext()) {
        String s = (String) e.Current;
        Console.WriteLine(s);
    }
}
```

This code excerpt uses ArrayList (namespace System.Collections), a class that can be used to store a collection of generic objects. The size of an ArrayList can change dynamically (whereas arrays have fixed sizes).

Initially, the cursor is placed just before the first element in the set. To access the first element, you must first call the MoveNext method and then access the Current property. Each call to MoveNext advances the cursor to the next element in the set. MoveNext returns false when the cursor has reached the last element in the set. At this point, your attempt to access the `Current` property raises an `InvalidOperationException`. If you want, you can call the `Reset` method, which once again places the cursor just before the first element in the set.

Note that enumerators are intended to be used only to read data in the set. They cannot be used to modify the underlying set.

Although the `MoveNext`/`Current` combination can be used to iterate over a set, the most common enumeration style under C# is using the `foreach` statement, as illustrated here:

```
// Project Enumeration

foreach(String s in a) {
    Console.WriteLine(s);
}
```

Not only is this style simpler to code, but it is also more robust than the earlier style. Behind the scenes, the C# compiler actually generates a `try-finally` block and, if the enumerator supports `IDisposable` (see Chapter 4), disposes the enumerator.

Robust Coding

In C#, always use `foreach` to enumerate over a set. Not only will the compiler prevent you from moving too far through the list, it will also generate code to dispose of the enumerator.

Implementation Considerations

Each call to `GetEnumerator` must return a new enumerator object. When the enumerator is constructed, it typically takes a snapshot of the elements currently in the set. Otherwise, the underlying set has to be locked down from any changes while the enumerator object is alive. Generally, this is not desirable.

As the enumerator object stores the snapshot, it is quite possible that two successive calls to `GetEnumerator` will return two different enumerators, each with different elements in their snapshots.

There are two common techniques for an enumerator to initialize its snapshot:

- Copy all elements in the set to the enumerator.
- Pass a reference to the set to the enumerator.

Choosing the right technique depends on your needs. The first technique costs more in terms of both speed and memory. This technique is best if the set contains a small number of elements or if it is important that the enumerator reflect the exact set of elements at a specific point in time. The second technique has lower overhead. However, as the set may change while the elements are being enumerated, the integrity of the enumerator might get compromised. This technique is best if the set remains static while being enumerated.

All the collection types under the framework use the second technique with a little twist. When any method is called on the enumerator, it checks if the underlying set has changed since the enumerator was initialized. If the set has indeed changed, the method throws an InvalidOperationException.

The following C# code excerpt illustrates a simple enumerator implementation that uses the second technique. Here, class Line consists of two points that can be enumerated over.

```
// Project EnumerationImpl

public struct Point {
    public int x;
    public int y;
};

public class Line : IEnumerable {
    // a line has two points
    private Point[] m_points = new Point[2];

    public IEnumerator GetEnumerator() {
      // simply return a new enumerator object
      return new Enumerator(m_points);
    }

    // A simple enumerator implementation
    class Enumerator : IEnumerator {
      private Point[] m_points;
      private int m_cursor;
      public Enumerator(Point[] points) {
        m_points = points; //  keep a reference
        m_cursor = -1;
      }
      public bool MoveNext() {
        if (m_cursor < m_points.Length) {
          m_cursor++;
        }
        return !(m_cursor == m_points.Length);
```

```
      }
      public object Current {
        get {
          if ((m_cursor < 0) ||
            (m_cursor == m_points.Length)) {
            throw new InvalidOperationException();
          }
          return m_points[m_cursor];
        }
      }
      public void Reset() { m_cursor = -1; }
    }
  }
```

Based on this code, a client can enumerate over the points of the line as follows:

```
// Project EnumerationImpl

Line l1 = new Line();
foreach(Point p in l1) {
  // do something with p
}
```

Strongly Typed Enumerators

Although our enumeration implementation will certainly work as expected, there are a couple of issues with the IEnumerable interface that are not that apparent. Notice that the Current property on IEnumerable returns the current object as System.Object, not the type of the object it actually represents (Point in our case). There are two problems with this.

First, the client has to cast the returned object to the more meaningful representation. In the client code shown earlier, the compiler was generating code to convert System.Object to Point behind the scenes. Although this cast operation succeeds, it hurts performance. Recall from Chapter 2 that each time a cast operation is performed, the runtime has to check if the requested cast is valid. If not, it generates an InvalidCastException.

There is yet another problem because of this type conversion when dealing with value type elements. When Current is called, the value type element is converted to its boxed equivalent. Moreover, the caller most likely will cast the boxed object back to its value type to use it. In our previous code, for example, value type Point is first boxed to System.Object and then unboxed back to Point in the client code. We know from Chapter 4 that for performance reasons, unnecessary boxing should be avoided whenever possible.

Fortunately, it is possible to write a strongly typed enumerator. The trick is not to use IEnumerable or IEnumerator interfaces when defining the class and to change the method signatures to return strong types instead of generic types. This is illustrated in the following code excerpt. The changes from the previous code have been highlighted:

```
// Project StronglyTypedEnumerator

public class Line /*: IEnumerable*/ {
    private Point[] m_points = new Point[2];

    public Enumerator /*IEnumerator*/ GetEnumerator() {
      return new Enumerator(m_points);
    }

    public class Enumerator /*: IEnumerator*/ {
      private Point[] m_points;
      private int m_cursor;
      public Enumerator(Point[] points) {
        m_points = points;
        m_cursor = -1;
      }

      public bool MoveNext() {
          if (m_cursor < m_points.Length) {
            m_cursor++;
          }
          return !(m_cursor == m_points.Length);
      }
      public Point /*object*/ Current {
        get {
          if ((m_cursor < 0) ||
            (m_cursor == m_points.Length)) {
            throw new InvalidOperationException();
          }
          return m_points[m_cursor];
        }
      }
      public void Reset() { m_cursor = -1; }
    }
}
```

You might be wondering if the removal of enumeration interfaces on the class will cause your beloved foreach statement to break. You will be pleased to know that the language was designed to handle this situation. As long as the GetEnumerator method is implemented on the enumerable class and the Current property is implemented on the enumerator class, the C# compiler lets you use the foreach statement.

Strongly Typed Enumerator Versus IEnumerator

If the C# code uses a foreach statement, the code generated by the compiler behaves differently depending on how GetEnumerator is implemented.

If GetEnumerator on the class returns the IEnumerator interface, then the compiler generates a try-finally block and disposes the enumerator in the finally block.

However, if GetEnumerator returns a strongly typed enumerator, the compiler is smart enough not to generate the try-finally block unless the enumerator implements IDisposable interface.

It is also possible to extend the preceding strong-typed implementation to support the enumeration interfaces. A typical implementation would forward the interface method calls to its noninterface counterparts, as illustrated here:

```
// Project StronglyTypedEnumerator

public class Line2 : IEnumerable {

    // non-interface implementation
    public Enumerator GetEnumerator() {
      return new Enumerator(m_points);
    }

    // interface implementation
    IEnumerator IEnumerable.GetEnumerator() {
      return GetEnumerator();
    }
    ...
}
```

Note that when expanding the foreach statement against a class that implements both GetEnumerator as well as IEnumerable.GetEnumerator, the C# compiler gives precedence to the former method.

It is worth mentioning that the .NET Framework provides strongly typed implementation of some frequently used collection classes. One such example is class StringCollection (namespace System.Collection.Specialized), which manages the collection of strings.

COLLECTION

Another common task under programming is to store and manage ordered sets of elements. Some common examples are the list of open files in an application, the set of rows returned from a database query, the group of users allowed to access an application, and so on.

Typically, dealing with elements of a specific type is encapsulated in a new type. Such a type is called a *collection* type. A collection type essentially lets you treat a set of elements as a single unit.

The BCL defines many useful collection types under the System.Collections and System.Collections.Specialized namespaces. The following are some common examples:

- ArrayList: An array of elements. The size of the array can grow dynamically.
- BitArray: A variable-size compact array of bit values.
- HashTable: A variable-size table of key–value pairs.
- Queue: A variable-size first in, first out (FIFO) queue of elements.
- SortedList: A variable-size sorted list of key–value pairs.
- Stack: A variable-size last in, first out (LIFO) stack of elements.
- StringCollection: A variable-size collection of String values.

The .NET Framework offers a formal definition of a collection as a type that implements a standard interface ICollection (namespace System.Collections). Here is the definition of the interface:

```
interface ICollection : IEnumerable {
    Int32 Count { get; }
    void CopyTo(Array array, Int32 index);
    Boolean IsSynchronized{ get; }
    Object SyncRoot { get; }
}
```

Property Count returns the number of elements in the collection. For some types, calculating the number of elements can be quite time consuming. Such a type may choose to throw a NotSupportedException instead of returning the count.

Method CopyTo can be used to copy a collection into an array.

Property IsSynchronized returns true if the collection has been designed to be thread-safe. For updating such a collection, no explicit thread-safety measures are needed.

Property `SyncRoot` returns an object that can be used to explicitly synchronize access to the collection in a multithreaded environment. Under C#, the returned value is typically used with a `lock` statement. Most implementations of `SyncRoot` simply return "this" object. Thread safety and the semantics of `lock` are covered in Chapter 8 when we discuss synchronization.

Note that almost all collection classes defined in the BCL are not thread-safe by default. It is up to the user of the collection to explicitly synchronize access to the collection, if necessary. The good news is that most of these collection classes implement a method called `Synchronized` that returns a synchronized wrapper around the underlying collection. Look in the SDK documentation for more information.

Let's now look at how to use some frequently used (BCL) collection classes.

Lists

Although a collection is formally defined using `ICollection`, the interface provides rather limited functionality. A collection type is more meaningful if it provides manageability functions such as adding and removing elements. Such collection types can expose their functionality by means of a standard interface, `IList`. Here is its definition:

```
public interface IList : ICollection {
    // Access individual element by its index
    Object this[Int32 index} {get; set;}

    // Adding elements
    Int32 Add(Object item);
    void Insert(Int32 index, Object item);

    // Removing elements
    void Remove(Object item); // Remove the specified item
    void RemoveAt(Int32 index); // Remove item at the index
    void Clear(); // Remove all items

    // Search
    Boolean Contains(Object item); // Return true if item found
    Int32 IndexOf(Object item); // Return the index of the item

    // Misc
    Boolean IsFixedSize { get; } // Return true if the set
                        // cannot be resized
    Boolean IsReadOnly { get; } // Return true if the set
                        // cannot be modified
}
```

As can be seen from the IList interface definition, any collection type that implements IList must also implement ICollection and IEnumerable interfaces. Types that implement IList expose a decent set of functionality for adding, removing, and searching elements in the collection.

An example of a BCL class that implements IList is ArrayList. This class stores generic objects. The following code excerpt shows how to use this class:

```
// Project ArrayList

class Foo {
    public Foo(int val) {m_Value = val;}
    public int Value { get {return m_Value;}}
    private int m_Value;
}

class MyApp {
    public static void Main() {
        ArrayList myList = new ArrayList();

        // Add some values
        myList.Add(new Foo(5));
        myList.Add(new Foo(10));
        myList.Add(new Foo(15));

        // enumerate values
        for(int i=0;i<myList.Count;i++) {
            Foo f = (Foo) myList[i];
            Console.WriteLine(f.Value);
        }

        // Remove the second value
        myList.RemoveAt(1);

        // enumerate values using foreach
        foreach(Foo f in myList) {
            Console.WriteLine(f.Value);
        }
    }
}
```

An important aspect of an IList-based collection type is that it provides indexed access to its elements; that is, you can access an element in the collection by its index, as illustrated here:

```
Foo f = (Foo) myList[i];
```

Note that indexes in this collection type are zero-based.

Internally, ArrayList uses an array to store the elements. As elements are added and removed, it automatically adjusts the size of the internal array by allocating and freeing memory as required. To optimize performance, the size of the internal array is adjusted in chunks. The class exposes a property, Capacity, that defines the number of elements the internal array can hold without requiring a reallocation. The initial value for the Capacity by default is 16, which implies that the first 16 elements added to the ArrayList do not result in any reallocation. When the 17th element is being added, the Capacity gets doubled; that is, the size of the internal array is reallocated to 32. When the 33rd element is added, the Capacity gets doubled once again, and so on.

In some situations, you may wish to define your own initial Capacity. ArrayList defines an overloaded constructor that can be used to specify the Capacity. The following code excerpt sets Capacity to 3.

```
// Project ArrayList

ArrayList myNewList = new ArrayList(3);
Console.WriteLine("Initial capacity: {0}", myNewList.Capacity);
```

It is also possible to change the Capacity property anytime during the execution. Just make sure that the specified value is greater than the number of elements the ArrayList object is holding. Otherwise, the runtime will throw an ArgumentOutOfRangeException.

Initialize Collections with Item Count

When using ArrayList or any other collection type under .NET, try to specify the initial capacity. This obviates unnecessary reallocations.

Note that when using ArrayList, each element is stored as a generic object (System.Object). There are two problems with this. First, when a value-type element is stored, it gets boxed. Second, when retrieved, the element typically requires a cast back to its original type.

So, can we create strongly typed collections; that is, collections where storing or retrieving elements does not require casting?

Custom Collections

The BCL provides a class, CollectionBase, which you can inherit to create a custom strongly typed collection. This class provides a property of type

`IList` called `List` that you can use to store and retrieve elements. The following code excerpt illustrates its usage:

```
// Project CustomCollector

class FooList : CollectionBase {
    public int Add(Foo f) {
       return List.Add(f);
    }

    public Foo this[int index] {
       get { return (Foo) List[index]; }
       set { List[index] = value; }
    }

    public new void RemoveAt(int index) {
       List.RemoveAt(index);
    }

    public new Enumerator GetEnumerator() {
       return new Enumerator(this);
    }
    ...
}
```

The enumerator class can be created as shown in the earlier section. To take a snapshot, this class can store as member field the enumerator from the `CollectionBase` class. This is illustrated in the following code:

```
// Project CustomCollector

class FooList : CollectionBase {
    ...
    public class Enumerator : IEnumerator {
       private IEnumerator m_BaseEnumerator;

       public Enumerator(IEnumerable baseEnumerable) {
          m_BaseEnumerator = baseEnumerable.GetEnumerator();
       }
       ...
    }
}
```

Note that implementing a strongly typed collection using `Collection-Base` doesn't really save on performance. The casts (and possible boxing for value types) still take place when the values are passed to and from the inner list. The only advantage is that the user code does not have to perform any explicit cast operations.

In the next release of the .NET Framework, Microsoft plans to offer an extension to C# called *generics*. Among other things, generics is intended to work with value types nicely without the need for boxing.

Why inherit from `CollectionBase` instead of `ArrayList`? Well, `CollectionBase` provides hooks to monitor addition and removal of elements from the collection. For example, one can override `CollectionBase`'s virtual methods `OnInsert` and `OnInsertComplete` to provide extra logic before and after inserting an element into the collection.

As a collection of strings is used so often in programming, it is worth noting that the BCL provides a strongly typed collection for strings called `StringCollection`.

Arrays

Although one can implement a strongly typed collection by hand, the .NET Framework provides a simpler mechanism to do so by means of arrays. An array defines a way to store a set of strongly typed elements. The only limitation on an array is that once it is allocated, its size cannot be changed.

In C#, creating and using arrays is quite similar to that in C++ or Java. The following code excerpt illustrates its usage:

```
// Project SimpleArray

int[] arr = new int[] {20, 10, 40, 30};
int [] newarr = new int[4];

// Method 1 of accessing elements
for(int i=0;i<arr.Length;i++) {
    newarr[i] = arr[i];
    Console.WriteLine(newarr[i]);
}
```

When dealing with arrays, there are two important differences that C++ programmers should be aware of. The first difference is that you cannot define a fixed-sized array declaratively. For example, the following lines of code are not valid under C#:

```
int arr[4]; // illegal
int[4] newarr; // illegal
```

However, you can define the size of the array using keyword new, as we did in our previous example. You can either define the size or initialize the array that indirectly defines the size:

```
int [] newarr = new int[4];
int[] arr = new int[] {20, 10, 40, 30}; // initialize with values
```

The second difference is that in C# (and in Java), creating an array of a reference type, as shown in the following code excerpt, does not create each individual element of the array. To illustrate this, consider the following code excerpt:

```
// Project SimpleArray

class Foo {
    ...
}

Foo[] foos = new Foo[2];
```

Creating an array only creates the placeholder for storing the elements, not the elements (unlike C++, which creates and initializes the elements as well). The individual elements can be created in two ways, as illustrated here:

```
// Project SimpleArray

// Method 1
Foo[] foos = new Foo[2] { new Foo(), new Foo() };

// Method 2. Use a loop.
for(int i=0;i<2;i++) {
    Foo[i] = new Foo();
}
```

Note that this extra initialization logic is needed only for reference type elements, not for value types.

Behind the scenes, an array gets derived from System.Array class. This class implements interface IList but hides some of the interface's methods such as Add and Remove that may result in changing the size of the array.

System.Array also provides methods for searching and sorting arrays. For example, the following line of code sorts our array in an ascending order:

```
Array.Sort(arr);
```

Array Covariance

Under C# specifications, for two reference types A and B, if there exists a conversion from A to B, then it is also possible to convert an array of A to an array of B. The following code excerpt illustrates this:

```
// Project SimpleArray

class Fruit {
  ...
};

class Orange : Fruit {
  ...
}

class TestFruits {
  public static void Test() {
    Orange[] oranges = new Orange[2];
    Fruit[] fruits = oranges;
    ...
  }
}
```

Essentially, this lets you convert a bag of oranges to a bag of fruits, which is not possible in C++. Java programmers, however, are used to this idea of array covariance.

It should be noted, that array covariance applies only to reference types. It does not apply to value types. For example, you cannot convert int[] to object[] or double[] to float[].

Dictionaries

All the collection types that we have dealt with so far store a set of single elements. Sometimes, it is desirable to store elements as key–value pairs. For example, a professor may wish to create a list of student grades where the key is the full name of the student and the value is the grade. Such a collection is referred to as a *dictionary*.

The .NET Framework offers a formal definition of a dictionary as a type that implements a standard interface IDictionary. Here is its definition (along with a short description of each method):

```
public interface IDictionary : ICollection {
    // access elements of the collection
    Object this[Object key] { get; set; } // indexed access
    ICollection Keys { get; } // return a collection of keys
    ICollection Values { get; }// return a collection of values
```

```
    new IDictionaryEnumerator GetEnumerator(); //The enumerator
    // Add, Remove, etc.
    void Add(Object key, Object value); // add a pair
    void Remove(Object key); // remove a pair by its key
    void Clear(); // clear the whole table

    // search
    Boolean Contains(Object key); // search for a given key

    // Misc
    Boolean IsFixedSize { get; } // Is the size fixed?
    Boolean IsReadOnly  { get; } // Is it just read-only?
}
```

As can be seen from the IDictionary interface definition, any class that implements IDictionary must also implement ICollection and IEnumerable.

Perhaps the most commonly used BCL implementation of IDictionary is the Hashtable class. The following code excerpt demonstrates how to create and use this class:

```
// Project HashTable

public static void Main() {
    Hashtable grades = new Hashtable();

    // Add some values
    grades.Add("Tom", 70);
    grades.Add("Dick", 60);
    grades.Add("Harry", 80);

    // display grade for a specific student
    int grade = (int) grades["Harry"];
    Console.WriteLine("Harry's grade={0}", grade.ToString());

    // enumerate values
    foreach(DictionaryEntry entry in grades) {
      Console.WriteLine("{0}={1}", entry.Key, entry.Value);
    }

    // Remove Dick
    grades.Remove("Dick");

    // enumerate values
    foreach(DictionaryEntry entry in grades) {
      Console.WriteLine("{0}={1}", entry.Key, entry.Value);
    }

}
```

Internally, a `Hashtable`'s storage is divided into a number of buckets. Each bucket can store at most one entry. When an entry is being added to the `Hashtable`, the table uses the hash code of the key to compute a suitable bucket location for storing the entry. The search algorithm is based on an algorithm called *double hashing* [Nist]. If the computed bucket has already been filled, then the algorithm tries to guess another bucket location using a different hash function, thus minimizing clustering. The guessing process continues until an empty bucket is found or a certain number of attempts have been exceeded.

For looking up a key, the `Hashtable` applies the same double hashing technique.

From the algorithm, there are two things that must be obvious. First, providing a good hash function on a class can significantly affect the performance of adding those objects to a hash table. In a hash table with a good implementation of a hash function, searching for an element takes constant time. In a hash table with a poor implementation of a hash function, the time for a search increases with the number of items in the hash table. Hash functions should also be inexpensive to compute.

Second, for faster inserts and lookups, the number of buckets should be more than the number of entries. The ratio of entries to buckets is called the *load factor* of the hash table. The default load factor for the `Hashtable` is 1.0, implying that there is one entry per bucket on an average. A load factor of less than 1.0 implies that when an entry is being added to the `Hashtable`, there is a good chance that an empty bucket will be found on the first attempt. Likewise, there is a good chance of looking up a key on the first attempt.

It is worth noting that the increased performance is achieved at the expense of higher memory consumption—a smaller load factor value implies that more buckets must be created.

A Good Load Factor for Hashtables

A load factor of 0.7 to 0.8 has been found to provide a good balance between performance and memory consumption.

The `Hashtable` provides many overloaded constructors that can be used to specify the load factor. The following line of code uses one such constructor.

```
// Project HashTable

Hashtable newgrades = new Hashtable(10, 0.7f);
```

The `Hashtable` constructor used in this code takes two parameters. The first parameter is used to specify the initial capacity of the `Hashtable` object. The second parameter is the load factor that the `Hashtable` object should use.

There is an important programming consideration when defining a type that may be used as a key in the `Hashtable`. When an entry is being added to the `Hashtable` or a key is being looked up, the `Hashtable` obtains the hash code by calling `Object.GetHashCode` on the key. The actual key is matched by calling `Object.Equals` on the key. Therefore, it is important for the key type to provide a suitable implementation of `GetHashCode` and `Equals` methods. Furthermore, these methods must produce the same results when called with the same parameters while the key exists in the `Hashtable`.

Note that the `Hashtable` stores keys and values as generic objects. It is possible to define a custom dictionary that is strongly typed. The framework provides a class, `DictionaryBase`, to make this job easier for the implementers. Defining a custom dictionary based on `DictionaryBase` is similar to defining a collection using `CollectionBase`, as we did earlier, and is left as an exercise for the readers.

The BCL also provides another `IDictionary`-based class called `List-Dictionary`. This class is a simple implementation of `IDictionary` using a singly linked list. If the number of elements being stored is 10 or less, this class provides better performance than a `Hashtable` and uses less memory.

The BCL provides one more class, `HybridDictionary`, which uses `ListDictionary` while the collection is small and then switches to `Hashtable` when the collection gets large. This class is recommended for cases in which the number of elements in the dictionary is unknown. However, be aware of the overhead of switching between the `ListDictionary` and the `Hashtable`.

Using a Different Hash Code Algorithm

A `HashTable` depends on the hash code of the object being inserted or retrieved. Recall that providing a good hash function on a class can significantly improve the performance of adding those objects to the hash table.

If the type being added to the hash table is owned by you, it is easy to override `Object.GetHashCode` and provide a suitable implementation. But what can you do about types that you don't own?

For cases where you cannot override `GetHashCode`, the BCL provides a different mechanism to provide your hash function—by way of interface `IHashCodeProvider`. Here is its definition:

```
public interface IHashCodeProvider {
    int GetHashCode(object o);
}
```

Some overloads of the Hashtable constructor take IHashCodePro-vider as a parameter. This gives you a chance to pass in an object that implements IHashCodeProvider and returns the hash code based on your logic.

A common example of a type that you don't own but might require a different hash function is String. The default implementation of String.GetHashCode computes the hash code that is based on the case-sensitivity of the string. However, you can now define your own hash code provider that returns a case-insensitive hash code. As a matter of fact, this case is so common that the BCL provides such a provider—class CaseInsensitiveHashCodeProvider. The BCL also provides a static instance of this class that can be accessed via CaseInsensitiveHashCodeProvider.Default.

Sorting a Collection

Consider the following code excerpt:

```
// Project CollectionSort

class Foo {
    public Foo(int val) {m_Value = val;}
    public int Value { get {return m_Value;}}
    private int m_Value;
}

class MyApp {
    public static void Main() {
      ArrayList myList = new ArrayList();

      // Add some values
      myList.Add(new Foo(10));
      myList.Add(new Foo(5));
      myList.Add(new Foo(15));

      // enumerate values
      foreach(Foo f in myList) {
        Console.WriteLine(f.Value);
      }
    }
}
```

The main program stores instances of class Foo in an ArrayList object and dumps the value of each instance back to the console. When the program is run, you see the following output:

```
10
5
15
```

Sometimes it is desirable to have a sorting order between items of a collection. In fact this is such a common programming request that BCL defines a method, Sort, on ArrayList (as well as Array). Our Foo items can be sorted, for example, using the following line of code:

```
myList.Sort();
```

However, if you execute this code, you will notice that the program throws an InvalidOperationException. The problem is that the system doesn't know how to compare one instance of Foo to another.

To impose a sorting order there must be some mechanism that allows two items to be compared. Under .NET, this mechanism is provided by means of a standard interface IComparer, defined as follows:

```
public interface IComparer {
   int Compare (Object x, Object y);
}
```

This simple interface defines just one method, Compare. The purpose of this method is to compare two objects and return an integer indicating which object should be placed before the other. The implication of the return value is shown in Table 5.1.

TABLE 5.1   Comparer Return Value

Return Value	Implication
A negative number	x is less than y. Therefore, x should be placed before y.
0	x and y are equal. Either can come first.
A positive number	x is greater than y. Therefore, x should be placed after y.

ArrayList supplies many overloaded versions of the Sort method. One such method takes a parameter of type IComparer that the method uses internally for comparing items in the collection. You can define a new type that implements IComparer and pass it to this method, as illustrated here:

```
// Project CollectionSort

class FooComparer : IComparer {
    public int Compare(Object x, Object y) {
```

```
            Foo f1 = x as Foo;
            Foo f2 = y as Foo;
            if ((null == f1) || (null == f2)) {
                throw new ArgumentException();
            }
            return (f1.Value - f2.Value);
        }
    }

class MyApp {
    public static void Main() {
        ...
        myList.Sort(new FooComparer());
    }
}
```

The BCL provides some useful utility classes that are based on IComparer. For example, you can use the class CaseInsensitiveComparer to perform case-insensitive comparisons on strings. The class provides a static instance that can be obtained using the property CaseInsensitiveComparer.Default. Likewise, if you are interested in case-sensitive comparisons, you can use another class Comparer or its static instance Comparer.Default.

Case-Insensitive Hash Table

If you wish to define a hash table that can store and retrieve keys in a case-insensitive fashion, you need to supply both a case-insensitive hash-code provider and a case-insensitive comparer to the hash table. This can be done using one of the overloaded constructors of Hashtable, as shown here.

```
Hashtable grades = new Hashtable(
    CaseInsensitiveHashCodeProvider.Default,
    CaseInsensitiveComparer.Default);
```

The BCL defines yet another mechanism to compare objects by means of an interface, IComparable (namespace System). Here is its definition:

```
public interface IComparable {
    int CompareTo(Object object);
}
```

Any object that implements IComparable is declaring that it knows how to compare itself with other objects. The interface method CompareTo serves comparing "this" object with the specified object. The following code excerpt illustrates this. It defines a new class `FooNew` that is a replacement for our old class `Foo`. The changes have been highlighted.

```
// Project CollectionSort

class FooNew : IComparable {
    public FooNew(int val) {m_Value = val;}
    public int Value { get {return m_Value;}}

    public int CompareTo(Object o) {
      FooNew f = o as FooNew;
      if (null == f) {
        throw new ArgumentException();
      }
      return (this.Value - f.Value);
    }

    private int m_Value;
}
```

When such a type is used with `Array` or `ArrayList`, there is no need to provide a separate comparer object for sorting. However, a separate comparer object is still useful if your collection contains objects of different types.

It is worth mentioning that almost all base datatypes defined in the BCL, such as `Int32`, `String`, `Double`, and so on, implement the `IComparable` interface.

How about keeping the keys of a dictionary in a sorted order? Well, a `Hashtable` doesn't provide such a sorting functionality. However, the BCL provides another `IDictionary`-based class called `SortedList` that can be used to sort the keys, either via the `IComparable` interface or the `IComparer` interface. Check the SDK documentation on how to use this class. Keep in mind, though, that operations on a `SortedList` tend to be slower than operations on a `Hashtable` because of the sorting.

You may be wondering why `IComparable` is defined in the `System` namespace and not in the `System.Collection` namespace. This is because this interface provides a general mechanism that is not just specific to collections.

CLONING

We know that when we assign one reference-type object to another, both the objects point to the same memory location after the operation is completed. If a member field in one object is changed, for example, it gets reflected in the other object.

Sometimes you might want to clone the object, i.e., create a duplicate copy of the object. The .NET Framework formalizes this notion of cloning by meaning of a standard interface, ICloneable. Here is its definition:

```
public interface ICloneable {
    Object Clone();
}
```

The interface defines just one method, Clone. The purpose of this method is to return a clone of the object. Any class that implements ICloneable must implement Clone and the necessary logic to duplicate the object.

Interface ICloneable is implemented by many classes in the BCL. All the collection classes that we covered earlier implement this interface.

The simplest implementation of Clone could just invoke System .Object.MemberwiseClone, as illustrated in the following code excerpt:

```
// Project Cloning

class Student : ICloneable {
    public String Name;
    public int Grade;

    public Object Clone() {
       return this.MemberwiseClone();
    }
}

class MyApp {
    public static void Main() {

       // Create s1
       Student s1 = new Student();
       ...

       // Clone s1 to s2
       Student s2 = (Student) s1.Clone();
       ...
    }
}
```

The MemberwiseClone method makes a shallow copy of the object; that is, if the object contains a reference-type field, the cloned object points to the same reference. Only the value-type fields are truly duplicated.

If this shallow copy behavior is not desired, it is up to you to provide your own deep-copy semantics when you implement Clone.

A related note on the collection classes: Most of them implement ICloneable as a shallow copy. If you require deep-copy semantics on, for example, an ArrayList, derive your own class from ArrayList and override the method Clone.

STREAMS

A common programming task is to read data from or write data to files, network sockets, or some other devices. The BCL formalizes this behavior by means of an abstract class Stream (namespace System.IO). Table 5.2 shows some frequently used methods available on this class.

TABLE 5.2   Some Methods Available on System.IO.Stream

Method	Description
CanSeek	Can you seek to a position within the stream?
CanRead	Can the stream be read?
CanWrite	Can the stream be written to?
Length	Length of the stream.
Position	Current cursor position.
Seek	Seek to a position.
Read	Read bytes from the stream.
Write	Write bytes to the stream.
Flush	Flush any buffered data to the underlying device.
Close	Close the stream and release any resources (such as sockets and file handles). Data is flushed before the stream is closed.

The Stream class also offers methods to perform asynchronous reads and writes. Check the SDK documentation for more information.

Why doesn't the table show any method to open a stream? The semantics of opening a stream depends on the underlying device. Stream is just an abstract class. Table 5.3 lists some common classes inherited from Stream.

TABLE 5.3   Some Common Stream-Based Classes

Name	Description
FileStream	A buffered stream based on a disk file
NetworkStream	An unbuffered stream based on a socket

TABLE 5.3   Some Common Stream-Based Classes (Continued)

Name	Description
BufferedStream	A wrapper class that adds buffering to an existing unbuffered stream
MemoryStream	A stream based on memory

How a stream is created depends on the mechanism provided by the underlying class. For example, a `FileStream` object can be created using the static methods `OpenRead` (for reading) or `OpenWrite` (for writing) that are available on a BCL class `File` (namespace `System.IO`). The following code excerpt, for example, opens a file for writing, writes some bytes to the stream, and closes it:

```
// Project FileStream

public static void Main() {
    // Store ASCII "hello" as bytes
    Byte[] data = new Byte[] {104, 101, 108, 108, 111};

    // Open a new file for writing. Write the data
    using (FileStream fs = File.OpenWrite("Output.Dat")) {
        fs.Write(data, 0, data.Length);
        fs.Close();
    }
}
```

Note that the `FileStream` object is scoped within a `using` block. This is to ensure that the file handle is properly disposed off in case of an error (or after it has been used).

Data Encoding

`Stream.Read` and `Stream.Write` let you read and write data as bytes. However, programmers in general prefer dealing with strings to bytes. It would be nice to have a mechanism to convert a string to a byte array and vice versa.

At this point, it is worth reinforcing the differences among bytes, characters, and strings under C# (and under .NET). A C# byte (`System.Byte`) is a single unsigned byte (8-bit), a C# char (`System.Char`) is a 2-byte Unicode character, and a C# string (`System.String`) is an array of Unicode characters.

The BCL provides a number of encoding classes under the `System.Text` namespace to convert between characters, bytes, and strings using various encoding schemes. These classes include `ASCIIEncoding`, `UnicodeEncoding`, `UTF7Encoding`, and `UTF8Encoding` to deal with ASCII, Unicode, UTF-

7, and UTF-8 encoding schemes, respectively. The namespace System.Text also provides another class called Encoding that exposes the encoding classes as static properties. The following code excerpt demonstrates how to use this class to convert between strings and byte arrays:

```
// Project Encoding

public static void Main() {
    // Convert ASCII-encoded bytes to UNICODE string
    Byte[] buf = new Byte[] {104, 101, 108, 108, 111};
    String s = Encoding.ASCII.GetString(buf);
    Console.WriteLine(s);

    // Convert the string back as ASCII-encoded bytes
    Byte[] asciiBuf = Encoding.ASCII.GetBytes(s);
    foreach(Byte b in asciiBuf) {
      Console.WriteLine(b);
    }

    // Convert the string to UNICODE-encoded bytes
    Byte[] unicodeBuf = Encoding.Unicode.GetBytes(s);
    foreach(Byte b in unicodeBuf) {
      Console.WriteLine(b);
    }
}
```

Readers and Writers

Using the encoding classes, it is now possible to convert bytes to strings each time they are read from a FileStream object and to convert strings to bytes just before writing them to the FileStream. It is desirable if you don't have to deal with raw byte input and output at all.

The BCL provides two classes, StreamReader and StreamWriter, to help you. StreamReader reads data from a stream as characters or lines. StreamWriter writes data to a stream as characters or lines. The specific encoding to use can be specified in the constructor. In the following code excerpt, an ASCII line is read from an input file and is saved back as a Unicode line in an output file:

```
// Project ReaderWriter

public static void Main() {
    // Open the file for reading and read one line
    String sLine;
    using (FileStream fsr = File.OpenRead("Readme.Txt")) {
```

```
using(StreamReader reader =
    new StreamReader(fsr,Encoding.ASCII)) {
  sLine = reader.ReadLine();
  reader.Close();
}
fsr.Close();
}

// Open a new file for writing. Write line as UNICODE
using (FileStream fsw = File.OpenWrite("NewReadme.Txt")) {
  using(StreamWriter writer =
      new StreamWriter(fsw, Encoding.Unicode)) {
    writer.WriteLine(sLine);
    writer.Close();
  }
  fsw.Close();
}
}
```

Note the use of using statements on `StreamReader` and `StreamWriter` objects. Both the classes implement `IDisposable` and release any unmanaged resources used via `Dispose` method.

Also note that both the classes define an overloaded constructor that takes as a parameter the filename to open (instead of a stream). If you use this constructor, you don't have to deal with stream objects separately.

`StreamReader` offers a particular feature that you should be aware of. If you are not sure of the encoding used in the input file, you can instruct the `StreamReader` object to detect the encoding during its construction. If the `detect-encoding` parameter is specified as `true`, the reader object looks at the first three bytes of the stream (called byte order marks [BOM]) to identify the encoding. The class is capable of automatically recognizing UTF-8 and Unicode (little-endian as well as big-endian) encoding schemes if the file starts with the appropriate BOM.

`StreamReader` and `StreamWriter` classes are great for character input and output, but what if you want to save and load other basic datatypes such as integer, boolean, float, and so on? To solve this problem, the BCL provides two more classes, `BinaryReader` and `BinaryWriter` under the namespace `System.IO`. These two classes provide methods for reading and writing many base datatypes to the stream. The following code excerpt illustrates the use of these classes. The program writes an integer and a double value to a file and reads it back. For simplicity, I am not wrapping any objects in the using block.

```
// Project BinaryData

public static void Main() {
    // Open a file for binary write
    FileStream fsw = File.OpenWrite("Output.bin");
    BinaryWriter bw = new BinaryWriter(fsw);

    // write some basic data types to the stream
    int iVal = 10;
    double dVal = 20.5;
    bw.Write(iVal);
    bw.Write(dVal);
    bw.Close();
    fsw.Close();

    // Open the file for reading
    FileStream fsr = File.OpenRead("Output.bin");
    BinaryReader br = new BinaryReader(fsr);

    // read data back
    int iValNew = br.ReadInt32();
    double dValNew = br.ReadDouble();
    br.Close();
    fsr.Close();
    Console.WriteLine("{0}, {1}", iValNew, dValNew);
}
```

Note that the `BinaryWriter` class can also be used to write strings. One of the overloaded `Write` methods on the class takes a string as an argument and writes it out as a stream of bytes (based on the encoding the `Binary-Writer` class is using).

SERIALIZATION

At this point, we are experts on reading and writing various datatypes to and from streams. However, what we haven't considered is dealing with perhaps the most important datatype, an object. How do you save an object to the stream and load it back such that it is in the same state when it was saved?

One way is to provide explicit save and load methods on your class that take a `Stream` object as an argument. Within each method, you can explicitly save or load each member field of the class.

There is nothing wrong with this technique; but when dealing with large numbers of classes, it soon becomes painful to add the logic to each of the classes. Why can't we write a generic mechanism to load and save any arbitrary object? After all, the metadata contains all the information about all the fields of a class. It would be easy to enumerate through all the fields of an object in a generic manner to save or to load them. .NET does provide such a generic mechanism.

The process of saving the state of an object into a stream is a common programming task, referred to as *serialization*.

Serialization is an important part of the .NET Framework. The remoting infrastructure and services depend on serialization. For example, the serialized representation of an object can be taken to a different machine where the object can be reconstructed. Given an efficient serialization framework, an object may simply be serialized to a stream of bytes in memory and transmitted to the remote machine.

Under .NET, the type that requires serialization has to indicate this by means of the System.SerializableAttribute class-level attribute. This is illustrated in the following code excerpt:

```
// Project Serialization

[Serializable]
class Foo {
    ...
}
```

If the serialization is attempted on a type that is not marked as Serializable, the system throws a SerializationException. This exception is also thrown if any object in the serialization graph is not marked as Serializable.

By default, all the member fields defined in the type get serialized. To omit a specific field from serialization, you can apply the System.NonSerializedAttribute attribute to the field. This is illustrated in the following code excerpt:

```
// Project Serialization

[Serializable]
class Foo {
    private int m_i;
    [NonSerialized] private double m_d;
    private string m_s;
    ...
}
```

The object is now ready for serialization, but how do you initiate the serialization process?

Formatters

Serialization can be initiated either by an application or by the runtime. The application initiates serialization, for example, to store the state of the object on a disk file when the application is being exited. The runtime initiates serialization, for example, when the object is being passed to a different application domain, perhaps to a different machine.

The format of the serialized data depends on why the object is being serialized. For example, if the object is being transferred to a different computer using HTTP, storing data in a SOAP-compliant XML format makes sense. However, if the object is being stored to a file or being transferred using TCP, storing data in a binary form is more efficient. Therefore, it makes sense to decouple the logic of serialization and the format of the serialized data.

Under .NET, the format of the output is controlled by what is called a formatter, or a type that implements a standard interface IFormatter. Here are some methods on the interface that are relevant to our current discussion:

```
public interface IFormatter {
    void Serialize(Stream stream, Object root);
    void Deserialize(Stream stream);
    StreamingContext Context {get; set;}
    ...
}
```

The Serialize method serializes an object (and all its children) to a stream.

The Deserialize method reads the data back from the stream and reconstructs the state of the object.

The Context property provides a mechanism for the initiator to supply additional information to the object being serialized. Its type, Streaming-Context, exposes two properties, State and Context.

The StreamingContext.State property is an enumeration of type ContextSreamingStates that is used to indicate why the data is being serialized. For example, a value of CrossMachine implies the serialized data is for a remote computer. A value of CrossProcess implies the data is for a different process on the local computer. Look into the SDK documentation for the rest of the enumeration values.

The `StreamingContext.Context` property provides a way to supply any additional information, in the form of an object, to the object being serialized.

Note that you are not required to specify a `StreamingContext` object in your code. The runtime provides an appropriate context to the object being serialized.

Enough with `IFormatter`! Let's see how we can use a formatter.

The BCL provides a formatter called `BinaryFormatter` to serialize an object to a binary format. The output is very compact and can be parsed quickly. The following code excerpt illustrates the use of this formatter:

```
// Project Serialization

public static void UseBinaryStream() {
    Foo f1 = new Foo(10, 20.5, "Jay");

    // Open a file for binary write
    FileStream fsw = File.OpenWrite("Output.bin");
    BinaryFormatter bf = new BinaryFormatter();
    bf.Serialize(fsw, f1);
    fsw.Close();

    // Open the file for reading and recreate Foo
    FileStream fsr = File.OpenRead("Output.bin");
    Foo f2 = (Foo) bf.Deserialize(fsr);
    fsr.Close();
}
```

It is worth noting that serialization of an object is not limited to its public member fields. To store the state of the object with complete fidelity, all the member fields, including the private ones, are serialized.

As the serialization logic is independent of the stream being used, it is relatively trivial to modify the preceding code to use a `MemoryStream` instead. Project `Serialization` also contains such an example.

There is yet another useful formatter the BCL provides called the `Soap-Formatter`. This formatter generates SOAP-compliant XML-based output. If you replace `BinaryFormatter` with `SoapFormatter` in the preceding code, here is how the output looks (project `SoapFormatter`):

```
<SOAP-ENV:Envelope
    xmlns:xsi="http://www.w3.org/2001/XMLSchema-instance"
    xmlns:xsd=http://www.w3.org/2001/XMLSchema
    xmlns:SOAP-ENC="http://schemas.xmlsoap.org/soap/encoding/"
    xmlns:SOAP-ENV="http://schemas.xmlsoap.org/soap/envelope/"
```

```
SOAP-ENV:encodingStyle=
    http://schemas.xmlsoap.org/soap/encoding/
xmlns:a1="http://schemas.microsoft.com/clr/assem/main">
<SOAP-ENV:Body>
  <a1:Foo id="ref-1">
    <m_i>10</m_i>
    <m_s id="ref-3">Jay</m_s>
  </a1:Foo>
</SOAP-ENV:Body>
</SOAP-ENV:Envelope>
```

A final note on formatters: Although the BCL-provided formatters will meet most of your needs, it is possible to create your own formatter. The BCL supplies an abstract base class called Formatter that provides some helper methods for implementing the IFormatter interface. Adventurous readers can implement their own formatter by inheriting from this class.

Custom Serialization

Occasionally, an object itself may wish to finely control how it gets serialized. For example, the object might want to save its internal state in a more compressed way if the data is being written to a file. Perhaps the object does not wish to save some data if it is being serialized for the purpose of being rebuilt on a different computer.

To provide custom serialization, a class has to support a standard interface, ISerializable. Here is its definition:

```
public interface ISerializable {
    void GetObjectData(SerializationInfo info,
      StreamingContext context);
}
```

When serialization is in progress, the framework checks if the object implements the ISerializable interface, in which case it calls GetObjectData on the object. This gives the object a chance to serialize itself. The parameter SerializationInfo holds the serialization data. The object can inject its own data into SerializationInfo by means of a method called AddValue. This is illustrated in the following code excerpt:

```
// Project CustomSerialization

[Serializable]
class Foo : ISerializable {
    ...
```

```
    public void GetObjectData(SerializationInfo info,
        StreamingContext ctx) {
      info.AddValue("My iVal", m_i);
      info.AddValue("My dVal", m_d);
      info.AddValue("My sVal", m_s);
    }
}
```

Method AddValue can be called multiple times to inject multiple entries. Each entry forms a key–value pair when the key is in the form of a string. The value could be of any base datatype. The SerializationInfo class provides many overloaded AddValue methods to deal with various base datatypes.

Parameter StreamingContext provides the contextual information. Recall that this information is set either explicitly by the application or implicitly by the runtime.

Note that implementing ISerializable on a class doesn't preclude the need for the [Serializable] attribute. Without this attribute present on the class, the common language runtime does not even consider serializing the instances of the class.

Deserialization

Now you know how to save an object's state. How do you read the data back to restore the state of the object? Implementing just the ISerialize interface is not enough. You also have to provide an overloaded constructor for your class that takes SerializationInfo and StreamingContext as the parameters. This is illustrated in the following code excerpt:

```
// Project CustomSerialization

[Serializable]
class Foo : ISerializable {
    ...

    public Foo(SerializationInfo info, StreamingContext ctx) {
      m_i = info.GetInt32("My iVal");
      m_d = info.GetDouble("My dVal");
      m_s = info.GetString("My sVal");
    }
}
```

During deserialization, the runtime calls this constructor, giving the object a chance to initialize its internal state. The parameter SerializationInfo provides many GetXXX methods to retrieve various base datatypes.

Deserialization Completion

Deserialization is quite simple for objects that have no dependencies on other objects. In real life, the root object being serialized points to many other objects that in turn point to other objects. Sometimes, from an object's perspective, it is desirable to know if the deserialization process is complete; that is, if the entire object graph has been deserialized.

An object that wants to receive a notification at the end of the deserialization must implement a standard interface, IDeserializationCallback. This interface defines just one method, OnDeserialization, that the runtime calls at the end of the deserialization. You can implement the interface as shown in the following code excerpt:

```
// Project Deserialize

[Serializable]
class Foo : ISerializable , IDeserializationCallback {
    ...
    public void OnDeserialization(Object sender) {
      Console.WriteLine("Deserialization complete");
    }
}
```

XML Serializer

In the new era of communication, XML has become a standard format for information exchange between businesses. The BinaryFormatter provides a compact format, but it works only between .NET applications. Serializing to XML creates a message that is readable on any platform by anyone. When developing business applications, it is becoming quite common to write to or read from XML documents. The format of the XML document typically conforms to a given XML Schema Definition (XSD) schema (.xsd) document.

.NET provides a class, XmlSerializer (namespace System.Xml .Serialization), that enables you to control how objects can be serialized into XML output and how objects can be rebuilt from XML input.

Technically, XmlSerializer belongs to the XML Class Library and not the BCL. However, I am covering it here because it is relevant to our current discussion on serialization.

Using XmlSerializer is similar to using a formatter. The following code excerpt demonstrates its usage. Here, an instance of class BookInfo is serialized to a document. Later the document is deserialized to create a new instance of BookInfo:

```
// Project XmlSerialize

public class BookInfo {
    public String ISBN {
       get{return m_ISBN;}
       set{m_ISBN = value;}
    }
    public String Title {
       get{return m_Title;}
       set{m_Title = value;}
    }
    public String Author {
       get{return m_Author;}
       set{m_Author = value;}
    }

    public float Price = 0.0f;
    private String m_Title = "";
    private String m_Author = "";
    private String m_ISBN = "";
}

static public void Run() {
    BookInfo b1 = new BookInfo();
    b1.ISBN = "0130886742";
    b1.Title = "COM+ Programming";
    b1.Author = "Pradeep Tapadiya";
    b1.Price = 40.0f;

    // Open a file for XML output
    FileStream fsw = File.OpenWrite("Output00.xml");
    XmlSerializer xs = new XmlSerializer(typeof(BookInfo));
    xs.Serialize(fsw, b1);
    fsw.Close();

    // Open the file for reading
    FileStream fsr = File.OpenRead("Output00.xml");
    BookInfo b2 = (BookInfo) xs.Deserialize(fsr);
    fsr.Close();
}
```

XmlSerializer serializes the public fields and properties of a type. Contrast this to a formatter, which can save even the private fields and does not do anything special for properties. Also, the serializer does not pay any attention either to the [Serializable] attribute or to the ISerializable interface.

Here is the output when the preceding program is executed:

```xml
<?xml version="1.0"?>
<BookInfo xmlns:xsi="http://www.w3.org/2001/XMLSchema-instance"
      xmlns:xsd="http://www.w3.org/2001/XMLSchema">
  <Price>40</Price>
  <ISBN>0130886742</ISBN>
  <Title>COM+ Programming</Title>
  <Author>Pradeep Tapadiya</Author>
</BookInfo>
```

As can be seen from the output, each of the public fields and properties is saved as an XML element. The name of the root node matches that of the class and the name of each XML element matches that of the corresponding field or property of the class.

The XML serialization mechanism, however, provides a flexible way to format the output. As I mentioned earlier, the format of the XML document typically conforms to a given XSD schema. Let's say, for example, that the XSD schema for the book is defined as follows:

```xml
<xsd:schema targetNamespace=""
    xmlns:xsd="http://www.w3.org/2001/XMLSchema" >
  <xsd:element name="book">
    <xsd:complexType>
      <xsd:sequence>
        <xsd:element name="name" type="xsd:string" />
        <xsd:element name="author" type="xsd:string" />
      </xsd:sequence>
      <xsd:attribute name="isbn" type="xsd:string" />
    </xsd:complexType>
  </xsd:element>
</xsd:schema>
```

Details about XSD schema can be found in the SDK documentation. The schema presented here essentially states that the root node should be named book, the ISBN should be an attribute named isbn, and the name and author are XML elements of type string. Given this, an instance of the output may look like the following:

```xml
<book isbn="0130886742">
  <name>COM+ Programming</name>
  <author>Pradeep Tapadiya</author>
</book>
```

To customize the output, you can define XML serialization attributes on the class and its public elements. Table 5.4 shows some common attributes and their usage.

TABLE 5.4   XML Serialization Attributes

Attribute	Description
XmlRoot	To identify the class or struct as the root node. Typically used to assign a different element name to the root other than the class name itself.
XmlElement	The public property or field should be serialized as an XML element. Typically used to name the element other than the field name itself.
XmlAttribute	The public property or field should be serialized as an XML attribute. Can also rename the attribute to a different value than the field itself.
XmlArray	The public property or field should be serialized as an array. Useful when an array of objects need to be serialized.
XmlArrayItem	To identify a type that can be placed into a serialized array.
XmlIgnore	Do not serialize the specific public property or field.

Using these attributes, we can revise our `BookInfo` class as follows:

```
// Project XmlSerialize

[XmlRoot(ElementName="book")]
public class BookInfo {
    [XmlAttribute(AttributeName="isbn")]
    public String ISBN {

      . . .

    }
    [XmlElement(ElementName="name")]
    public String Title {

      . . .

    }

    [XmlElement(ElementName="author")]
    public String Author {

      . . .

    }

    [XmlIgnore]
    public float Price = 0.0f;

    . . .

}
```

Serializer versus Formatter

Although `SoapFormatter` also can be used to serialize an object into XML, formatters and the XML serializer solve two different problems. A formatter is used to serialize an object with the utmost fidelity. The XML serializer, on the other hand, is used to process XML documents that typically conform to a given XSD schema. It is not associated with the runtime serialization architecture as formatters are and is controlled by a different set of attributes than those used by the formatters.

Although the ability to produce XML documents that conform to a given schema is very powerful, it also has some limitations that you should be aware of. One such limitation that we have already seen is that the private fields cannot be serialized. Another limitation is that if an object graph contains circular references, then the object cannot be serialized.

As XSD schemas are so frequently used to specify XML formats, the SDK provides a tool called the XML Schema Definition Tool (`xsd.exe`) that lets you generate a strongly typed C# class based on existing XSD schema. For example, assuming the XSD schema for the book is defined in file `Book-Schema.xsd`, the following command generates an output file, `Book-Schema.cs`, containing the corresponding C# class:

```
xsd.exe BookSchema.xsd /c
```

It is also possible to generate an XSD schema either from the XML output definition or from an assembly that defines the type to be serialized. The following command line, for example, uses XML instance data from the file `BookInstance.xml` and generates an XSD schema in the file `BookInstance.xsd`:

```
xsd.exe BookInstance.xml
```

The samples dealing with `xsd.exe` can be found under the project `UsingXSD`. More information on `xsd.exe` can be found in the SDK documentation.

STRINGS

No discussion about a foundation class library would be complete without talking about the capabilities it provides for storing and manipulating strings. We have already covered some aspects of string manipulation, such as converting bytes to strings using various encoding schemes. In this section, let's look at some other important string manipulation classes provided by the .NET Framework.

The system.string class that we are used to by now stores a string of Unicode characters. This class offers many useful features, such as the following:

- Obtaining the length of the string
- Checking if two strings are equal
- Comparing two strings for a lexical relationship
- Concatenating one or more strings to create a new string
- Replacing a substring with another
- Splitting a string into an array based on a delimiter
- Changing cases
- Trimming characters from both ends of the string

The following code excerpt illustrates many of these features:

```
// Project Strings

// Length
String s1 = "hello";
Console.WriteLine(s1.Length);

// Equality
bool b = ("Hello" == "hello"); // false
b = ("Hello".Equals("hello")); // false

// Case-sensitive comparison
int val = String.Compare("Hello", "hello"); // 1

// Case-insensitive comparison
val = String.Compare("Hello","hello", true); // 0

// Compare substrings "ello." Case-sensitive
val = String.Compare("Hello", 1, "hello", 1, 4, false);// 0

// Concatenation
String s2 = String.Concat("Hello", " ", "World");

// Replace
String s3 = "How can I help you?";
String s4 = s3.Replace("I", "we");

// Split
String[] sArray = s3.Split(' ');

// Trim
String s5 = " blah ".Trim();
String s6 = " blah ".TrimEnd();
```

Formatting

It is also possible to format one or more objects into a textual representation. The `String` class provides a method, `Format`, to accomplish this. The following code excerpt illustrates its use:

```
// Project Strings

int i = 2;
int j = 4;
String s = "equal to";

// s1 = "2 and 2 is equal to 4"
String s1 = String.Format("{0} and {0} is {1} {2}", i, s, j);
```

The first parameter specifies the format string. Within this format string, an object that is passed as an argument to `Format` can be represented in the form `{N}`, where `N` represents the zero-based index of the argument.

Note that the format string used in `Format` is similar to that in `Console.WriteLine`. Internally, `Console.WriteLine`, and many other class methods that deal with formatted strings, end up calling `String.Format` for their formatting needs.

It is also possible to specify special formatting codes for an argument. This can be done using the representation `{N:formatString}` where `formatString` represents the string of formatting codes. Look in the SDK documentation for applicable formatting codes for base datatypes. The help topic labeled "Formatting Strings" is a good starting point. The following code excerpt, for example, formats an integer into a decimal (Base-10) representation. The minimum number of digits to display is 5:

```
// Project Strings

int i = 2;

// s2 = "00002";
String s2 = String.Format("{0:d5}", i);
```

How does `String.Format` know how to represent an object in its textual form? It doesn't. It relies on the object to return the string representation. `System.Object.ToString` should ring a bell here.

What about the formatting codes? `System.Object.ToString` doesn't seem to take the format string as a parameter.

Custom Formatting

A datatype that wishes to handle formatting beyond what System.Object
.ToString offers must implement a standard interface, IFormattable.
Here is its prototype:

```
public interface IFormattable {
    public String ToString(String format,
       IFormatProvider formatProvider) {
}
```

When an object needs to be formatted, the runtime first checks if the
object implements IFormattable. If it does, then the runtime calls IFor-
mattable.ToString on the object, passing the formatting information. Otherwise, it calls System.Object.ToString as usual.

In our earlier code, for example, System.Int32 implements IFormattable. Therefore, the runtime calls IFormattable.ToString on the object
passing "d5" as the format string. This method knows how to deal with the
formatting code.

Parameter formatProvider is used to format strings based on specific
culture, and it is typically null when called by the runtime.

The following code excerpt shows how to call ToString directly to format an integer using the formatting code:

```
// Project Strings

int i = 2;

// s = "00002";
s = i.ToString("d5", null);
```

The following code excerpt shows how to implement the IFormattable
interface. Here, method ToString on class Foo takes any formatting code
and returns the same string in uppercase:

```
// Project Strings

class Foo : IFormattable {
    public String ToString(String format,
        IFormatProvider formatProvider) {
      return format.ToUpper();
    }
}

// Client code
Foo f = new Foo();
String s = String.Format("{0:abc}", f); // returns ABC
```

String to Base Datatypes

So far we have looked at representing objects, including the base datatypes, in their string form. How about converting a string to a base datatype?

The BCL provides a class, `System.Convert`, that defines static methods to convert strings to many base datatypes. For example, the following code excerpt converts a Base-10 string representation of a number to its integer form:

```
// Project Strings

int i = Convert.ToInt32("12", 10);
```

The `System.Convert` class defines many other static methods to convert one datatype to another. Check the SDK documentation for more information.

Mutable String Class

You may have wondered why the methods in the `System.String` class don't modify the string, but always return a new copy of the string. It's because although string is a reference type, it needs to be used as a value type.

Members that change the value of a class are called *mutators*, and a class that doesn't have any mutators is called an *immutable* class. Immutable classes are the way to create a class that behaves like a value class, but can't be written as a value class. Class `String` is an example of an immutable class.

There are situations in which it is desirable to modify a string without recreating a new string on each modification. For these situations, the BCL provides a class, `StringBuilder` (namespace `System.Text`). This class provides methods to remove, replace, and insert characters or strings to the existing string. The following code excerpt illustrates this:

```
// Project Strings

StringBuilder s = new StringBuilder("Hello");
s.Append(" Worldx"); // Hello Worldx
s.Replace('x', '!'); // Hello World!
String sNew = s.ToString();
```

SUMMARY

The BCL defines hundreds of useful interfaces and classes to boost a developer's productivity. In this chapter, we covered many important ones. Table 5.5 summarizes some of these interfaces and classes. As an exercise, I suggest that you cover the right-hand column and try to remember the idea behind each interface or class.

TABLE 5.5.   BCL Interfaces and Classes

Name	Description
IEnumerable	Represents enumerable object. Makes `foreach` keyword in C# work.
IEnumerator	Represents enumerator object. Returned by the enumerable object via `GetEnumerator` method.
ICollection	Represents a collection. Inherits `IEnumerable`.
IList	Represents a manageable collection. Inherits `ICollection` and `IEnumerable`.
ICloneable	Provides the semantics of deep copy on an object.
ArrayList	A class that stores weakly typed objects. Implements `IList`, `ICollection`, `IEnumerable`, and `ICloneable`.
BitArray, Queue, SortedList, Stack, StringCollection	Various collection types.
CollectionBase	A helper class that can be inherited to create a strongly typed collection.
Array	A class that represents an array of strongly typed items. Once allocated, the size cannot be changed.
IDictionary	Represents a collection of key–value pairs.
Hashtable	Dictionary holding key–value pairs.
IHashCodeProvider	Provides a way to define your own hash code function.
IComparer, IComparable	Provides a way to compare two objects.
SortedList	Sorted dictionary.
ListDictionary	An efficient implementation of a dictionary useful for less than 10 items.
DictionaryBase	A helper class that can be inherited to create a strongly typed dictionary.
Stream	An abstract base class for reading and writing data.
FileStream	Read or write data from or to a file.
Encoding	Exposes various encoding classes as static properties.
StreamReader, StreamWriter	Read or write data as characters and lines.
BinaryReader, BinaryWriter	Read or write basic datatypes in binary format.
Serializable	An attribute that indicates that the object can be serialized.

TABLE 5.5.   BCL Interfaces and Classes (Continued)

Name	Description
ISerializable	Helps in customizing serialization on an object.
IFormatter	Represents a formatter.
BinaryFormatter	Serializes an object in binary format.
SoapFormatter	Serializes an object in SOAP format.
XmlSerializer	Serializes an object in XML format.
IFormattable	Provides custom formatting to strings.
String	Stores a string.
StringBuilder	Mutable string class.

At this point, you should be fairly comfortable in developing programs using the BCL classes. We will be using many of these classes in the rest of the book.

REFERENCE

[Nist]   *Double Hashing, Dictionary of Algorithms, Data Structures, and Problems*, National Institute of Standards and Technology. *hissa.nist.gov/dads/HTML/doublehashng.html*

CHAPTER 6

Distributed Computing

In this chapter, we look at how to develop distributed applications under .NET that can communicate within intranets as well as over the Internet. We will see how .NET remoting offers seamless remote activation and remote method calls, among other things. We examine how to develop intranet applications using this support. Over the Internet, Web services have become the building blocks for distributed Web-based applications. We will look at the support offered by ASP.NET to create and deploy Web services. By the end of this chapter, readers will be comfortable developing applications using the common language runtime object-remoting and will be fairly conversant with ASP.NET Web services development.

APPLICATION DOMAINS

Operating systems typically provide some form of isolation between different applications running on the same system. This isolation is necessary to ensure that code running in one application does not adversely affect other (most likely unrelated) applications.

Historically, most OSs, including Windows, achieve this isolation using process boundaries. Under this model, there is one process per executing application and a crash in one application cannot affect any other executing application.

The common language runtime has similar needs for the isolation. However, there are many scenarios in which isolation at the process boundary is too expensive in terms of performance: A process switch involves a thread switch, saving and restoring call stack, and so on. For this reason, .NET advocates running multiple applications within the same process.

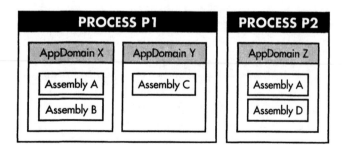

FIGURE 6.1   Application domains.

Although multiple .NET applications can run in the same process, the need for isolation is still there. You do not want one errant application to bring down the whole process. This isolation is achieved by means of application domains.

An *application domain* (or AppDomain for short) is the common language runtime's equivalent of an OS process in many respects. User code and data are isolated to the AppDomain in which they are loaded. In other words, the user code from one AppDomain cannot be called from the user code from another AppDomain directly and data cannot be shared directly between application domains.

A process can have multiple application domains. However, an application domain cannot span multiple processes, just as a process cannot span multiple machines. This relationship is illustrated in Figure 6.1.

Under .NET, assemblies can be loaded and the user code can be executed only within the context of an application domain. When the common language runtime is first loaded within a process, it automatically creates a default application domain to execute the user code. However, more application domains can be created (within the same process) either by the common language runtime host or by the user code.

An application domain has a friendly name, assigned to it at the time of its creation. The default application domain gets its name from the filename of the first assembly it loads.

The following code excerpt demonstrates obtaining the friendly name of an application domain:

```
// Project AppDomain/AppDomainName

class MyApp {
    public static void Main(){

Console.WriteLine(AppDomain.CurrentDomain.FriendlyName);
    }
}
```

The BCL provides a class, AppDomain (namespace System), to create and manage application domains. This class has a static property, Current-Domain, that returns an AppDomain object representing the application domain where the method is called. The preceding code displays the FriendlyName property for the current application domain.

It is possible to programmatically create new application domains. This is typically done by applications hosting the common language runtime. For example, ASP.NET hosts all the ASP.NET applications on the machine within a single process; each application is hosted in a separate application domain. However, .NET provides the necessary isolation among the application domains.

Listing Application Domains

Is there a way to list all the application domains within a process?

Here is the trick. Just run the command-line debugger (cordbg.exe) that comes with the SDK and enter the command pro at the prompt. This command displays all the managed processes running on the system along with the list of application domains for each process.

You can also get the list of loaded assemblies within an application domain. Again, using cordbg, attach to the process that you are interested in by typing the command a <pid>, where pid is the process identifier. Then you can type ap to dump a list of all the application domains within the process along with their loaded assemblies. Remember to detach the process (command de) before you quit the debugger. Otherwise, the attached process terminates prematurely.

The fact that application domains are isolated from each other also makes it possible to unload an application domain without causing the process to become unstable. You can use static method AppDomain.Unload for this purpose. If you are writing a custom runtime host, you can also use ICorRuntimeHost::UnloadDomain to unload an application domain. Check the SDK documentation for more information on these APIs.

So, why would you unload an application domain? Well, sometimes you may wish to unload an assembly, perhaps for the purpose of upgrading it.

However, an assembly, once loaded, cannot be unloaded directly. A type from one loaded assembly could be using a type from another loaded assembly. It is not possible to unload an assembly without unloading all other assemblies it is interacting with. However, as assemblies are loaded in the context of an application domain, unloading the application domain can unload all the assemblies within the application domain. An exception to this case is domain-neutral assemblies (covered shortly). Domain-neutral assemblies are not unloaded until either the process is shut down or the host unloads the common language runtime itself by using ICorRuntimeHost::Stop method.

It should be noted that the default domain will not be unloaded until the process is shut down or the host unloads the common language runtime.

Global Exception Handler

We know that under .NET, an exception thrown from a method, if not caught by any of the callers in the call chain, will result in terminating the application abruptly. Wouldn't it be a boon for forgetful programmers to have a mechanism that will let you catch any uncaught exceptions? You can then either deal with the exception or do some housekeeping work and quit the program more gracefully. Fortunately, .NET provides such a mechanism. You can define an exception handler at the application domain level. Any uncaught exception within the application domain will get caught by this handler. The following code snippet illustrates this mechanism:

```
// Project AppDomain/ExceptionHandler

class MyApp {
    static void MyExceptionHandler(Object sender,
      UnhandledExceptionEventArgs e) {
      Console.WriteLine(e.ExceptionObject.ToString());
    }

    public static void Main()
    {
      // add an exception handler to the current appdomain
      AppDomain ad = AppDomain.CurrentDomain;
      ad.UnhandledException += new
        UnhandledExceptionEventHandler(MyExceptionHandler);

      // throw an exception
      throw new Exception("Houston! We have a problem.");
    }
}
```

This program throws an exception that is not caught by any caller on the call chain. However, the program passes the exception to the exception handler, which gracefully writes a message to the console and returns.

Note that the exceptions are caught at the application domain level. If you have more than one application domain within your process, you may wish to register the exception handler for each application domain.

Domain-Neutral Assemblies

Assemblies are loaded within the context of an application domain. If a single application is used by several applications in the same process, by default the common language runtime will load multiple copies of the assembly, one for each domain in which the assembly is used. To maintain isolation, each domain gets its own copy of the user's code and data.

When the common language runtime is being hosted, it is possible to configure the runtime such that the assembly's code (but not its data) can be shared by all domains referencing the assembly. This reduces the amount of memory used at runtime. An assembly whose code is being shared by all domains in the process is said to be *domain-neutral.*

A host can specify the runtime startup configuration via `startupFlags` parameter to `CorBindToRuntimeEx` (Chapter 4). The choices are:

- STARTUP_LOADER_OPTIMIZATION_SINGLE_DOMAIN: Do not load any assembly as domain-neutral. This setting is commonly used when the host is running just a single application in the process.
- STARTUP_LOADER_OPTIMIZATION_MULTI_DOMAIN: Load all the assemblies as domain-neutral. This setting is useful when multiple domains within the process are likely to run the same code.
- STARTUP_LOADER_OPTIMIZATION_MULTI_DOMAIN_HOST: Load only the strong-named assemblies as domain-neutral. This setting is useful if the host intends to run a different application in each of the domains. For example, ASP.NET runs many different applications. However, most of these applications are likely to use some common strong-named assemblies such as `System.WebForms` and `System.Data`. By using this setting, ASP.NET can optimize the use of shared assemblies.

To decide whether or not to load assemblies as domain-neutral, you must make a tradeoff between reducing memory use and performance. Although domain-neutral code consumes less memory, it runs a bit more slowly. The slower performance is related to the way in which the assembly's static variables and methods are accessed. The common language runtime has to ensure that only the user-code gets shared but not the user-data. To make sure that data doesn't leak across domains, the common language runtime maintains a separate copy of static variables per domain. The common language runtime also maintains tables that map a given caller to the appropriate copy of the static variables. The indirection through these lookup tables causes the code to run more slowly.

It should be noted that the above optimization settings do not affect non-static data and methods. For these fields, performance is affected by how the objects are marshaled across the domains, which we will cover later.

MsCorLib.DLL is Special

In chapter 4, I mentioned that the Base Class Library (BCL) is spread over two assemblies—MSCorLib.DLL and System.DLL. It is interesting to know why the BCL was not placed in just a single assembly.

The common language runtime always loads MSCorLib.DLL as domain-neutral, irrespective of the loader optimization settings. Moreover, the execution engine (MsCorWks.DLL and MsCorSvr.DLL) caches all the entry-points and offsets into MsCorLib's code and metadata. So Microsoft wanted to keep MsCorLib as small as possible. As a result, MSCorLib is not allowed to have references to any assemblies. Any type present in MsCorLib has all its transitive closures present in MsCorLib. For example, MsCorLib implemented type System.String refers to type CultureInfo and Encoding. Therefore, both these types are also defined in MsCorLib. All other BCL types that end up accessing external assemblies, directly or indirectly, were put in System.DLL.

Let's recap what we have learned so far about application domains. A process contains one or more application domains. The application domains can be loaded and unloaded dynamically. Assemblies are loaded and objects are housed within the context of an application domain. Objects from one application domain cannot interact directly with objects from another application domain.

Under the .NET Framework, it turns out that application domains are not the lowest level of isolation. There is yet a finer level of isolation within an application domain. This isolation is provided by an entity called the context.

CONTEXTS

Under .NET, a class can be configured to require certain services such as synchronization, transaction, just-in-time activation, security, and so on. These configuration settings together define a runtime environment for the instances of the class to live in. This runtime environment is referred to as the *context* and the configuration settings are called *context attributes.*

A context holds one or more like-minded objects. Whenever a new object is created, the runtime examines whether the creator's context is compatible with the context attributes specified on the object. If the context is found to be compatible, the object is created in this context. Otherwise, the runtime creates a new context and places the object there. Once created, the context remains fixed and immutable until all the objects within the context are deactivated.

An application domain holds one or more contexts. When an application domain is created, the runtime creates a default context within the AppDomain. Subsequently, more contexts may get created within the domain as more objects are created. The relationship among objects, contexts, and application domains is illustrated in Figure 6.2.

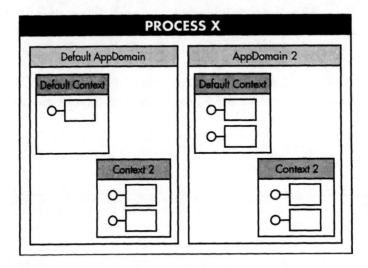

FIGURE 6.2   Objects, contexts, and AppDomains.

Note that objects live in contexts. When we refer to an object from an AppDomain, it automatically implies an object from a context within an AppDomain. Also note that a context cannot span multiple application domains, just as an application domain cannot span multiple processes.

The .NET Framework encapsulates the context environment in a class called `Context` (namespace `System.Runtime.Remoting.Contexts`). The context that a thread is currently executing under can be obtained using a static method, `Thread.CurrentContext` (class `Thread` is defined under namespace `System.Threading`). The following code excerpt displays the context identifier for the current context. A context identifier is a numeric value that uniquely identifies a context within an application domain.

```
// Project AppDomain/ContextID

public static void Main(){
   Context cur = Thread.CurrentContext;
   Console.WriteLine("Context ID={0}", cur.ContextID);
}
```

When this code is executed, it outputs a value of 0, which is the context identifier for the default context. Note that the context identifier is unique only within the scope of an application domain. Two contexts from two different application domains can have the same identifier.

Now that we have a fairly good understanding of contexts and application domains, let's take a look at how objects can communicate across contexts (and application domains).

MARSHALING

Earlier, I stated that .NET lets multiple applications run within a single process under different application domains and that the runtime provides isolation between application domains. Let's see how this is done.

To provide isolation, the runtime ensures that an object from one application domain cannot directly invoke a method on another object that belongs to a different AppDomain. For the same reason, an object from one AppDomain cannot be directly passed to another AppDomain. This holds true irrespective of whether the domains reside in the same process, two different processes on the same machine, or processes on two different machines. From the runtime's perspective, an object that belongs to a domain that is different than that of the caller is deemed a remote object and is treated the same way no matter where the domain resides.

Methods on a remote object thus cannot be called directly, so how does one develop a distributed application if one cannot communicate across processes and across machines? Is there some indirect way to communicate with the remote object?

.NET remoting has been designed so that you don't really need to do anything special in your code to deal with remote objects. Just call the method on the remote object as if you are calling a method on a local object, pass in the method parameters, and obtain the method result. The infrastructure hides the complexity of calling methods on remote objects and returning the results.

Behind the scenes, when a remote object is created or an object is passed to another domain as a method parameter, the runtime transforms the object into a block of memory suitable for transmitting to the other context. This process is referred to as marshaling. Subsequently, the importing domain can unmarshal the block of data; that is, decode it to obtain a new object that is a copy of the original object.

Strictly speaking, cross-domain marshaling automatically implies cross-context marshaling. However, if the contexts belong to the same AppDomain, and if the object exhibits certain characteristics, the runtime may eliminate marshaling altogether. Essentially, the object can be accessed directly from any context within the AppDomain. Such an object is called a *context-agile object*. Context-agile objects live in the default context of the AppDomain. The behavior of a context-agile object is illustrated in Figure 6.3.

Essentially, the role of an AppDomain is to form the boundary for the context agility of an object (and to house contexts).

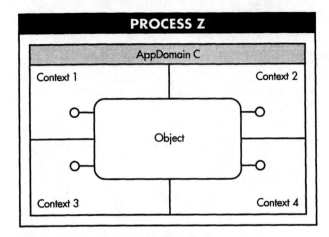

FIGURE 6.3   Context-agile object.

For marshaling purposes, .NET classifies objects into three distinct groups: marshal-by-value, marshal-by-reference, and nonremotable. Let's examine each of them. For our discussion, we may loosely interchange the terms AppDomain and context, but the idea should be clear.

Marshal-by-Value Objects

An object that is marked with the [Serializable] custom attribute is referred to as a *marshal-by-value* (MBV) object. When such an object is passed as a parameter to a remote AppDomain, the runtime serializes the object and transports it to the destination AppDomain, where the data is then deserialized to create a duplicate copy of the original object. Recall from Chapter 5 that the serialization mechanism uses reflection to serialize the member fields and that it is possible to customize the default serialization mechanism by further implementing the ISerializable interface.

Once the copy is in the destination AppDomain, any call to the object within the destination AppDomain is automatically directed to the copy.

The behavior of MBV objects is illustrated in Figure 6.4.

You should use MBV objects when it is desirable to move the entire state of object to the target AppDomain. This reduces time- and resource-consuming round trips across network, process, and AppDomain boundaries. Keep in mind, though, that the caller is working on the copy; any change made in the state of the copy is not reflected in the original object. Likewise, any change made to the original object is not reflected in the copy.

Note that MBV objects are duplicated only when they cross their home AppDomain. Within an AppDomain, MBV objects are context-agile. Also note that all the base datatypes under .NET are marked as [Serializable]; that is, these datatypes are always marshaled by value.

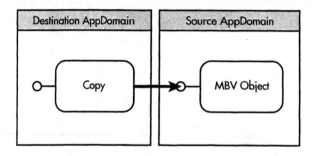

FIGURE 6.4 Marshal-by-value object.

Marshal-by-Reference Objects

An object that is derived from the standard class `MarshalByRefObject`, either directly or indirectly, is referred to as a *marshal-by-reference* (MBR) object. When such an object is passed from the original AppDomain to a different AppDomain, the runtime transparently creates a proxy object in the destination AppDomain and returns to the caller a reference to the proxy. The proxy object represents the actual object; that is, it implements the same methods and properties as the actual object. However, each time the caller invokes a method on the proxy, the runtime intercepts the method call and performs the following operations:

1. Marshal the parameters.
2. Switch to the object's actual context or AppDomain and apply any context-specific policies (e.g., synchronization, transaction, etc.).
3. Unmarshal the parameters.
4. Execute the call.
5. Marshal the return value.
6. Switch back to the caller's context.
7. Unmarshal the return value and make it available to the caller.

The behavior of MBR objects is illustrated in Figure 6.5.

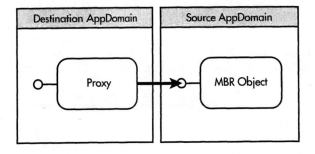

FIGURE 6.5   Marshal-by-reference object.

Let's write a program to create a new application domain and to display information about the default application domain as well as the newly created application domain.

The following code excerpt defines a class `Foo` containing a method `DisplayDomainInfo` that displays the application domain information:

```
// Project AppDomain/RemotableObject

public class Foo : MarshalByRefObject  {
    public void DisplayDomainInfo() {
        String s = "Domain="
            + AppDomain.CurrentDomain.FriendlyName
            + " Thread ID="
            + AppDomain.GetCurrentThreadId()
            + " Context ID="
            + Thread.CurrentContext.ContextID;
        Console.WriteLine(s);}
}
```

In this code, class Foo is derived from MarshalByRefObject, which implies that any instance of Foo is an MBR object. Method DisplayDomain-Info displays three fields: the friendly name of the current domain, the identifier of the thread executing the code, and the context identifier of the current thread.

The following is our main application logic. Here, two instances of Foo are created, one in the default domain and one in a domain called MyNewApp-Domain:

```
// Project AppDomain/RemotableObject

class MyApp {
    public static void Main()
    {
      // Display default domain info
      Foo fDefault = new Foo();
      fDefault.DisplayDomainInfo();

      // Create a new appdomain. Name it MyNewAppDomain
      AppDomain ad = AppDomain.CreateDomain("MyNewAppDomain");

      // Load RemotableObject.exe assembly in the new appdomain
      // and create an instance of Foo
      Foo fNew = (Foo)
        ad.CreateInstanceAndUnwrap("RemotableObject", "Foo");
      fNew.DisplayDomainInfo();
    }
}
```

The method CreateInstanceAndUnwrap creates an instance of specified type Foo from the specified assembly RemotableObject.exe in the domain on which the method is called. However, what gets stored in the variable fNew is a proxy object. If you compile this code as RemotableObject.exe and execute it, you will witness that the call to DisplayDomainInfo on fNew takes place in the newly created application domain. This is how .NET provides isolation among application domains.

As an exercise, remove `MarshalByRefObject` as the parent class on class `Foo` and add the `[Serializable]` attribute instead. When you compile and execute the new code, both the calls to `DisplayDomainInfo` happen in the default AppDomain.

Wrapped Objects

You may be wondering what the `AndUnwrap` part of `AppDomain.CreateInstanceAndUnwrap` stands for. When an object is passed from one AppDomain to another, typically the metadata for the object's type gets loaded in the new AppDomain. However, the .NET Framework provides an optimization wherein you can pass a different object that wraps the original object such that loading of metadata is deferred until the object is unwrapped.

The wrapped object is represented by the class `ObjectHandle`. You can obtain the `ObjectHandle` by calling `AppDomain.CreateInstance` and you can call `ObjectHandle.Unwrap` to obtain the original object (or its proxy if called from a different AppDomain).

You may be wondering what the behavior would be if an object inherits from `MarshalByRefObject` and is marked with the `[Serializable]` attribute. In this case, inheriting from `MarshalByRefObject` takes precedence. A remote domain receives a proxy object.

It must be clear that when you make a call on the proxy of an MBR object, the runtime intercepts the call and executes the call in the MBR object's AppDomain. There is just one exception to this rule—any static method on the MBR class is always executed in the caller's AppDomain. This is because static methods are not associated with an object, but the class itself. The interception occurs only if an object is accessed.

Application Domains and Threads

When you execute `RemotableObject.exe`, notice that the thread identifier displayed for both application domains is the same because threads do not have any affinity to application domains (or contexts). Application domains and contexts are spatial objects, whereas threads are temporal objects. A thread can traverse multiple contexts and application domains. Multiple threads can execute over the same application domain.

When an application domain is being unloaded, all threads that are executing in the domain must be unwound out of the domain. For any thread traversing

through the domain, the runtime throws an exception of type `ThreadAbortEx-`
`ception`. For the last transition out of the domain for a given thread, this
`ThreadAbortException` is turned into an `AppDomainAbortException`.

Context-Bound Objects

At this point, it should be reasonably clear that the creator of an MBR object
gets either a raw reference (if the object is created in the creator's AppDomain) or a proxy (in a different AppDomain).

Within an AppDomain, the context agility of an object can create problems in certain cases. Let's say the object has certain context attributes. For
proper operation, the object depends on the context (the runtime environment) in which it was created. If a raw reference of this object were shared
with another context in the same AppDomain, for example by using a global
variable to store the reference, the context that is used during method execution is that of the caller, not that of the object. This results in a completely
unpredictable behavior. For example, if the object relied on the same transaction service or security service to be available during method execution, it
might not get one. Worse yet, it may get the caller's settings (which may be
completely different). Almost all configured services would malfunction if
the call were processed in the wrong context.

If the caller, however, had a reference to the proxy object instead, the
runtime could intercept any call on the proxy and run appropriate configuration services before invoking the call on the method.

To prevent the context agility of the object, the .NET remoting architecture provides a base class, `ContextBoundObject` (namespace `System`). Any
object that is based on `ContextBoundObject` is context bound; that is, the
object can never leave the context it is created in. Any other context, even
within the same AppDomain, can only get a proxy to this object. This behavior is illustrated in Figure 6.6.

Any method call made on the proxy is intercepted by the runtime. The
subsequent operations are similar to that of an MBR object, as discussed earlier. As a matter of fact, the `ContextBoundObject` class itself is derived from
`MarshalByRefObject`.

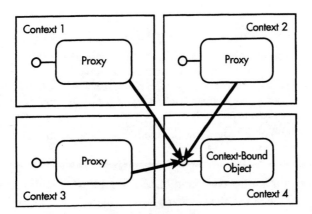

FIGURE 6.6 Context-bound object.

You define your own context-bound class by inheriting from Context-BoundObject. In addition, you can specify one or more context attributes on the class. This is illustrated in the following code excerpt:

```
// Project Contexts/ContextAttributes

[Synchronization(SynchronizationAttribute.REQUIRED)]
public class Foo : ContextBoundObject   {
    public void DisplayInfo() {
        Console.WriteLine("Foo Context ID: {0}",
            Thread.CurrentContext.ContextID);
    }
}
```

This code uses a context attribute, SynchronizationAttribute (namespace System.Runtime.Remoting.Contexts). This attribute is used to provide synchronized access to an object. The value Synchronization-Attribute.REQUIRED tells the runtime that an instance of Foo should be created in a context that participates in synchronization. Such a context guarantees that no two threads can enter the context concurrently. One thread has to exit the context before another thread can enter it. We will learn more about synchronization in Chapter 8.

When to Use Context-Bound Objects

When should you use `ContextBoundObject` instead of `MarshalByRefObject`? If you intend to specify any context attributes on the class, then you should derive your class from `ContextBoundObject`. As a `ContextBoundObject` inherits from `MarshalByRefObject`, you get all the features of `MarshalByRefObject` as well.

For all other remotable cases, you can use `MarshalByRefObject` or `[Serializable]` as appropriate.

Instantiating a context-bound class is no different than instantiating any other class. You can use the standard new keyword in C#, as highlighted here:

```
public static void Main() {
    Console.WriteLine("Default Context ID={0}",
      Thread.CurrentContext.ContextID);
    Foo f1 = new Foo();
    ...
}
```

Here is the partial output from the application:

```
Default Context ID=0
Foo Context ID=1
```

When this code is run, Main is invoked from the default context (represented by the context ID=0). When Main creates an instance of Foo, the runtime checks if the caller's context is compatible with the context requirements for Foo. As the caller's context is not set to participate in synchronization, the runtime creates a new context, places the object in the new context (represented by context ID=1), and returns a proxy to the caller.

At this point, it is worth mentioning that there is yet another way to create instances using .NET. The BCL defines a class, Activator (namespace System), to deal with object activation[1] issues. Using the static method Activator.CreateInstance, you can create a new object. The following two lines of code are equivalent in functionality:

```
Foo f1 = new Foo();
Foo f2 = (Foo) Activator.CreateInstance(typeof(Foo));
```

---

1. For now, you can assume instantiation and activation are the same. The difference will become clear when we discuss the concept of object pooling in a later chapter.

An interesting overload of `Activator.CreateInstance` is the one that lets you define one or more context attributes during activation. The attributes can be built in an array and passed as a parameter to the method. The following code excerpt illustrates this:

```
Bar b1 = (Bar) Activator.CreateInstance(
    typeof(Bar),
    null,
    new object[] {new SynchronizationAttribute(
      SynchronizationAttribute.REQUIRES)});
```

The first parameter to `Activator.CreateInstance` is the type of the object to be created. The second parameter is used to pass arguments to the constructor of class `Bar`. Passing a value `null`, as we have done here, invokes the default constructor. The third parameter is used to specify the required context attributes. In our case, we pass just one attribute, `Synchronization-Attribute`.

Okay, we are done with context-bound objects. In a later chapter on enterprise services, we will learn more about an important derivation of `ContextBoundObject`, `ServicedComponent`. This class lets you use COM+ runtime services such as transaction and object pooling.

Nonremotable Objects

An object that is neither inherited from `MarshalByRefObject` nor marked with the `[Serializable]` attribute is a nonremotable object. These objects can never leave their domain. Trying to pass such an object to a remote domain results in an exception of type `SerializationException`.

REMOTING ARCHITECTURE

Establishing communication between two objects from two different domains or contexts, either on the same machine or on two different machines, is a common programming task. Traditionally, this requires in-depth knowledge of transport protocols, communication APIs, security mechanisms, and so on. The .NET Framework, however, makes it easy to develop such distributed applications by providing a number of services, utility classes, and tools. Figure 6.7 illustrates the process of general remoting.

Under .NET remoting, a client simply creates an instance of the server class. The remoting layer creates a proxy object and returns it to the client.

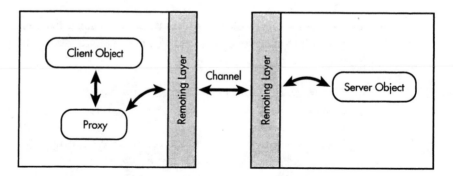

FIGURE 6.7 Remoting model.

When the client makes a method call on the proxy, the remoting layer (in the client domain) intercepts the call, packs the call information into a message, and sends it over a communication channel to the server domain. The remoting layer in the server domain picks up this message, unpacks it, and invokes the appropriate method on the real object.

Channels

Channels transport messages between the remoting boundaries. A channel can either listen to an endpoint for inbound messages, send outbound messages, or both. The architecture allows you to plug in a wide range of protocols.

The .NET Framework provides channel classes to deal with some frequently used transport protocols such as TCP and HTTP. The `TcpChannel` class (namespace `System.Runtime.Remoting.Channels.Tcp`) transports the stream to the destination using TCP. By default, it uses a binary formatter (see Chapter 5) to serialize a message into a binary stream. The `HttpChannel` class (namespace `System.Runtime.Remoting.Channels.Http`) transports the data stream over HTTP. By default, it serializes messages using the SOAP–XML formatter. All the required SOAP headers are added to the stream before the data is transported.

It is possible to configure the TCP channel to use the SOAP formatter or the HTTP channel to use the binary formatter. The architecture is open enough to support even third-party formatters.

Channel classes such as `TcpChannel` and `HttpChannel` implement the channel logic for the client side as well as for the server side. The .NET Framework also provides the classes `TcpServerChannel` and `HttpServer-Channel`, which implement only the server-side channel logic. Likewise, the classes `TcpClientChannel` and `HttpClientChannel` implement only the client-side channel logic.

At this point, it is worth understanding the activation model of the .NET remoting architecture. .NET classifies remote objects as either server-activated objects or client-activated objects, depending on who controls the lifetime of the object. Let's look at the server-activated objects first.

Server-Activated Objects

A server-activated object is an object with a lifetime that is directly controlled by the server. In this mode, the server application publishes the information on a type and assigns it a name. Although not necessary, the name is generally human-readable. Clients can use this name to look up the remote object. For this reason, a server-activated object is also referred to as a well-known object (WKO). The well-known name is referred to as the Uniform Resource Identifier (URI).

Consider the following code excerpt, which defines a class `HelloUser` that we wish to expose as a server-activated type:

```
// Project SingleCallObjects/Greeting

public class HelloUser : MarshalByRefObject  {
    public String GetGreeting(String user) {
        String retVal = String.Format(
          "Hello {0} from {1}:{2}",
          user,
          AppDomain.CurrentDomain.FriendlyName,
          this.GetHashCode());
        Console.WriteLine(retVal); // debugging aid
        return retVal;
    }
}
```

In this code, method `GetGreeting` takes as input a user name and returns a formatted string containing a greeting, the user name, the friendly name of the domain executing the method, and the hash code of the instance of `HelloUser`. The hashcode can serve as a unique identifier for the instance.

Note that class `HelloUser` is inherited from `MarshalByRefObject`. Without this, our discussion about distributed client–server computing would not make much sense.

Compile this code into a library assembly named `Greeting.dll`. Let's now expose `HelloUser` as a server-activated type, as shown in the following code excerpt:

```
// Project SingleCallObjects/MyHost

class MyApp {
    public static void Main() {
        ChannelServices.RegisterChannel(
          new TcpServerChannel(8085));
        RemotingConfiguration.RegisterWellKnownServiceType(
          Type.GetType("HelloUser, Greeting"),
          "GetHello",
          WellKnownObjectMode.SingleCall);

        // Keep the server alive
        Console.WriteLine("Press any key to quit server");
        Console.Read();
    }
}
```

To expose a WKO for remoting, a server application has to go through the following general steps:

1. Register one or more server-side channels for communication.
2. Register the identity of the remote types.
3. Provide a mechanism to keep the server application alive.

First, the server application has to register one or more server-side channels with the remoting layer. These are the channels on which remoting will intercept calls for the WKO. The framework provides a class, ChannelServices (namespace System.Runtime.Remoting.Channels), that can be used to perform this and many other remoting-related operations. Method RegisterChannel on this class can be used to register a channel. In our example, we registered the TCP channel at port 8085.

A channel that is registered is global only within the context of the registering AppDomain. Each AppDomain is required to register the channel exclusively; that is, if the AppDomain intends to supply objects for remoting.

Also note that a port number cannot be shared between two AppDomains on the same machine. If you have a client and a server application that are running on the same machine, make sure that they use different port numbers.

Registering just the channels is not enough. All remote types also have to be registered with the .NET remoting framework before clients can access them. The framework provides a class, RemotingConfiguration (namespace System.Runtime.Remoting), for this purpose. In our code, we called a static method RegisterWellKnownServiceType on this class to register type HelloUser and gave it the URI GetHello. The last parameter to RegisterWellKnowServiceType dictates the mode of the server-activated object and is discussed shortly.

Obtaining Type Information

Recall from Chapter 3 that under .NET, a type can be represented by a display name. The syntax for the display name is:

```
Namespace.TypeName <,assembly name>
```

To obtain type information on type HelloUser from assembly Greeting.dll, one can call a static method, System.Type.GetType, passing it the display name HelloUser, Greeting as a parameter. This method returns an instance of class System.Type, a class that encapsulates all the information about a type.

Note that under C#, the type information can also be obtained using the typeof keyword. However, to use this keyword, the assembly containing the type has to be referenced during the compilation.

Given the fact that the type HelloUser has been published as GetHello on TCP port 8085, clients can access an instance of HelloUser using the lookup string tcp://machinename:8085/GetHello, where machinename is the IP name of the machine. This lookup string is referred to as the Uniform Resource Locator (URL) of the remote type. The syntax of the URL is dictated by the channel in use and can be found in the SDK documentation.

The final couple of lines of the preceding code implement a logic to keep the server alive until you press any key on the keyboard.

Compile this code as an assembly, MyHost.exe.

You may be wondering why we broke the server-side logic into two different assemblies, Greeting.dll and MyHost.exe. From a deployment perspective, doesn't it seem logical to create just one assembly with all the necessary code? If you examine the server registration code in MyHost.cs, you will see that the logic is so generic that it can be used to host more than one type. Thus, you can have your types spread over many assemblies but still host them using one generic hosting executable.

There is yet another reason for this separation. It is also possible to publish the types from Greeting.dll in other hosts, such as ASP.NET, eliminating the need for writing a separate host application. Later, we will see how this can be done.

Let's now look at how the client can activate and use the remote object. The following is the relevant code excerpt:

```
// Project SingleCallObjects/MyClient

class MyApp {
    public static void Main() {
      ChannelServices.RegisterChannel(new TcpClientChannel());

      HelloUser user = (HelloUser) Activator.GetObject(
        typeof(HelloUser),
        "tcp://localhost:8085/GetHello");

      String greeting = user.GetGreeting("Jay");
      Console.WriteLine("Return value: {0}", greeting);

      greeting = user.GetGreeting("Jay");
      Console.WriteLine("Return value: {0}", greeting);
    }
}
```

Before activating a remote object, a client has to register a client-side channel that it wishes to use. This is done by calling the familiar `Chan-nelServices.RegisterChannel` method.

It is not necessary for a client to register a channel explicitly. The default installation of the runtime sets up a machine-wide configuration that makes a TCP channel or an HTTP channel registered as necessary when activating the remote object. For details, look into the `configuration/system.run-time.remoting/application/channels` section in the global configuration file (`Machine.Config`).

Once a client channel is registered, the remote object is activated by calling a static method, `Activator.GetObject`. The first parameter to the method specifies the type of object that the client is interested in and the second parameter specifies the URL of the remote type.

When `GetObject` is called, a proxy object is created and returned to the client. This proxy object internally holds necessary information for communication, such as the type of channel used, the port number of the channel, the name of the remote machine, and so on. However, the client can treat the proxy object as though it is a direct reference to the remote object.

It is interesting to note that even though the runtime creates a proxy object on the call to `GetObject`, it does not create the corresponding remote object on the server, at least not yet. The remote object is created only when the first method call is made on the proxy object.

Compile the client code as `MyClient.exe` and execute it. Be sure to run `MyHost.exe` first. For our sample, both programs need to run on the same machine (machine name `localhost` is a standard DNS name representing the local machine).

Here is the output from our client program:

```
Return value: Hello Jay from MyHost.exe:58
Return value: Hello Jay from MyHost.exe:61
```

The client application calls `GetGreeting` twice on the proxy object and displays the string returned from each call. The domain name returned is `MyHost.exe`, confirming that the code was actually executed in the server application.

Also note that the hash code of the remote object returned is different for each method call. This implies that two different instances of the remote type were created even though only one proxy object was activated. How is this possible?

Single-Call and Singleton Objects

Under .NET, a server-activated object can be published in two possible modes, single-call and singleton. Each mode indirectly lets the server application control the lifetime of the remote object. A single-call object mode implies that the remote object is created on each method call and torn down after the call returns. A singleton object mode implies that the remote object is created just once on the first method call and is reused on subsequent method calls.

The mode of the object is defined at the time of registering the object by calling `RegisterWellKnownServiceType`. The last parameter to this method can be either `WellKnownObjectMode.SingleCall` for single-call mode or `WellKnownObjectMode.Singleton` for singleton mode.

Our earlier program sample registered the type in the single-call mode, so you saw two different instances of the remote type. If you edit `MyHost.cs` and change the object mode to singleton, as follows, then you will see that the hash code returned is the same for both the method calls made by the client:

```
// Project SingletonObjects/MyHost

    ...
    RemotingConfiguration.RegisterWellKnownServiceType(
      Type.GetType("HelloUser, Greeting"),
      "GetHello",
      WellKnownObjectMode.Singleton);
```

At this point, it is worth understanding the usage implications of each of the object modes. For a single-call mode, as a new object is created on each method call, the client cannot use it to store instance-specific data between two method calls. Even for a singleton object, it is not a good idea to store instance-specific data between method calls. As the same object is shared among all the clients, there is no guarantee that the data set by one client will not be overridden by another client. Moreover, as we will see later, there is also a lifetime issue to deal with. Server-activated objects, single-call or singleton, are generally designed to perform atomic operations; the client sends as method parameters any data that is needed by the server and gets back the result in a single method call.

If instance-specific data should be shared between method calls, then the server must publish client-activated types instead.

Client-Activated Objects

Client-activated objects (CAOs) are objects with a lifetime that is controlled by the client, just as they would be if the object were local to the client.

A server publishes a client-activated type using a static method, `Remot-ingConfiguration.RegisterActivatedServiceType`, as shown in the following code excerpt:

```
// Project ClientActivated/MyHost

class MyApp {
    public static void Main() {
        ChannelServices.RegisterChannel(
          new TcpServerChannel(8085));
        RemotingConfiguration.RegisterActivatedServiceType(
          Type.GetType("HelloUser, Greeting"));

        // Keep the server alive
        Console.WriteLine("Press any key to quit server");
        Console.Read();
    }
}
```

This code publishes our earlier defined class `HelloUser` (in assembly `Greeting.dll`) as a client-activated type. This class is available at TCP port 8085, which can be represented in URL form as `tcp://<machine-name>:8085`.

A client instantiates a client-activated type using `Activator.Cre-ateInstance`, a method we saw earlier. However, the URL information for the type has to be made available to `CreateInstance`. This is done by way of a context attribute called `UrlAttribute`. Here is our client code:

```
// Project ClientActivated/MyClient

class MyApp {
    public static void Main() {
        ChannelServices.RegisterChannel(new TcpClientChannel());

        HelloUser user = (HelloUser) Activator.CreateInstance(
            typeof(HelloUser),
            null,
            new object[] {
                new  UrlAttribute("tcp://localhost:8085")
            });

        String greeting = user.GetGreeting("Jay");
        Console.WriteLine("Return value: {0}", greeting);

        greeting = user.GetGreeting("Jay");
        Console.WriteLine("Return value: {0}", greeting);
    }

}
```

When the client tries to create an instance of a client-activated type, a remote object is created on the server and a proxy is returned to the client. Contrast this to a server-activated object, where the remote object is not created until a method call is made on the proxy. The returned proxy represents a specific remote object. If two new remote objects are created, two different proxy instances are returned to the client. The client can use the returned proxy as if it were a local object. The client can even store instance-specific data between two method calls.

It is important to note that the remote object may get destroyed even before the client releases the proxy object. This seems contrary to the intuition that as long as the client keeps a reference to the proxy object alive, the corresponding remote object should stay alive. This is because of the way .NET remoting manages the remote object's lifetime. We cover this later when we discuss lifetime leases.

Creating Proxy Classes

In Chapter 4, we learned that the common language runtime requires access to the metadata for the managed code. This holds true even if a client application is accessing a remote object; the metadata for the remote object must be available locally and should be accessible by the common language runtime. For example,

`MyClient.exe` does not execute properly if it cannot access `Greeting.dll`, the assembly that stores the type information for the `HelloUser` class.

There are cases in which it is not acceptable to install the server assemblies on a client's machine. Perhaps the server does not wish to expose the implementation details, or perhaps it is not practical to keep a copy of the server assemblies on each client.

No matter what the reason is, there is no real need for a client to be able to access the implementation of remote classes. All that the client really needs is local access to the metadata of the referenced classes. This is where the Soapsuds tool (`soapsuds.exe`) comes into play.

The Soapsuds tool comes with the .NET Framework SDK. This tool can extract metadata information from an assembly and can save the information in various output formats such as XML schema, C# classes, and .NET assembly. Check the SDK documentation for more details. The following command line, for example, reads an assembly `Greeting.dll` as input and generates a C# source file `Greeting.cs`:

```
soapsuds -ia:Greeting -gc
```

The source code used in creating `Greeting.dll` can be found under Project `Soapsuds`. It essentially defines a class `HelloUser` as follows:

```
// Project Soapsuds/Greeting

public class HelloUser : MarshalByRefObject {
    public HelloUser() {...}

    public String GetGreeting(String user) {
      ...
    }
}
```

Here is the relevant portion of the code generated by the Soapsuds tool:

```
public class HelloUser :
    System.Runtime.Remoting.Services.RemotingClientProxy
{

    public Object RemotingReference {
        get{return(_tp);}
    }

    public String GetGreeting(String user) {
        return ((HelloUser) _tp).GetGreeting(user);
    }
}
```

The generated proxy class maintains all the public methods (with matching signatures) found in the original class. A client can use this proxy class to satisfy the metadata requirement of the runtime.

Note that the proxy class inherits from a class `RemotingClientProxy`. This class provides some frequently used properties when dealing with Soapsuds-generated proxies. For example, you can specify user authentication information such as the user name, password, and so on. If the client is behind a firewall, you can also specify the proxy server to use.

If inheriting from `RemotingClientProxy` is not desired, you can specify the `-nowp` command-line switch to `Soapsuds.exe`. In this case, the generated proxy class inherits from `MarshalByRefObject`.

Instead of generating the source code as the output, it is also possible to specify the Soapsuds tool to generate an assembly containing the proxy class. This is illustrated in the following command line:

```
soapsuds -ia:Greeting -oa:ClientGreeting.dll
```

Either way, the output of the Soapsuds tool can be consumed by the client code to generate the client-side executable, as illustrated here:

```
csc -t:exe -r:ClientGreeting.dll MyClient.cs
```

There is no need to reference the original assembly anymore when building the client code. As a result, the original assembly need not be installed on the client machine.

Using URLs

The Soapsuds tool can also take its input from an HTTP URL. This feature is useful when the server assembly is not available to the client.

Project `Soapsuds` hosts the server class using an HTTP channel. Here is the relevant code excerpt for the host:

```
// Project Soapsuds/MyHost

class MyApp {
public static void Main() {
    ChannelServices.RegisterChannel(
      new HttpServerChannel(8085));
    RemotingConfiguration.RegisterWellKnownServiceType(
      Type.GetType("HelloUser, Greeting"),
      "Greeting/GetHello.soap",
      WellKnownObjectMode.SingleCall);
    ...
    }
}
```

Note that the URI has the extension `.soap`. Although not necessary, the convention is to have an extension of either `.soap` or `.rem`. The global configuration file `Machine.config` defines HTTP remoting handlers to handle a request that ends with either of these two extensions. This is the default behavior. You can also add your own extensions, if desired. Look at `<httpHandlers>` tag for configuration details.

Given this URI and HTTP port number, a client can access the WKO using the URL `http://localhost:8085/Greeting/GetHello.soap`.

If a remote application is set up to use the HTTP channel, then the Soapsuds tool can be run against an HTTP URL as illustrated in the following command line:

```
soapsuds -url:http://localhost:8085/Greeting/GetHello.soap?wsdl
    -oa:MyGreeting.dll
```

This command reads the input from the specified URL and generates an assembly containing the proxy class.

Note that the URL has to be suffixed with `?wsdl`. The remoting layer is set up to handle this suffix and generate the necessary WSDL information that Soapsuds can consume.

Remoting Configuration

Although servers can register an object by hard-coding the publishing information in the source, as we did in our earlier examples, it is also possible to put the type information in external XML-based files. This provides the flexibility of configuring registration parameters without the need to recompile the source code.

The syntax for the configuration file can be found in the SDK documentation under the topic "Remoting Settings Schema."

Host Settings

Using the configuration file, one or more types to be hosted and one or more channels to be used can be specified. The following server-side configuration settings publish three types in three different remote object modes (Project `RemotingConfig/MyHost`):

```
<configuration>
  <system.runtime.remoting>
    <application name="MyRemotingHost">
      <service>
        <wellknown type="Foo,Greeting" mode="SingleCall"
        objectUri="GetFoo" />
```

```
        <wellknown type="Bar,Greeting" mode="Singleton"
        objectUri="GetBar" />
        <activated type="Baz,Greeting" />
      </service>
      <channels>
        <channel port="8085" ref="http" />
      </channels>
    </application>
  </system.runtime.remoting>
</configuration>
```

This configuration implies:

- Class Foo is exposed as a single-call object on the HTTP channel at port number 8085.
- Class Bar is exposed as a singleton object on the HTTP channel at port number 8085.
- Class Baz is exposed as a client-activated object on the HTTP channel at port number 8085.

The configuration setting file can be loaded using a static method RemotingConfiguration.Configure. The name of the configuration file must be passed as a parameter to this method, as shown in the following code excerpt:

```
// Project RemotingConfig/MyHost

class MyApp {
    public static void Main() {
      RemotingConfiguration.Configure("MyHost.cfg");

      // Keep the server alive
      Console.WriteLine("Press any key to quit server");
      Console.Read();
    }
}
```

It is easy to guess that the Configure method internally calls ChannelServices.RegisterChannel to register the channels and RegisterWellKnownServiceType or RegisterActivatedServiceType to register the types to be remoted. However, placing the connection information in an external file makes it easy to administer the parameters, and this is the preferred way.

Client Settings

Remoting configuration settings are not just limited to the server side. Similar settings can be specified on the client side as well, although the syntax is slightly different. The following configuration settings make our just published server-side objects available to the client:

```
<configuration>
    <system.runtime.remoting>
        <application name="ThisIsMyClient">
            <client>
                <wellknown type="Foo,Greeting"
                url="http://localhost:8085/GetFoo" />
                <wellknown type="Bar,Greeting"
                url="http://localhost:8085/GetBar" />
            </client>
            <client url="http://localhost:8085/">
                <activated type="Baz,Greeting" />
            </client>
        </application>
    </system.runtime.remoting>
</configuration>
```

The configuration file needs to be loaded in the client's AppDomain using the `RemotingConfiguration.Configure` method. Once the configuration is loaded, the client can instantiate the remote objects using the `new` operator as illustrated in the following code:

```
// Project RemotingConfig/MyClientNew

class MyApp {
    public static void Main() {
        RemotingConfiguration.Configure("MyClientNew.cfg");

        // FOO
        Foo foo = new Foo();
        String greeting = foo.GetGreeting("Foo");
        Console.WriteLine("Return value: {0}", greeting);

        // BAR
        Bar bar = new Bar();
        greeting = bar.GetGreeting("Bar");
        Console.WriteLine("Return value: {0}", greeting);

        // BAZ
        Baz baz = new Baz();
        greeting = baz.GetGreeting("Baz");
        Console.WriteLine("Return value: {0}", greeting);
    }
}
```

Note that clients can also use `Activator.CreateInstance` or `Activator.GetObject` to override the configuration file settings for specified types.

Internally, `RemotingConfiguration.Configure` calls the method `RegisterWellKnownClientType` to associate a type with the URL of the remote server-activated object and method `RegisterActivatedClientType`, to associate a type with the URL of the remote client-activated type. You can use these methods directly if you do not wish to use a client-side configuration file. This is illustrated in the following code:

```
// Project RemotingConfig/MyClientUsingNew

public static void Main() {

    // Configuring object information programmatically

    // Foo - Single-call object
    RemotingConfiguration.RegisterWellKnownClientType(
        typeof(Foo),
        "http://localhost:8085/GetFoo");

    // Bar - Singleton object
    RemotingConfiguration.RegisterWellKnownClientType(
        typeof(Bar),
        "http://localhost:8085/GetBar");

    // Baz - Client-activated object
    RemotingConfiguration.RegisterActivatedClientType(
        typeof(Baz),
        "http://localhost:8085/");

    // Now instantiating classes using "new" operator
    Foo foo = new Foo(); // Foo
    ...
}
```

As may be obvious, if a type is not associated with a remote URL, the new operator ends up creating a local object.

Note that `RegisterWellKnownClientType` and `RegisterActivatedClientType` register well-known types only for the `AppDomain` they are invoked from. Each AppDomain that wishes to use the new operator for remote objects should call these methods (or load the configuration file).

Hosting under ASP.NET

Earlier, I mentioned that a reason to separate the main business logic (Greet-ing.dll in our case) from the hosting logic (MyHost.exe) is that it is possible to publish classes under ASP.NET, thus eliminating the need for a hosting executable. Let's see how this can be done.

Under ASP.NET, classes are published using a configuration file. The file is named web.config and the configuration format is similar to one we saw earlier for the server-side settings. There are just a few differences:

1. Under ASP.NET, classes are always published using the HTTP channel. Therefore, channel information should not be present in web.config.

2. ASP.NET recognizes only two extensions for the URI, .rem or .soap. These two extensions are defined in the global configuration file (Machine.config). If need be, you can add your own extension by editing this file.

3. The <application> element should not have any name attribute. When ASP.NET gets loaded for a specific Web application, it automatically sets the name of the application to the alias name of the IIS virtual directory in which it is being hosted.

Here is the modified version of our server-side configuration file that can be used under ASP.NET (Project WebApplication):

```
<configuration>
  <system.runtime.remoting>
    <application>
      <service>
        <wellknown type="MyCompany.Foo, Greeting"
        mode="SingleCall" objectUri="GetFoo.rem" />
        <wellknown type="MyCompany.Bar, Greeting"
        mode="Singleton" objectUri="GetBar.rem" />
        <activated type="MyCompany.Baz,Greeting" />
      </service>
    </application>
  </system.runtime.remoting>
</configuration>
```

To avoid any naming conflicts, I have defined the remote types under the namespace MyCompany. Using the company name as a namespace is a good coding guideline.

To host ASP.NET, you need to have IIS Web server running on your machine.

Here are the steps needed to host our assembly under ASP.NET:

1. Create a new virtual directory under IIS. Give a suitable name for the alias and point the virtual directory (also called the virtual root or vroot) to the directory where web.config resides. This is an important step. ASP.NET expects web.config to be present in the vroot (although it is possible to customize the behavior for a subdirectory under vroot by defining another web.config in the subdirectory). For our experiment, let the alias name be Greeting and the directory be C:\DotNetProgramming\Ch06-DistributedComputing\WebApplication.

2. Create a subdirectory called bin under this directory and copy the required assemblies to this directory. In our case, Greeting.dll has already been built in C:\DotNetProgramming\Ch06-Distributed-Computing\WebApplication\bin directory. The default PrivatePath configuration setting for ASP.NET is defined as bin. If you wish, you can customize this setting for your needs.

We are ready to go. A client can now access the published types at the URL http://<machinename>/<alias>/<objectUri>. In our experiment, for example, this translates to http://localhost/Greeting/GetFoo.rem for accessing class MyCompany.Foo, as shown in the following code excerpt:

```
// Project WebApplication/MyClient

class MyApp {
    public static void Main() {
        ChannelServices.RegisterChannel(new HttpChannel());

        String url = "http://localhost/Greeting/";
        // FOO
        Foo foo = (Foo) Activator.GetObject(
          typeof(Foo),
          url + "GetFoo.rem");
        String greeting = foo.GetGreeting("Foo");
        Console.WriteLine("Return value: {0}", greeting);
        ...
    }
}
```

Recall that our implementation of Foo.GetGreeting returns the greeting along with the name of the assembly and the hash code of the instance of Foo. Here is the partial output when the client program is executed:

```
Return value: Hello Foo from
    /LM/W3SVC/1/Root/Greeting-1-126572344064463520:181
```

Notice the strange assembly name returned for `Greeting.dll`. This is because ASP.NET uses a mechanism called *shadow copy*. Using this mechanism, ASP.NET makes a "shadow" copy of an assembly to be used, which is then locked and loaded. As the original assembly is not locked, it gives a chance for the developers or administrators to replace the assembly with a newer version even while the Web server is running. Furthermore, any changes to the original assembly can automatically be detected by ASP.NET, and, if needed, the assembly is shadow-copied once again. The newer incoming requests are automatically redirected to the newer copy of the assembly.

A final word on hosting .NET remoting applications either under ASP.NET or using an HTTP channel directly: Although the communication is based on HTTP and SOAP, the way the SOAP messages are formatted, not many non-.NET platforms are capable of interpreting the message. There have been some success stories with PocketSOAP (*www.pocketsoap.com/ weblog/soapInterop/base.html*) and Apache (*www.apache.org/~rubys/Apache ClientInterop.html*). Later in the chapter, we look at Web services, a different mechanism for exposing types for remoting. The SOAP format used by Web services can be consumed by a wide range of platforms.

Lifetime Leases

For a CAO, it seems intuitive that as long as the client keeps a reference to the proxy the remote object stays alive and that when the client releases the last reference to the proxy, the remote object gets garbage collected. However, don't count on this.

In a distributed system, if a reference counting mechanism is used on an object, there needs to be a mechanism in place to adjust the object's reference count in case a client is not reachable anymore. Perhaps the client has terminated unexpectedly. Traditionally, this check is achieved by requiring the server to ping the clients periodically. Those who have worked with DCOM are familiar with this concept. Although this technique of periodically pinging the clients works well for a small number of clients per service, it doesn't scale well when there are a huge number of clients per service.

.NET uses a leased-based technique to manage the lifetime of MBR objects. An MBR object, either client-activated or singleton, can be associated with a lifetime lease. When the lease expires, the object is destroyed (garbage collected). This is the default behavior. As we will see shortly, there are various ways to extend the lease.

A lease implements the ILease interface (all lifetime-related interfaces and classes are defined in the namespace System.Runtime.Remoting .Lifetime). Here is its definition:

```
interface ILease {
    LeaseState CurrentState {get; } // Initial, Active, etc.
    TimeSpan InitialLeaseTime {get; set;}
    TimeSpan RenewOnCallTime {get; set; }
    TimeSpan CurrentLeaseTime {get; } // remaining lease time

    // Renew a lease
    TimeSpan Renew(TimeSpan renewalTime);

    // Sponsorship related
    void Register(ISponsor)
    void Register(ISponsor, TimeSpan)
    void Unregister(ISponsor)
    TimeSpan SponsorshipTimeout (get; set;}
}
```

Property ILease.InitialLeaseTime defines the time the object will be kept alive once it is remoted, irrespective of whether a client makes a method call or not. If a call comes in during this time, the remaining lease time (ILease.CurrentLeaseTime) is automatically adjusted to the greater of ILease.CurrentLeaseTime and ILease.RenewOnCallTime. The default value for the initial lease time is five minutes and for the renew-on-call time is two minutes. This means that once a client obtains a remote object, if the client doesn't make a call within five minutes, the remote object is destroyed, leaving the client with a dangling proxy (and we all know how much that hurts). If the unsuspecting client makes a call on such a proxy, the runtime throws an exception of type RemotingException.

Let's say the client makes a call on the remote object after four minutes. The runtime adjusts the remaining lease time (which should be one minute at this point) to two minutes (the default value for ILease.RenewOnCallTime). The client must now continue to make calls on the object at least once every two minutes, failing which the remote object is garbage collected.

The default lease parameters for an MBR object can be adjusted before the object leaves the context. A type can control its own lifetime policy by overriding the MarshalByRefObject.InitializeLifetimeService method, as shown in the following code excerpt:

```
// Project LifetimeLeases/Greeting

public class HelloUser : MarshalByRefObject {
    public override Object InitializeLifetimeService() {
        ILease lease =
          (ILease) base.InitializeLifetimeService();
        if (lease.CurrentState == LeaseState.Initial) {
          lease.InitialLeaseTime = TimeSpan.FromSeconds(30);
          lease.RenewOnCallTime = TimeSpan.FromSeconds(10);
        }
        return lease;
    }
    ...
}
```

The runtime calls InitializeLifetimeService when the object is being remoted. A typical override implementation obtains the lease by calling the base class InitializeLifetimeService, modifies the lease parameters, and returns it to the runtime. A null value can be returned, indicating that no lease can be created for the associated object, giving the object an infinite timeout.

Note that the runtime may call InitializeLifetimeService multiple times but the lease parameters can be adjusted only when the lease is in its initial state (LeaseState.Initial).

Each AppDomain contains a lease manager that is responsible for administering leases in its domain. The lease manager periodically checks all leases for expired leases. If the lease expires, the corresponding object is garbage collected. Note that a lease comes into play only when the object is remoted out of its AppDomain, not just out of its context.

There are two ways for the clients to extend the lease. The first way is to call ILease.Renew whenever appropriate and specify a new expiration time period. This is illustrated in the following code excerpt:

```
// Project LifetimeLeases/MyClient

public static void Main() {

    HelloUser user =
       (HelloUser) Activator.CreateInstance(...);

    ILease lease = (ILease) user.GetLifetimeService();
    lease.Renew(TimeSpan.FromMinutes(3));
    ...
}
```

The lease for an object can be obtained by calling `MarshalByRefObject` `.GetLifetimeService`. The preceding code obtains the lease and sets the new expiration time to three minutes.

The second technique for extending the lease is based on a sponsorship mechanism. A client can register an object, referred to as the *sponsor object*, with the lease manager. When the lease for an object expires, the lease manger first walks through all the sponsors for the object to see if any sponsor wishes to renew the lease. If no sponsor renews, only then is the object destroyed.

A sponsor object implements an interface, `ISponsor`. The interface definition is shown here:

```
interface ISponsor {
    TimeSpan Renewal(ILease lease)
}
```

When the lease expires for an object, the lease manager calls `Renewal` on each of the sponsors of the object. Each sponsor can return the new expiration time period, and the lease manager uses the maximum of the returned values as the new lease period.

A sponsor might not respond immediately, perhaps because of network problems such as latency, delays, and so on. To account for this, the lease manager waits for the `ILease.SponsorshipTimeout` time period for a response. If the response doesn't come within this period, the sponsor is removed from the list and the lease manager moves on to the next sponsor. The default value for `SponsorshipTimeout` is two minutes, but it can be set to a different value when initializing lifetime services.

A type can refuse to accept any sponsor by setting `SponsorshipTimeout` to a value `TimeSpan.Zero`.

A client can register a sponsor by calling `ILease.Register`, as shown in the following code excerpt:

```
// Project LifetimeLeases/MyClient

public class MySponsor : MarshalByRefObject, ISponsor {
    public override Object InitializeLifetimeService() {
        return null;
    }

    public TimeSpan Renewal(ILease lease) {
        Console.WriteLine("Renewal at {0}", DateTime.Now);
        return TimeSpan.FromSeconds(20);
    }
}
```

```
class MyApp {
    public static void Main() {
        ChannelServices.RegisterChannel(new TcpChannel(8086));

        HelloUser user =
           (HelloUser) Activator.CreateInstance(...);

        ILease lease = (ILease) user.GetLifetimeService();
        lease.Register(new MySponsor());
        ...
    }
}
```

Once a sponsor object is registered, a client can unregister it anytime by calling `ILease.Unregister`.

Note that the sponsor object has to be marked as remotable (either serializable or MBR). In addition, if the sponsor object is of the MBR type, then it also has to take care of its own lifetime.

In the preceding code, the client is using a `TcpChannel` instead of `TcpClientChannel`. Recall that `TcpChannel` implements client-side as well as server-side logic for the TCP channel. As the client-local object `MySponsor` is implemented as an MBR object and is being sent to a remote AppDomain, in a way, the client is now acting as a server. This explains the need for a server-side channel.

Technically, if `TcpChannel` is initialized using the default constructor, the implementation of `TcpChannel` sets up only the client channel and does not listen on any ports. Using a constructor that takes the port number as a parameter indicates that the server channel also has to be set up. Obviously, the port number to be used should not conflict with any other application.

 Automatic Port Number Selection

If you are not sure of the port number to use, pass in the value 0 to the constructor of `TcpChannel` or `HttpChannel`. The remoting system automatically chooses an available port for you.

Note that this mechanism is meaningful for a client that may act as a server. When a client passes a local MBR object to a remote AppDomain, the object carries with it all the necessary information, including the port number, to connect back to the client. Therefore, the remote AppDomain need not explicitly know the port number of the client. Contrast this to a client trying to obtain an object by calling `Activator.GetObject` or `Activator.CreateInstance`. In this case, the client and the server have to agree on the port number to use.

ASP.NET Web Services

The Internet is evolving from a collection of isolated Web sites and applications into a general communication bus for distributed applications. Recall from Chapter 1 that Microsoft and many other companies believe that the components of the distributed applications will communicate with each other using Web services. A Web service (more specifically, XML Web service) is a service that can be programmatically accessed over the Web. It is based on industry standards such as SOAP and WSDL.

ASP.NET makes it easy to create and test Web services.

Providing Web Services

Let's define a simple Web service class that defines a method to add two numbers. Here is the code:

```
<%@ WebService Language="C#" Class="MyCompany.MyCalculator" %>

// Calculator.asmx - Project Calculator

using System.Web.Services;

namespace MyCompany {

    [WebService(Namespace="http://localhost/WSRemoting/")]
    public class MyCalculator : WebService {

      [WebMethod]
      public int Add(int a, int b) {
        return (a+b);
      }
    }
}
```

Under ASP.NET, a Web service source file is saved with the extension .asmx. The first line of the source file contains a directive for ASP.NET. The Language attribute specifies the programming language being used for the code and the Class attribute specifies the name of the class that should be published as a Web service.

The rest of the source defines the code for the MyCompany.MyCalculator Web service.

It is also possible, and recommended, to keep the code in a separate file. In this case the code must be compiled and the generated assembly must be placed in a subdirectory named Bin. The name of the generated assembly

does not matter. ASP.NET scans all the assemblies in the `Bin` directory looking for the class specified in the `Class` attribute.

If you use the Visual Studio .NET Wizard to generate the Web service,
the wizard creates a file, `Service.asmx`, to store the `WebService` directive
and another file `Service.asmx.cs` (or `.vb` for Visual Basic) to store the
code, where `Service` is the name of your service. Using Visual Studio .NET
to generate a Web service is a good idea. The wizard also creates a virtual
directory under IIS and configures it to allow program execution. However, if
you already have an existing IIS virtual directory that you wish to use, you
can select the project template called New Project in Existing Folder to create
your Web service project.

CodeBehind **Attribute**

A Visual Studio.NET Web service project automatically adds an attribute `Code-`
`Behind` to the `WebService` directive. This attribute is not used by ASP.NET. Visual
Studio .NET uses it to associate an `.asmx` file with a source file (`.cs` or `.vb`).

A Web service class is typically inherited from a standard class `WebSer-`
`vice` (namespace `System.Web.Services`). This makes it possible to
directly access certain ASP.NET intrinsic objects such as those for application and session state. By default, Web service classes created using Visual
Studio .NET inherit from the `WebService` class.

It is not a requirement for your Web service class to inherit from `Web-`
`Service`. Your class can still access the ASP.NET intrinsic objects from a
static property, `System.Web.HttpContext.Current`.

Whether or not your Web service inherits from `WebService`, there are a
few requirements your class must meet.

First, the class must be marked as public and must have a public default
constructor. This makes it possible for ASP.NET to create an instance of your
Web service class.

Second, and more important, your class must support MBV semantics,
not MBR. ASP.NET Web services are about loosely coupled systems. MBR
objects provide for distributed identity and are not supported under ASP.NET.
For the same reason, MBR objects should not be returned from ASP.NET
Web services.

Finally, each method that should be exposed as part of the service must
be attributed with the [`WebMethodAttribute`] token, as shown in the earlier
code. The `WebMethodAttribute` attribute contains several properties for
configuring the behavior of the method. For example, you can add a brief

description of your Web service method, or you can enable or disable the ASP.NET session state for the method. Check the SDK documentation for a complete list of supported properties.

The simple datatypes that a Web method can support can be found in the section Built-In Datatypes of the XML Schema Part 2: Datatypes specifications (*www.w3.org/TR/xmlschema-2/*). Examples include `int`, `float`, `string`, and so on. Web methods also support compound types such as structures and array for method parameters as well as the return value. Check the World Wide Web Consortium (W3C) site for more details (*www.w3.org/TR/ SOAP/#_Toc478383532*).

A Web service class can optionally be marked with the `WebServiceAttribute` attribute. This lets you add extra information to your Web service, such as the description of the service and the namespace the Web service belongs to. A Web service's namespace is not the same as assembly namespaces that you have been used to seeing, although the concept is the same—to resolve naming conflicts. A Web service namespace is identified by a URI. If not specified, the default namespace is `http://tempuri.org/`.

Let's test this little program of ours. First, create a virtual directory under IIS. In my case, the alias for the virtual directory is `WSRemoting` and the root directory for this alias is `D:\DotNetProgramming\Ch06-Distributed-Computing\Calculator`. This is where the file `Calculator.asmx` is stored.

No explicit compilation is needed to run the Web service. Behind the scenes, when a call is made on the Web service, ASP.NET automatically compiles the code and generates a .NET assembly. Subsequently, ASP.NET continues to monitor the source files and recompiles the code if it detects a change in the files.

ASP.NET Web Services versus .NET Remoting

In the previous section, we saw that the .NET remoting framework is capable of providing services over an HTTP channel, which by default uses the SOAP formatter. The server application can also produce WSDL-compliant XML schema. This makes you wonder why there is any need for a different technology to create Web services.

Although it is true that both ASP.NET and .NET remoting can serialize objects in SOAP format, the two serialization mechanisms have entirely different goals. The goal of the SOAP formatter under .NET remoting is to serialize any .NET object with true fidelity. You can change the formatter from binary to SOAP and the chances are your managed code will not break. The goal of the ASP.NET serializer is to provide interoperability across various development platforms. It does not necessarily support everything in the common language runtime.

Another subtle difference is that ASP.NET uses XMLSerializer (Chapter 5) for serializing objects. This class serializes only the public fields of a class. Contrast this to the SOAP formatter used by .NET remoting—it serializes the public as well as the private fields (to maintain true fidelity).

If you know that the server and all its clients are running the common language runtime on their systems, then there is nothing wrong with using .NET remoting. Perhaps this should be your choice. Not only do you get full fidelity for the .NET objects but you can also get performance improvement by using the binary formatter. Plus, you get a choice of TCP, HTTP, or any other proprietary channel.

It may be a while before the common language runtime will be available on all systems. In fact, it may never be available on some platforms. Therefore, if interoperability is your concern, then you should use the ASP.NET Web services architecture.

ASP.NET also takes care of generating the WSDL definition for the class. From Microsoft Internet Explorer, for example, if you type http://localhost/WSRemoting/Calculator.asmx?wsdl (note ?wsdl at the end), then you will see the WSDL definition being displayed.

There is much more. Entering http://localhost/WSRemoting/Calculator.asmx?disco in Internet Explorer, causes ASP.NET to automatically produce the discovery document. A discovery document provides clients with information on available Web services and their descriptions. Discovery documents are typically stored in .disco files.

Finally, ASP.NET also makes it easy to test a Web service. For example, from Internet Explorer, if you type http://localhost/WSRemoting/Calculator.asmx, the resulting Web page shows the methods that are available in the Web service. When you click on a method, ASP.NET automatically generates a page that you can use for testing the method. A snapshot of the test page is shown in Figure 6.8.

Consuming Web Services

The NET SDK ships with a tool called the Web Services Description Language tool (wsdl.exe) that can be used to generate a proxy class for a Web service. The proxy class defines all the methods that are exposed as part of the Web service. A client can simply invoke these methods, which in turn communicate with the Web service over the network. The proxy takes care of generating the appropriate SOAP messages and converting the resulting SOAP responses to the common language runtime types.

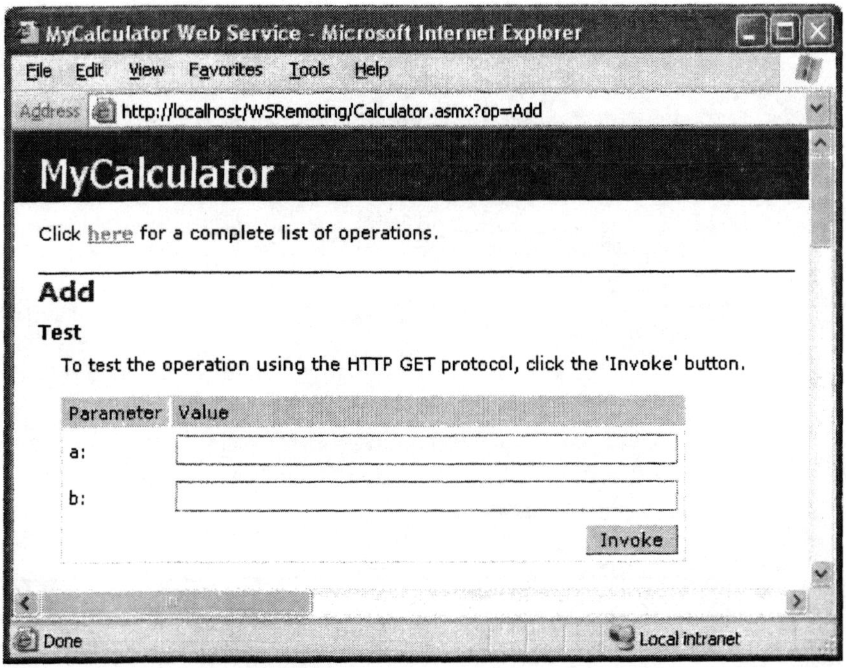

FIGURE 6.8   A snapshot of an ASP.NET generated test page.

The following command line generates the proxy class for `MyCalculator` Web service. The code is saved in file `Proxy.cs`:

```
wsdl.exe -o:Proxy.cs \
    http://localhost/WSRemoting/Calculator.asmx?wsdl
```

By default, the code is generated in C# but a different programming language can be specified by means of a command-line switch.

Here is the code excerpt for the generated proxy class:

```
public class MyCalculator :
    System.Web.Services.Protocols.SoapHttpClientProtocol {
    public MyCalculator() {
      this.Url =
        "http://localhost/WSRemoting/Calculator.asmx";
    }

    public int Add(int a, int b) {
      ...
    }
}
```

Note that the proxy class inherits from a class `SoapHttpClientProto-col`. This class provides some frequently used properties when dealing with `Wsdl.exe`-generated proxies. For example, you can specify security credentials for Web service client authentication (we will see this in Chapter 9). If the client is behind a firewall, you can also specify the proxy server to use, as illustrated in the following client-side code:

```
MyCalculator calc = new MyCalculator();
calc.Proxy =
    new System.Net.WebProxy("http://myproxyserver:8080");
```

Note the code in the constructor of the generated `MyCalculator` class. By default, the proxy class points to the URL of the Web service that was used to generate the proxy class. However, it is possible to point to a different URL at runtime by setting the URL property of the `SoapHttpClientProto-col` class as shown here:

```
calc.Url = "http://Machine/Alias/File.asmx";
```

Here is our actual client code:

```
// Project Calculator/MyClient

// File MyClient.cs
class MyClient {
    public static void Main() {
        MyCalculator calc = new MyCalculator();
        int retVal = calc.Add(10, 20);
        Console.WriteLine(retVal);
    }
}
```

Compile the client code as follows:

```
csc -out:MyClient.exe MyClient.cs Proxy.cs
```

When `MyClient.exe` is executed, it calls the `Add` method on the Web service and displays the return value.

 ## Watching SOAP Traffic

As you start playing with Web services, at some point you will want to look at the SOAP packets being exchanged between your client and a Web service. Here are two excellent tools.

PCapTrace is a free packet capture tool that can be downloaded from *www.pocketsoap.com/pcaptrace/*. Simply run this tool and specify the server and port your code is connecting to. The tool captures and displays all the data. You can also log the data.

ProxyTrace is yet another free tool that acts as an HTTP proxy server. It can be downloaded from *www.pocketsoap.com/tcptrace/pt.asp*. The only drawback with this tool is that you need to modify your client code to go through a proxy server.

At this point, it is worth mentioning that Visual Studio .NET makes it easy to generate a Web service client. In the Solution Explorer, right-click your project and select Add Web Reference. Enter the URL for the Web service in the ensuing dialog box. The wizard discovers and displays the Web service(s). Clicking the Web service generates a proxy class for the Web service and adds it to your project. By default, the namespace of the generated proxy class is the host name of the URL. For example, selecting our Calculator Web service from localhost generates a proxy class localhost.MyCalculator. However, you can change the localhost namespace to something more meaningful by selecting the localhost folder in the Solution Explorer and renaming it.

Managing State in ASP.NET Web Services

Inheriting a Web service class from WebService makes it easy to access the state management options of ASP.NET. The WebService class contains many of the common ASP.NET objects, including the Application and Session objects.

The Application object provides a mechanism for storing data that is accessible to all code running within the Web application. The following code excerpt demonstrates a simple example of how the Application object can be used to track the usage of the Web application.

```
// Project Calculator. File Calculator.asmx

[WebMethod(Description=
    "Number of times this application has been used")]
public int ApplicationUsage() {
    String USAGE = "Usage";
    if (Application[USAGE] == null) {
      // First time
      Application[USAGE] = 0;
    }
```

```
        // Increment the usage count.
        Application[USAGE] = ((int) Application[USAGE]) + 1;
        return  (int) Application[USAGE];
    }
```

The `Application` object stores each bit of state information as a name–value pair. In the preceding code, a counter is being stored under the name USAGE. Each time the method is called, the counter is incremented by one.

Whereas the `Application` object is used to store data at the application level, irrespective of the number of clients connected to the application, the `Session` object allows data to be stored on a per-client session basis. The following code excerpt shows how to create a hit counter for per-user session:

```
// Project Calculator. File Calculator.asmx

[WebMethod(EnableSession=true)]
public int PerUserSessionUsage() {
    String USAGE = "Usage";
    if (Session[USAGE] == null) {
      // First time
      Session[USAGE] = 0;
    }

    // Increment the usage count.
    Session[USAGE] = ((int) Session[USAGE]) + 1;
    return  (int) Session[USAGE];
}
```

As can be seen, using the `Session` object is similar to using the `Application` object. The important thing to note is that to use the `Session` object, the session state must be enabled on the Web service method. This is done by setting the `EnableSession` property of the `WebMethod` attribute to true.

ASP.NET keeps track of the session by means of a client-side cookie. The client code should be enabled to store the cookie. This is done by setting the `CookieContainer` property to a new `System.Net.CookieContainer` object, as highlighted in the following code:

```
// Project Calculator/MyClient

calc.CookieContainer = new System.Net.CookieContainer();
int count = calc.PerUserSessionUsage();
count = calc.PerUserSessionUsage();
count = calc.PerUserSessionUsage();
```

Customizing the Web Service Interface

Sometimes it may be necessary to control the auto-generated WSDL document and the contents of the SOAP messages. In this section, we explore some important possibilities.

Protocols

By default, ASP.NET supports three different HTTP protocols for communication: HTTP-GET, HTTP-POST, and HTTP-SOAP. A client application can use any of these three protocols to communicate. When you're ready to go to production, however, you'll probably want to stick to just SOAP. Most Web service implementations today rely on HTTP-SOAP because it offers a much more robust and extensible protocol. For example, SOAP defines standards for encoding data and communicating error information.

To exclude HTTP-GET and HTTP-POST from your Web service's WSDL, you need to add the `configuration\system.web\webServices\protocol` XML path in your application's `web.config` file. You need to add a `<remove>` element for each protocol that you want to remove, as shown here:

```
<configuration>
    <system.web>
        <webServices>
            <protocols>
                <remove name="HttpPost" />
                <remove name="HttpGet" />
            </protocols>
        </webServices>
    </system.web>
</configuration>
```

Configuring your Web service this way has the following effects:

1. The removed protocols are excluded from the service's WSDL document.

2. The clients receive an error if they attempt to use these protocols to invoke the Web service.

3. Disabling HTTP-GET disables the autogenerated test page. Although not a big deal during development, removing the protocols you don't use is an important step before a Web service goes into production.

SOAP Message Formatting

WSDL defines two styles for how a Web service method can be formatted in a SOAP message: document and RPC. Document formatting is designed for XML document-based messaging. It doesn't have, for example, the notion of method parameter ordering. RPC formatting states that all parameters are encapsulated within a single XML element named after the XML Web service method and that each XML element within that XML element represents a parameter named after the parameter it is representing. More information about RPC formatting can be found in Section 7 of the SOAP specifications (*www.w3.org/TR/SOAP/#_Toc478383532*).

By default, ASP.NET Web services use `document` formatting. However, it is possible to specify RPC formatting on a Web service method. This is done using the attribute `SoapRpcMethodAttribute` (namespace `System .Web.Services.Protocols`), as illustrated in the following code excerpt:

```
// Project Calculator/Calculator.asmx

[SoapRpcMethod]
[WebMethod]
public int Multiply(int a, int b, out int c) {
    c = a * b;
    return c;
}
```

There are many properties that can be set on `SoapRpcMethodAt-tribute`. For example, the `OneWay` property can be set to true, in which case the client call does not have to wait for the Web server to finish processing the message. Check the SDK documentation for `OneWay` as well as all other properties available on the attribute.

Tracing ASP.NET Web Services

A discussion on ASP.NET Web services will not be complete without talking about how to trace the Web services.

ASP.NET provides a class `TraceContext` that makes it easy to add trace statements to your applications, and to capture and view them while the application is executing. The class implements two methods, `Write` and `Warn`, that you can use for adding traces to your application.

The `TraceContext` object is available as a property `Trace` on the current HTTP context. That is, the object can be accessed as `HttpContext .Current.Trace` anywhere from the ASP.NET application or as `Context`

`.Trace` in case of `WebService` methods, as illustrated in the following code excerpt:

```
// Project Calculator. File Calculator.asmx

[WebService(Namespace="http://localhost/WSRemoting/")]
public class MyCalculator : WebService {

    // Simple Web Service Demo
    [WebMethod]
    public int Add(int a, int b) {
        Context.Trace.Write("Add called");
        return (a+b);
    }
}
```

Just adding the trace statements to your code is not enough; tracing has to be enabled in order to be able to view the traces. You can enable application-level tracing by adding a `<trace>` element to your `Web.config` file, as illustrated below:

```
<configuration>
  <system.web>
    <trace enabled="true" requestLimit="40" />
  </system.web>
</configuration>
```

When application-level tracing is enabled, ASP.NET writes the output details to an application-wide trace viewer application called `Trace.axd`. `Trace.axd` is an HTTP handler that you can use to watch a bunch of requests. The number of requests to be saved can be configured with an optional `requestLimit` attribute in your `Web.config` file. The default value (and the minimum) is ten. Once the number of requests reaches `request-Limit`, tracing is automatically disabled.

To view the traces, issue the URL `http://<Machine>/<AppRoot>/Trace.axd` from Internet Explorer, where `<Machine>` is the machine on which your ASP.NET application is running and `<AppRoot>` is the name of the IIS virtual directory of your application. And don't worry that the trace viewer (`Trace.axd`) does not physically exist as a file in the root directory of your application.

The trace viewer lets you view your executed trace statements. It also lets you get detailed information on a specific trace.

Note that the trace viewer does not update the view automatically. You will need to hit the refresh button (F5) from your browser to get an up-to-date view.

This concludes our discussion on developing and using ASP.NET Web services. In Chapter 8, we will look at how to invoke Web services asynchronously. In Chapter 9, we will look at how to secure your ASP.NET Web services. In Chapter 10, we will see how Web services can participate in a transaction. If you wish to experiment with Web services, I suggest that you use the Web Services Wizard that comes with Visual Studio .NET. Besides generating the Web services template, it also creates the necessary configuration (`web.config`) and discovery (`.disco`) files. For a good article on getting started with Web services using Visual Studio .NET, check out [MS-02].

REMOTING INTERNALS

In this section, we look at the internals of remoting. You can skip this section and revisit it later if you wish to.

Recall from the earlier section that when an object is passed from the original context or AppDomain to the client's context or AppDomain, the runtime transparently creates a proxy object in the client's context and returns to the client a reference to the proxy. When the client makes method calls on the proxy, the runtime takes care of packaging the data as a message and sending it over the transport channel to the server.

For the sake of our discussion in this section, an object refers to either a context-bound object or a context-agile object that will be remoted to a different AppDomain. Such an object always requires marshaling.

The overall structure of how the message flows from the client to the server is shown in Figure 6.9.

Don't get daunted by the complexity of Figure 6.9. By the time you are done with this section, you won't have any problems drawing this figure out and impressing your officemates.

As messages form the basis of the flow, let's examine them first.

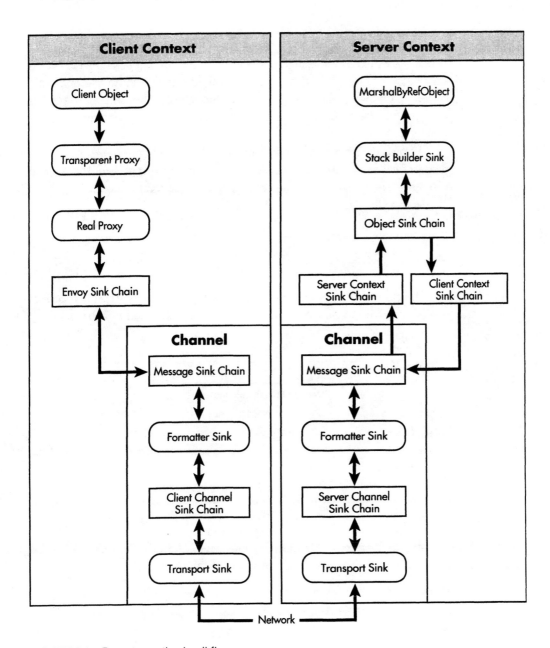

FIGURE 6.9 Remote method call flow.

Messages

When a method call is made on the proxy, the runtime packages the necessary data such as name of the method, method arguments, and so on, into a message. On return, the runtime packages the return values into a message. A message is simply composed of properties, each of which is uniquely identified by a name.

A message is represented by a standard interface, IMessage. This interface is further classified as IMethodCallMessage (to represent the method call) and IMethodReturnMessage (to represent the return value).

Here is the definition of interface IMessage:

```
interface IMessage {
    IDictionary Properties {get; }
}
```

The property Properties returns a dictionary that represents a collection of properties. Some basic message properties are listed in Table 6.1.

TABLE 6.1   Basic Message Properties

Name	Description
__MethodName	Name of the remote method being called
__MethodSignature	Parameter types and return value type of the method
__TypeName	Complete type name of the remote object
__Args	Actual arguments being passed to the method
__CallContext	The logical call context of the method
__Return	Holds the return value of the method

Project Utilities on the companion Web site defines a method MyRemoteUtils.DumpMessage that you may find useful. This method can be used to dump the contents of a message to the console.

Message Sinks

One of the goals of the .NET remoting architecture was to provide an extensible mechanism so that developers can intercept various stages of the message pipeline and monitor or massage the message according to their needs. This interception capability is provided in the form of an interface IMessageSink. You create your message sink class that implements IMessageSink and insert it into the pipeline. More than one message sink can be inserted into the pipeline as a singly linked chain.

Here is the definition of the IMessageSink interface:

```
interface IMessageSink {
    public IMessageSink NextSink {get; }
    public IMessage SyncProcessMessage(IMessage msg);
    public IMessageCtrl AsyncProcessMessage(
        IMessage msg, IMessageSink replySink);
}
```

The NextSink method returns the handle to the next sink in the chain. A typical implementation of a message sink stores this handle as a member field.

When a synchronous method call is made on the proxy, the runtime calls SyncProcessMessage on the first message sink in the chain. This gives the sink a chance to inspect or modify the message. A typical implementation would eventually forward the message to the next sink in the chain. However, a sink may choose to manufacture a return value and short-circuit the method call.

When an asynchronous method call is made on the proxy, the runtime calls AsyncProcessMessage on the first message sink in the chain. Parameter replySink is used to post the reply of the message. The return value, IMessageCtrl, provides a way to cancel the asynchronous call that is in progress. A typical implementation just forwards the incoming message to the next sink in the chain.

Here is a vanilla implementation of IMessageSink. The only extra functionality this code provides is to display the synchronous method call message and the return value to the console:

```
// File Utilities\MyUtils.cs

[Serializable]
public class MyMessageSink : IMessageSink {
    private IMessageSink m_nextSink;

    public MyMessageSink(IMessageSink nextSink) {
        m_nextSink = nextSink;
    }

    public IMessageSink NextSink { get { return m_nextSink; } }

    public IMessage SyncProcessMessage(IMessage msg) {
        MyRemoteUtils.DumpMessage(msg);
        IMessage retmsg = m_nextSink.SyncProcessMessage(msg);
        MyRemoteUtils.DumpMessage(retmsg);
```

```
        return retmsg;
    }

    public IMessageCtrl AsyncProcessMessage(
        IMessage msg, IMessageSink replySink) {
        return m_nextSink.AsyncProcessMessage(msg, replySink);
    }
}
```

Note the [Serializable] attribute on the message sink. This ensures that the sink runs in the context it is intended for, even if it initially gets created in a different context.

Always Use [Serializable] on Message Sinks

Without this attribute on the message sink, the sink methods may execute in the wrong context.

As we go through the rest of this section, we will discover the stages in the pipeline where an IMessageSink-based sink can be used.

Contexts

A .NET object lives in a context, which stores objects that have context attributes compatible with it.

A context is represented by a class Context. Here are some useful methods available in this class:

```
public class Context {
    public virtual int ContextID {get;}
    public virtual IContextProperty[] ContextProperties {get;}
    public virtual IContextProperty GetProperty(string name);
    ...
}
```

The property ContextID returns an identifier for the context that is unique within the context's AppDomain.

A context stores one or more properties. A context property is represented by an interface, IContextProperty, and is uniquely identified by a name within the context. A context property can be accessed by its unique name by calling GetProperty on the context. All the context properties can be obtained by calling ContextProperties.

A context also stores zero or more message sinks. In this case, the message sinks are referred to as the context sinks.

When a context-bound class is instantiated, the runtime queries each of its context attributes for compatibility with the current context. If any of the attributes are not compatible, the runtime creates a compatible context and houses the object in the new context.

Context Attributes

Context attributes serve three purposes:

1. They inform the runtime if a context-bound object is compatible with the specified context.

2. They contribute properties to the new context. These properties can be programmatically accessed at runtime from within a type's methods.

3. They contribute zero or more message sinks.

A context attribute is defined by a class that inherits from the class `System.Attribute` and implements an interface `IContextAttribute` (namespace `System.Runtime.Remoting.Contexts`).

Let's develop a simple context attribute that contributes the name of the developer as a context property. Here is an example of its usage:

```
[Developer("Jay")]
public class Foo : ContextBoundObject {
    . . .
}
```

The .NET Framework provides a class, `ContextAttribute`, that simplifies developing context attributes. The following code excerpt shows an implementation that inherits from this class:

```
// Project ContextProperties/DeveloperAttribute

[AttributeUsage(AttributeTargets.Class)]
public class DeveloperAttribute : ContextAttribute {
    private String m_Name;
    public DeveloperAttribute(String name):base("MyDevAttr") {
      m_Name = name;
    }
```

```
public override void GetPropertiesForNewContext(
    IConstructionCallMessage ctor) {
  DeveloperProperty dev = new DeveloperProperty(m_Name);
  ctor.ContextProperties.Add(dev);
}

public override bool IsContextOK(Context ctx,
    IConstructionCallMessage ctorMsg) {
  DeveloperProperty prop =
    ctx.GetProperty(DeveloperProperty.KEY) as
      DeveloperProperty;
  if (null == prop) {
    return false;
  }
  bool contextOK = (this.m_Name == prop.Developer);
  return contextOK;
}
}
```

Here is what happens when an instance of class Foo is instantiated. The runtime instantiates DeveloperAttribute and calls IsContextOK to check if the caller's context is compatible with the attribute. If the method returns false, the runtime obtains the context property by calling GetProperties-ForNewContext, creates a new context, and places the property into the new context.

The logic in IsContextOK ensures that no two developers can share the same context. Don't try this at work. Creating a context for each developer may not be a good idea for real applications.

Note that the context attribute object can add as many properties as desired by calling ContextProperties.Add repeatedly.

The context attribute object is not needed again until a new context-bound object is instantiated.

Let's now examine our context property class, DeveloperProperty.

Context Properties

A context property is defined by a class that implements IContextProp-erty. Here is its definition and description:

```
interface IContextProperty {
        // The runtime uses the property name to
        // uniquely identify the property
        public String Name { get; }

        // The runtime creates a new context and calls this
        // method to check if the new context is compatible
```

```
    public bool IsNewContextOK(Context ctx);
    // The runtime calls this to indicate that no more
    // properties can be added to the context
    public void Freeze(Context ctx);
}
```

Here is some of the relevant code from our implementation:

```
// Project ContextProperties/DeveloperAttribute

[Serializable]
public class DeveloperProperty : IContextProperty {
    public static readonly String KEY = "Developer";
    private String m_Name; // Store the developer's name

    public String Name {
        get {return KEY;} // return the identifier
    }

    public String Developer {
        get {return m_Name; }
    }

    public bool IsNewContextOK(Context ctx){
        // We will force a new context for each developer.
        DeveloperProperty prop =
            ctx.GetProperty(KEY) as DeveloperProperty;
        if (null == prop) {
            return false;
        }
        bool contextOK = (Developer == prop.Developer);
        return contextOK;
    }
    ...
}
```

The code is self-explanatory. Just note that a property class must be marked as [Serializable]. The importance of this will become evident when we discuss context sinks.

We are finished creating the context attribute and the context property. It is now time for us to apply it on a class. The following code demonstrates how to apply DeveloperAttribute on a context-bound object and how the name of the developer can be obtained within the context during runtime.

```
// Project ContextProperties/Foo

[Developer("Pradeep")]
public class Foo : ContextBoundObject {

    public int Add(int x, int y) {
      DeveloperProperty prop =
      Thread.CurrentContext.GetProperty(DeveloperProperty.KEY)
        as DeveloperProperty;
      throw new Exception("Contact " + prop.Developer);
      return (x+y);
    }
}
```

Straightforward, isn't it?

It is interesting to note that if you apply more than one Developer attribute on the same class, the runtime picks just one attribute and simply ignores the rest.

Context Sinks

Context sinks provide an interception point in the communication. They allow you to hook the messages as they enter and leave contexts. There are four kinds of context sinks, each of which serves a different purpose. A *server context sink* is used to install a context-wide interceptor for calls entering the server context. This sink is represented by the interface IContributeServerContextSink. A *client context sink* is used to install a context-wide interceptor for calls leaving the server context. This sink is represented by the interface IContributeClientContextSink. An *object sink* is used to install a per-object interceptor in the server context. This sink is represented by the interface IContributeObjectSink. An *envoy sink* is used to install a per-object interceptor in the client context. This sink is represented by the interface IContributeEnvoySink.

Note that the envoy sink is the only one that is installed in the client context. All others are meant to be installed in the server context.

From an implementation perspective, all the context sink interfaces are similar. All of these interfaces have just one method of the following type:

```
IMessageSink GetXxxSink(IMessageSink nextSink);
```

The method name is different for each interface. For example, IContributeEnvoySink has the method GetEnvoySink. However, all of them essentially return a message sink when queried for.

A context sink interface is implemented on the context property object. Recall that the runtime obtains one or more context property objects from the context attribute by calling `GetPropertiesForNewContext`. Later, when the first out-of-context call comes in, the runtime checks if the context property object supports any of the context sink interfaces. For each interface that is found, the runtime calls an appropriate `GetXxxSink` method on the context property object, obtains the message sink, and inserts it in the appropriate sink chain.

Here is a code excerpt that defines an envoy sink on a context property. The complete source can be found on the companion Web site.

```
// Project EnvoySink/MyTraceSink

[Serializable]
public class MyTraceProperty :
    IContextProperty, IContributeEnvoySink
{
    ...
    public IMessageSink GetEnvoySink(
      MarshalByRefObject mbro, IMessageSink nextSink)
    {
      return new MyMessageSink(nextSink);
    }
}
```

The first parameter to `GetEnvoySink` represents the object for which the interceptor is being installed.

Note that the runtime mandates that a context property be marked as `[Serializable]`. Without this, the remoting layer throws a `SerializationException`.

Call Contexts

While we are on the subject of contexts, .NET provides another type of context that you should be aware of, the *call context*. The call context represents the logical thread of the execution code path. Objects can be added to the call context as it travels down and back up the execution code path, and examined by various objects along the path. This makes it possible for either the developers or the runtime to pass extra information about a specific execution code path.

The call context is encapsulated in the `CallContext` class (namespace `System.Runtime.Remoting.Messaging`). All the methods in this class are static and operate on the call context of the current thread. The static method `SetData` can be used to store an object in a named data slot, whereas the static method `GetData` can be used to retrieve an object by the name of the data slot. Another static method, `FreeNamedDataSlot`, can be used to empty a named data slot.

It is interesting to note that although any object can be stored in the call context, only those objects that implement a standard interface `ILogicalThreadAffinative` can propagate to a different AppDomain. Internally, when a call is made on an object from a different AppDomain, the runtime generates an instance of the class `LogicalCallContext` and sends it along with the remote call. Objects that do not support `ILogicalThreadAffinative` are not transmitted in `LogicalCallContext`.

The SDK includes a sample that shows how extra information can be passed in the call context.

Transparent and Real Proxies

There are two proxy objects in the remoting infrastructure that work together to make calls from a client to a remote server. The proxy object that the client object deals with is actually an instance of a runtime class called `TransparentProxy`. The majority of the work is done by a helper object of type `RealProxy`. When the client makes a method call, the `TransparentProxy` checks the call against its type information, bundles the call parameters into a message object, and hands it over to the `RealProxy` object. The `RealProxy` object is then responsible for forwarding the message across the configured channel.

For every `TransparentProxy` object, there is a corresponding `RealProxy` object. You can obtain the `RealProxy` object from the `TransparentProxy` object by calling a static method, `RemotingServices.GetRealProxy`. Likewise, you can obtain the `TransparentProxy` from the `RealProxy` by calling the method `GetTransparentProxy` on it.

Casting a Transparent Proxy

Consider the following line of code:

```
Foo f = (Foo) Activator.GetObject(…);
```

You know that `Activator.GetObject` eventually returns a `TransparentProxy` object to the caller. Here is what happens when you cast the `TransparentProxy` object to the type `Foo`.

A `RealProxy` object implements a standard interface, `IRemotingTypeInfo`. When the caller casts the `TransparentProxy` object to a specific type, the `TransparentProxy` object calls the `IRemotingTypeInfo.CanCastTo` method on the RealProxy object to check if the cast is supported. If the method returns true, the cast is accepted.

You can implement CanCastTo on your own RealProxy derived class and support casting the TransparentProxy object to any other unrelated type. The SDK includes an example that demonstrates this.

In general, the proxy object pair is created when:

1. A client activates an MBR object that is not compatible with the current AppDomain or context.

2. An MBR object is passed as a method parameter or a return value from one context to another.

Object References

When an MBR object is passed from its context or AppDomain to another context or AppDomain, the runtime needs to transfer the whereabouts of the MBR object to the other context so that remote method calls can be made on the MBR object. The runtime packages the whereabouts of the MBR object in an object of type ObjRef. The ObjRef contains the information that describes the type of the object being marshaled, the URI of the specific object, and information on how to reach the application domain or context where the object lives, such as channel information, and so on.

When the MBR object is marshaled, the runtime creates an ObjRef object representing the MBR object, serializes the ObjRef object, and transfers it to the remote AppDomain, possibly in another process or computer. In the target domain, the information is deserialized and an ObjRef is created. The runtime then proceeds to create a RealProxy object, passing in ObjRef as a parameter. The RealProxy object then creates a TransparentProxy object and returns it to the client.

Things are slightly different for a server-activated object. Although the proxy pair gets created when Activator.GetObject is called, the remote object, and hence its ObjRef, are not created until a method call is made on the object. On the first method call, the remote object is created, its ObjRef is obtained, and it is passed back to the RealProxy in the client's AppDomain.

Custom Proxies

The remoting architecture had a purpose in separating the proxy into a TransparentProxy object and a RealProxy object. Whereas the TransparentProxy is an internal class that cannot be extended, the RealProxy class can be extended. This is useful for many purposes:

1. To trace the method calls being made on the proxy object.
2. To perhaps handle some method calls locally, thus saving network round trips.
3. To support casting a transparent proxy to another type.
4. To perform load balancing (depending on the load on the servers, routing the call to an appropriate server).

The SDK includes a few samples that show how to extend the `Real-Proxy` class to create your own custom proxy. I have also included a sample (Project `CustomProxy`) on the companion Web site that demonstrates how a custom proxy can be associated with a given context-bound type such that instantiating the type automatically creates the custom proxy for the type. For those interested, this is achieved by means of extending an attribute called `ProxyAttribute`. This sample is based on a sample posted on *www.gotdot-net.com*, which, by the way, is a good source of developer information on .NET technology.

Channels

Channels are objects responsible for transporting messages across remoting boundaries. When a method call is made, the client channel is responsible for serializing the message object (using a formatter) into a stream and transporting it. The server channel is responsible for receiving the stream data and transforming it back to a message object that can then be forwarded to the context sink. On return, the process is reversed. The server channel serializes the data (using a formatter) and sends it back to the client channel, where it is transformed back to a message object.

Some commonly used channel classes in .NET are `TcpChannel` and `HttpChannel`.

Channels must expose the `IChannel` interface. Client channels must expose `IChannelSender`, a derivation of `IChannel`. Server channels must expose `IChannelReceiver`, another derivation of `IChannel`. The `TcpChannel` and `HttpChannel` classes implement both these interfaces so that they can be used to send and receive information.

Channels can be registered in two ways, either by calling the familiar `ChannelServices.RegisterChannel` method or by loading them from the remoting configuration file.

Information in the remoting configuration file can be specified in two ways. You can either declare a channel template, and then reference this channel in your application, or specify all channel information directly in your application. Channel settings must be defined under the `configura-tion\system.runtime.remoting\channels` path.

The global configuration file `Machine.Config` defines some templates, such as `tcp` and `http`, that should be sufficient for most applications. Within your application file, you can refer to these templates using the `ref` attribute and adding any additional information such as the port number, and so on. An example is shown next. Here, the channel template referred to is `tcp` and additional information is the port number 8085:

```
<configuration>
    <system.runtime.remoting>
      <application name="MyRemotingHost">
        <channels>
          <channel port="8085" ref="tcp" />
        </channels>
      </application>
    </system.runtime.remoting>
</configuration>
```

A channel is uniquely identified by a name within the AppDomain in which it is registered. The default name for `TcpChannel` is `tcp` and for `HttpChannel` is `http`. If you wish to register more than one instance of the same type of channel, you need to provide a different name for the channel during registration. Both classes take an overloaded constructor that takes a parameter of type `IDictionary`. You can create a dictionary object, set the name, port, and any other information (e.g., proxy server to use for HTTP requests) and pass this object to the constructor. This is illustrated in the following code excerpt:

```
// Project Channels/MultipleChannels

public static void Main() {
    IDictionary prop = new Hashtable();
    prop["name"] = "MySecondChannel";
    prop["port"] = "8087";
    HttpChannel channel2 = new HttpChannel(prop, null, null);
    ChannelServices.RegisterChannel(channel2);

    ...

}
```

The project also shows how to enumerate through the registered channels in an application.

Formatter Sinks

Formatter sinks serialize the message object into a message stream and vice versa. Some standard formatter sinks are `BinaryClientFormatterSink` and `SoapClientFormatterSink` on the client side and `BinaryServerFormatterSink` and `SoapServerFormatterSink` on the client side. The binary formatter sinks internally use `BinaryFormatter` and the SOAP formatter sinks internally use `SoapFormatter`.

A client formatter sink is typically the first sink in the client channel, although, as we will see shortly, it is possible to insert additional message sinks before the formatter sink. Likewise, a server formatter sink is typically the first sink in the server channel.

The function of a formatter is to generate the necessary headers and serialize the message object to the stream. After the formatter, the message object is still forwarded to each of the sinks in the sink chain. However, as the message has already been serialized, changing the message does not change the information in the stream.

By default, the TCP channel is set to use the binary formatter and the HTTP channel is set to use the SOAP formatter. However, you can change this behavior for your application by associating a formatter with a specific channel. The simplest way to do this is to reference the formatter templates that are defined in `Machine.Config`. The following configuration, for example, associates a binary formatter with the HTTP channel:

```
<application name="MyRemotingHost">
  <channels>
    <channel ref="http" port="8090" name="MyBinaryHttp">
      <clientProviders>
        <formatter ref="binary" />
      </clientProviders>
      <serverProviders>
        <formatter ref="binary" />
      </serverProviders>
    </channel>
  </channels>
</application>
```

A formatter can also be associated with a channel programmatically at runtime. The overloaded constructors for `TcpChannel` and `HttpChannel` take additional parameters just for this purpose.

Although the standard formatter sinks provided should suffice for most applications, it is also possible to provide your own formatter sink. Look into the SDK documentation for IClientFormatterSinkProvider and IServerFormatterSinkProvider.

Channel Sinks

After transforming the message object to the message stream, the formatter forwards the message object and the stream object to the first channel sink in the channel.

A channel has at least one channel sink, the transport sink. The transport sink is the last sink in the client sink chain and the first sink in the server sink chain. These sinks are built into the channel and cannot be extended.

It is possible to create one or more custom channel sinks and insert them into the channel sink chain, which is useful if you wish to inspect or modify the message stream.

To create a client channel sink, you need to implement the interface IClientChannelSink; to create a server channel sink, you need to implement IServerChannelSink.

In addition to implementing a channel sink, you also need to implement a provider for the channel sink. When creating the sink chain, the runtime queries each channel sink provider to obtain the respective channel sink object.

A client channel sink provider implements IClientChannelSinkProvider and a server channel sink provider implements IServerSinkProvider.

Let's create a client channel sink provider. However, we will not create a full-fledged client channel sink. The system provides a way to create a message sink as a client channel sink. This message sink can then be placed before the formatter sink in the channel.

Here is the partial code for the client channel sink provider. The complete source can be found on the companion Web site:

```
// Project MessageSink/MyMessageSink

public class MyClientSinkProvider: IClientChannelSinkProvider {
    private IClientChannelSinkProvider
      m_nextChnlSinkProvider = null;

    public MyClientSinkProvider () { }

    public MyClientSinkProvider(
      IDictionary properties, ICollection providerData) { }

    public IClientChannelSink CreateSink(
      IChannelSender channel,
      string url, object remoteChannelData) {
      return new MyMsgSink(
```

```
        m_nextChnlSinkProvider.CreateSink(
          channel,url,remoteChannelData));
    }

    public IClientChannelSinkProvider Next {
       get { return m_nextChnlSinkProvider; }
       set { m_nextChnlSinkProvider = value; }
    }
}
```

The channel sink providers themselves form a chain. The runtime sets the Next property on each provider to define the next provider.

The runtime then calls CreateSink on the first provider in the chain, passing in some channel-specific information. This method is responsible for creating its sink as well as the next sink, and chaining them together. The method then returns its sink.

Here is a code excerpt for MyMsgSink:

```
// Project MessageSink/MyMessageSink

public class MyMsgSink :
        BaseChannelObjectWithProperties,
        IMessageSink, IClientChannelSink
{
    private IMessageSink m_nextMsgSink = null;
    private IClientChannelSink m_nextChnlSink = null;

    public MyMsgSink(object nextSink) {
       m_nextMsgSink = nextSink as IMessageSink;
       m_nextChnlSink = nextSink as IClientChannelSink;
    }

    // IMessageSink methods (already familiar)
    public IMessage SyncProcessMessage (...) {...}
    public IMessageCtrl AsyncProcessMessage(...) {...}
    public IMessageSink NextSink { get {...} }

    // IClientChannelSink Methods
    public IClientChannelSink NextChannelSink {
       get { return m_nextChnlSink; }
    }

    // These methods just throw an exception
    public void AsyncProcessRequest(...) {...}
    public void AsyncProcessResponse(...) {...}
    public Stream GetRequestStream(...) {...}
    public void ProcessMessage(...) {...}
}
```

Our client channel sink implements `IClientChannelSink` and `IMes-sageSink`. Of course, any of the `IClientChannelSink` methods are not to be used, so their implementation simply throws an exception.

`MyMsgSink` is derived from `BaseChannelObjectWithProperties`. This standard class provides a base implementation of a channel object.

Now the only thing left to do is to place the provider information in the application configuration file. This is done using the `<provider>` tag, as shown here:

```
<channels>
  <channel ref="http">
    <clientProviders>
      <provider type="MyClientSinkProvider, MyMessageSink" />
      <formatter ref="soap" />
    </clientProviders>
  </channel>
</channels>
```

To make a client channel sink act as a message sink, the key is to place the provider information before the formatter information.

Intraprocess Communication

Have you been wondering what channel is used for cross-context or cross-App-Domain communication within the same process? Clearly, using a TCP channel or an HTTP channel in this scenario may be overkill.

Your guess is right. For intraprocess communication, the runtime uses a combination of the private classes `CrossContextChannel` or `CrossAppDomainChannel`, as appropriate. Both classes can be found in `MSCorLib.dll` under the namespace `System.Runtime.Remoting.Channels`.

The Complete Picture

In this section, we covered a number of advanced topics. Let's put all them together and see if Figure 6.9 makes sense now.

When an MBR object is marshaled from its AppDomain or context to another AppDomain or context:

1. The runtime creates a `RealProxy` object corresponding to the MBR object.

2. The `RealProxy` object in turn creates a `TransparentProxy` object.

3. The `TransparentProxy` object returns it to the caller.

When a client makes a synchronous method call on the proxy, the `TransparentProxy` object reads the parameters from the stack, builds an `IMessage` object, and hands it over to the `RealProxy` object.

The `RealProxy` object forwards the message to the first context envoy sink in the envoy sink chain. The envoy sink in turn forwards it to the next envoy sink in the chain. The last sink in the chain forwards the message to the message sink chain in the channel.

The last sink in the message sink chain is the formatter sink. This sink converts the message object to a message stream and forwards it to the first item in the client channel sink chain. The original message object is also passed along, but at this point it can only be inspected.

The last sink in the client channel sink is the transport sink. This sink takes the message stream, adds the necessary headers, and then writes this stream out to the wire.

On the server side, the server transport sink reads requests off the wire and passes the request stream to the server channel sink chain. The server formatter sink at the end of this chain deserializes the request into a message object and forwards it to the server context sinks.

The last sink in the complete chain is the stack builder sink. This sink takes the message object, recreates the stack, and invokes the actual method on the MBR object.

On return, the return value is converted to a message object and then to a message stream in the server channel and is sent to the client channel. The client channel reconstructs the message stream and forwards it to the client channel sink. Eventually, the return value comes back to the client object.

A similar, more complex, process takes place for asynchronous method calls. The extra complexity arises from the fact that a sink has to keep track of the response message.

At this point, it is worth mentioning an optimization technique that the .NET remoting architecture provides. If a method is not expected to return any value to the caller, it can be attributed with `OneWayAttribute` (namespace `System.Runtime.Remoting.Messaging`), as illustrated here:

```
// Project OneWayMethod/Demo

public class Foo : MarshalByRefObject {

    [OneWay]
    public void DoSomething() {
        ...
    }
}
```

When a method is marked as one way, the client channel does not have to wait for a response from the server. Therefore, when a client makes a call on a one-way method, the call returns immediately to the caller. The server, however, continues to execute the call.

Ideally, a method marked with `OneWayAttribute` must have a `void` return value and must take only `[in]` type method parameters. However, the .NET remoting mechanism lets you annotate any method with this attribute. This includes methods that have a non-`void` return value or `[out]` type parameters. The server-side `StackBuilder` simply discards the return values. If the executing method throws any exception, this too is caught by the `StackBuilder` and simply discarded.

SUMMARY

Application domains provide isolation between different applications running on the same system.

A context provides a runtime environment for compatible objects to live in. It contains one or more context properties and context sinks. Context properties provide passive services. Context sinks provide active interception-based services.

When an object is activated, the runtime houses the object in the caller's context if the context attributes on the object are compatible with the caller's context. If not, the runtime creates a compatible context and houses the object in the new context.

An application domain holds one or more contexts. When an application domain is created, the runtime creates a default context within the AppDomain. Subsequently, more contexts may be created within the domain as more objects are created.

When a remote object is created or an object is passed to another domain as a method parameter, the runtime transforms the object into a block of memory suitable for transmitting to the other context. This process is referred to as marshaling. Subsequently, the importing domain can unmarshal the block of data and create a new object that has similar characteristics to the original object.

Under .NET, objects are classified as MBV objects, MBR objects, and nonremotable objects. When an MBV object is moved to a different domain, an exact copy of the object is made in the target domain. When an MBR object is moved to a target domain, the runtime creates a proxy object in the target domain and returns it to client. Any call on the proxy object is intercepted by the runtime and is forwarded to the original object in the remote domain. These objects cannot leave their domain.

MBR objects are further classified as context-bound objects or context-agile objects. Context-bound objects are bound to a context and require proxy marshaling if moved to a different context, even if the context is in the same AppDomain. A context-agile object does not require any marshaling within the AppDomain but needs to be marshaled when moved to a different AppDomain.

A remote object can be created as a server-activated object or a client-activated object. Server-activated objects are those objects with a lifetime that is directly controlled by the server. The lifetime of a client-activated object is controlled by the client. Server-activated objects are usually identified by a name, so they are also called well-known objects.

Server-activated objects can be published in two modes, single-call or singleton. A single-call object mode implies that the remote object be created on each method call and torn down after the call returns. A singleton object mode implies that the remote object be created just once on the first method call and be reused on subsequent method calls.

.NET uses a lease-based technique to manage the lifetime of MBR objects. An MBR object, either client-activated or singleton, can be associated with a lifetime lease. When the lease expires, the object is destroyed (garbage collected). However, .NET provides various ways to extend the lease.

It is possible to store the object activation information in external configuration files. This provides flexibility to the administrator in configuring an application. The configuration files can be created on the server side and the client side.

.NET remoting applications can also be hosted under ASP.NET. However, this requires a client to be on the .NET platform. True platform independence can be achieved by creating Web services. ASP.NET makes it easy to develop and test Web services. The .NET platform also makes it convenient for clients to consume the Web services.

The .NET remoting framework provides full managed code type–system fidelity over the network. The mechanism is open to use TCP, HTTP, or any other proprietary channel. The message can be formatted in binary, SOAP, or using a custom formatter. In addition, different types of sinks can be added at various stages in the remoting pipeline.

REFERENCES

[MS-02]   Microsoft Visual Studio Team, "Getting Started with XML Web Services in Visual Studio .NET," MSDN Library, February 2002.
msdn.microsoft.com/library/en-us/dv_vbvcstechart/html/vbtchGettingStartedWithXML-WebServicesInVisualStudioNET.asp

CHAPTER 7

Interoperability

$\mathbf{T}$he .NET Framework provides support for managed code to interoperate with unmanaged code. The unmanaged code could either be COM-based or be in native DLLs. The .NET Framework has been designed to provide smooth interoperability. In this chapter, we examine the support for interoperability provided by the .NET Framework. By the end of the chapter, readers will be comfortable making calls from managed code into unmanaged code and vice versa.

INTRODUCTION

.NET provides a number of features, such as garbage collection and managed memory, that make programming easier and safer than before. However, there are millions of lines of existing code that are here to stay for a considerable time. One of the goals of the .NET Framework designers was to provide smooth interoperability between managed and unmanaged code.

Let's refresh our understanding of managed and unmanaged code. Managed code is the code that is written according to the specifications of the common language runtime (e.g., providing metadata). Managed code can take advantage of the services provided by the common language runtime such as garbage collection and enhanced security. Unmanaged code on the other hand is any code that does not target the common language runtime and hence cannot take advantage of the services offered by runtime. Existing COM components, native DLLs, and so on, fall under the unmanaged code category.

The common language runtime supports:

- Managed code making calls into native DLLs.
- Managed code making calls into COM components.
- Wrapping .NET code as COM components so that unmanaged code can deal with them.

To support marshaling across native DLLs as well as COM components, the .NET Framework defines a collection of classes under the namespace `System.Runtime.InteropServices`. Some examples of these classes are `Marshal`, `DllImportAttribute`, and `MarshalAsAttribute`. Later in the chapter, we will see how these classes, and many others, let us define and control the marshaling behavior. Unless otherwise explicitly mentioned, any class related to interoperability that we discuss in this chapter can be assumed to belong to the `System.Runtime.InteropServices` namespace.

At this point it is worth mentioning that the primary purpose of .NET's support for interoperability is to deal with existing Windows-based code. Keep in mind that .NET assemblies making calls to the unmanaged code may not be portable to other platforms.

Finally, it is worth mentioning that Microsoft has added extensions (called Managed Extensions) to Visual C++ language to support mixing managed and unmanaged code freely. Obviously, the unmanaged code will not be able to take advantage of the services provided by the common language runtime. However, Managed Extensions do provide the ability for you to port your existing code incrementally, without incurring the cost of porting the whole application at once. You can maintain your existing code base as unmanaged but still write newer code as managed code to take advantage of the new features of the .NET Framework. As a matter of fact, you can simply compile your existing C++ code with the `-clr` compiler switch to produce an output that is compatible with the common language runtime (what Microsoft calls "It Just Works."). Covering Managed C++ is beyond the scope of this book. Two good references on Managed Extensions to C++ are [Sel-01] and [Ras-01].

MANAGED CODE TO NATIVE DLLS

The common language runtime provides a service that enables managed code to call unmanaged functions implemented in DLLs. This service is known as *platform invoke,* or *PInvoke* for short.

To understand how PInvoke works, let's start with making a call to `MessageBox`, a Win32 API that is implemented in `user32.dll`. Making calls to Win32 APIs is the most likely scenario you will run into. In the first version of the .NET runtime, many of the Win32 features have not been provided in the .NET Framework Class Libraries, requiring you to obtain the desired feature by invoking the Win32 API from your managed code.

Note that the .NET Framework already defines a `MessageBox` class under `System.Windows.Forms` namespace. You would never need to call the Win32 `MessageBox` API, but it provides a good example of how PInvoke works.

A Simple Example

Here is the Win32 API prototype for `MessageBox`:

```
int WINAPI MessageBox(HWND hWnd, LPCTSTR lpText,
    LPCTSTR lpCaption, UINT uType);
```

Here is a C# example that invokes `MessageBox`:

```
// Project PInvoke/SimplePInvoke

using System;
using System.Runtime.InteropServices;

class MyApp {
    [DllImport("user32.dll")]
    public static extern intMessageBox(System.IntPtr h,
      string m, string c, uint type);

    public static void Main() {
      int retval =
        MessageBox((IntPtr) 0, "Hi!", "Greetings!", 0);
    }
}
```

As shown in the code, there are three things that are needed to set up a function for PInvoke:

1. The DLL function that needs to be invoked must be marked as `public static extern`.
2. The DLL to which the function belongs to should be indicated with the attribute `DllImportAttribute`.
3. The parameters and return value should be matched with their C# equivalents. This way, the runtime knows how to marshal data to and from the function. Some basic Win32 datatypes and their C# equivalents are shown in Table 7.1.

TABLE 7.1   PInvoke Datatypes

Win32	Managed Class	C#
HWND, HANDLE, HMODULE, Any handle	System.IntPtr	System.IntPtr (no real equivalent)
BYTE	System.Byte	byte
SHORT	System.Int16	short
WORD	System.UInt16	uint
INT, LONG	System.Int32	int
UINT, ULONG, DWORD	System.UInt32	uint
BOOL	System.Int32	bool
CHAR	System.Char	char
LPSTR, LPWSTR, LPCSTR, LPCWSTR	System.String or System.StringBuilder	string
FLOAT	System.Single	float
DOUBLE	System.Double	double

By default, the name of the function in the method definition is the same as the name of the function in the DLL. However, the .NET Framework allows you to rename the function within your managed code. This is accomplished by means of the `EntryPoint` attribute field, as shown here:

```
// Project PInvoke/SimplePInvoke

[DllImport("user32.dll", EntryPoint="MessageBox")]
public static extern int MsgBox(System.IntPtr h, string m,
    string c, uint type);

public static void Main() {
    ...
    retval = MsgBox((IntPtr) 0, "Hi!", "Greetings!", 0);
}
```

Developers familiar with the Win32 API will know that there really isn't a `MessageBox` function, but rather two versions, `MessageBoxA` (for ANSI) and `MessageBoxW` (for Unicode). One of the interesting things about PInvoke is that it is aware of such differences. By default, it internally maps the API to the ANSI version. However, you can explicitly specify the character set by means of the `CharSet` attribute, as shown here:

```
// Project PInvoke/SimplePInvoke

[DllImport("user32.dll", EntryPoint="MessageBox",
    CharSet=CharSet.Auto)]
public static extern int SmartMsgBox(System.IntPtr h, string m,
    string c, uint type);

public static void Main() {
    ...
    retval = SmartMsgBox((IntPtr) 0, "Hi!", "Greetings!", 0);
}
```

Character set CharSet.Auto indicates the runtime to pick the appropriate version automatically. For example, on Windows NT, it automatically calls the Unicode version, whereas on Win9x it would call the ANSI version.

Behind the scenes, the runtime marshals the data from the managed side to the unmanaged side so that the data can be understood by the unmanaged code. For example, System.String gets marshaled into null-terminated char or WCHAR arrays (depending on the definition). Once the unmanaged function returns, some marshaling might be required to deal with the return value and the parameters that return data.

The .NET Framework defines a few more attribute fields that can be used to adjust the method definition. Check the SDK documentation for more details.

PInvoke and Performance

The interop marshaler has to perform two extra operations before invoking the actual PInvoke method.

First, the security mechanism under .NET triggers a stack walk to ensure that all the callers have the necessary security permission (referred to as Unmanaged-Code permission) to invoke the unmanaged code. However, this step can be eliminated by applying the attribute SuppressUnmanagedCodeSecurityAttribute either to the PInvoke methods or to the class containing the PInvoke methods. This results in substantial performance savings. Be warned, though, that incorrect use of this attribute can create security weakness. The implementer of the class must ensure that the class is secure.

Second, the marshaler has to create a stack frame that is compatible with the unmanaged code. Microsoft has put much effort into optimizing this step. In the best case scenario, setting up the stack frame and invoking the method takes very few machine language instructions.

With this basic understanding of PInvoke, let's move on to some more interesting scenarios.

String Type as Output

In the previous example, we looked at passing strings as input to an unmanaged function. However, it is also possible to pass in a string-type parameter as a buffer to the unmanaged function and let the unmanaged function fill the buffer. There are many Win32 APIs that fit this bill. Let's see how to invoke one such function.

For our example, we look at a Win32 API, GetTempPath. Here is its Win32 definition:

```
DWORD GetTempPath(
   DWORD nBufferLength,   // size of buffer
   LPTSTR lpBuffer        // path buffer
);
```

The function GetTempPath returns the path for the temporary directory on the local machine. The string value is returned in parameter lpBuffer.

Recall from Chapter 5 that the String class under .NET is invariant. Therefore, for cases where String is used as an output parameter, you cannot use the String class. Instead, you should use the StringBuilder class.

Here is the prototype declaration for GetTempPath in C#:

```
[DllImport("kernel32") ]
public static extern uint GetTempPath(uint size,
    StringBuilder buf);
```

The following code shows how to use this function:

```
// Project PInvoke/StringOutput

public static void Main() {
    const int size = 255;
    StringBuilder path = new StringBuilder(size);
    GetTempPath(size, path);
    Console.WriteLine(path);
}
```

It is important to allocate a proper size to the buffer being passed before calling the unmanaged API, as shown in the preceeding code.

There is one case of string output that requires special attention—when a function returns a pointer into the process' environment or similar kernel data structure. Consider, for example, the Win32 API GetCommandLine:

```
LPTSTR GetCommandLine(VOID);
```

The function GetCommandLine returns a pointer to the command-line string. As it points into the process' environment, the caller must not free the returned string. However, if the return value is declared as string type in the managed code, the PInvoke marshaler assumes that the memory should be freed.

To ensure that the returned pointer does not get freed, the return type must be declared as IntPtr and not string, as shown here:

```
[DllImport("Kernel32", CharSet=CharSet.Auto)]
public static extern IntPtr GetCommandLine();
```

The framework provides a collection of static methods, Marshal.Ptr-ToStringXXX, to obtain a copy of the native string. For example, Mar-shal.PtrToStringAuto automatically detects if the native string is ANSI or Unicode and obtains a copy of it as string. This is illustrated in the following code excerpt:

```
// Project PInvoke/StringOutput

public static void Main() {
    ...
    IntPtr p = GetCommandLine();
    String cmd = Marshal.PtrToStringAuto(p);
    Console.WriteLine(cmd);
}
```

Besides converting pointers to strings, the Marshal class provides a number of useful methods dealing with managed and unmanaged transitions. Check the SDK documentation for more information. We cover some of these methods later in the chapter.

Pointers

We know that .NET uses garbage collection for managing heap memory. Because of the nature of garbage collection, the memory being used by a variable may be relocated during the collection. This is not a problem for managed code. The garbage collector freezes the execution of the code during the collection, effectively preventing the managed heap from being accessed. After the collection is performed, the execution resumes with the variables pointing to the relocated memory locations.

For unmanaged code, however, the runtime has no control over how the code accesses the memory. Therefore, if a garbage collection occurs while some unmanaged code is executing, the code may access an invalid memory location, resulting in unpredictable behavior, possibly a crash.

To prevent such unpredictable behavior, the .NET Framework provides for freezing the memory location for a variable. Essentially, the variable gets "pinned" to the memory location. Let's see how to pin a variable. Consider the following Win32 API for reading data given a file handle. It requires a pointer to a buffer to be passed as a parameter. On successful return, this buffer is filled with the read data:

```
BOOL ReadFile(
    HANDLE hFile,                    // handle to file
    LPVOID lpBuffer,                 // data buffer
    DWORD nNumberOfBytesToRead,      // number of bytes to read
    LPDWORD lpNumberOfBytesRead,     // number of bytes read
    LPOVERLAPPED lpOverlapped        // overlapped buffer
);
```

Here is the managed code declaration for this API:

```
// Project PInvoke/Pinning

[DllImport("kernel32", SetLastError=true)]
static extern unsafe bool ReadFile(IntPtr hFile,
    void* lpBuffer, uint nBytesToRead,
    uint* nBytesRead, IntPtr overlapped);
```

The mapping for the first four parameters to ReadFile is straightforward. The fifth parameter is a pointer to a structure used for overlapped input operation. As we are not interested in using this feature, we can get away with declaring this pointer as IntPtr.

Use `IntPtr` for Any Opaque Pointer

If an unmanaged API takes a pointer as a parameter and you do not intend to use the pointer within your managed code, you can declare the pointer as `IntPtr`, irrespective of the datatype the pointer is pointing to.

Recall that Win32 HANDLE is an example of such an opaque pointer. We don't use the handle directly within the managed code. We obtain it via one Win32 API, such as `CreateFile`, and just pass it around to other Win32 APIs, such as `ReadFile`.

Note that the function `ReadFile` is declared as `unsafe`. Recall from Chapter 4 that under C#, pointers can be used only within unsafe code and you need to compile your code with the `-unsafe` compiler switch.

The declaration also introduces a new argument to the `DllImport` constructor, `SetLastError`. Many Win32 APIs, including `ReadFile`, generate an unsigned 32-bit error code on failure. This error code can be retrieved using the Win32 API `GetLastError`. The error code is valid only for the last call to a Win32 API. Before you get a chance to retrieve it from the managed code, the runtime internally may call some other Win32 API, effectively wiping away your error code. If `SetLastError` is set to true, the runtime will fetch the error code and cache it on the logical thread. You can obtain this error code from the managed code using a static method `Marshal.GetLast-Win32Error`. If you wish to obtain the error code as an HRESULT, you can call `Marshal.GetHRForLastWin32Error` instead.

Before calling `ReadFile` from the managed code, the buffer being passed to the function has to be pinned. In C#, this can be done using the keyword `fixed`, as illustrated here:

```
// Project PInvoke/Pinning

public unsafe uint Read(byte[] buffer, uint bytesToRead) {
    uint bytesRead = 0;
    fixed (byte* p = buffer) {
       ReadFile(m_handle, p, bytesToRead,&bytesRead, NULL);
    }
    return bytesRead;
}
```

Statement `fixed` pins the specified variable within its scope. Once the scope is exited, the pinned variable automatically gets unpinned and is subject to garbage collection.

PInvoke and Memory Pinning

From the interop marshaler's point of view, a managed datatype can be classified as isomorphic or nonisomorphic. An isomorphic datatype has its memory representation identical in both the managed and the unmanaged world. An example of such a type is the class `System.Int32`. Managed structures with sequential layout type (covered shortly) can also be isomorphic. For such a datatype, the interop marshaler pins the managed memory and passes the pinned memory location to the unmanaged code. For all other cases, a conversion from managed representation to unmanaged representation is required. The interop marshaler allocates memory (using the COM API `CoTaskMemAlloc`) to hold a copy of the managed data in a layout that the unmanaged code expects and passes the location of the new memory to the unmanaged code. When the code returns, any out parameter is converted back to its managed representation.

As an optimization, when the String or StringBuilder class is marshaled by value, the interop marshaler passes a direct pointer to the internal Unicode buffer instead of copying it to a new buffer.

When a String object is passed by reference, the marshaler makes a copy of the input. This way, even if the callee modifies the contents, the immutability of the original string is maintained.

When a StringBuilder object is passed by reference, the marshaler passes a direct string to the internal Unicode buffer. In this case, the caller is responsible for creating a string of adequate length, as discussed earlier.

Note that C# does not let you assign a managed variable to a pointer without using the fixed statement. You would get an error from the compiler.

The statement fixed can pin only one variable. If you need to pin more than one variable, you can do that by nesting fixed statements.

Looking at the earlier code excerpt, you may be wondering why variable bytesRead was not pinned. This is because garbage collection is performed on the heap, not on the stack (see Chapter 4). Thus, there is no need to pin stack-based variables, such as bytesRead in this example.

At this point, it is worth mentioning that under .NET it is also possible to programmatically allocate space on the stack. Under C#, this can be done using the keyword stackalloc, as shown in the following code:

```
byte* buffer = stackalloc byte[256];
```

Note that stackalloc can be used only within an unsafe context. It is useful primarily for interoperability.

Safe Declarations

The previous example requires the use of pointers, but not all .NET languages support pointers. Yet all languages need to be able to invoke APIs such as ReadFile. Hence, .NET supports marshaling pointers, and many other unmanaged datatypes, in a way such that the APIs can be invoked from any programming language. The declaration of the Win32 API ReadFile from the previous example can be re-declared as follows:

```
[DllImport("kernel32", SetLastError=true)]
static extern bool ReadFile(IntPtr hFile,
    byte[] lpBuffer, uint nBytesToRead,
    ref uint nBytesRead, IntPtr overlapped);
```

Note that the `lpBuffer` parameter type has been changed from `byte*` to `byte[]` and the `nBytesRead` parameter type has been changed from `uint*` to `ref uint`.

Also note that the method is not marked as `unsafe`. By replacing pointer type parameters, we have eliminated the need for unsafe code.

Based on this declaration, our method `Read` from the previous example can be redefined as follows:

```
// Project PInvoke/SafePInvoke

public uint Read(byte[] buffer, uint bytesToRead) {
    uint bytesRead = 0;
    ReadFile(m_handle, buffer, bytesToRead, ref bytesRead,
      NULL);
    return bytesRead;
}
```

When `ReadFile` is declared this way, the runtime takes care of pinning the buffer; there is no need for explicit pinning in the code.

Structures

The .NET runtime interop layer also supports marshaling complex datatypes such as structures between managed and unmanaged code.

Consider the Win32 API `GetSystemTime` that returns the current date and time on the local machine:

```
VOID GetSystemTime(LPSYSTEMTIME lpSystemTime);
```

The function `GetSystemTime` takes a pointer to structure `SYSTEMTIME` as the parameter:

```
typedef struct _SYSTEMTIME {
    WORD wYear;
    WORD wMonth;
    WORD wDayOfWeek;
    WORD wDay;
    WORD wHour;
    WORD wMinute;
    WORD wSecond;
    WORD wMilliseconds;
} SYSTEMTIME, *PSYSTEMTIME;
```

To represent this structure in the managed code, each field of the structure must be represented by its corresponding managed type. This is illustrated in the following C# code excerpt:

```
[StructLayout(LayoutKind.Sequential)]
public struct SystemTime   {
     public ushort year;
     public ushort month;
     public ushort dayOfWeek;
     public ushort day;
     public ushort hour;
     public ushort minute;
     public ushort second;
     public ushort milliSeconds;
}
```

As can be seen, mapping the structure's fields under managed code is relatively straightforward.

Note that the structure is marked with the StructLayout attribute. The .NET Framework provides for developers to specify the layout of a structure's fields. This is done by means of a LayoutKind enumeration. A LayoutKind.Sequential value indicates that the fields should be laid out in the order in which they are declared. By default, the layout order is LayoutKind.Auto, which means that the runtime is free to rearrange the fields as it deems optimal.

Here is the code to declare and call the API:

```
// Project PInvoke/Structure

public class Win32 {
    [DllImport( "Kernel32.dll")]
    public static extern
      void GetSystemTime(ref SystemTime st);
}

class MyApp {
    public static void Main() {
      SystemTime st = new SystemTime();
      Win32.GetSystemTime(ref st);
      ...
    }
}
```

Note that when the native structure is represented as a C# struct, the ref directive is needed on the parameter in the imported method declaration.

Otherwise, because of the semantics of a value type, a copy of the structure is placed on the stack.

Also note that I have encapsulated the imported function in a separate class. At this point, I am also introducing a good software practice: Wrap all the imported functions as static methods within one class.

It is also possible to represent the native structure with a C# class instead of a C# `struct`. We examine this case when we discuss directional attributes later in the chapter.

Controlling the layout is important if the structure is being passed to unmanaged code that expects a specific layout. In most cases, specifying `LayoutKind.Sequential` suffices. However, it is also possible to define the layout explicitly using the layout enumeration value `LayoutKind.Explicit` and specifying each field's layout by means of the `FieldOffset` attribute. This is illustrated in the following code excerpt:

```
[StructLayout(LayoutKind.Explicit)]
public struct SystemTimeEx  {
    [FieldOffset(0)] public ushort year;
    [FieldOffset(2)] public ushort month;
    [FieldOffset(4)] public ushort dayOfWeek;
    [FieldOffset(6)] public ushort day;
    [FieldOffset(8)] public ushort hour;
    [FieldOffset(10)] public ushort minute;
    [FieldOffset(12)] public ushort second;
    [FieldOffset(14)] public ushort milliSeconds;
}
```

Explicit layout is quite useful if you wish to represent C-style unions in the managed code. All the fields within the union can be declared with the same `FieldOffset` value. Consider, for example, the following union definition:

```
union MyUnion {
    int i;
    double d;
}
```

This union can be represented in the managed code as follows:

```
[StructLayout(LayoutKind.Explicit)]
public struct MyUnion  {
    [FieldOffset(0)] public int i;
    [FieldOffset(0)] public double d;
}
```

Marshaling Hints

Most datatypes have a common representation in both managed and unmanaged memory. The interop marshaler has built-in rules to handle datatype transformations. As we have seen in previous examples, all that is needed is to let the interop marshaler know the equivalent managed datatype for an unmanaged datatype.

There are cases in which the default marshaling behavior is not what is desired or the interop marshaler simply does not know how to transform the given type. This can happen if a given type can be marshaled to multiple types. For example, class String can be marshaled as LPSTR, LPWSTR, LPTSTR, or even a COM-style string, BSTR. In such cases, the interop marshaler requires hints from the developers on how to transform the managed data.

The marshaling hints are supplied in the form of two BCL types—the class MarshalAsAttribute and the enumeration UnmanagedType. These hints can be applied to each parameter of a function, each field of a structure, and the function's return value.

Consider, for example, the Win32 structure OSVERSIONINFO. This structure is used in calls to Win32 API GetVersionEx to obtain the version information of the Windows OS on the local machine:

```
typedef struct _OSVERSIONINFO
{
    DWORD dwOSVersionInfoSize;
    DWORD dwMajorVersion;
    DWORD dwMinorVersion;
    DWORD dwBuildNumber;
    DWORD dwPlatformId;
    TCHAR szCSDVersion[128];
}OSVERSIONINFO;


BOOL GetVersionEx(LPOSVERSIONINFO lpVersionInfo);
```

A reminder is in order that you will never have to call this function directly. The .NET Framework already provides a static method Environment.OSVersion that returns the current version number of the OS.

OSVERSIONINFO defines a field szCSDVersion that is a fixed-sized character array. Recall from Chapter 5 that there is no declaration of fixed-sized arrays under the .NET programming model. The best you can do is to define a field of type array, as shown here:

```
public struct OSVersionInfo1
{
    ...
    public char[] versionString;
}
```

The fact that this field represents an array that has to be imported by value can be represented using the `MarshalAs` attribute with an enumeration value `UnmanagedType.ByValArray`. The size of the array can be defined using the field `MarshalAs.SizeConst`. The following code illustrates this:

```
// Project PInvoke/AdjustMarshal

[StructLayout(LayoutKind.Sequential)]
public struct OSVersionInfo1
{
    ...
    [MarshalAs(UnmanagedType.ByValArray, SizeConst=128)]
    public char[] versionString;
}
```

There is yet another way to represent fixed-sized character arrays, using the enumeration value `UnmanagedType.ByValTStr`. In this case, the managed datatype can be conveniently declared as of type `String`, as the following code excerpt illustrates:

```
// Project PInvoke/AdjustMarshal

[StructLayout(LayoutKind.Sequential, CharSet=CharSet.Auto)]
public struct OSVersionInfo2
{
    ...
    [MarshalAs(UnmanagedType.ByValTStr, SizeConst=128)]
    public String versionString;
}
```

Note that the character type used by `ByValTStr` can be specified by means of applying the `CharSet` attribute to the structure. Obviously, the same `CharSet` attribute should also be specified on the imported function.

`UnmanagedType` provides many other enumeration values that serve different purposes. Look into the SDK documentation for more information.

Directional Attributes

Under certain circumstances, the interop marshaler needs to know the direction of marshaling for the parameters. This is done by way of attributes on the parameter. Possible choices are `[In]` for one-way marshaling from managed to unmanaged code, [Out] for one-way marshaling from unmanaged to managed code, or [In, Out] for two-way marshaling.

Consider the case of calling GetSystemTimeEx. The function takes a pointer to a structure. Earlier, we declared the native structure as a C# struct. However, it is also possible to define the native structure as a class instead of a struct. However, as a class already is of the reference type, the instances of the class are already treated as pointers. Hence, the imported method can be declared as follows:

```
public static extern void GetSystemTimeEx(SystemTimeEx st);
```

This is semantically equivalent to declaring the function as:

```
public static extern
    void GetSystemTimeEx([In, Out] SystemTimeEx st);
```

As the parameter is used only to receive data, the method declaration can be further refined as:

```
public static extern
    void GetSystemTimeEx([Out] SystemTimeEx st);
```

Note that the imported method declaration should not contain a ref directive. Otherwise, as a class is already a reference type, the interop marshaler passes a pointer to a pointer, resulting in unpredictable behavior.

This concludes our discussion of the PInvoke mechanism. .NET also makes it possible to invoke COM components from .NET and vice versa. The services provided by PInvoke form the groundwork for the COM Interop layer.

As accessing COM components from .NET code will be more likely than the other way around, let's look at this case first.

ACCESSING COM COMPONENTS FROM .NET

The companion Web site contains a project called Test to build a DLL-based COM component that we will use for our demonstrations. The executable is named test.dll. Here is some relevant information about the component, taken from its IDL file:

```
// Project ComFromNet/Test

[
    uuid(653E70B3-4243-4A25-B713-0BFA7A271D02),
    oleautomation,
    ...
]
```

```
interface IMyFoo : IUnknown {
    HRESULT GetGreeting([in] BSTR user, [out] BSTR* greeting);
};

[
    uuid(B879FF11-EEAF-474C-B28C-F214B893A4B7),
    version(1.0),
    ...
]
library TestLib
{
    [uuid(FADA4A73-76DC-443C-838E-E6B98251E428)]
    coclass MyTest
    {
        [default] interface IMyFoo;
    };
};
```

As can be seen from the IDL definition, the component exposes a COM class `MyTest` that implements a COM interface `IMyFoo`. Interface `IMyFoo` defines a method `GetGreeting` that takes a BSTR `user` as input and returns a BSTR `greeting` as output.

The implementation of `GetGreeting` can be found on the companion Web site. It essentially creates a string as `"Hello " + user` and returns it as output. For example, if the input user is `Jay`, the output greeting is `Hello Jay`.

Note that `IMyFoo` is automation compatible. Any custom interface that is marked with the `oleautomation` attribute is automation compatible. In addition, `dispinterface`-based or `IDispatch`-based interfaces are also automation compatible.

What's the significance of a COM interface being automation compatible? Recall that the .NET programming model is built around metadata information. To consume COM-style interfaces, .NET requires the metadata for the interfaces. As you may know, COM provides a mechanism called type libraries to store metadata for automation-compatible COM interfaces. As we will see shortly, .NET is capable of consuming the metadata from a type library.

Note that, for interoperability, it is not necessary that a COM interface be automation compatible or that a type library be available for .NET's consumption. In such cases, however, you will have to construct the interface metadata manually in your managed code.

A type library contains metadata (in binary format) for one or more automation-compatible interfaces. A type library can either be created as a stand-alone binary file or be embedded in the executable itself. In our case, the type library is embedded in the executable `Test.dll`. This type library stores metadata information on the COM class `MyTest` as well as the interface `IMyFoo`.

To extract the metadata from the type library, the .NET SDK provides a tool called the Type Library Importer (`tlbimp.exe`). This tool converts the type definitions found within a type library into equivalent definitions in a .NET assembly. The generated assembly is referred to as an *interop assembly*. The tool contains many options to customize interop assemblies. The following command line, for example, produces an interop assembly from our COM component `Test.dll`. The interop assembly is named `TestImport.dll` and the imported types are wrapped in the namespace `MyImports`:

```
tlbimp.exe Test.dll /out:TestImport.dll /namespace:MyImports
```

Here is a partial output from `TestImport.dll` as produced from the IL disassembler:

```
.namespace MyImports
{
    .class interface public abstract auto ansi import IMyFoo
    {
    .method public hidebysig newslot virtual abstract
      instance void  GetGreeting(
        [in] string  marshal( bstr) user,
        [out] string&  marshal( bstr) greeting)
          runtime managedinternalcall
      {
      } // end of method IMyFoo::GetGreeting
    } // end of class IMyFoo

    .class public auto ansi import MyTestClass
      extends [mscorlib]System.Object
      implements MyImports.IMyFoo
    {
      ...
    } // end of class MyTestClass
} // end of namespace MyImports
```

As can be seen, the type library importer wraps the COM object in an interop layer. This interop layer is referred to as the runtime-callable wrapper (RCW). The RCW takes care of transforming each call to the COM object to the COM calling convention. For example, it transforms .NET strings to COM-style BSTR and vice versa. A close inspection of the declaration of `GetGreeting` from the disassembler's output would make this clear.

At this point, it is worth mentioning that Visual Studio .NET makes the job of generating the RCW easy. Just select Add Reference from the context menu of a project. The ensuing dialog box lets you select any of the registered type libraries on the local machine. You can also navigate through directories and select a specific COM component. Visual Studio .NET runs TlbImp.exe to generate the RCW and adds the generated interop assembly as a reference to your project.

A Simple Example

To access the COM component, all that is needed now is for the managed code to reference the generated assembly and use the defined types. Here is a code excerpt in C# that illustrates this:

```
// Project ComFromNet/NetClient

using MyImports;

class MyApp {
    public static void Greet01() {
        IMyFoo foo = new MyTestClass();
        String greeting;
        foo.GetGreeting("Jay", out greeting);
        Console.WriteLine(greeting);
    }
}
```

COM programmers will notice that there is no need to call the COM API CoCreateInstance to create the COM object, call QueryInterface to obtain the IMyFoo interface, or call Release to release the object. This is because behind the scenes, the RCW calls CoCreateInstance as well as other IUnknown methods, AddRef, QueryInterface, and Release as needed. Essentially, the RCW makes the COM object appear as a native .NET object and makes the .NET client appear to the COM object just as if it were a standard COM client. This is illustrated in Figure 7.1.

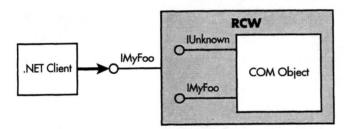

FIGURE 7.1 Accessing COM components from .NET.

The RCW goes beyond what is needed for COM interoperability. It goes through all the interfaces that are defined in the `coclass` section and makes the interface methods available as part of the imported class. This eliminates the need to explicitly obtain the interface to make a method call, as illustrated in the following code excerpt:

```
// Project ComFromNet/NetClient

public static void Greet02() {
    MyTestClass x = new MyTestClass();
    String greeting;
    x.GetGreeting("Jay", out greeting);
    Console.WriteLine(greeting);
}
```

To run the .NET application, the runtime should be able to locate the interop assembly. One option is to copy the interop assembly to the application's private path. However, it may be better to install the interop assembly in the GAC so that the COM component is available to any .NET application that needs it. Recall from Chapter 3 that only strong-named assemblies can be installed in the GAC. The type library importer provides a switch, `-keyfile`, to specify the file containing the strong-named key pair that should be used to sign the resulting interop assembly.

Lifetime Management

The RCW makes the COM object appear as a managed object. Naturally, the managed object has to follow the rules of the common language runtime. An interesting result of this is that the COM object is released only when the corresponding .NET object is garbage collected.

Recall from Chapter 4 that the garbage collection may happen much later than the last time a managed object is used. To hold the COM object until the .NET object is garbage collected may not be desirable in some cases (e.g., if the COM object holds some expensive resources).

The RCW has been designed to handle this situation. You can explicitly control the lifetime of the COM object from the managed code. The .NET Framework defines a static method, `Marshal.ReleaseComObject`, that you can use to explicitly release a COM object. This is illustrated in the following code excerpt:

```
// Project ComFromNet/NetClient

public static void LifetimeMgmtDemo() {
    MyTestClass x = new MyTestClass();

    ... // use x

    // explicit release
    Marshal.ReleaseComObject(x);

    // Don't use x anymore
}
```

Once the COM object has been explicitly released, any call made on the corresponding native object results in an exception of type `InvalidComObjectException`.

Error Handling

COM APIs and COM interface methods always have a return value of type `HRESULT`. COM applications check this return value to see if the called API or interface method succeeded. In case of failure, a COM object can return additional error information by means of a standard interface, `ISupportErrorInfo`.

The .NET programming model, on the other hand, is based on raising exceptions to indicate error conditions.

To provide the needed compatibility, the .NET interop layer internally checks for COM method call failures and automatically raises .NET style exceptions. These .NET style exceptions for COM style errors are of the type `COMException`. All that a .NET application has to do is to catch and process this type of exception, as illustrated in the following code excerpt:

```
// Project ComFromNet/NetClient

public static void DisplayException() {
    try {
      // some code
    }catch(COMException e) {
      Console.WriteLine("Exception: {0} (0x{1:x})",
        e.Message, e.ErrorCode);
    }
}
```

COM Apartments

A COM apartment is a logical container within a process that enforces certain threading requirements on COM objects. A thread must enter an apartment before it can access a COM object. Apartments are either single-threaded (STA) or multithreaded (MTA). COM objects instantiated in an STA can be directly accessed only from the STA thread that instantiated it. COM objects instantiated in an MTA can be directly accessed from any MTA thread. Accessing an object from an incompatible apartment requires marshaling. A process can contain zero or more STAs and at most one MTA.

Although the .NET Framework itself doesn't use apartments to access .NET objects, it still provides for a managed thread to enter a specified apartment. Otherwise, managed code will not be able to access any COM object.

The apartment that a managed thread must enter can be specified by setting the ApartmentState property of the thread to one of the values from ApartmentState enumeration. Meaningful values are ApartmentState.MTA (for MTA) and ApartmentState.STA (for STA). The following code excerpt sets the apartment state of the current thread to MTA:

```
// Project ComFromNet/NetClient


public static void Main() {


    Thread.CurrentThread.ApartmentState = ApartmentState.MTA;
    ...
}
```

By default, the apartment state of the thread is set to ApartmentState.Unknown, in which case .NET automatically initializes the thread to MTA when making the first COM call from the thread.

There is a subtle difference between managed and unmanaged threads with regards to their apartment states that is worth noting. An unmanaged thread can enter and leave an apartment as many times as desired. A managed thread, however, can enter the apartment only once. Once the managed thread enters an apartment, it stays in that apartment until it is terminated.

Finally, it is also possible to specify the apartment a thread must enter by means of STAThread or MTAThread attributes on the thread entry point method. The following code excerpt, for example, sets the apartment of the main thread to STA:

```
// Project ComFromNet/NetClient

  [STAThread]
  public static void Main() {
    ...
  }
```

DataTypes

The type library importer does a good job of wrapping most COM datatypes into their managed counterparts. COM datatype BSTR is mapped to `System.String`, as we saw earlier. Two COM datatypes, variants and safe arrays, deserve a little more attention.

Variants

Some programming languages such as VBScript forego the notion of typed data in favor of increased programming simplicity. These typeless languages support only one datatype called a *variant*. A variant can contain any type of data. Even many typed languages, such as Visual Basic, support variants natively.

The COM SDK defines a discriminated union to deal with variants. It is called VARIANT. The COM SDK performs APIs to deal with variants, such as converting basic datatypes to variants and vice versa, or to copy one variant to another.

Under .NET, the RCW maps a VARIANT datatype to `System.Object` and vice versa. The underlying datatype is preserved and can be obtained by casting `System.Object` appropriately.

Consider the following IDL method declaration:

```
// Project ComFromNet/Test

interface IMyFoo : IUnknown {
    HRESULT GetDataType(
      [in] VARIANT vin, [out] VARIANT* retVal);
    ...
}
```

The implementation of `GetDataType` examines the datatype of parameter `vin` and returns the type information as a BSTR in the parameter `retVal`.

The RCW wraps this method as:

```
void GetDataType(System.Object vin, out System.Object retVal);
```

Invoking this method is straightforward, as can be seen in the following code excerpt:

```
public static void VariantDemo() {
    MyTestClass test = new MyTestClass();

    object retVal;
    test.GetDataType("Hello", out retVal);
    String s = retVal as String;
    Console.WriteLine(s);

    test.GetDataType(20, out retVal);
    Console.WriteLine(retVal);
}
```

Safe Arrays

Programming languages such as C++ support arrays intrinsically. However, most do so without any index protection, size limit, and initialization. An array is just a pointer to a random memory location. Even experienced C++ programmers are reluctant to use raw arrays. Many of them write protect wrapper classes to deal with arrays.

On the other hand, Visual Basic (and now .NET) provides a more protected way of dealing with arrays; it stores the array bounds and does a runtime check to ensure that the boundaries are not violated.

To deal with arrays, the COM SDK defines a data structure called SAFE-ARRAY. A SAFEARRAY is an array of other automation-compatible datatypes.

Under .NET, the RCW wraps safe arrays into a managed array of the corresponding datatype.

Consider the following IDL method definition:

```
// Project ComFromNet/Test
interface IMyFoo : IUnknown {
    HRESULT Concatenate([in] SAFEARRAY(BSTR) psa,
      [out, retval] BSTR* retVal);
    ...
}
```

The implementation of method Concatenate (Project Test) takes the safe array of strings as a parameter and returns a new concatenated string.

The RCW makes method Concatenate appear as follows in the managed code:

```
System.String Concatenate(System.String[] psa);
```

The safe array is imported as a single-dimensional array with a lower bound that starts from zero.

Here is the code excerpt that demonstrates calling this method:

```
public static void SafeArrayDemo() {
   MyTestClass test = new MyTestClass();

   String[] nameList = new String[] {"Jay", "Pradeep"};
   String s = test.Concatenate(nameList);
   Console.WriteLine(s);
}
```

The RCW is also capable of wrapping a safe array into a more generic form of .NET arrays, the System.Array type. This is done by means of -sysarray switch on the type library importer. Doing so in our example results in the managed code representation as follows:

```
System.String Concatenate(System.Array psa);
```

The advantage of this mechanism is that the arrays can be multidimensional or can have nonzero lower bounds. The downside is that you lose information about the type of element (although it is captured in a custom attribute).

Custom Wrapper

Availability of a type library makes it easy to develop managed code that accesses COM objects, as we saw in the previous sample. Just running tlbimp.exe against the type library generates all the necessary metadata and marshaling information that the interop marshaler needs.

It is also possible under .NET to define the metadata for COM interfaces within the managed code. This is useful in many cases:

1. For some reason, the type library is not accessible during code development.

2. The interface to be accessed is not automation compatible. COM cannot save the metadata for such an interface in the type library.

3. Under some cases, the type library is not capable of truly representing the marshaling information. An example of such a case is conformant arrays. A conformant array is an array whose size (called conformance)

is specified at runtime. Although the conformance can be represented correctly in the IDL definition, the IDL compiler conveniently drops this information while generating the type library.

Let's define a custom wrapper for a COM interface. Specifically, we will target marshaling a conformant array:

Here is the definition for the COM interface we will write the custom wrapper for:

```
// Project ComFromNet/Test
// File: Custom.idl

[
    uuid(018D9CF7-7C5F-4161-8114-99ECE2EAB361),
    ...
]
interface IMyBaz : IUnknown {
    HRESULT GetId([out, retval] long* pValue);
    HRESULT GetArray([in] long cElem,
        [out, size_is(cElem)] long array[]);
};
```

Method GetId returns an integer. I am adding this method primarily for testing purposes.

Method GetArray returns an array of integers. The caller allocates the array and specifies the size during the method call. The method implementation just fills the array with some values.

Here is how this interface can be represented in C#:

```
// Project ComFromNet/CustomWrapper
// File: CustomWrapper.cs

[
    ComImport,
    Guid("018D9CF7-7C5F-4161-8114-99ECE2EAB361"),
    InterfaceType(ComInterfaceType.InterfaceIsIUnknown)
]
public interface IMyBaz {

    [return : MarshalAs(UnmanagedType.I4)]
    int GetId();

    void GetArray([In, MarshalAs(UnmanagedType.I4)] int cElem,
      [Out, MarshalAs(UnmanagedType.LPArray,
        SizeParamIndex=0)]
        int[] array);
}
```

Attribute `ComImport` informs the runtime that the interface was originally defined as a COM interface. Attribute `Guid` specifies the identifier for the interface. Attribute `InterfaceType` is used to indicate whether an interface is `dual`, `IDispatch` only, or `IUnknown` based. The code indicates that the interface type is `IUnknown` based.

Interface `IMyBaz` defines two methods—`GetId` and `GetArray`. Note that neither the name of the interface nor the name of the method needs to match its counterparts in the original COM interface. What is important is that the GUID and the layout (including the order of methods) of the interfaces match.

Attribute target `return` on method `GetId` is applied to the return value. The code specified that the return value be marshaled as a 4-byte integer.

Although the preceding code explicitly specifies that a C# `int` type be marshaled as a 4-byte integer, it is not necessary to do so for basic data types. By default, the framework defines the right marshaling behavior for `int` as well as many other basic datatypes.

Take note of the attribute definition on the `array` parameter of method `GetArray`. Attribute `Out` indicates that the parameter is used only as an output type. The `MarshalAs` definition indicates that the parameter must be marshaled as an array (`UnmanagedType.LPArray`) and that the size of the array is defined by the first parameter to the method (`SizeParamIndex=0`). Parameter indexes are zero-based.

Let's also go ahead and define a dummy C# class, `MyTestClass`, to represent the original COM `coclass`. The following code excerpt shows the COM `coclass` in the IDL file and its representation under C#:

```
// Project ComFromNet/Test

// File Test.idl
    [
      uuid(FADA4A73-76DC-443C-838E-E6B98251E428),
      ...
    ]
    coclass MyTest
    {
      ...
    };

// Project ComFromNet/CustomWrapper
    [
      ComImport,
      Guid("FADA4A73-76DC-443C-838E-E6B98251E428")
    ]
    public class MyTestClass {
    }
```

As with interfaces, the class definition specifies attributes `ComImport` and `Guid`. The parameter to the GUID represents the CLSID of the `coclass`.

Here is the code excerpt that shows how the custom-defined class and the interface can be used for COM interop:

```
// File CustomWrapper.cs

IMyBaz baz = (IMyBaz) new MyTestClass();

Console.WriteLine(baz.GetId());

int[] prms = new int[] {-1, -2, -3};
baz.GetArray(prms.Length, prms);
Console.WriteLine(prms.Length);
for(int i=0;i<prms.Length; i++) {
   Console.WriteLine(prms[i]);
}
```

Before running this application, remember to build and register the proxy-stub DLL for `Test.dll`.

It is left as an exercise for you to extend this example to marshal an array of interface pointers. Those who are busy can take a peek at the sample code on the companion Web site.

The .NET interop marshaler provides a great deal of support for many other COM interop issues. For example, it is possible to allocate memory in the COM component (e.g., via `CoTaskMemAlloc` or `SysAllocString`) and to free the allocated memory in the managed code. Look at the SDK documentation for more details on COM interop. In particular, examine the COM interop methods provided by the class `Marshal`.

Late Binding

The RCW example that we have looked at so far is that of early binding, meaning that the developer requires access to the metadata at the time of building the assembly.

COM programmers are aware that COM supports the notion of late binding; that is, a method that is called is bound to at runtime instead of compile time. This late binding is possible for COM components that support `IDispatch` interface.

The .NET Framework supports late binding for COM components supporting the `IDispatch` interface.

Consider the following interface definition:

```
// Project ComFromNet/Test

interface IMyBar : IDispatch{
    HRESULT Add([in] long param1, [in] long param2,
        [out,retval] long* value);
}
```

Interface IMyBar is a dual interface in the sense that it supports the interface IDispatch as well as the custom interface IMyBar.

For our demonstration, this interface is implemented in a COM component with the PROGID Test.MyBar. The implementation of IMyBar.Add adds the two numbers that are passed as input parameters and returns the sum as output in the third parameter.

The following code shows how to use this COM component from .NET in a late-binding fashion:

```
// Project ComFromNet/LateBinding

    public static void LateBindingExample() {
        // Obtain type based on prog id
        Type t = Type.GetTypeFromProgID("Test.MyBar");

        // Create an instance using Activator
        Object o = Activator.CreateInstance(t);

        // input parameters
        Object[] prms = new object[] {2, 3};

        // make the call
        int val = (int) t.InvokeMember("Add",
            BindingFlags.InvokeMethod, null, o, prms);

        Console.WriteLine(val);
    }
```

Static method Type.GetTypeFromProgID returns the .NET type of the COM object whose PROGID is specified. This method returns null if the object does not implement the IDispatch interface.

If you have the CLSID available instead of the PROGID, you can call another static method Type.GetTypeFromCLSID to obtain the .NET type.

Once you have the type available, you create the COM object using Activator.CreateInstance and call the method using Type.InvokeMember. You need to specify the name of the method, the type of method (method or property), the object you are calling this method on, and the parameters to the method.

`Type.InvokeMember` returns the logical return value from the interface method (e.g., that is, the parameter marked with `retval`).

A final word on method `GetTypeFromProgID`: One of its overloads can be used to obtain a type from the specified machine. This enables you to create an object from a remote machine and invoke methods on the object (assuming the DCOM gods are happy with your DCOM configuration).

This covers the basics of accessing COM components from .NET. The SDK contains some good sample programs on COM interoperability such as hosting Internet Explorer ActiveX controls within your managed code. David Platt's article in *MSDN Magazine* [Pla-01] is also worth a read.

ACCESSING .NET COMPONENTS FROM COM

It is also possible to access .NET components as COM components, although this scenario is not that common. To support this case, the .NET Framework creates a COM-callable wrapper (CCW) around the .NET object, as shown in Figure 7.2.

Let's expose our console greeting .NET application from Chapter 2 as a COM component. Here is the code for the .NET application:

```
// Project NetFromCom/ConsoleGreeting

namespace MyGreeting {

    public interface IGreeting {
        String UserName { set; }
        void Greet();
    }

    public class ConsoleGreeting : IGreeting {
        private String m_userName;

        public ConsoleGreeting() {}

        public String UserName {
            ...
        }

        public void Greet() {
            ...
        }
    }
}
```

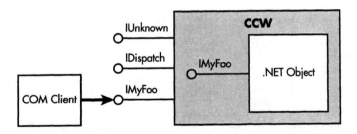

FIGURE 7.2   Accessing .NET components from COM.

The code defines an interface IGreeting and a class ConsoleGreeting that implements this interface. Strictly speaking, it is not necessary to define interfaces in managed code for the purpose of COM interoperability. The interop layer is capable of exposing .NET classes as COM interfaces, as we will see shortly.

Note that to expose a .NET class as a COM class, the .NET class must provide a default constructor; that is, a constructor that does not require any parameters. The COM API to create an object, CoCreateInstance, does not know how to pass parameters to the object that it creates.

Let's compile this code into the assembly ConsoleGreeting.dll. The command line is shown here:

```
csc.exe -t:library ConsoleGreeting.cs
```

Now we need to make the .NET assembly act as a COM component. The .NET SDK provides a tool called the Assembly Registration tool (regasm.exe) to do this. The tool reads metadata from a .NET assembly and adds the necessary entries to the registry. Here is the command line to register our assembly:

```
regasm.exe -tlb:ConsoleGreeting.tlb ConsoleGreeting.dll
```

The switch -tlb can be used to generate a type library for COM clients to consume. Here is a partial output from ConsoleGreeting.tlb when viewed through the OLE Viewer (oleview.exe):

```
[
  uuid(71EB53FD-FBDB-3A97-828E-6747B61E6CE4),
  dual,
  oleautomation,
]
interface IGreeting : IDispatch {
  [id(0x60020000), propput]
```

```
    HRESULT UserName([in] BSTR rhs);

    [id(0x60020001)]
    HRESULT Greet();
};


[
  uuid(A4E92664-EC8E-30B4-9D4E-CD6F1459CD44),
  dual,
  oleautomation,
]
interface _ConsoleGreeting : IDispatch {
};


[
  uuid(38CA9DFF-762B-31AA-B052-836243916D06),
  custom(0F21F359-AB84-41E8-9A78-36D110E6D2F9,
    MyGreeting.ConsoleGreeting)
]
coclass ConsoleGreeting {
    [default] interface _ConsoleGreeting;
    interface _Object;
    interface IGreeting;
};
```

Note that the CCW exposes the .NET class as a COM coclass Con-soleGreeting that supports interfaces IGreeting, IDispatch (through inheritance), _ConsoleGreeting, and _Object. Interface _Object represents System.Object and can be found in mscorlib.tlb.

Interface _ConsoleGreeting represents the class ConsoleGreeting itself. It is interesting to note that whenever you export a .NET class for use from COM, the class' public methods do not appear in the corresponding COM interface (as can be seen in the generated type library). However, you can change this behavior by applying an attribute ClassInterfaceAttribute passing in the class interface type as an enumeration value ClassInterface-Type.AutoDual. This is illustrated in the following code excerpt.

```
[ClassInterface(ClassInterfaceType.AutoDual)]
public class ConsoleGreeting : IGreeting {
    ...
}
```

Regasm.exe registers with Windows the type library associated with the specified assembly, irrespective of whether or not you have specified the -tlb switch. If you just wish to create the type library file from an assembly but have no interest in registering it, then you must instead use the Type Library Exporter (tlbexp.exe), another tool provided in the .NET SDK. The following command line, for example, generates a type library Foo.tlb from the assembly ConsoleGreeting.dll.

```
tlbexp.exe ConsoleGreeting.dll -out:Foo.tlb
```

Here is a partial list of registry entries that regasm.exe adds, shown in regedit format. You can obtain the complete list using the -reg switch on the tool:

```
[HKEY_CLASSES_ROOT\MyGreeting.ConsoleGreeting]
@="MyGreeting.ConsoleGreeting"

[HKEY_CLASSES_ROOT\MyGreeting.ConsoleGreeting\CLSID]
@="{38CA9DFF-762B-31AA-B052-836243916D06}"

[HKEY_CLASSES_ROOT\CLSID\{38CA9DFF-762B-31AA-B052-836243916D06}]
@="MyGreeting.ConsoleGreeting"

[HKEY_CLASSES_ROOT\CLSID\{38CA9DFF-762B-31AA-B052-836243916D06}\
          InprocServer32]
@="C:\WINDOWS\System32\mscoree.dll"
"ThreadingModel"="Both"
"Class"="MyGreeting.ConsoleGreeting"
"Assembly"="ConsoleGreeting, Version=0.0.0.0, Culture=neutral,
          PublicKeyToken=null"
"RuntimeVersion"="v1.0.3215"

[HKEY_CLASSES_ROOT\CLSID\{38CA9DFF-762B-31AA-B052-836243916D06}\
          ProgId]
@="MyGreeting.ConsoleGreeting"
```

Essentially, the .NET class is exposed as a COM component with the PROGID MyGreeting.ConsoleGreeting. The component is registered with ThreadingModel set to both.

Note that the server associated with the COM class is mscoree.dll, the DLL that contains the common language runtime execution engine. The execution engine in turn loads the assembly specified by the Assembly entry.

Also note that managed objects do not have any thread affinity. Internally, the runtime effectively aggregates the free threaded marshaler (FTM) when exposing managed objects to COM. It is the responsibility of the developer to guard the managed code against possible multithreading issues.

An exception to the managed objects having no thread affinity are *serviced components*. These managed objects act strictly as if they are COM+ objects, even when called from other managed objects. We cover serviced components in Chapter 10 when we discuss enterprise services.

Here is the C++ client code that accesses the COM component:

```
// Project NetFromCom/Client

#import "ConsoleGreeting.tlb"

int _tmain(int argc, _TCHAR* argv[])
{
    // Initialize COM
    HRESULT hr = ::CoInitialize(NULL);

    // Create an instance of ConsoleGreeting and obtain
    // interface IGreeting
    ConsoleGreeting::IGreetingPtr spGreeting;
    hr = spGreeting.CreateInstance(
        __uuidof(ConsoleGreeting::ConsoleGreeting));

    // Invoke properties and methods on the interface
    spGreeting->UserName = "Jay";
    spGreeting->Greet();

    // Release the object and uninitialize COM
    spGreeting = NULL;
    ::CoUninitialize();
    return 0;
}
```

Compile the program as Client.exe.

To run Client.exe, you need to copy ConsoleGreeting.dll into the same directory as Client.exe. Otherwise the runtime will not be able to locate the assembly. The mechanism of specifying the assembly search path via configuration files is available only to .NET applications, not to COM applications.

If you expect that your .NET assembly may be used by multiple COM applications, it may be a good idea to sign the assembly with a strong name and install the assembly in the GAC. This way the assembly is accessible to any COM application, irrespective of the directory the application resides in.

Here is what happens behind the scenes when you execute the COM client. When the COM client calls CoCreateInstance to create the .NET object, the registered COM server, mscoree.dll, gets loaded in the process space. The execution engine in turn loads the assembly containing the .NET class and creates a CCW on the fly. The CCW converts all the method parameters and return values from native COM types to .NET equivalents. For example, BSTRs are converted to .NET strings. We have already discussed the mechanism of datatype conversion earlier in the chapter.

The CCW also coverts .NET exceptions to COM-style error code, with support for the interface ISupportErrorInfo. The sample code on the companion Web site demonstrates how the error description can be obtained when a call fails.

Lifetime Issues

It is worth noting that when you release the COM object in your unmanaged code, the corresponding .NET object is not destroyed until the next garbage collection takes place. Unlike the RCW, where you can control the lifetime of the COM object by using Marshal.ReleaseComObject, there is no equivalent functionality from the unmanaged code to dispose of a .NET object. This could be a problem if the .NET object is holding one or more COM objects that were passed to it from the unmanaged code. Not knowing that there are still some COM objects alive, the unmanaged code may close the COM library by calling CoUninitialize. This may result in unpredictable behavior when the COM objects are released later.

The recommended solution is to add a method such as Close or CleanUp on the .NET object that does the necessary clean up and call this method explicitly from the unmanaged code.

Adjusting Interop Attributes

When regasm.exe is run against a .NET assembly, by default the tool generates all the necessary COM identifiers such as GUIDs for interfaces, type libraries, and coclasses, as well as dispids for interface methods. However, .NET provides many attribute classes that can be applied to the managed source code to customize this behavior. For example, the following code shows the use of the class GuidAttribute to specify the GUID for interface IGreeting:

```
[Guid("71EB53FD-FBDB-3A97-828E-6747B61E6CE4")]
public interface IGreeting {
   ...
}
```

The GuidAttribute can also be applied to a .NET class.

By default, the generated PROGID of the class is `<Namespace>`, `<ClassName>`. However, you can explicitly specify a PROGID using the `ProgIdAttribute` attribute, as shown here:

```
[ProgId("MyCompany.MyDemo")]
public class InteropAdjustDemo {
    ...
}
```

Check the SDK documentation for all other applicable attributes.

Hiding Interfaces

By default, all the public interfaces, classes, and methods in the managed code are made available to COM applications. However, it is possible to hide some of the information by using an interop attribute `ComVisible`.

When this attribute is applied with a value `False`, the code this attribute is applied to is not accessible from COM.

This attribute can be applied to interfaces, classes, methods, and even the whole assembly.

This covers the basics of invoking .NET objects from unmanaged code. It is also possible to host .NET controls as COM ActiveX controls. Interested readers may wish to look at [Noy-01].

SUMMARY

.NET supports interoperability with APIs in native DLLs as well as with COM components. The SDK defines a collection of classes under the namespace `System.Runtime.InteropServices` to support this interoperability.

The ability to access APIs in native DLLs is offered through a mechanism called PInvoke, which offers a great deal of support for marshaling basic datatypes, pointers, and even structures.

The default marshaling options used by the interop marshaler try to make interoperability as seamless as possible. In cases where there is an ambiguity on how a managed type can be marshaled, the .NET Framework defines a mechanism to let the developers provide marshaling hints to the interop marshaler.

The framework also defines a mechanism to invoke COM components from .NET applications and .NET components from COM applications. For accessing COM objects, the interop layer creates an RCW around the COM object and makes it appear as a .NET object to managed code. For accessing .NET objects, the interop layer creates a CCW around the .NET object and makes it appear as a COM object to the unmanaged code.

In a later chapter on enterprise services, we will look at how .NET preserves the context information across the .NET–COM interop layer. This makes it possible, for example, for .NET as well as COM components to participate in a transaction.

REFERENCES

[Sel-01]   Sells, Chris, "Managed Extensions Bring .NET CLR Support to C++," *MSDN Magazine*, July 2001.
msdn.microsoft.com/msdnmag/issues/01/07/vsnet/vsnet.asp

[Ras-01]   Restrepo, Tomas, "Introducing Managed Code to C++," *Visual Systems Journal*, February 2001.
www.vsj.co.uk/archive/feb2001/hoc1-0102.asp

[Pla-01]   Platt, David, "Get Ready for Microsoft .NET by Using Wrappers to Interact with COM-Based Apps," *MSDN Magazine*, August 2001.
msdn.microsoft.com/msdnmag/issues/01/08/Interop/Interop.asp

[Noy-01]   Noyes, Brian, "Exploit COM Interop in .NET," *Visual Basic Programmer's Journal*, June 2001.
www.devx.com/premier/mgznarch/vcdj/2001/06jun01/ce0106/ce0601-1.asp

Symmetric Cryptography
· encrypt with key K : $C = E_K(M)$ } DES
· decrypt $M = D_K(C)$ → it's fast

·NET Symmetric Cryptography.

public static main(String[] args) {
    // 4 values to use   Symmetric Alg SO = DES.
        byte[] key;   Create
        byte[] iv;
        Cipher Mode mode
        Padding Mode

using System;
using System IO;
using System. Security. Cryptography;
using System. Security;
using System. Text;

// display byte array in Hex

public static void Disp(Byte[] b){
        String Builder sb = new StringBuilder();

ASSYMMETRIC
· to encrypt $C = E(M, Public Key)$ } RSA
· to decrypt $M = D(C, Private Key)$ } Digital Signature Algorithm
                                             Elliptic Curve Cryptography

Digital Signatures. $M =$ "transfer 50000".
○ Anyone can & comp: $h(M)$
· Sign by computing $S = E[h(M), Private Key)$.
· To verify signature compute $h'(M) = D(S, Public Key)$
        and check if $h'(M) = h(M)$

$$((hash value)^d mod N)^e mod n$$

Concurrency

Under Windows, and most other modern OSs, a process can execute multiple threads concurrently, each of which carry out a specific task. The .NET Framework supports developing multithreaded applications in two ways—by supporting the creation and use of threads and by providing a mechanism to make asynchronous calls. In this chapter, we examine both these techniques in detail. We also look at various issues involved with multithread programming and the support provided by the .NET Framework in developing classes that are safe from concurrent access.

MULTITHREAD PROGRAMMING

First, a little background on processes and threads as defined by the OS is in order.

A thread is the basic unit of execution on the Win32 platform, to which the OS allocates processor time. A process represents a running application that consists of a private virtual address space, code, data, and other OS resources such as files, pipes, and synchronization objects that are visible to the process. A process also contains one or more threads that run in the context of the process. A thread can execute just one task at a time. To perform multiple tasks concurrently, a process can create multiple threads. Even though only one thread can execute at any time,[1] the Windows OS preemp-

---

1. More specifically, thread execution is processor based. A multiprocessor machine can have multiple threads executing simultaneously.

tively switches execution from one thread to another. The switching is so fast that all the threads appear to run at the same time.

All threads within a process share the virtual address space and global variables of that process. However, each thread has its own stack. Therefore, when a thread is executing, any program variables that are created on the stack are local to the thread.

A thread is uniquely identified by a numeric value. This numeric identifier is unique only within a process. In other words, two processes can each have a thread that has the same thread ID.

Threads are scheduled for execution based on their priority. Thread priorities specify the relative priority of one thread over another and can be adjusted programmatically. The OS can also adjust the thread priority dynamically.

Often, it is necessary to maintain thread-specific data. However, a static or global variable cannot be used for this purpose because it has the same value across all the threads. To address this problem, the OS provides a feature called thread local storage (TLS). With TLS, it is possible to create a unique copy of a variable for each thread within a process.

This information is in the context of the unmanaged world. Things are slightly different in the managed environment of .NET. For example, a global variable is global only within an application domain, not at the process level. Also, a managed thread can be assigned a name, which is useful for debugging purposes.

The .NET SDK provides classes that deal with thread creation, manipulation, and synchronization. The SDK also provides comprehensive documentation on their usage.

With this brief background information, let's develop a simple application that demonstrates the use of the .NET classes in creating and manipulating threads. As we go along in the chapter, we will pick up any other thread-related information that we need.

A Simple Example

The following code excerpt creates a thread and displays the thread identifier from both the main thread and the spawned thread:

```
// Project Threads/SimpleThread

using System;
using System.Threading;
```

```
public class Foo {

    public static void MyThreadProc() {
      Console.WriteLine("I am in thread: {0}",
        AppDomain.GetCurrentThreadId());
    }
}

class MyApp {
    public static void Main() {
      Console.WriteLine("Main thread: {0}",
        AppDomain.GetCurrentThreadId());
      Thread t = new Thread(
        new ThreadStart(Foo.MyThreadProc));
      t.Start(); // start the thread
      t.Join();  // wait for the thread to finish
    }
}
```

Namespace System.Threading provides classes and interfaces that deal with multithreaded programming. The class Thread encapsulates the creation and manipulation of a managed thread. This class has a public constructor that takes a delegate ThreadStart as a parameter. Here is the definition of the delegate:

```
public delegate void ThreadStart();
```

Essentially, ThreadStart can be used to specify the entry point for the thread. In our example, the entry point is a static method Foo.MyThreadProc. However, a nonstatic method can also be specified as the entry point.

Chaining Multiple Methods

As ThreadStart takes a multicast delegate, it is possible to add more than one method to the delegate. In this case, the thread executes the methods in the order in which they were added.

Creating an instance of thread doesn't spawn the physical thread. To create and execute the thread, you need to call Start on the thread. This method creates the physical OS thread, attaches the Thread object to it (using the TLS), and starts executing the specified entry point method.

Managed Threads and OS Threads

Any code is always executed on a physical OS thread. The .NET runtime creates an OS thread and installs a `Thread` object in the TLS of the OS thread. A managed thread is essentially an OS thread with the `Thread` object attached.

The runtime uses a similar technique when an unmanaged thread enters the runtime through, for example, a CCW. The runtime checks if the unmanaged thread already has a `Thread` object installed in the TLS. If not, it creates one on the fly and installs it.

Note that one should not assume a relationship between the OS thread identifier and the corresponding managed thread. A sophisticated runtime host, for example, can move a managed thread between different OS threads.

To wait for the spawned thread to complete its execution, the main thread calls `Join` on the instance of the thread. This method blocks the calling thread until the waited-on thread terminates. However, it is possible to specify the time to wait by using an overloaded `Join` method that takes the wait time as a parameter.

Tada! We just finished writing our first multithreaded program.

Besides `Start` and `Join`, there are many other thread-manipulation methods available in the `Thread` class. Table 8.1 describes some useful methods and their Win32 counterparts for reference.

TABLE 8.1. Some Useful Methods on the Thread Class

Method	Description	Win32 API
`Thread.Start`	Start a thread	`CreateThread`/`ResumeThread`
`Thread.Abort`	Terminate a thread forcefully	`TerminateThread`
`Thread.Suspend`	Suspend a thread's execution	`SuspendThread`
`Thread.Resume`	Resume a suspended thread	`ResumeThread`
`Thread.Current-Thread`	Return the `Thread` object of the current thread	`GetCurrentThread`
`Thread.Priority`	Adjust thread's priority	`SetThreadPriority`
`Thread.Name`	Assign or obtain the name of a managed thread	No equivalent
`Thread.IsBackground`	Background or foreground thread	No equivalent
`Thread.Join`	Wait for the thread to complete	`WaitForSingleHandle`
`Thread.Apartment-State`	Set or get the COM apartment state	Close to `CoInitializeEx`

Background Threads

Under .NET, managed threads are classified as foreground threads and background threads. The .NET runtime waits for only the foreground threads to complete before quitting the application. By default, any explicitly spawned thread, such as the one in our previous example, has a foreground status. Therefore, it is not necessary for the main thread to explicitly wait for the spawned thread to complete before quitting the application.

Class `Thread` provides a `bool` property, `IsBackground`, that can be used to check or set the background status of a thread. For example, adding the following line in the thread entry point method of the previous example changes the status of the spawned thread from foreground to background:

```
Thread.CurrentThread.IsBackground = true;
```

Setting a thread to background status is useful if you do not wish to wait for the thread to complete when quitting the application.

Aborting a Thread

A thread can be aborted by calling `Abort` on the `Thread` object, as illustrated in the following code:

```
// Project Threads/ThreadAbort

class MyApp {
    public static void Main() {
        Thread t = new Thread(
          new ThreadStart(Foo.MyThreadProc));
        t.Start(); // start the thread
        Thread.Sleep(5*1000);// give the other thread
                   // a chance to execute
        t.Abort(); // abort the thread
        t.Join();  // wait for the thread to finish
    }
}
```

When `Abort` is called on a managed thread, the runtime raises a `ThreadAbortException` in the thread. `ThreadAbortException` is a special exception in that although it can be caught by the executing code, it is automatically raised once again at the end of the `catch` block. Whether or not you catch this exception, the runtime eventually executes all the `finally` blocks in the call chain and then terminates the thread.

Note the call to Join following the call to Abort on the thread. As the catch and the finally blocks are being executed, the thread may end up executing an unbound computation. Calling Join on the thread guarantees that the thread has indeed been terminated.

Aborting a Thread During an Unmanaged Call

When Abort is called on a managed thread that is executing an unmanaged call into the native DLLs, the common language runtime does not have much control on the thread. However, the common language runtime marks the thread for abort and takes control of the thread when it reenters the managed side.

Incidentally, the code introduces a new static method, Thread.Sleep. Calling this method causes the execution of the current thread to be temporarily suspended. The parameter to the method is used to specify the time in number of milliseconds for which the thread execution should be suspended.

When Thread.Sleep is called, the runtime may switch the context to a different thread. If you intend to suspend the execution of your thread for a very short time, and you do not wish to give up the rest of the time slice allocated to your thread, you can use a static method, Thread.SpinWait. This method causes the executing thread to wait in a tight loop without causing a context switch. The parameter to the method specifies the number of iterations for the loop.

In general, SpinWait is useful on a multiprocessor system. However, it is not easy to compute an appropriate value for the SpinWait iterations. Moreover, finding a case that justifies the use of SpinWait is not easy. My advice is to avoid using this method as much as possible.

Resetting an Abort

When Abort is called on a thread, the thread is terminated after the execution of the catch blocks and the finally blocks. However, .NET also provides an option to the thread being aborted to override the abort directive. This is done by calling the static method Thread.ResetAbort within the catch block, as highlighted in the following code:

```
// Project Threads/ThreadAbort

public class Foo {
    public static void MyThreadProc() {
        while(true) {
            try {
                Console.WriteLine("I am in thread: {0}",
```

```
                  AppDomain.GetCurrentThreadId());
                Thread.Sleep(20*1000); // sleep for 20 seconds
            }catch(Exception e) {
                Console.WriteLine("Exception: {0}", e);
                Thread.ResetAbort();
            }finally {
                Console.WriteLine("Executing finally");
            }
        }
    }
}
```

MULTITHREADING ISSUES

Multithreading is a powerful technique that can improve the performance and responsiveness of your application. At the same time, multithreading introduces some complexities into your code that, if not properly attended to during the design and development cycle, may lead to disastrous results. In this section, we look at some important multithreading issues and the support .NET provides to handle them.

Shared Data Conflicts

If two threads have access to the same variable (more precisely, the same memory location), updating the variable from both the threads may leave the variable's value in an inconsistent state. Consider, for example, the following code:

```
// Project SharedData\SharedDataConflict

public class Foo {
    public int m_Counter = 10;

    public void Increase() {
      int temp = m_Counter;
      m_Counter = temp + 10;
    }
    ...
}
```

The initial value of the member field m_Counter is 10. The method Increase bumps up the value of m_Counter by 10. If two threads executed the method Increase, you would expect the value of m_Counter to be 30. However, the problem is that the operation is not atomic—one thread can get preempted by the OS after executing the first line of code. In this case, the other thread will pick up the same value of m_Counter as the first thread. Both the threads will add 10 to this value. After the result is stored back, the final value of m_Counter is 20 and not 30.

Although the example code was a bit convoluted, it does illustrate the fact that shared data conflicts may arise in multithreaded applications. Shared data conflicts may manifest themselves in a number of ways. In fact, even if one thread updates the data while other threads are reading it, the data may get into an inconsistent state. Consider, for example, the BCL collection class ArrayList. This class internally maintains an array and a field, _size, that indicates the total number of items in the list. Let's say one thread removes an object from the list. Internally, this results in updating the array as well as adjusting the field _size to reflect the new total. If the thread is preempted before _size is updated, a different thread picks the wrong value of _size and may try to access an object that has already been deleted. This results in either a NullReferenceException or some other unpredictable behavior.

If a memory location (or any other resource for that matter) can potentially be accessed concurrently from more than one thread, it is the responsibility of the developers to provide some explicit mechanism to synchronize access to such shared resources.

Fortunately, the .NET Framework provides many primitives to protect a shared resource. Let's examine some of the important ones.

Critical Section

A critical section locks access to a block of code. While a thread owns the lock to the critical section, no other thread can access the block of code.

Although critical sections imply that sections of code are critical, the semantics of critical sections are more often used to guard data against concurrent access.

Under .NET, the critical section functionality is provided by a BCL class, Monitor (namespace System). Using Monitor, you lock an object, execute a section of the code, and unlock the object. No other thread can lock the object while it is locked by one thread. Essentially, as long as all the threads agree to lock the object before using it, the object is safe from concurrent access.

Using the Monitor class, our previous code can be modified as follows:

```
// Project SharedData/SafeSharing

public class CriticalSectionDemo {
    public int m_Counter = 10;

    public void Increase() {
```

```
            Monitor.Enter(this);
            int temp = m_Counter;
            m_Counter = temp + 10;
            Monitor.Exit(this);
        }
        ...
    }
```

The static method `Monitor.Enter` is used to lock an object and static method `Monitor.Exit` is used to unlock an object that was previously locked in the same thread. The object to be guarded is passed as the parameter to the static methods. Multiple objects can be locked by calling `Monitor.Enter` on each object.

If a thread attempts to lock an object that has already been locked by a different thread, then a `Monitor.Enter` call blocks until the other thread unlocks the object. However, `Monitor` also provides a nonblocking method, `TryEnter`. This method tries to acquire a lock on the object and, if unsuccessful, immediately returns a `false` value. An overloaded version of `TryEnter` also lets you specify a time period to wait to acquire a lock.

Use `Perfmon` for Contentions

You can observe the resource contention behavior for your .NET application by watching a performance counter `Total # of Contentions` under the object `.NET CLR LocksAndThreads`. This counter is incremented each time `Monitor.Enter` fails to acquire a lock immediately or each time `Monitor.TryEnter` fails.

You may be wondering why I locked object `this`, an instance of `Foo`, instead of a more granular object `m_Counter`. After all, it is this field that we are trying to guard against concurrent access. Well, it just so happens that `m_Counter` is a value type. If you try to lock this field, it will silently get boxed into an object and the object will be locked. When a second thread tries to lock the field, it once again will be boxed into an object. However, this object in reality is not the same as the object that has been locked in the earlier thread. In essence, you end up locking a different object and not really guarding the field that you intended to.

In fact, a similar problem arises when you try to unlock a value type variable locked earlier on the same thread. The variable will get boxed into a new object during the call to `Monitor.Exit`. Essentially, you are trying to unlock an object that was never locked. This results in a `SynchronizationLockException`.

You could get smart and explicitly box the value type field to an object up front, as illustrated in the following code:

```
public void Increase() {
  Object o = m_Counter;
  Monitor.Enter(o);
  ...
  Monitor.Exit(o);
}
```

Although you managed to get rid of the exception, this code still has the problem discussed earlier. The objects being created in different threads are not the same and therefore do not guard the intended field.

Robust Coding

There is a slight problem in the way we have coded `Increase` in our previous example. If an exception gets thrown in the middle of the locked section, `Monitor.Exit` will never be called. As a result, the object will stay locked forever.

To ensure that `Monitor.Exit` is always called, you can wrap your code in a `try-finally`, as shown here:

```
public void Increase() {
  Monitor.Enter(this);
  try {
    int temp = m_Counter;
    m_Counter = temp + 10;
  }finally {
    Monitor.Exit(this);
  }
}
```

In fact, this style of coding is used so often that C# provides a keyword, `lock`, to achieve the same behavior. Using `lock`, the code can be rewritten as follows:

```
public void Increase() {
  lock(this) {
    int temp = m_Counter;
    m_Counter = temp + 10;
  }
}
```

Mutual Exclusion

A `mutex` is a synchronization primitive that grants exclusive access to a shared resource to only one thread at a time. If a thread acquires a mutex, the second thread that tries to acquire the mutex is suspended until the first thread releases the mutex.

Under .NET, the functionality of a mutex is abstracted in the class `Mutex`. You can call the `WaitOne` method to request ownership of a mutex and can call `ReleaseMutex` to release ownership of the mutex. This is illustrated in the following code:

```
class MutexDemo {
    private Mutex m_Mutex = new Mutex(false);
    private int m_Counter = 10;

    public void Increase() {
      m_Mutex.WaitOne();
      try {
        int temp = m_Counter;
        m_Counter = temp + 10;
      }finally {
        m_Mutex.ReleaseMutex();
      }
    }
    ...
}
```

A mutex can be owned by the creating thread at the time of creation. By passing a value of `false` to the constructor, we are indicating that the mutex is not owned by the creating thread. This way, any thread, including the creating thread, that wishes to access a shared resource must always call `WaitOne` to own the mutex.

When should we use `Mutex` instead of `Monitor`? Well, there are two good cases.

First, `Mutex` wraps the synchronization handle provided by the underlying Windows OS. Therefore, a `Mutex` object can be used to synchronize between managed and unmanaged code.

Second, a `Mutex` object can also be used to synchronize across processes. So far we have looked at unnamed mutexes, but a mutex can also be named. An overloaded constructor of `Mutex` takes this name as a parameter. The name is treated uniquely within all the processes on the machine. If the named mutex already exists at the time of creation, the `Mutex` object attaches to the existing mutex. Otherwise, a new mutex is created. Using a named mutex, you can synchronize access to a machine-wide resource.

For all other cases, using `Monitor` is preferred over `Mutex`. `Monitor` is more portable and it is also efficient in terms of OS resources.

Single-Writer-Multiple-Readers

Generally speaking, a *reader thread* (or simply *reader*) is the thread that wishes to examine the contents of a shared resource and has no intention of modifying it. A *writer thread* (or simply *writer*) is a thread that wishes to examine as well as modify the contents of a shared resource.

Note that readers and writers are not mutually exclusive. A thread in a reader state could be in a writer state later and vice versa.

A shared resource requires protection only if there is the possibility of a thread modifying the data while some other thread is reading or writing to it. Therefore, it would be okay for multiple readers to access the resource as long as there is no writer accessing the resource. However, if a writer is accessing a resource, no other readers or writers must be allowed to access it until the writer is done accessing the resource. Such functionality is referred to as single-writer-multiple-readers (SWMR).

Classes `Monitor` and `Mutex` do not distinguish between a reader and a writer thread. They simply provide exclusive ownership to a resource, irrespective of whether the owner thread is a reader or a writer.

However, the .NET Framework does provide a reader–writer-aware synchronization primitive in the form of the `ReaderWriterLock` class. Using `ReaderWriterLock`, a reader calls `AcquireReaderLock` to own the reader lock, examines the shared resource, and calls `ReleaseReaderLock` to release the lock. Likewise, a writer calls `AcquireWriterLock` to own the writer lock, potentially modifies the data, and calls `ReleaseWriterLock` to release the lock. This is illustrated in the following code excerpt:

```
// Project SharedData/SafeSharing

class SWMRDemo {
    private ReaderWriterLock rwl = new ReaderWriterLock();
    private int m_Counter = 10;

    public void SafeRead() {
      rwl.AcquireReaderLock(Timeout.Infinite);
      try {
        Console.WriteLine("Read: Value={0}", m_Counter);
      }finally {
        rwl.ReleaseReaderLock();
      }
    }
```

```
public void SafeWrite() {
  rwl.AcquireWriterLock(Timeout.Infinite);
  try {
    int temp = m_Counter;
    m_Counter = temp + 10;
    Console.WriteLine("Write: Value={0}", m_Counter);
  }finally {
    rwl.ReleaseWriterLock();
  }
}
...
}
```

Note that ReaderWriterLock provides the capability to timeout if a lock cannot be acquired within the specified time. The preceding code uses a time-out value of Timeout.Infinite that tells the method to wait indefinitely until the lock is acquired.

Should you always use ReaderWriterLock instead of Monitor or Mutex? Keep in mind that compared to Monitor or Mutex, ReaderWriter-Lock is more expensive in terms of OS resources, so you should use the class sparingly.

Sharing a Field

If you intend to share a single field among multiple threads, then it is not necessary to use any of the previously discussed synchronization primitives such as Monitor, Mutex, and so on. A read or a write to a field is atomic. However, sharing a field has one problem. In its zeal to optimize performance, the JIT compiler may cache the value of a field (perhaps storing it in the hardware register). As a result, when the writer thread updates the field (in the memory), the reader thread may not pick the updated value.

To prevent the JIT compiler from performing such optimizations, a shared field must be marked with an attribute volatile, as shown in the following code excerpt:

```
class Foo {
    private volatile bool m_bStatus;
    ...
}
```

For a volatile field, the JIT compiler does not store the value in the register. Instead, the compiler produces code to obtain the field's value from the memory each time the field is accessed. This guarantees that you always get the updated values.

Interlocking

Sometimes, read and write operations on a field must be performed as a single atomic operation. Obviously, locking the field using `Monitor` is quite efficient for such cases. However, for accessing a single field of type `int`, .NET provides a more efficient class, `Interlocked`. Some of the `Interlocked` methods can also be used on the types `long`, `float`, and `object`.

Table 8.2 lists the methods available on `Interlocked` along with their description and the types they can be applied to.

TABLE 8.2   Interlocked Methods

Method	*Description*	*Type Supported*
Increment	Increment the variable	int, long
Decrement	Decrement the variable	int, long
Exchange	Exchange the value of a variable	int, object, float
CompareEx-change	Compare and exchange the value of a variable	int, object, float

From the description of the `Interlocked` methods, it should be clear that these methods are useful when a read and a write to the same memory location must to be performed as one atomic operation.

The following code excerpt uses the `Increment` method to increment the value of variable `m_Counter` by 1.

```
public class InterlockedDemo {
    public int m_Counter = 10;

    public void Increase() {
      Interlocked.Increment(ref m_Counter);
    }
    ...
}
```

Synchronized Methods

.NET also provides a way to synchronize access at the method level. This is done using the `MethodImpl` attribute with the `MethodImplOptions.Synchronized` option on the method, as shown in the following code:

```
    [MethodImpl(MethodImplOptions.Synchronized)]
    public void Increase() {
      int temp = m_Counter;
```

```
    m_Counter = temp + 10;
}
```

The `MethodImpl` attribute is present in the `System.Runtime.Compil-erServices` namespace. The synchronized option specifies that the method can be executed by only one thread at a time. The end result is a behavior that is similar to enclosing the entire method in `lock(this)`.

In general, using `lock` is better than using this attribute primarily because `lock` gives you better granularity on the region of the code to lock.

Synchronization Contexts

Under .NET, a context can be configured such that the runtime provides intrinsic call serialization across all the objects in the context. No two threads can enter the context concurrently, one thread has to exit the context before another thread can enter it.

Developers of a class specify the synchronization requirement of the class by means of the configurable context attribute `SynchronizationAt-tribute` (namespace `System.Runtime.Remoting.Contexts`), as illustrated in the following code excerpt:

```
// Project SharedData/SafeSharing

[Synchronization(SynchronizationAttribute.REQUIRED_NEW)]
class SyncContextDemo : ContextBoundObject {
    private int m_Counter = 10;

    public void Increase() {
        int temp = m_Counter;
        Thread.Sleep(10*1000);
        m_Counter = temp + 10;
    }
    ...
}
```

Recall from Chapter 6 that context attributes are applicable only to classes that are inherited from `ContextBoundObject`.

The constructor for `SynchronizationAttribute` takes an enumeration value of type `SynchronizationOption` as the parameter. The possible synchronization options are listed in Table 8.3.

TABLE 8.3   Synchronization Options

Value	*Description*
NOT_SUPPORTED	The class will be instantiated in a context that cannot participate in synchronization.
REQUIRED	The class will be instantiated in a context that is configured for synchronization. If the creator's context is not compatible, a new context will be created.
REQUIRES_NEW	A new context configured for synchronization will be created and the class will be instantiated in the new context.
SUPPORTED	The class does not care if the context has synchronization.

The synchronization option that we used in the earlier code causes a new context to be created when the class is instantiated. The instance is then housed in this new context. Any call made to any nonstatic method on this object, or any other object that may reside in this context, is serialized. Only one thread can enter the context at any time.

The synchronization is achieved by means of a context-wide sink that intercepts and serializes any call entering the context. Recall from Chapter 6 that such a sink has to support the IContributeServerContextSink interface.

Finally, it is worth noting that .NET provides another SynchronizationAttribute class under the namespace System.EnterpriseServices. This class relies on COM+ services to provide synchronization. Unless you require COM+ interoperability in your .NET application, you should use the native .NET implementation of the SynchronizationAttribute class.

Deadlock and Reentrancy

The preceding mechanism ensures that only one thread can enter a context at a time but it creates the possibility of a deadlock. Consider, for example, two objects A and B that belong to two different contexts from two different processes. Consider the case of nested method calls where A calls a method on B, and B calls a method on A. When the client calls a method on A's proxy, A's context gets locked for all other threads. Object A then proceeds to call a method on B. This is a blocking call waiting for the response from B. Now B tries to make a call on A. This call comes back to A's context on a different thread that is provided by the underlying communication channel, but A's context is already locked. We now have a situation where the call from A to B is blocked and the call from B to A is blocked as well. A deadlock, indeed! This scenario can easily be extended to any number of objects making a chain of calls on the same call stack.

To prevent such deadlocks, .NET remoting uses the call context (Chapter 6), which you can think of as the logical ID of a stack of nested calls. Due to the synchronous nature of method invocations, the call context has a single logical thread of execution throughout the network, despite the fact that several physical threads may be used to service the calls.

The call context begins when a thread makes the first call to a managed method. The common language runtime generates a call context object and tags it to this method call and to all the subsequent nested calls from object to object, process to process, even across host machines. As the call progresses, each context covered gets locked with the identity of the call context. If an incoming call arrives while a context is locked, the runtime checks if the call context identity of the incoming call matches that of the one that locked the context. If the identities match, the runtime lets the call be serviced. If the incoming call is from a different call context, the runtime correctly blocks its entrance to the activity. Thus, by allowing reentrancy from the same caller, the synchronization context sink solves the deadlock problem.

Project `SharedData/SyncDomain` shows reentrancy in action.

Synchronizing Collections

In Chapter 5, we looked at using BCL-defined collection classes. Let's look at their proper usage in a multithreaded application.

The following class `Foo` contains a member field `m_List` of type `Array-List`:

```
// Project SharedData/SafeCollection

class MyApp {
    private ArrayList m_List = new ArrayList();
    ...
}
```

Our requirement is to protect `m_List` against concurrent access. If your first reaction is to lock `m_List`, then congratulations! It shows that you understand the fundamentals of locking. However, .NET distinguishes between a collection type object and its synchronization access point, or synchronization root as it is called. This provides the flexibility for multiple datatypes to share the same synchronization root. All the standard collection types support a property, `SyncRoot`, that returns the synchronization root object. The `ArrayList` object in our sample can be locked using its `SyncRoot` property, as shown in the following code excerpt:

```
class MyApp {
    private ArrayList m_List = new ArrayList();

    public void DoIt() {
        lock(m_List.SyncRoot) {
          ...
        }
    }
}
```

You may recall from Chapter 5 that SyncRoot is actually defined on the interface ICollection. Therefore, for guaranteed thread safety, you should always lock the SyncRoot property on any ICollection-based types, including regular arrays.

Synchronize Arrays If They Are Shared

A regular array also represents a collection type and hence supports the SyncRoot property. Always lock this property while accessing an array that is being shared in multiple threads.

Why are the standard collection types designed not to be thread-safe? The primary reason is to avoid the overhead of thread safety if these classes are to be used within a single thread. However, the .NET Framework also provides thread-safe wrapper classes for many collection classes and a few classes in the System.IO namespace (namely TextReader and Text-Writer). This gives developers the choice of either the standard class or its wrapper class, depending on their needs.

The thread-safe wrapper is obtained by calling the Synchronized method on the collection class, as illustrated in the following code:

```
class MyApp {
    private ArrayList m_List =
      ArrayList.Synchronized(new ArrayList());
    public void DoIt() {
      Console.WriteLine(m_List.IsSynchronized);
      ...
    }
}
```

The collection classes also support a property, IsSynchronized, that you can use to determine if you are using the original collection or its thread-safe version.

The thread-safe wrappers essentially lock the original collection's Syn-cRoot property for all mutating methods. It is important to understand that only the mutating methods are protected from concurrent access. Other operations, such as enumerating through a collection, are intrinsically not thread-safe. You still have to lock the collection during the enumeration.

Why bother with the thread-safe wrappers if you still have to lock the collection in some cases? Well, the wrappers occasionally take advantage of some implementation details to avoid unnecessary contention. The wrapper is aware of the internal optimizations of the original collection and provides an abstraction that can take advantage of these internal optimizations. It is generally better to use the thread-safe wrappers for shared collections.

State Changes

Most modern OSs provide some sort of signaling mechanism for inter-thread communication. One or more threads wait for a specific type of signal, which typically indicates a change in state. On receiving the signal, the threads can process the changed state.

Under .NET, the wait mechanism is encapsulated in a base class, WaitHandle, that provides methods to set a signal or wait for one or more signals. .NET classes that are based on WaitHandle include AutoResetEvent, ManualResetEvent, and Mutex. These classes wrap the corresponding synchronization handle provided by the OS.

Events

Under .NET, events come in two varieties: AutoResetEvent and ManualResetEvent. Both types of events, once signaled, remain signaled until a wait request is satisfied. In the case of AutoResetEvent, the state is automatically set to nonsignaled once a wait request is satisfied. In case of ManualResetEvent, the state remains signaled until Reset is called explicitly.

The following code excerpt implements a producer–consumer mechanism using a Queue object and an AutoResetEvent object. The producer adds items to the queue. Each time it adds an item, it sends a signal to the consumer thread. On receiving the signal, the consumer thread processes items from the queue.

```
// Project StateChanges/Events

class MyQueue {
    private Queue m_Queue = new Queue();
    private AutoResetEvent m_NewData =
      new AutoResetEvent(false);
```

```
// producer
public void AddData(int value) {
  lock(m_Queue.SyncRoot) {
    m_Queue.Enqueue(value);
  }
  m_NewData.Set(); // signal
}

// dedicated consumer thread
public void ConsumerThread() {
  while(m_NewData.WaitOne()) {
    lock(m_Queue.SyncRoot) {
      while(m_Queue.Count > 0) {
        int value = (int) m_Queue.Dequeue();
        Console.WriteLine(value);
      }
    }
  }
}
}
```

The constructor for the `AutoResetEvent` takes a boolean parameter to indicate the initial state of the signal. A value of `false` implies that the state will remain nonsignaled initially.

The producer adds data to the queue and signals the consumer thread by calling `Set` on the event object. The consumer thread waits for the event by calling `WaitOne` on the event object. This method, which actually is defined on `WaitHandle`, blocks indefinitely until a signal is received. Upon receiving the signal, the consumer thread processes the data from the queue.

Note that event signaling and protecting data from concurrent access are two different concepts (although used in conjunction most of the time). As the queue is being shared between multiple threads, each thread still needs to lock the queue before accessing it.

Besides `WaitOne`, `WaitHandle` provides many other forms of waits. For example, it is possible to wait for one signal from a group of signals using the static method `WaitAny` or to wait for all the signals from the group using another static method, `WaitAll`. It is also possible to specify a wait timeout using both these methods.

Finally, `WaitHandle` objects internally store synchronization handles from the OS. These handles are limited in number and should not be held if not needed. To let you dispose of handles, `WaitHandle` implements `IDisposable`. Although not shown in the sample code, you should always implement `IDisposable` on a class that contains an `IDisposable`-based field such as `AutoResetEvent`.

Monitor Signals

`WaitHandle` objects represent Windows OS waitable objects. Hence, they are not portable on other platforms. However, the framework provides a portable version of event signaling via `Monitor`, a class that we have already used earlier for protecting shared objects. Using Monitor, our previous sample can be rewritten as follows:

```
// Project StateChanges/UsingMonitor

class MyQueue {
    private Queue m_Queue = new Queue();

    public void AddData(int value) {
      lock(m_Queue.SyncRoot) {
        m_Queue.Enqueue(value);
        Monitor.Pulse(m_Queue);
      }
    }

    public void ConsumerThread() {
      lock(m_Queue.SyncRoot) {
        while(Monitor.Wait(m_Queue)) {
          while(m_Queue.Count > 0) {
            int value = (int) m_Queue.Dequeue();
            Console.WriteLine(value);
          }
        }
      }
    }
}
```

Static method `Monitor.Pulse` is used to raise a signal for the specified object. Static method `Monitor.Wait` is used to wait for a signal on the specified object. The object must be locked before either of these two methods can be called.

Looking at the code, the consumer thread locks the queue in the beginning and never seems to release it. You may be wondering how the method `AddData` ever gets to lock the queue. Actually method `Monitor.Wait` is implemented such that it temporarily releases the lock and waits to reacquire the lock. This gives other threads a chance to lock the object and update the data. When `Monitor.Pulse` is called, it causes the waiting thread to move to the active queue so that it can relock the object as soon as the other thread unlocks it.

`Monitor` has been implemented as a purely managed class, that is, it is not tied to any native synchronization primitives. This makes it fully portable. Also, it is more efficient in terms of OS resource requirements.

So when does using `WaitHandle`-based objects make sense? Here are two good cases:

1. `WaitHandle` objects can be used to synchronize between managed and unmanaged code.

2. It is possible to wait on more than one `WaitHandle` object at once using the static method `WaitHandle.WaitAll`.

Thread Affinity

On the Win32 platform, certain resources have thread affinity; that is, such resources can only be used by a specific thread. Some examples follow:

1. Mutexes have thread affinity. For example, you cannot own a mutex on one thread and release it from another thread.

2. A TLS by its definition has thread affinity. A TLS from one thread is not available in any other thread.

3. Windows Forms controls can be executed only from the thread in which they are created. If you want to get or set properties of a control, or call methods from a worker thread, the call must be marshaled to the thread that created the control.

In the case of Windows Forms, there are a few methods on the control (a control is represented by the class `Control`) that can be called from any thread. These methods include `Invoke`, `BeginInvoke`, and `EndInvoke`. The `Invoke` method invokes a delegate synchronously, whereas the `BeginInvoke`/`EndInvoke` pair is used for asynchronous operations. When any of these methods are called from a worker thread, the runtime marshals the call to the control's thread.

Certain applications also may have a special need to store data on a per-thread basis. Under .NET, the simplest way to accomplish this task is to define a static variable and annotate it with the `[ThreadStatic]` attribute as shown here:

```
class Foo {
    [ThreadStatic] private static int Value;
    ...
}
```

A variable that is marked as thread static is static to the thread and the application domain or context. Each thread stores a local copy of the variable. However, the copy is still bounded by the application domain (and context if the object is context-bound); that is, as a thread passes through a different domain or context, the domain or context has its own static copy.

There is yet another way to create thread-specific and context-specific data—by means of data slots. A data slot stores a data value. A data slot is typically identified by a name, although it is possible to have unnamed data slots.

Under .NET, the data slot is encapsulated in the class `LocalData-StoreSlot` (namespace `System`). However, the functionality of dealing with data slots is defined as static methods on the `Thread` class. Table 8.4 describes some `Thread` methods dealing with data slots.

TABLE 8.4 Data Slot Methods

Method	Description
Thread.AllocateDataSlot	Create a data slot
Thread.AllocateNamedDataSlot	Create a named data slot
Thread.GetNamedDataSlot	Get a named data slot
Thread.FreeNamedDataSlot	Free a previously allocated data slot
Thread.SetData	Store data in the data slot
Thread.GetData	Get data from the data slot

The following code excerpt demonstrates using a data slot. The code keeps track of the number of times a specific thread called the `Process` method:

```
// Project Threads/ThreadLocalStorage

class Foo {
    readonly String SLOTNAME = "My TLS Slot";

    public void Process() {
        LocalDataStoreSlot dataSlot =
            Thread.GetNamedDataSlot(SLOTNAME);

        Object obj = Thread.GetData(dataSlot);
```

```
        int val = 0;
        if (null != obj) {
          val = (int) obj;
        }

        val++;
        Console.WriteLine("Thread {0} accessed {1} times",
          AppDomain.GetCurrentThreadId(), val);
        Thread.SetData(dataSlot, val);
      }
    }
```

Of course, using a ThreadStatic variable instead of using a data slot can simplify the program, as illustrated here:

```
// Project Threads/ThreadLocalStorage

class Bar {
    [ThreadStatic] private static  int m_Counter = 0;

    public void Process() {
      m_Counter++;
      Console.WriteLine("Thread {0} accessed {1} times",
        AppDomain.GetCurrentThreadId(), m_Counter);
    }
}
```

Performance

Another issue to consider when writing multithreaded programs is performance. Using more threads doesn't necessarily translate into better performance, because:

- Each thread consumes some system resources. If the resources available to the OS decrease, the overall performance degrades.
- Thread switching is a very expensive operation. The OS has to save the thread context (the register values, etc.) of the executing thread and load the thread context of the new thread.

It may be useful to look at the performance characteristics of your application using Perfmon. .NET provides many useful counters under the .NET CLR LocksAndThreads object.

In a later section, we will look at how thread pools can be used to improve performance for a specific case of tasks.

At this point, you should be reasonably comfortable with multithread programming under .NET, the issues associated with it, and the support provided by the .NET Framework to solve these issues. Let's now move on to a different way of multithreading programming, by means of making asynchronous calls.

ASYNCHRONOUS PROGRAMMING

In the previous section, we were explicitly creating threads and managing their lifetime. In this section, we let the common language runtime do the grungy work for us.

Under the .NET asynchronous programming model, when a call is made to a .NET class method, the call returns immediately. The common language runtime sets up the actual method to be executed in a different thread. This makes it possible for the calling thread to continue forward with its execution. Contrast this to the synchronous programming model where the call blocks until the method is completely processed.

Once the method execution completes, the common language runtime provides two ways to obtain the results of the execution. You can call a specific method to obtain the results. You can also provide a callback function with your initial call so that the common language runtime can automatically invoke the callback function after the method execution is completed.

Asynchronous programming is supported in many areas of the .NET Framework, including:

- Asynchronous delegates
- Web services
- File IO, Socket IO
- Networking (HTTP, TCP)

Let's look at a few important areas of asynchronous programming.

Asynchronous Delegates

Asynchronous delegates provide the ability to call a synchronous method in an asynchronous manner. Consider the following code excerpt:

```
// Project AsyncProgramming/AsyncDelegate

public class Foo {
    public String GetGreeting(String user) {
        String retVal = "Hello " + user;
        return retVal;
    }
}
```

Let's see how we can invoke GetGreeting on the Foo object using an asynchronous delegate. The first step is to declare a delegate for the method, as shown here:

```
public delegate String GreetingProc(String user);
```

When compiled, this declaration results in a class that looks as follows:

```
public class GreetingProc : MulticastDelegate {
    public GreetingProc(Object o, int method);
    public IAsyncResult BeginInvoke(String user,
      AsyncCallback callback, Object o);
    public String EndInvoke(IAsyncResult result);
    public String Invoke(String user);
}
```

The methods that can be used for asynchronous programming are BeginInvoke and EndInvoke.

BeginInvoke is used to begin the asynchronous call. The method definition contains two more parameters than the original method to be invoked. The second to the last parameter is used to optionally specify a callback method. When the invoked method completes, the runtime automatically calls the specified callback method. The last parameter is used to pass the state information, which is any information you deem appropriate, wrapped as an object. This state object is simply made available to the callback method.

BeginInvoke returns a value of type IAsyncResult. This return value can be used later to obtain the outcome of the invoked method.

The return value of the actual method that is invoked, or the output type parameters, can be obtained by calling EndInvoke. The method definition contains all the ref type and out type parameters from the original method plus a parameter to pass in the return value from BeginInvoke.

Note that EndInvoke is a blocking call. It returns only when the invoked method completes.

If the invoked method throws an exception, you can catch the exception by putting a try-catch block around EndInvoke. You do not have to call

EndInvoke unless you are interested in processing the outcome of the invoked method.

Using BeginInvoke and EndInvoke, here is one way to call the method GetGreeting asynchronously:

```
public class SimpleDemo {
    public static void DoIt() {
        Foo f = new Foo();
        GreetingProc proc = new GreetingProc(f.GetGreeting);
        IAsyncResult iar = proc.BeginInvoke("Jay", null, null);

        String greeting = proc.EndInvoke(iar);
        Console.WriteLine(greeting);
    }
}
```

Note that we passed in null for the callback function because the main thread explicitly calls EndInvoke to get back the results. The call to EndInvoke blocks until the common language runtime finishes processing the delegate method (Foo.GetGreeting in our case). However, it is also possible to specify a callback function that the common language runtime can call after it has processed the delegate method. This is illustrated in the following code:

```
public class AsyncCBDemo {
    public static void FinishProcessing(IAsyncResult iar) {
        // Get the state object, if need be
        Object stateObj = iar.AsyncState;

        // Get the delegate object
        GreetingProc proc =
          (GreetingProc)((AsyncResult)iar).AsyncDelegate;

        // Call EndInvoke on the delegate object
        String greeting = proc.EndInvoke(iar);
        Console.WriteLine(greeting);
    }

    public static void DoIt() {
        Foo f = new Foo();

        GreetingProc proc = new GreetingProc(f.GetGreeting);

        // The example uses a dummy state object.
        // You should pass in a more meaningful object.
        Object stateObj = new Object();
```

```
IAsyncResult iar = proc.BeginInvoke("Jay",
    new AsyncCallback(AsyncCBDemo.FinishProcessing),
    stateObj);

    Console.WriteLine("Waiting for FinishProcessing
        to be called...");
    WaitHandle wh = iar.AsyncWaitHandle;
    wh.WaitOne();
    }
}
```

After the common language runtime finishes processing Foo.GetGreet-ing, it stores the return results in an object of type AsyncResult (namespace System.Runtime.Remoting.Messaging). As our main method DoIt speci-fies FinishProcessing as the callback method, the common language run-time then invokes FinishProcessing and passes the AsyncResult object as the parameter.

FinishProcessing needs to call EndInvoke on the delegate object, which can be obtained from the AsyncDelegate property on AsyncResult, as highlighted in the code.

When FinishProcessing calls EndInvoke on the delegate, this time EndInvoke returns immediately with the results, as the delegate method (Foo.GetGreeting) has already been processed.

Note the extra logic in the main thread for asynchronous call completion. When BeginInvoke is called, the common language runtime invokes the original method using a thread from an internal thread pool. The threads in the pool are marked as background threads. Recall that the common language runtime does not wait for background threads to complete while quitting the application. Therefore, we need a way to ensure that the asynchronous call does not get aborted. Fortunately, the IAsyncResult interface that is returned from BeginInvoke provides a wait handle by means of an Asyn-cWaitHandle property. We can wait on this handle by calling our familiar method WaitOne (or any of its variations).

There is still one problem with waiting on AsyncWaitHandle. The wait state is signaled when the asynchronous call has been completed, not when the callback method finishes. As a result, there is no guarantee that the call-back method has completed when the wait state is signaled.

A common technique to deal with this problem is to raise an event before returning from the callback method. The main thread can wait on this event instead of AsyncWaitHandle. The modified code is shown here:

```
// Project AsyncProgramming/AsyncDelegate

class ProperAsyncCBDemo {
    private AutoResetEvent m_Event = new AutoResetEvent(false);

    public void FinishProcessing(IAsyncResult iar) {
        GreetingProc proc =
            (GreetingProc)((AsyncResult)iar).AsyncDelegate;
        String greeting = proc.EndInvoke(iar);
        Console.WriteLine(greeting);
        m_Event.Set(); // Let the main thread know
    }

    public void DoIt() {
        Foo f = new Foo();
        GreetingProc proc = new GreetingProc(f.GetGreeting);
        IAsyncResult iar = proc.BeginInvoke("Jay",
            new AsyncCallback(this.FinishProcessing), null);

        Console.WriteLine("Waiting for the callback to
            complete...");
        m_Event.WaitOne();
    }
}
```

What would happen if the delegate method throws an exception while processing? Where does the exception go? The common language runtime catches and stores this exception. Whenever you call EndInvoke, the exception is re-thrown back. Therefore, if you expect your delegate method to throw an exception, you must set up a try-catch block while calling End-Invoke.

What about one-way methods; that is, methods marked with OneWayAttribute (Chapter 6)? Asynchronous delegates work equally well with one-way methods. Of course, calling EndInvoke for one-way methods is redundant; the runtime discards return values, return parameters, or exceptions thrown from one-way methods.

We are done with asynchronous delegates. At this point, it is worth noting that the .NET Framework extends this model seamlessly to .NET remoting. The preceding asynchronous delegate example can very easily be extended to .NET remoting. It is left as an exercise for you to make class Foo a remote object.

Web Service Clients

The .NET Framework also makes it possible to call a Web service method asynchronously. Given a WSDL description, the framework generates appropriate client-side proxy code containing the necessary BeginXXX and EndXXX methods for each Web service method where XXX is the name of the method.

Let's look at using the Calculator Web service that we developed in Chapter 6. For your convenience, I have listed the Web service code here:

```
public class MyCalculator : WebService {
    [WebMethod]
    public int Add(int a, int b) {
      return (a+b);
    }
}
```

Recall that the client-side proxy code for a Web service is generated using the tool wsdl.exe. For my setup, the proxy code is generated using the following command line:

```
wsdl.exe -o:Proxy.cs
    http://localhost/WSRemoting/Calculator.asmx?wsdl
```

Tool wsdl.exe generates a class that looks as follows:

```
    public class MyCalculator {
      public int Add(int a, int b);
      public IAsyncResult BeginAdd(int a, int b,
        AsyncCallback callback, object state);
      public int EndAdd(IAsyncResult asyncResult);
    }
```

Why do I get this feeling that you already know how to call the Web method Add asynchronously? Your smile probably gave it away.

Although the client-side implementation of an asynchronous Web method call is similar to that of an asynchronous delegate, there is one thing that is different. For the asynchronous Web method, the runtime passes the WebClientAsyncResult object to the callback (recall that for the asynchronous delegates, the object passed to the callback is of AsyncResult type). AsyncResult supports a property AsyncDelegate to obtain the original delegate object and call EndInvoke on it. However, currently WebClientAsyncResult does not support any property that will let you obtain the original Web service object and call EndXXX on it. The workaround that I use is to pack the Web service object in the state object and pass it to BeginXXX. This is illustrated in the following client-side code for the MyCalculator Web service.

```
// Project AsyncProgramming/AsyncWebServiceClient

class MyClient {
    class MyStateObject {
        public AutoResetEvent Event = new AutoResetEvent(false);
        public MyCalculator Calc = new MyCalculator();
    }

    public static void MyFinishProc(IAsyncResult iar) {
        MyStateObject o = (MyStateObject) iar.AsyncState;
        int val = o.Calc.EndAdd(iar);
        Console.WriteLine(val);
        o.Event.Set(); // let the main thread know
    }

    public static void Main() {
        MyStateObject stateObject = new MyStateObject();

        IAsyncResult iar = stateObject.Calc.BeginAdd(10, 20,
          new AsyncCallback(MyFinishProc), stateObject);

        Console.WriteLine("Waiting for the callback to
          complete...");
        stateObject.Event.WaitOne();
    }
}
```

Thread Pooling

Many applications use multiple threads, but quite often these threads spend a great deal of time in a sleeping state waiting for an event to occur. Other times, threads might enter a sleeping state and wake up only periodically to do some processing and then go back to sleep again. Such applications can benefit from using a thread pool, which maintains a pool of worker threads. A thread pool is best suited for small tasks that require multiple threads. Using a thread pool has many advantages:

- The management of the thread pool is usually abstracted away from you so that you can focus on application tasks rather than pool management.
- A well-written thread pool class can optimize throughput and thread time slices based on available system resources.

The .NET Framework uses thread pools for several purposes. One that we have already seen is for asynchronous calls. Other uses include socket connections and asynchronous I/O completion.

Under .NET, a thread pool is implemented under a class `ThreadPool`. There is one `ThreadPool` object per AppDomain. However, at the physical level, there is only one thread pool per process (at least in the first version of the framework).

Here is the definition of the class `ThreadPool`. For simplicity, I have shown only those methods that are relevant for our current discussion:

```
public sealed class ThreadPool {
    // Add items to the queue
    public static bool
      QueueUserWorkItem(WaitCallback cb, object stateObj);
    public static RegisteredWaitHandle
      RegisterWaitForSingleObject(WaitHandle wh,
        WaitOrTimerCallback callback, Object state,
          int timeOut, bool justOnce);

    // Thread pool status
    public static void GetAvailableThreads(
      out int workerThreads, out int completionPortThreads);
    public static void GetMaxThreads(
      out int workerThreads, out int completionPortThreads);
    ...
}
```

The static method `QueueUserWorkItem` can be used to add a task (called a *work item* in .NET) to the thread pool. This method takes as a parameter a delegate of type `WaitCallback`. The definition of this delegate type is shown here:

```
public delegate void WaitCallBack(object stateObject);
```

Essentially, each work item method takes a state object as parameter and has a `void` return value. The state object is any object that you want your queued method to have access to.

Here is a simple code that adds a work item, `MyTask`, to the thread pool:

```
// Project Threads/ThreadPool

class Foo {
    private AutoResetEvent m_Event = new AutoResetEvent(false);

    void MyTask(Object stateObject) {
```

```
      Console.WriteLine("In");
      m_Event.Set(); // let the main thread know
   }

   public void DoIt() {
      ThreadPool.QueueUserWorkItem(new WaitCallback(Task));

      // Wait for completion (if need be)
      m_Event.WaitOne();
   }
}
```

The common language runtime uses one of the threads from the pool to invoke the work item MyTask. The implementation of the MyTask method uses an event to signal its completion to the main thread, a technique that we have seen and used in the past.

In the preceding code, the state object provided to the callback is null. However, an overloaded version of QueueUserWorkItem lets you specify a state object that the runtime passes over to the work item.

The thread pool class also lets you associate a wait handle with a work item such that the work item is executed if the wait handle is signaled. Further, you can also configure it such that the work item is executed if the wait handle is not signaled within a certain timeout period. All this is made possible through the static method ThreadPool.RegisterWaitForSingleObject. The signature for this method was shown earlier. The delegate type WaitOrTimerCallback that this method uses is defined as follows:

```
public delegate void WaitOrTimerCallback(Object state,
      bool timedOut);
```

The first parameter, state, is the state object as set by the caller to RegisterWaitForSingleObject. The second parameter, timedOut, indicates the reason the callback was invoked. A value false implies that the wait handle was signaled within the specified timeout interval.

Here is a sample code excerpt that illustrates the use of this method:

```
// Project Threads/ThreadPool

class Bar {
    void MyTask(Object stateObject, bool timedOut) {
       Console.WriteLine("In: {0}", timedOut);
    }

    public void DoIt() {
```

```
    AutoResetEvent e = new AutoResetEvent(false);

    ThreadPool.RegisterWaitForSingleObject(
        e,
        new WaitOrTimerCallback(MyTask),
        null,
        -1,
        true);

    Thread.Sleep(5*1000);
    e.Set();
    }
}
```

The roles of the first three parameters to RegisterWaitForSingleObject are obvious from the signature of the method and need no further explanation. The fourth parameter, timeOut, defines the time period in milliseconds to wait for the signal. A value of –1 indicates an indefinite wait. The fifth parameter, justOnce, indicates whether to wait just once or reset the wait timer each time the callback is called.

By setting the fourth parameter to a suitable timeout period and the fifth parameter to false, as shown in the following code excerpt, you can create a simple scheduler where a method is automatically called periodically.

```
    ThreadPool.RegisterWaitForSingleObject(
        e,
        new WaitOrTimerCallback(MyTask),
        null,
        10*1000, // wait for 10 seconds
        false);
```

Thread Pool Internals

There is only one ThreadPool object per application domain. The thread pool is created the first time you call ThreadPool.QueueUserWorkItem, or when a registered wait operation queues a callback method. Once submitted, a work item cannot be canceled.

The initial size of the pool (i.e., the number of worker threads in the pool) is one. As each item is queued, the thread pool checks if any thread in the pool is available for reuse. If not, it spawns a new worker thread and adds it to the pool. Each worker thread runs with the default stack size and priority, and in the multithreaded apartment. When processing the work item or the callback, the worker thread switches to the correct application domain.

The .NET Framework defines a limit on the maximum number of worker threads per process (not per application domain). The limit is determined based on the number of CPUs in the machine. Currently, this limit is defined as 25 per CPU. However, a runtime host is allowed to change the limit to a more suitable value (using the API `CorSetMaxThreads`).

Besides spawning the worker threads, the thread pool may also spawn up to two more threads for internal housekeeping functions.

The restriction on the number of worker threads does not impose a limit on the number of work items that can be added. These work items are limited only by the amount of available memory. If a work item is added, and all the worker threads are busy, then the work item is just queued until a worker thread becomes available.

Finally, it is worth mentioning that there are times when you may want to create your own thread pool mechanism instead of using the system-provided `ThreadPool` class. Here are some reasons:

- You want to place a thread into a single-threaded apartment (all `Thread-Pool` threads are placed in the multithreaded apartment).
- You need to run a task at a particular priority.
- You need to dedicate a specific thread in the thread pool for certain tasks.

SUMMARY

The .NET Framework supports multithreaded programming in two ways:

1. By letting you explicitly create and use threads.
2. By letting you make asynchronous calls.

Using the class `Thread`, you can create a thread, abort a thread, or wait for a thread to complete. You can also adjust the properties of a thread, such as the priority and the COM apartment model.

Class `Thread` and all other thread-related classes are defined under the namespace `System.Threading`.

You can use asynchronous delegates to make asynchronous calls. In this case, .NET uses threads from a thread pool to serve your request. You can use `BeginInvoke` to execute a method asynchronously and optionally use `End-Invoke` to retrieve output parameters. The asynchronous delegates work seamlessly with .NET remoting.

Asynchronous calls are also provided by the .NET Web services Framework. Use `BeginXXX` and `EndXXX` calls to begin and end a Web method.

Multithreaded programming requires careful designing. Some important issues with multithreading are shared resource conflicts, interthread communication, and performance.

To protect shared resources, the framework provides many classes, including the following:

- `Monitor`: Provides exclusive access to objects.
- `Mutex`: Provides exclusive access to a section of code (and therefore data).
- `ReaderWriterLock`: SWMR lock.
- `Interlocked`: An efficient mechanism for updating a variable.
- `MethodImpl`: An attribute that synchronizes access to a method.
- `SynchronizationAttribute`: An attribute that synchronizes access to all the objects in a context.
- `SyncRoot` property: For synchronizing collections.

For interthread signaling, the framework provides the following classes:

- `AutoResetEvent`: An event that, once raised, gets reset automatically.
- `ManualResetEvent`: An event that requires explicit resetting.
- `Monitor`: A portable version of event signaling.

More threads doesn't necessarily imply better performance because of the costs associated with creating a thread. Also, context switching between threads is an expensive operation.

The framework provides a thread pool and a `ThreadPool` class to access it. Some specific tasks can benefit from using the thread pool.

Security

T he .NET Framework offers two security mechanisms—code access security and role-based security. Both security mechanisms are built on top of the security provided by the underlying OS. Code access security keeps track of where the assemblies come from and what security permissions should be granted to them. Role-based security enables the code to make security decisions based on the role of the user executing the code.

In this chapter, we look at the concepts underlying code access security and role-based security. We also examine the classes and services provided by the .NET Framework to facilitate the use of these security mechanisms.

Security is also an important consideration for ASP.NET applications. ASP.NET applications need to authenticate clients and provide restricted access to any sensitive data, based on the client credentials. In addition, the ASP.NET applications may also have to act on behalf of the client in some cases to access OS secured resources such as NTFS files. In this chapter, we also examine various security features that ASP.NET provides to deal with authentication, authorization, and impersonation.

INTRODUCTION

Windows is a secure OS. The security offered by the OS protects the local machine from any unauthorized user operation. Each secured resource under the OS, such as the Windows registry or an NTFS file, can be configured to allow access to some users, while denying access to others. This approach, however, fails to address an important security issue: users acquiring and running third-party applications that potentially could be malicious. Today, users obtain the applications from many sources. They have no idea what the application code does internally. The code may delete some important files on the local disk. Worst yet, the code may leak your private data. The quality of the code may be poor; it might contain bugs or vulnerabilities that some other malicious code may take advantage of. The ease of downloading components over the Internet has exacerbated this security issue.

Microsoft has put a lot of thought into designing the .NET Framework so that the number of bugs can be reduced in the code that you develop. Here are some examples:

- A common source of security bugs is that developers fail to check the error codes. Under .NET, all the standard classes throw exceptions in case of an error. This forces developers to check the error conditions.

- Array bounds are always checked, eliminating many sources of buffer overruns.

- All variables are guaranteed to be initialized. This avoids people being able to read random bits of memory.

- During JIT compilation, by default a verification process examines whether the metadata and the MSIL instructions of the method to be JIT compiled are type safe (there is a way to override this default behavior using a security action called SkipVerification, which we will see later). Type-safe code can access only the memory locations that it is authorized to access. It is disallowed from accessing all other memory locations. This isolation helps ensure that assemblies can execute in the same process without adversely affecting each other.

Although these built-in precautions are good security measures, they don't (and cannot) address the fact that a third-party assembly may contain malicious code.

To ensure that untrustworthy assemblies do not harm your computer, the .NET Framework provides a security mechanism called Code Access Security (CAS). Based on CAS, code obtained from unknown origins can be configured to run with restricted permissions, thereby reducing the chances of the code being able to harm your computer. For example, if you were visiting a Web page that caused managed code to be downloaded and run on your local system, CAS would prevent it from formatting your hard drive even though you, as the user, might have the appropriate Windows NT permissions to do so.

The CAS mechanism enforces security based on the identity of the code, not that of the user. There are times, however, when an application may wish to make security decisions based on the user's identity and group member-

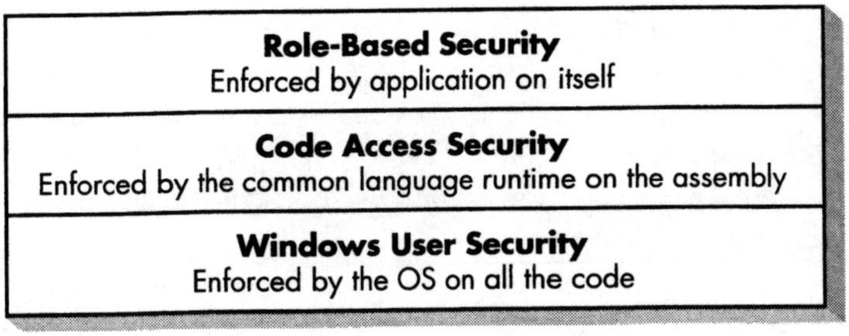

| **Role-Based Security** |
| Enforced by application on itself |
| **Code Access Security** |
| Enforced by the common language runtime on the assembly |
| **Windows User Security** |
| Enforced by the OS on all the code |

FIGURE 9.1   Security levels for .NET applications.

ship. To address this, .NET provides another security mechanism referred to as role-based security. This security mechanism enables the code to make security decisions based on the role the user belongs to.

The relationship between OS security and .NET security can be envisioned as three levels, each level influencing the ones above it, as depicted in Figure 9.1.

Let's look at the concepts underlying CAS and role-based security.

CODE ACCESS SECURITY

To understand CAS, let's develop a simple program that accesses the local file system. Here is the relevant code excerpt:

```
// Project Evidence/Foo

[assembly: AssemblyVersionAttribute("1.2.3.4")]
[assembly: AssemblyKeyFileAttribute(@".\Bin\MyKey.snk")]

public class Foo {
    public void Store(String s){
        FileStream f = new FileStream("Foo.log",
          FileMode.Append, FileAccess.Write);
        StreamWriter w = new StreamWriter(f);
        w.WriteLine(s);
        w.Close();
        f.Close();
    }
}
```

Method `Store` simply opens a local file `Foo.log`, appends the specified string to the file, and closes the file.

We will build this code as a library application, Foo.dll. Note that the assembly is signed with a strong name. This is needed because we will download the assembly over the network and install it in the download cache later in the experiment.

Here is the code excerpt for the client application, built as MyClient.exe:

```
// Project Evidence/MyClient

public class MyApp {
    public static void Main() {
        Foo f = new Foo();
        f.Store("Hello World!");
    }
}
```

Copy Foo.dll and MyClient.exe in a directory and run MyClient.exe. You will see that a file Foo.log is created in the local directory. If you open this file using Notepad, you will see that it contains the string "Hello World!"

Now set up a virtual directory under IIS on the local machine. Copy Foo.dll to the root of the virtual directory. For my experiment, I am using an alias name SecurityDemo for the virtual directory. This allows Foo.dll to be accessible using the URL http://localhost/SecurityDemo/Foo.dll.

Copy MyClient.exe to a new directory. Do not copy Foo.dll to this directory. Instead, create an application configuration file in this directory, MyClient.exe.Config, that contains the codeBase entry for Foo.dll that points to this URL. Recall from Chapter 3 that the assembly pointed by the codeBase entry is automatically downloaded and installed in the current user's download cache.

Run MyClient.exe from the new directory. The program will abort with an exception that the code in Foo.dll does not have the security permission of type FileIOPermission.

In both the test cases, it is the same program and the same user. Yet one case succeeded and the other failed. The only difference is that in the first case Foo.dll was being accessed from the local directory, whereas in the second case the assembly originated, or was perceived to be originating, from a different machine on the intranet.

This is the essence of CAS under .NET. Based on certain evidence about the origin or the author of the assembly, the assembly is granted certain security permissions such as reading or writing files, changing environmental variables, displaying dialog boxes, and so on. The exact set of permissions to be granted is controlled by a security policy on the local machine. The standard classes under .NET that deal with any security sensitive operations are designed to perform the appropriate security check. If the assembly does not have the needed permissions, the security mechanism throws an exception of type `SecurityException`.

The security provided by CAS is above and beyond the security provided by the underlying OS. Even if some code successfully gets past the CAS, it still is subjected to the access checks provided by the OS.

Before we go any further, it is worth understanding that although the permissions are granted at the assembly level, the CAS check is performed on the complete call chain. To see why this is necessary, consider two assemblies, A and B. Based on the evidence, let's assume A is trustworthy and is granted complete permissions, whereas B is not that trustworthy and is granted minimal permissions. Now consider the case when B makes a call into A. We have a problem. Although B has restricted permissions, it can lure A into doing evil things (e.g., destroying your private documents, or leaking them out).

To avoid such luring attacks, the common language runtime walks the whole stack and verifies that every caller in the call chain has the permissions demanded by the operation. If even one caller in the call chain does not have the requisite permissions, the runtime throws the security exception.

Now let's delve further into various aspects of the CAS.

Code Access Permissions

Code access permissions protect resources and operations from unauthorized use. Each code access permission is implemented as a class. Table 9.1 summarizes the code access permission classes that are currently implemented by the .NET Framework.

TABLE 9.1 Code Access Permissions

Permission	Description
`DirectoryServicesPermission`	Controls access to Active Directory classes (under the namespace `System.Directory-Services`).
`DnsPermission`	Controls access to DNS servers on the network.
`EnvironmentPermission`	Controls read and write access to individual environment variables.

TABLE 9.1 Code Access Permissions (Continued)

Permission	Description
EventLogPermission	Controls read and write access to event log services.
FileDialogPermission	Allows read-only access to files that have been selected by the interactive user in an Open dialog box.
FileIOPermission	Controls read, write, and append access to individual files and directory trees.
IsolatedStorageFilePermission	Controls access to the isolated storage file system. Isolated storage provides a unique file system for an assembly.
IsolatedStoragePermission	Controls access to the isolated storage.
MessageQueuePermission	Controls access to Microsoft Message Queue (MSMQ).
OleDbPermission	Controls access to databases using Object Linking Embedding Database.
PerformanceCounterPermission	Controls access to performance counters.
PrintingPermission	Controls access to printers.
ReflectionPermission	Allows access to view assembly metadata using Reflection.
RegistryPermission	Controls read, write, create, and delete access to registry keys, subkeys, and values.
SecurityPermission	This is really a metapermission, as it governs the use of the security infrastructure itself. Several unrelated permissions are also grouped under this category. This includes the ability to execute managed code, call into unmanaged code, skip code verification, extend the infrastructure (e.g., adding context sinks), and so on.
ServiceControllerPermission	Controls access to Windows services, both running and stopped.
SocketPermission	Allows making or accepting connections on a transport address.
SqlClientPermission	Allows access to SQL databases.
UIPermission	Controls access to user interface functionality such as clipboard, user input, and so on. Can also be used to restrict window usage to "safe" windows so that the code cannot spool system dialog boxes and ask for sensitive information such as passwords.
WebPermission	Controls access to specific or all Internet resources (identified by their URLs).

A CAS class is required to inherit from a standard class, CodeAccess-
Permission (namespace System.Security). This class defines some standard methods to deal with permissions. As we go through the rest of this section,
we will see many of these methods in action.

Demanding Permissions

Instead of relying on the underlying security-aware .NET class to throw a
security exception, a component can perform the security check directly.
Class CodeAccessPermission defines a method, Demand, that can be called
to explicitly request a specific permission. If the requested permission has not
been granted to any of the callers in the call stack, the method throws a SecurityException. This is illustrated in the following code excerpt, where
method Store explicitly requests the permissions to append to a file and, if
permission is not granted, takes a different action:

```
// Project Permission/SecurityChecks

public class Foo {
    public void StoreDemand(String s){
        String fullPath = Path.GetFullPath("Foo.log");
        CodeAccessPermission perm =
          new FileIOPermission(FileIOPermissionAccess.Append,
            fullPath);
        try {
          perm.Demand(); // Request for the permission
          ... // Proceed with opening the file
        }catch(SecurityException) {
          Console.WriteLine("Not permitted to append to
            file {0}", fullPath);
        }
    }
}
```

At this point, it is useful to remember that even if the code clears the
.NET FileIOPermission check, it is still subject to the security check provided by the underlying OS. For example, if Foo.log is marked as a read-
only file, then the preceding code will throw a System.UnauthorizedAc-
cessException.

Implied Permissions

Before we go further, it is important to understand that some permissions,
when granted, imply others. For example, if you are granted all access to the
directory C:\Temp, you are implicitly granted all access to its children in the
hierarchy (C:\Temp*.*, C:\Temp\Foo*.*, C:\Temp\Bar*.*, etc.).

To check if a permission is a subset of another permission, you can call the IsSubsetOf method of CodeAccessSecurity. This is illustrated in the following code excerpt.

```
// Project Permissions/SecurityChecks

public static void SubsetTest() {
    CodeAccessPermission p1 = new FileIOPermission(
      FileIOPermissionAccess.AllAccess, @"C:\Temp");
    CodeAccessPermission p2 = new FileIOPermission(
      FileIOPermissionAccess.Append,
@"C:\Temp\Foo\Bar.txt");
    bool b = p2.IsSubsetOf(p1);
    Console.WriteLine(b);
}
```

This code, when executed, indicates that p2 is a subset of p1.

The presence of implied permissions makes it convenient to administer security policies. The common language runtime automatically compares a demanded permission to see if it is a subset of a granted permission.

Restricted Permissions

If an assembly is installed locally, it most likely will have wide-ranging or even completely unrestricted code access permissions. Imagine if one of these highly trusted assemblies were to make a call into an unknown, perhaps untrustworthy, assembly.

Although the security policy is likely to ensure that the untrustworthy assembly is granted limited permissions, even the calling assembly can restrict the effective permissions before making the call. CodeAccessServices provides a method, Deny, to place an extra restriction in the current stack frame. It is also possible to group a number of permissions together as one set and deny the entire set. The collection of permissions is represented by a class PermissionSet. The following code excerpt illustrates the use of the PermissionSet object to deny access to certain resources:

```
// Project Permissions/SecurityChecks

public static void DenyPermissions() {
    PermissionSet ps =
      new PermissionSet(PermissionState.None);
    ps.AddPermission(new EnvironmentPermission(
      PermissionState.Unrestricted));
    ps.AddPermission(new UIPermission(
      PermissionState.None));
```

```
    ps.AddPermission(new FileIOPermission(
      FileIOPermissionAccess.Append,
      Path.GetFullPath("Foo.log")));
    ps.Deny();

    Foo f = new Foo();
    f.StoreDemand("Hello World!");
    ...
    CodeAccessPermission.RevertDeny();
}
```

The code places extra restrictions on the current stack frame. This means that if `Foo.Store` tries to access any environmental variable, sneak a peek at the contents of the clipboard, or access the file `Foo.log`, the operation will fail. The restrictions are also applicable to any other component that `Foo.Store` tries to access.

Note that each stack frame can have at the most one permission set used for denial. If `Deny` is called twice, the second call effectively overwrites the first.

When the method that called `Deny` returns, the denial permission set is automatically removed from the current stack frame. However, you can explicitly empty the denial permission set yourself by calling a static method, `CodeAccessPermission.RevertDeny`, as shown in the previous code.

If you find yourself denying lots of individual permissions, you might find it easier to take a different approach: instead of denying permissions, grant only specific permissions. This is done by calling the `PermitOnly` method, either on the `CodeAccessSecurity` object or the `PermissionSet` object. Obviously, this works only if you know exactly which permissions you'd like to allow. As with the denial permission set, the permit-only permission set is automatically emptied when the caller returns. However, you can also call a static method, `CodeAccessPermission.RevertPermitOnly`, explicitly to revert back to the original status.

Suppressing the Stack Walk

The stack-walking mechanism is great for avoiding luring attacks like the one described earlier. However, it also creates a problem for trustworthy assemblies.

Imagine a class that is designed to provide service to other assemblies. Our `Foo` class is a good example. Its `StoreDemand` method can be used to log errors at one central place. As `Foo` is a well-written class from a trusted source, the security policy grants it full access to the local file. Now consider the case when another assembly with restricted permissions tries to invoke the StoreDemand method on Foo. The stack-walking mechanism checks if every caller in the chain has the requisite FileIOPermission. As the calling code does not have this permission, it generates a SecurityException, although Foo has been deemed safe for use by the security policy.

To deal with such cases, the security mechanism provides for the code to assert its own authority. The code can assert the permissions that it needs by calling the method Assert (available on CodeAccessSecurity and hence any of its derivations). This is illustrated in the following code excerpt:

```
// Project Permissions/Foo

public class Foo {
    public void StoreAssert(String s){
       String fullPath = Path.GetFullPath("Foo.log");
       CodeAccessPermission perm =
          new FileIOPermission(FileIOPermissionAccess.Append,
             fullPath);
       perm.Assert();

       ... // Continue opening the file
    }
}
```

The method StoreAssert asserts a File-IO permission before opening the file. Each stack frame has the potential to have an asserted permission set. When the stack walk reaches the stack frame, it considers the asserted permission satisfied. The stack walk won't continue further unless there are other permissions being demanded that aren't satisfied by the asserted permission set.

Note that you can assert only those permissions that your assembly has been granted by the security policy.

Similar to denial and permit-only permission sets, the asserted permission set is torn down when the calling method returns. However, one can explicitly call CodeAccessPermission.RevertAssert to empty the asserted permission set.

At this point, it is worth mentioning that the ability to assert permissions can clearly be abused. For example, a rogue component can call Foo.Store-Assert and send very large strings to fill up the user's hard disk. So, even though Foo is considered safe, attacks can still occur simply because of the assertion.

Do not just avoid using Assert because of issues like these. Instead, ask your peers to review any use of this feature.

One instance in which assertions are absolutely essential is when invoking unmanaged code from the managed code. Consider the system-defined FileStream class as an example. Clearly, this class needs to make calls to the underlying OS (which is implemented as unmanaged code) to open, close, read, and write files. The interop layer demands a SecurityPermission (with flag SecurityPermissionFlag.UnmanagedCode) when these calls are made. If this demand were to propagate up the stack, no code would be allowed to access files unless also granted permission to make calls into unmanaged code.

From a design standpoint, it is worth noting that FileStream does not simply assert the UnmanagedCode permission. It first ensures that the callers have the permission for file IO by demanding a FileIOPermission in its constructor. If this permission is not satisfied, the object itself can never be constructed.

Finally, because assertion is a powerful facility with the potential for abuse, its usage is also governed by a SecurityPermission (with flag SecurityPermissionFlag.Assertion).

Permission Attributes

So far we have used the security actions (Demand, Deny, PermitOnly, Assert) programmatically. However, it is also possible to define these actions declaratively. Each of the code access permission classes that we listed in Table 9.1 has a corresponding attribute class. For example, FileIOPermission has a corresponding attribute class, FileIOPermissionAttribute, and RegistryPermission has a corresponding attribute class, RegistryPermission-Attribute.

The following code excerpt is a variation of our earlier defined method to append strings to a file. Here, FileIOPermissionAttribute is used to assert the file-append permission:

```
// Project Permissions/Foo

public class Foo {
    [FileIOPermission(SecurityAction.Assert,
        Append=@"C:\Temp\Foo.log")]
    public void StoreAssertEx(String s){
        // proceed with opening the file and appending
        // the string. No explicit assertion needed.
        ...
    }
}
```

The biggest advantage of defining security actions using attributes is that the attributes become part of the metadata and thus can be discovered easily via Reflection. This would allow you, for example, to write a tool that shows various permissions required for your classes and methods.

The main drawback of this approach is that it is impossible for the method to catch an exception if the permission being asserted or demanded is denied. This particular drawback applies only to asserting or demanding permissions. You will never have this problem if you are using declarative attributes to simply restrict permissions.

A second drawback of this approach is that arguments passed to the attribute should be known at compile time. For example, in the preceding code, the absolute path name of the file has to be known at compile time. Constructing the path name at runtime, as we did in our earlier examples, is not an option.

The permission attribute classes take the first parameter an enumeration of type `SecurityAction`. Table 9.2 describes the options available on the enumeration, along with the time at which the option is considered by the runtime.

TABLE 9.2.   SecurityAction Enumeration

Action	Description	Time of Action
LinkDemand	Check demand only on the immediate caller.	JIT compilation
InheritanceDemand	Check demand on any derived class or an overridden method in the derived class.	Load time
Demand	Check demand on all the callers in the call stack.	Execution time
Assert	Check callers in the call stack only up to the point where the asserted permission is satisfied.	Execution time
Deny	Deny a specific permission to successive calls in the current call stack.	Execution time
PermitOnly	Allow only specific permissions to successive classes in the current call stack.	Execution time
RequestMinimum	The request for minimum permissions required for the code to run. This option can be used only at the assembly level.	Grant time
RequestOptional	The request for optional permissions. The code still executes if the requested permissions are not granted. This option can be used only at the assembly level.	Grant time
RequestRefuse	The request to deny specific permissions. This option can be used only at the assembly level.	Grant time

The last three options in Table 9.2 are available only at the assembly level. We revisit these options later.

Evidence

The common language runtime grants permissions to an assembly based on the information it obtains about the assembly. This information, called *evidence*, includes items such as the origin or the author of the assembly.

The security policy gathers the evidence for an assembly in the form of the following questions:

- From which site was this assembly obtained? An example of a site is *www.somecompany.com.*
- From which URL was this assembly obtained? An example of the URL is *www.somecompany.com/Demo/Foo.dll.* An asterisk can be used as a wildcard character at the end of the URL, as in *somecompany/Demo/*.*
- From what zone was this assembly obtained? .NET defines five zones: Internet, Local intranet, Trusted Sites, Untrusted Sites, and My Computer. The first four zones are the same as those found under Internet Explorer. The last zone represents the local computer.
- Who is the publisher of this assembly? This is obtained from the Authenticode digital signature of the assembly, if present.
- What is the strong name of this assembly?
- What is the hash value of this assembly?
- What is the directory name of this assembly? The security policy can be configured such that all the assemblies in the specified directory or its child directory can be granted specific permissions.

The evidence is gathered either by the common language runtime itself or the hosts of the common language runtime such as ASP.NET and the shell host (which launches .NET applications from the shell). The evidence is then submitted to the common language runtime, which in turn grants proper permissions to the assembly.

It is worth noting that the host itself must be trusted to not submit false evidence. This is the reason that the host is required to have a special security permission, `ControlEvidence`. The common language runtime itself is naturally trusted to provide evidence—after all, it is trusted to grant proper permission.

Identity Permissions

The .NET Framework also defines a different type of permission called the identity permission. Identity permissions represent characteristics that identify an assembly. The common language runtime grants identity permissions to an

assembly based on the evidence provided by the hosts. Some examples of identity permissions are SiteIdentityPermission (representing the Web site
where the assembly originated) and StrongNameIdentityPermission (representing the strong name of the assembly).

Identity permissions have a set of functionality that is common with code access
permissions. For example, identity permissions can be asserted or can be
demanded. In fact, identity permissions inherit from the same base class as code
access permissions, CodeAccessPermission.

Let's now look at how the common language runtime grants code access
permissions to an assembly.

Security Policy

Once the host and the common language runtime have gathered as much evidence as possible, they submit the evidence to the common language runtime.
Based on the evidence, the common language runtime grants permission to
an assembly.

The exact permissions that are granted to an assembly are based on an
entity on the local machine called the *security policy*. The security policy
defines the mapping between the evidence of the assembly and the permissions to be granted to the assembly.

The .NET Framework provides two tools to view and modify the security
policy. The first tool is a command-line program called the Code Access
Security Policy Tool (caspol.exe). The second one is a GUI tool called the
.NET Framework Configuration tool (MsCorCfg.msc). Choosing which tool
to use is a matter of personal preference. Both provide similar functionality,
although the GUI-based tool is a bit more user-friendly.

Figure 9.2 shows a snapshot of the security policy from the .NET Framework Configuration tool.

As shown in Figure 9.2, the security policy can be configured at three
levels: enterprise, machine, and user. The significance of these levels will
become clear when we will discuss how the security policy is evaluated
against an assembly.

The enterprise level describes the security policy for the entire enterprise.
The security settings are stored in XML format in the file <windir>\Microsoft
.NET\Framework\v<CLRVersion>\config\enterprisesec.config.

The machine level describes the security policy for all the assemblies on
the local machine. This XML file can be found at <windir>\Microsoft
.NET\Framework\v<CLRVersion>\config\security.config.

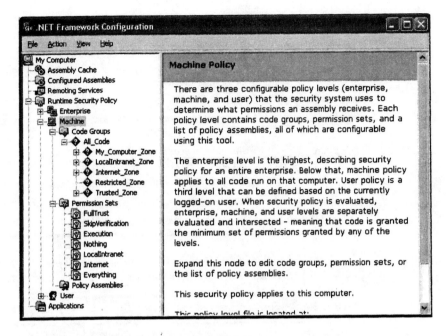

FIGURE 9.2 Security policy configuration.

The user level describes the security policy for the user currently running the application. This XML file can be found at `<UserProfile>\Application Data\Microsoft\CLR Security Config\v<CLRVersion>\security.config`.

Not visible in Figure 9.2 is yet another level of security policy, the application domain level. It is possible to programmatically create a policy level (represented by the class `PolicyLevel`) and set it on an application domain by calling the method `AppDomain.SetAppDomainPolicy`. The AppDomain policy level is optional and is typically provided by the host.

Figure 9.2 also shows that the security policy at a security level is composed of a linear list of objects called the permission sets and a hierarchical list of objects called the code groups. Let's examine what they represent.

Permission Sets

A permission set is a named set of permissions. Table 9.3 shows some standard permission sets under .NET.

TABLE 9.3   Built-In Permission Sets

Name	Description
Nothing	No permissions. Deny access to all the secure resources, including the right to execute.
Execution	Permits execution.
FullTrust	Unrestricted access to all the secure resources. Permissions in the set cannot be modified.
Everything	Unrestricted access to all the secure resources. An administrator can change any permission in the set.
Internet	Default rights given to applications originating from the Internet.
LocalIntranet	Default rights given to applications on the local intranet.
SkipVerification	Grants right to bypass the verification.

A permission set can contain any number of permissions. As an example, Table 9.4 lists permissions available in the LocalIntranet permission set.

TABLE 9.4   LocalIntranet Permissions

Permission	Access Allowed
EnvironmentPermission	Read only USERNAME variable
FileDialogPermission	Unrestricted
IsolatedStorageFilePermission	Isolated by user; fixed disk quota
ReflectionPermission	Reflection/Emit
SecurityPermission	Assert granted permissions; enable code execution
UIPermission	Unrestricted
DnsPermission	Unrestricted
PrintingPermission	Default printer; safe printing through a dialog box
EventLogPermission	Write to local event log

It is also possible to define a custom permission set. The .NET Framework Configuration tool provides a wizard to help you create a permission set. Alternatively, you can create an XML file that defines the permission set and add it to the policy using caspol.exe with the -addpset switch. Check the SDK documentation for the format of the XML file.

Code Groups

A code group maps specific evidence to a specific permission set. The evidence is represented as a membership condition. The structure of the code

```
┌─────────────────────────────┐
│     LocalIntranet_Zone      │
├─────────────────────────────┤
│  Membership Condition :=    │
│  (Zone = Local Intranet)    │
├─────────────────────────────┤
│     Permission Set =        │
│     (Local Intranet)        │
└─────────────────────────────┘
```

FIGURE 9.3 Code group.

group is shown in Figure 9.3. Here, LocalIntranet_Zone is the name of the code group that represents the local intranet.

The code groups that are available on your machine can be seen from the .NET Configuration tool (Figure 9.2), or you can run caspol.exe, as shown in the following command line:

```
caspol.exe -a -listgroups
```

In this command line, switch -a stands for all policy levels (if not specified, only the machine-level settings are displayed) and the switch -listgroups tells the tool to list the code groups.

Here is the partial output from caspol.exe:

```
1. All code: Nothing
    1.1. Zone - MyComputer: FullTrust
    1.2. Zone - Intranet: LocalIntranet
        1.2.1. All code: Same site Web.
        1.2.2. All code: Same directory FileIO - Read
    1.3. Zone - Internet: Internet
        1.3.1. All code: Same site Web.
```

Note that caspol.exe assigns a number to each code group. This number is not actually a part of the code group; it is generated by caspol.exe as an identity so that users can modify a code group using this identity.

At each policy level, code groups are organized in a hierarchical fashion, as illustrated in Figure 9.4. The common language runtime takes the gathered evidence, matches it up to the nodes in the hierarchy, and ends up with a merged list of permissions that can be granted to an assembly at that policy level.

Figure 9.4 represents a partial snapshot of the default security policy at the machine level. The root code group, All_Code, matches any code (from anywhere). The code groups immediately under All_Code, except for My_Computer_Zone, represent the zones that you see under Internet

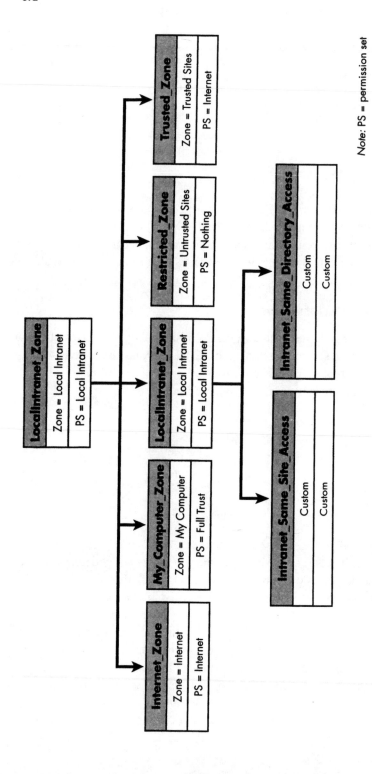

FIGURE 9.4   Code groups hierarchy.

Note: PS = permission set

Explorer's zone settings. `My_Computer_Zone` matches the assemblies that are installed locally, perhaps using an installation program. These assemblies are granted unrestricted code access permissions. `LocalIntranet_Zone` matches the assemblies downloaded from the local intranet, either over HTTP or from a shared network drive. These assemblies are granted the right to use isolated storage, full user interface access, some reflection capability, and limited access to the environment variables. `Internet_Zone` represents the assemblies downloaded over the Internet. These assemblies are granted very limited permissions.

Identifying Intranet versus Internet Sites

The common language runtime uses Windows LAN Manager APIs to identify if a computer is part of an intranet or Internet. For example, if you use a fully qualified domain name (FQDN) as the machine name, the site is treated as an Internet site. This is true even if the machine belongs to the local intranet.

If you plan to use the FQDN to identify a machine on the local intranet, you may wish to add the FQDN to the trusted zone under Internet Explorer.

Executing Internet-Downloaded Applications

The first release of the .NET Framework by default grants the permission to execute code for the assemblies in the `Internet_Zone`. This allows, for example, use of the `href` tag in a Web page to download an assembly (in the download cache) and execute it. However, it is interesting to note that Service Pack 1 (SP1) for .NET has removed this permission as default. In fact, assemblies in the Internet zone have no permissions at all (`PermissionSet=Nothing`). This has been done to make your computer more secure. Despite the fact that CAS provides a tight security mechanism, hackers are bound to find some security holes in the mechanism. After all, it is the first release of the CAS. Disabling code execution for applications downloaded over the Internet reduces the chances of some rogue application hacking into your computer.

Starting with the SP1 release, to run an Internet downloaded assembly, you will need to explicitly create a code group to match the assembly evidence, and give the code group the permissions to execute. My recommendation is to use the publisher's digital signature as the membership condition as much as possible. This also puts a pressure on the software vendors to sign their assemblies with a digital signature.

Recall that we have four levels of policy: enterprise, machine, user, and AppDomain. The evaluation process to obtain the merged list of permissions is run at each policy level. In the final step, only those permissions that are common to each policy level are selected. This is the final list of permissions that is granted to the assembly being evaluated.

For the purpose of policy evaluation, the enterprise level gets the top priority, followed by machine, user, and AppDomain levels in that order. Lower level policies cannot increase permission granted at the higher levels. However, lower level policies can decrease permissions. Furthermore, you can assign a `LevelFinal` attribute to a node. If this attribute is discovered on a matching node, no further policy levels are evaluated (except the AppDomain level which is always evaluated). This allows administrators, for example, to define security settings at the machine level that cannot be changed by individual users editing user-level policy.

The bulk of the policy, by default, is defined at the machine level.

So far we haven't discussed why code groups are organized in a hierarchy. The hierarchical structure helps the common language runtime prune down its search for the matching nodes. The traversing of the hierarchy is based on two rules:

1. A child node is visited only if the parent node matches. In other words, if a node does not match, none of its children are tested for matches.

2. If a matching node has been assigned an `Exclusive` attribute, only the permission set for that node is used. Naturally, it doesn't make sense for two matching nodes in a policy level to have this attribute, and therefore, is considered an error.

The root node of the hierarchy, `All_Code`, is just a starting point for the traversal. Hence, it matches all code and by default points to the permission set `Nothing`—a set containing no permissions.

To check the code groups an assembly belongs to, you can run `caspol.exe` with the switch `-resolvegroup`, as shown in the following command line for our assembly `Foo.dll` which was available over the local intranet.

```
caspol.exe -a
-resolvegroup http://localhost/SecurityDemo/Foo.dll
```

Alternatively, you can obtain the same information from the .NET Configuration tool. Select Evaluate Assembly menu item from the Runtime Security Policy context menu. A security wizard pops up that helps you evaluate the matching code groups. Figure 9.5 shows a snapshot of the output.

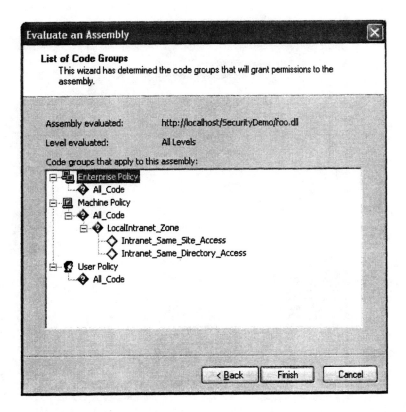

FIGURE 9.5 Resolving code groups.

Once you have the list of matching code groups, you can figure out the final set of permissions that can be granted to the assembly.

Better still, you can just select an option in the security wizard to give you the final set of permissions. Figure 9.6 shows a snapshot of such an output.

As can be seen from Figure 9.6, our `Foo.dll` assembly that was downloaded from the local intranet does not have `FileIOPermission`. Now you know why our experiment failed.

As an exercise, run the security wizard once again. This time, however, specify the complete path to `Foo.dll` on the local disk. The assembly will then be seen as having unrestricted permissions.

You can also use `caspol.exe` to resolve the set of granted permissions using the switch `-resolveperm`. This is illustrated in the following command line:

```
caspol.exe -a
    -resolveperm http://localhost/SecurityDemo/Foo.dll
```

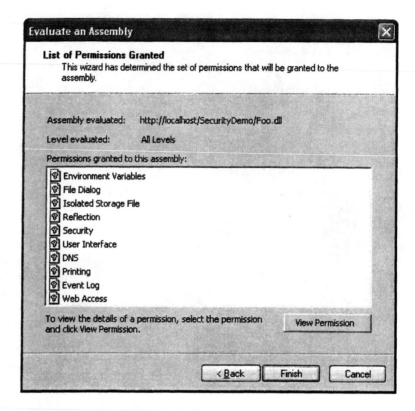

FIGURE 9.6 Permissions granted to `Foo.dll`.

An interesting aspect of using `caspol.exe` to resolve the code access permissions is that it also shows the identity permissions that have been granted to the assembly.

Here is an interesting question: If you trust the source of an assembly, how can you set the security policy so that the necessary permissions are granted to the assembly, even if the assembly is downloaded from the Internet? What you are thinking is absolutely right; just create a new code group with an appropriate membership condition and a proper permission set.

The simplest way to create a code group is by using the .NET Configuration tool.

For `Foo.dll`, the requisite permission was not granted by the security policy at the machine level (the enterprise level and the user level grant `FullTrust` to any code by default). Therefore, it makes sense to add the code group at the machine level. Defining code groups at the machine level is the most likely scenario for any downloaded assembly.

Naturally, the code group node has to be created only under a matching node. Otherwise, it will never be traversed. However, the decision to pick a parent becomes difficult when there are many matching nodes. For example, as seen in Figure 9.5, some of the matching code groups for *http://localhost/ SecurityDemo/Foo.dll* are `All_Code` and `LocalIntranet_Zone`. For such cases, selecting a parent depends on what your final goal is. You can create a code group under `LocalIntranet_Zone` and add the permission set that grants `FileIOPermission`. Remember that this permission set will be merged with the permission set of the parent node, `LocalIntranet_Zone`. Or, you can create a code group under the `All_Code` node and define all the necessary permissions that are needed by the assembly.

Sometimes choosing a proper parent for the code group also depends on the membership condition specified on the code group. For `Foo.dll`, for example, the membership condition can be either the URL of the source or the strong name of the assembly. There is an advantage of using the strong name as the membership condition and creating the code group directly under `All_Code`. The permissions granted to the assembly will be the same irrespective of whether the assembly comes from the local computer, intranet, or the Internet. If you use just the public key for the strong name (assembly name and version are optional), then any assembly matching the public key will be granted the same permissions. Generally, assemblies coming from the same publisher tend to have the same public key.

The recommended way to define the membership condition is by using the publisher's credentials. By doing so, we show our level of trust for the publisher, not the specific assemblies, which generally is true. Obviously, to use the publisher's credentials as the membership condition, the assembly has to be signed with a digital certificate.

It is left as an exercise for you to define an appropriate code group for `Foo.dll` and obtain the final list of granted permissions by running the assembly evaluation wizard. Hint: Use the public key for `Foo.dll` for the match.

Modify the Security Policy Cautiously

Do not blindly add Web sites to the trusted zone. Instead, define newer code groups using either the public key of the assembly or the publisher's credentials.

Note that when you try to resolve either the code group or the code access permissions against a URL, the assembly pointed to by the URL is downloaded and installed in the user's download cache (recall from Chapter 3 that each user has a different download cache). Also note that, besides the strong name, each downloaded assembly is further identified by its evidence. For example, if you download the same Foo.dll from two different URLs, you will see two assemblies in the download cache with the same name, version, and public key token. As a matter of fact, the following three commands produce three entries in the download cache, despite the fact that all the commands are accessing the same assembly from the same machine. Here, mydev is the name of my local machine and mydev.mycompany.net is its FQDN.

```
caspol.exe -resolveperm http://localhost/SecurityDemo/Foo.dll
caspol.exe -resolveperm http://mydev/SecurityDemo/Foo.dll
caspol.exe -resolveperm
    http://mydev.mycompany.net/SecurityDemo/Foo.dll
```

It is interesting to note that the permission set returned for the third command is that of the Internet. As the machine name is specified as an FQDN, the runtime by default assumes that the machine is part of the Internet.

If you want the machine with an FQDN to be treated as part of the intranet, then add the FQDN to the intranet site from the Internet Explorer.

Finally, it is worth mentioning that a code group is represented by an abstract base class called CodeGroup. It is possible to create a new class by inheriting from CodeGroup to represent a code group that programmatically returns the name of the permission set. The membership condition for the code group can also be specified by implementing a class that implements a standard interface, IMembershipCondition.

Requesting Permissions

Once the common language runtime builds the list of permissions that can be granted to an assembly from the three policy levels, a final step allows the assembly itself to dictate the permissions that it needs or doesn't need.

Recall from Table 9.2 that the SecurityAction enumeration provides three actions that can be applied at the assembly level: SecurityAction.RequestMinimum, SecurityAction.RequestOptional, and SecurityAction.RequestRefuse.

RequestMinimum is used to define the minimum set of permissions requested by the assembly. If these permissions are not granted by the security policy, the assembly won't run. The following are two common examples that show how an assembly-level attribute can be defined that uses this security action:

```
// Project Permissions/Foo

[assembly:SecurityPermissionAttribute(
    SecurityAction.RequestMinimum,
    Flags = SecurityPermissionFlag.UnmanagedCode)]

[assembly:SecurityPermissionAttribute(
    SecurityAction.RequestMinimum,
    Flags = SecurityPermissionFlag.SkipVerification)]
```

The first example is useful if your assembly intends to make calls into the unmanaged code. The second example is useful if your assembly contains unsafe code and you don't want the common language runtime to verify your code for type safety. If the requested permissions cannot be granted to the assembly, the common language runtime ensures that the assembly does not get loaded at all.

Note that these examples represent the common cases of requesting assembly-level permission attributes. Assembly-level permission attributes by no means are limited just to `SecurityPermissionAttribute`; any code access permission attribute can be used.

Requesting the minimum permissions your code requires ensures that it either receives those permissions or does not run. By requesting minimum permissions, you don't have to worry that your code will crash in some unexpected way because it was not granted a permission it absolutely needed to function. Also, by doing the work up front to determine what permissions your code requires, you make it easier on users and administrators. The .NET Framework provides a tool called the Permission Request Viewer (`Perm-View.exe`) that you can run on an assembly to see what permissions the assembly requires. For example, systems administrators can determine if your code will run from a network share under their current corporate policy or whether they need to modify the policy to grant extra rights to your code.

Be careful about how you use this security action. For instance, if you ask for all the permissions your assembly might need, the assembly would fail to load in more circumstances than might be necessary. Moreover, this may lead an administrator to loosen up his or her security policy more than necessary to allow your assembly to run.

`RequestRefuse` allows you to simply deny yourself permissions that you might have been granted by the security policy. It is good programming advice to refuse the permissions that you know your assembly doesn't need. It certainly cannot hurt to play it safe.

`RequestOptional` allows you to specify optional permissions. Your assembly can use these permissions if granted. If not granted, your assembly is still expected to handle the situation gracefully and continue to execute.

Finally, instead of requesting individual permissions, you can also request any of the following built-in permission sets: `Nothing`, `Execution`, `FullTrust`, `Internet`, `LocalIntranet`, and `SkipVerification`. This is done using the `PermissionSetAttribute` class with the `Name` property representing the permission set, as illustrated in the following code excerpt:

```
[assembly:PermissionSetAttribute(
    SecurityAction.RequestMinimum,
    Name = "LocalIntranet")]
```

Note that you can request only those permission sets that do not change from system to system. This means that you cannot request custom-named permission sets or the `Everything` built-in permission set (which is modifiable).

This concludes our discussion on CAS. Interested readers may wish to read [Bro-01a] for an excellent introduction to CAS.

ROLE-BASED SECURITY

Many applications require that different users be grouped based on the privileges they have. Typically, these applications check the group, or role, of a user and provide access to the resources based on the role. For example, an employee salary management application may provide access to employee salaries only if the current user belongs to the Manager role. Even Windows NT (Windows 2000 and all subsequent versions are based on Windows NT technology) was built with a role-based security architecture: It grants or denies access to secured resources based on the local group to which a user belongs. A Windows NT user that belongs to the Administrators role has complete and unrestricted access to the computer, whereas a user that belongs to the Guests account has limited access to the computer.

Users and Roles

Under the .NET security model, the identity of a user is encapsulated in an interface, `IIdentity`, and the role of the user is encapsulated in an interface, `IPrincipal`. Both these interfaces, and most other types discussed in this section, can be found under the namespace `System.Security.Principal`. Here are the definitions of these interfaces:

```
interface IIdentity {
    string Name { get; }
    bool IsAuthenticated {get; }
    string AuthenticationType {get; }
}

interface IPrincipal {
    IIdentity Identity {get; }
    bool IsInRole(string role);
}
```

Interface IIdentity provides the name of the user and the authentication information. Authentication is the process of verifying if a user is who he or she claims to be. The commonly used authentication mechanisms are basic, digest, Microsoft Passport, NTLM, and Kerberos. The latter two mechanisms are provided by the Windows OS.

The interface IPrincipal encapsulates the identity of the user along with the roles the user may belong to. You can use the IsInRole method to check if the user belongs to a specific role. There is no direct way to obtain a list of the roles a user belongs to.

Note the complete lack of reliance on the Windows security model in defining these interfaces. The .NET security model makes it possible to use any standard authentication mechanism. You can even create your own authentication mechanism by implementing these two interfaces and still take advantage of the .NET security infrastructure.

To be clear, these interfaces do not let you authenticate a user. Rather, they represent the result of the authentication. During the steady state operation of your application, these interfaces indicate whether the request is anonymous or has been authenticated.

The .NET Framework comes standard with a few identity providers, as listed in Table 9.5. The table also shows the associated principal class, if any.

TABLE 9.5. Standard Identity Providers

Identity Class	Principal Class	Description
GenericIdentity (System.Security.Principal)	GenericPrincipal	Represents a generic user
WindowsIdentity (System.Security.Principal)	WindowsPrincipal	Represents a Windows user

TABLE 9.5. Standard Identity Providers (Continued)

Identity Class	Principal Class	Description
PassportIdentity (System.Web.Security)		Represents a Passport identity
FormsIdentity (System.Web.Security)		Represents an identity based on forms authentication

Here is a code excerpt from a program that displays the identity information of the Windows user currently running the application:

```
// Project RoleBasedSecurity/WhoAmI

public static void WindowsUserDemo() {

    IIdentity id = WindowsIdentity.GetCurrent();

  Console.WriteLine("Name={0}\nAuthenticated={1}\nType={2}",
      id.Name, id.IsAuthenticated, id.AuthenticationType);
    ...
}
```

Here is the output of the program when executed under the Windows account myguest on the machine MYDEV:

```
Name=MYDEV\myguest
Authenticated=True
Type=NTLM
```

If you are interested in just the name of the user running the application, you can also use two static methods, UserDomainName and UserName, from the class System.Environment, as shown in the following code excerpt:

```
// Project RoleBasedSecurity/WhoAmI

public static void WindowsUserDemo() {
    ...
    // Second method (using System.Environment)
    Console.WriteLine("Name: {0}\\{1}",
      System.Environment.UserDomainName,
      System.Environment.UserName);
}
```

At this point, it is worth understanding a little about the security mechanism provided by the underlying OS, Windows NT.

Under Windows NT, there are two types of security contexts—one of the process and another of the thread. The process under which an application is running has the security context of the user (principal) who was responsible for executing the application. Any thread created within the process does not have a security context associated with it by default. However, the executing code can obtain the security context of a user (not necessarily the same user as that of the process) and associate the current thread with this security context. The thread is said to be under impersonation. At some later stage, the code can remove the security context from the current thread.

For those interested in the Win32 APIs, the security context of a user can be obtained by calling the Win32 API `LogonUser` and passing the name and password of the user. The Win32 API to impersonate a user is `Impersonate-LoggedOnUser` and to remove the impersonation token is `RevertToSelf`.

Note that the OS-provided security context for a user is also referred to as the *security token* or simply *token*.

Virtually any Windows API that does any access check (e.g., `Create-File`) uses the security token of the current thread if the thread is under impersonation. Otherwise, the API uses the security token of the process.

In our earlier example, `WindowsIdentity.Current` (the same holds true for `System.Environment.UserName`) returns the identification of the Windows principal associated with the OS thread that executed the method. If the OS thread is not under impersonation, then the method returns the identification of the principal under which the process is running.

Managed Thread Principal

Similar to Windows NT, where a thread within a process can be associated with a security principal, .NET also supports the notion of associating a security principal with a managed thread within an AppDomain.

The principal under which the current managed thread is executing can be obtained by calling a static method, `Thread.CurrentPrincipal`.

The type of principal to be used at the thread level is dictated by the principal policy that is set on the AppDomain under which the thread is currently executing. The principal policy is represented by an enumeration of type `PrincipalPolicy`. Table 9.6 describes possible enumeration values for `PrincipalPolicy`.

TABLE 9.6   PrincipalPolicy Enumeration

Value	Description
NoPrincipal	No principal should be associated with the thread.
UnauthenticatedPrincipal	Create a principal of type GenericIdentity. By default, the name is set to an empty string and the authentication flag is set to false.
WindowsIdentity	Use the Windows identity for executing the thread.

By default, the principal policy for the AppDomain is set to Unauthen-ticatedPrincipal. However, you can change the principal policy by calling the SetPrincipalPolicy method on the AppDomain. This is illustrated in the following code excerpt:

```
// Project RoleBasedSecurity/WhoAmI

public static void ThreadPrincipalDemo() {
    AppDomain.CurrentDomain.SetPrincipalPolicy(
      PrincipalPolicy.WindowsPrincipal);

    IPrincipal pr = Thread.CurrentPrincipal;
    Console.WriteLine(pr.Identity.Name);
}
```

Thread Principal and Remoting

In the first version of the .NET Framework, the thread principal is not carried to a remote object. However, if it is desired that you pass the identity information, you can use the call context (Chapter 6) to store such information. The SDK includes a sample program under Samples\Technologies\Remoting that illustrates this.

It is also possible to explicitly assign a principal to a thread. The SDK includes an example that shows how to create a new generic principal and a few generic roles (using GenericIdentity and GenericPrincipal classes), and assign the principal to the thread. Here, I present an example that uses WindowsIdentity. This example is a bit complex in that to create a new WindowsIdentity object, first the security token of the user account has to be obtained by calling a Win32 API, LogonUser. Once the security token is no longer needed, it has to be closed by calling another Win32 API, CloseHandle. Both the APIs are encapsulated as imported functions in a class Win32, as shown here:

```
// Project RoleBasedSecurity/WhoAmI

public class Win32 {
    // logon type
    public static readonly UInt32 LOGON32_LOGON_INTERACTIVE=2;

    // logon provider
    public static readonly UInt32 LOGON32_PROVIDER_DEFAULT = 0;

    [DllImport("AdvApi32.Dll", SetLastError=true)]
    public static extern bool LogonUser(
      String userName,
      String domain,
      String password,
      UInt32 logonType,
      UInt32 logonProvider,
      out IntPtr token);

    [DllImport("Kernel32.Dll")]
    public static extern void CloseHandle(IntPtr token);
}
```

Here is the code that creates a Windows user principal and assigns it to the current thread:

```
// Project RoleBasedSecurity/WhoAmI

public static void ThreadPrincipalDemo() {

    // Step 1: Get user token
    IntPtr token;
    bool b = Win32.LogonUser("myguest", "", "mypassword",
      Win32.LOGON32_LOGON_INTERACTIVE,
      Win32.LOGON32_PROVIDER_DEFAULT, out token);

    // Step 2: Create a Windows identity and principal
    WindowsIdentity newIdentity =
      new WindowsIdentity(token);

    WindowsPrincipal pr1 = new WindowsPrincipal(newIdentity);

    // Step 3: Change the current principal
    Thread.CurrentPrincipal = pr1;
    DumpPrincipals();

    // Step 4: Once done, close the user token
    Win32.CloseHandle(token);
}
```

Here is the implementation of DumpPrincipals:

```
public static void DumpPrincipals() {
    Console.WriteLine("\nPrincipals from managed APIs:");
    Console.WriteLine("Win32 Thread (or Process): {0}\\{1}",
      System.Environment.UserDomainName,
      System.Environment.UserName);
    Console.WriteLine("Managed thread: {0}",
      Thread.CurrentPrincipal.Identity.Name);

    String processUser, threadUser;
    Win32.GetPrincipals(out processUser, out threadUser);

    Console.WriteLine("\nPrincipals from unmanaged APIs:");
    Console.WriteLine("Win32 Process: {0}", processUser);
    Console.WriteLine("Win32 Thread: {0}", threadUser);
}
```

Win32.GetPrincipals is an imported method that is implemented in DumpPrincipal.dll. It returns the names of the principals associated with the current OS process and the current OS thread. If the current OS thread is not under impersonation, an empty string is returned. The source code for this DLL can be found on the companion Web site under the project Role-BasedSecurity\DumpPrincipal.

At this point, it is worth mentioning that the ability to replace principal objects opens up a security hole. Some malicious code can claim an untrue identity or role. For this reason, applications that require changing the identity must be granted the code access permission SecurityPermission that has the ControlPrincipal enumeration value applied to it.

Impersonation

Recall that the security infrastructure provided by the common language runtime is completely separate from that of the underlying OS. If you are running on an OS based on Windows NT, you will have processes and threads that have user tokens attached to them. You will be subjected to the security policy of the OS when you perform operations on security objects such as NTFS files.

However, when you are running on Windows 98 or Windows CE, there is no security infrastructure on these systems. You can open any file that you like. Note, however, that the CAS as well as the role-based security still exist on these platforms. They continue to function because they are abstracted from the underlying OS.

This abstraction means you need to pay attention to two security contexts on secure OSs, the one of the managed code and the one of the underlying OS.

Here is the output from running `ThreadPrincipalDemo` from our previous example:

```
Principals from managed APIs:
Win32 Thread (or Process): MYDEV\pradeep
Managed thread: MYDEV\myguest

Principals from unmanaged APIs:
Win32 Process: MYDEV\pradeep
Win32 Thread:
```

Note from the output that although the managed thread is associated with a principal, it does not imply that the underlying physical thread is under impersonation. These are two orthogonal concepts. Each can be customized independent of the other. Moreover, the managed thread can be associated with a `GenericPrincipal`, whereas the underlying physical thread (and process) will always have a Windows principal (if the OS is based on Windows NT).

With Windows NT, when the managed code makes a call into the unmanaged world, the security context of the managed thread is not automatically mapped to the security context of the physical thread. The implication of this is that the unmanaged code will use the security context of the process to perform any security access checks.

If the security context from the managed thread needs to be mapped to the security context of the unmanaged thread, it has to be done explicitly by calling the method `WindowsIdentity.Impersonate`. This is illustrated in the following code excerpt:

```
// Project RoleBasedSecurity/WhoAmI

public static void ImpersonationDemo() {
    ...

    // Step 1: Get user token
    IntPtr token;
    bool b = Win32.LogonUser("myguest", "", "mypassword",
        Win32.LOGON32_LOGON_NETWORK_CLEARTEXT,
        Win32.LOGON32_PROVIDER_DEFAULT, out token);

    // Step 2: Create a Windows identity
    WindowsIdentity id = new WindowsIdentity(token);

    // Step 3: Impersonate.
```

```
        // Store the original security context away
        WindowsImpersonationContext ctx = id.Impersonate();

        Console.WriteLine("Impersonation on...");
        IPrincipal pr = Thread.CurrentPrincipal;
        Console.WriteLine(pr.Identity.Name);

        // Step 4: Revert to the old user context
        ctx.Undo();

        // Step 5: Close the Win32 handle
        Win32.CloseHandle(token);
}
```

Once impersonation is no longer needed, it is a good idea to restore the original user's security context. `WindowsIdentity.Impersonate` returns the original context as an object of type `WindowsImpersonationContext`. Calling the method `Undo` on this object causes the thread to revert to the old user context.

For those who are curious, here is the output from running `ImpersonationDemo`:

```
Principals from managed APIs:
Win32 Thread (or Process): MYDEV\myguest
Managed thread:

Principals from unmanaged APIs:
Win32 Process: MYDEV\pradeept
Win32 Thread: MYDEV\myguest
```

Role-Based Security Checks

Once the authentication mechanism has been defined and the roles have been identified for your application, it is time for you to add security checks in your code to determine if a particular principal object is a member of a known role. You can do this by calling `IsInRole` on the `IPrincipal` interface. The following code excerpt illustrates this:

```
public static void DirectRoleCheck() {
    IPrincipal pr = Thread.CurrentPrincipal;
    bool b = pr.IsInRole(@"BUILTIN\Administrators");
    if (!b) {
      throw new Exception("Only administrators allowed!");
    }

    Console.WriteLine("Okay to proceed...");
}
```

The method checks if the Windows principal associated with the current thread is part of the local administrative group. If not, the method throws an exception. Any security-sensitive code can be placed after the code that does this check.

For the built-in user groups under Windows, it is also possible to use a .NET-defined standard enumeration, `WindowsBuiltInRole`. Using this enumeration, the preceding implementation can be revised as follows:

```
public static void DirectRoleCheckBuiltIn() {
    WindowsPrincipal pr =
        (WindowsPrincipal) Thread.CurrentPrincipal;
    b = pr.IsInRole(WindowsBuiltInRole.Administrator);
    if (!b) {
        throw new Exception("Only administrators allowed!");
    }

    Console.WriteLine("Okay to proceed...");
}
```

Removing the hard-coded string for the role makes the code safe from localization issues.

Note that this code assumes that the AppDomain security policy is set to use `WindowsPrincipal`.

Debugging Windows Identities

If you are planning to use Windows identities in your application, then using Windows 2000 or a later OS may simplify testing your application under various user accounts. The OS provides a utility, `runas.exe`, that can be used to execute an application under a specific user account. You can even spawn a command window that runs under a different user account, as shown here:

```
runas.exe /user:MYDOMAIN\account cmd.exe
```

When executed, `runas.exe` prompts you for the user's password.

The technique of explicitly checking the role is perfectly fine and is necessary in many cases. However, it turns out that the role-based security model follows the footsteps of the CAS model. The role-based security model defines a permission object, `PrincipalPermission`, that is similar in functionality to the code access permission objects. For example, `PrincipalPermission` can be demanded at runtime to check if the current principal matches the specified user and role.

The constructor of the PrincipalPermission object takes two parameters. The first parameter is a string that represents the user to be matched. Passing the null identity string indicates that the identity of the principal can be anything. The second parameter is a string that represents the role to be matched. Passing a null role string indicates that the principal can be a member of any role.

Note that it is possible to combine multiple PrincipalPermission objects into one object by calling the Union method on one object repeatedly for each of the other objects.

Using the PrincipalPermission object is similar to using the CAS permission object; you can use it either imperatively or declaratively.

Imperative Role Checks

Using the PrincipalPermission class, our earlier role check code can be written slightly different. The following is the revised code excerpt:

```
public static void ImperativeRoleCheck() {
    PrincipalPermission perm =
      new
PrincipalPermission(null,@"BUILTIN\Administrators");
    perm.Demand();

    Console.WriteLine("Okay to proceed...");
}
```

The result is the same basic behavior as the earlier implementation. If the principal associated with the current thread is not in the Administrators role, a security exception will be thrown. Any security-sensitive code can be placed after the call to Demand. This sensitive code is executed only if the principal permission Demand succeeds.

Declarative Role Checks

Much along the lines of CAS, the role-based security mechanism defines an attribute, PrincipalPermissionAttribute, that can be used declaratively to perform the role check. The following code excerpt is yet another revision of our earlier implementation:

```
[PrincipalPermission(SecurityAction.Demand,
     Role=@"BUILTIN\Administrators")]
public static void DeclarativeRoleCheck() {
    Console.WriteLine("Okay to proceed...");
}
```

In this case, the common language runtime demands that the principal associated with the current thread is in the Administrators role and will generate an exception if the demand is not satisfied.

Note that `PrincipalPermissionAttribute` is not a context attribute. This makes it possible to apply this attribute to any object, context-bound or not.

An advantage of the declarative role check is that you can simply apply it to an entire class instead of each individual method. Another advantage is that you can use Reflection to read the principal permission attribute from an assembly. This should make it easy to generate documentation for your classes, including which roles are allowed access to which classes and methods.

This completes our discussion on role-based security under .NET. In the next chapter, we will look at another role-based security mechanism that is actually a part of COM+ services but is available to .NET applications.

ASP.NET WEB SERVICES SECURITY

Security is an important issue for many Web sites, whether they are serving Web pages or running Web services. This is especially true if the Web site is exposed on the Internet. The site might contain sensitive data that, in the wrong hands, could cause substantial damage to the company or the individuals. Such a site may wish to allow only specific users to be able to access the site. The site may wish to authenticate the user; that is, verify the user is the one he or she claims to be. The site might want to implement some kind of authorization such as role-based security so that users get restricted access to the data, based on their privileges. Finally, under some circumstances, the executing code might wish to impersonate the user so that certain secured objects at the OS level can be accessed.

In this section we examine how ASP.NET provides support for handling these security issues. Although our focus will be from the Web services perspective, the same principles are applicable if you are serving Web pages using any server-side code.

Before we go further, it is important to understand how ASP.NET applications are hosted under IIS and the security context under which the ASP.NET applications run.

Hosting ASP.NET under IIS

Figure 9.7 illustrates how ASP.NET applications are executed under IIS.

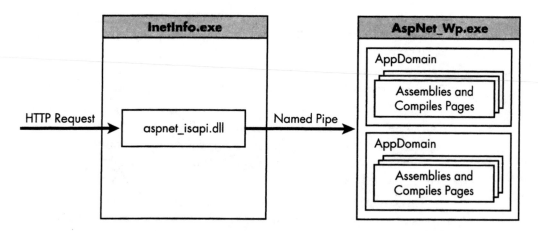

FIGURE 9.7 Hosting ASP.NET Applications under IIS.

Under IIS, any HTTP request to ASP.NET files such as `.asmx`, `.aspx`, and so on, is handled by an ISAPI DLL called `aspnet_isapi.dll`. This ISAPI DLL always runs inside the core IIS server process, `InetInfo.exe`. The DLL doesn't do much except to forward incoming requests to an ASP.NET worker process called `aspnet_wp.exe` over a named pipe. The ASP.NET worker process is automatically created if it doesn't exist.

The ASP.NET worker process hosts your ASP.NET code. It compiles your server-side pages as need be and executes your code, loading whatever assemblies are necessary.

No matter how many ASP.NET applications you are running on your system, all are hosted in just one ASP.NET worker process. To provide isolation between the applications, each application is run under a separate AppDomain.

ASP.NET Changes in IIS 6.0

IIS 6.0 is currently slated to be released along with Windows .NET Server. Under IIS 6.0, `aspnet_wp.exe` does not exist. Instead, IIS provides the worker processes for ASP.NET as well as other applications. At the time of this writing, Microsoft plans to connect `Inetinfo.exe` to the worker processes using local procedure calls (LPCs) instead of named pipes.

By default, `aspnet_wp.exe` runs under an account name ASPNET. This is a low-privileged user account that is created at the time of .NET Framework installation.

Although running the ASP.NET worker process under a low-privileged account is desirable from a security perspective, it is possible to configure `aspnet_wp.exe` to run under a different account. This is done by modifying the `<processModel>` XML element in the global configuration file, `Machine.config`. This element is used to define various process settings by means of XML attributes. These attributes are well-documented in the SDK. A limited explanation of these attributes is also available in the configuration file.

The two attributes that are important to us are `username` and `password`. The default settings for these two attributes are:

```
userName="machine" password="AutoGenerate"
```

This setting causes `aspnet_wp.exe` to run under the ASPNET account.

To run `aspnet_wp.exe` under the local SYSTEM account, which is a high-privileged administrator account, you can define the settings as follows:

```
userName="SYSTEM" password="AutoGenerate"
```

User names `machine` and `SYSTEM` are special tokens that ASP.NET is aware of. The password value of `AutoGenerate` can be applied only to these two accounts, eliminating the need to enter the actual passwords.

To run `aspnet_wp.exe` under a specific account, you can specify an explicit user name and password, as shown here:

```
userName="jay" password="jayspassword"
```

Be aware that `Machine.config` is readable by anyone who has physical access to the machine. You might have to take extra precautions to secure access to the machine.

This concludes the short introduction to how ASP.NET applications are hosted and executed. Interested readers can read [Bro-01b] for more details.

Authentication

Authentication is the process of accepting credentials from a user and validating those credentials against a designated authority. The client must provide credentials to allow the server to verify the client's identity.

In the case of ASP.NET, the clients have to go through two different authentication checks. The first-level authentication is done by IIS and the second-level authentication is done by ASP.NET.

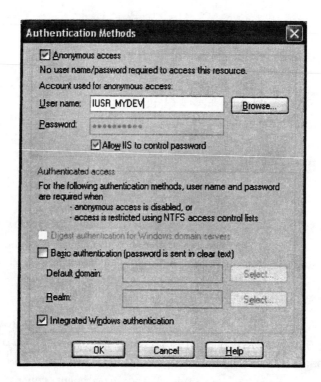

FIGURE 9.8   Authentication Methods under IIS.

IIS Authentication

IIS offers four basic modes of authentication:

1. Anonymous access
2. Integrated Windows authentication
3. Basic authentication
4. Digest authentication

An IIS virtual directory can be set to use one or more of these authentication modes. A snapshot of the Authentication Methods dialog box is shown in Figure 9.8.

The client code has to provide proper credentials to IIS to clear the authentication check. Let's see how this can be done in the client code for each of the four modes.

For our experiment, we use the following Web service class (creating Web services was discussed in Chapter 6):

```
// Project WebSecurity. File MyTest.asmx

<%@ WebService Language="C#" Class="MyCompany.MyTest" %>

[WebService(Namespace="http://localhost/Demo/")]
public class MyTest : WebService {

    [WebMethod]
    public String WhoAmI() {
        return Thread.CurrentPrincipal.Identity.Name;
    }
}
```

The Web service class MyTest implements a method WhoAmI that simply returns the name of the identity associated with the managed thread on which the method is called.

For the experiment, the Web service is hosted on the local machine under the IIS virtual directory Demo. This allows the Web service to be accessed as *http://localhost/Demo/MyTest.asmx.*

Recall that it is the responsibility of the client to provide the credentials to the server. Under .NET, the client's credentials are represented in a standard interface ICredentials. The framework also comes standard with two classes based on this interface, NetworkCredential and Credential-Cache. The NetworkCredential class provides credentials for password-based authentication schemes such as basic, digest, NTLM, and Kerberos. The CredentialCache provides storage for multiple credentials. We use these classes later in our examples.

Note that the types ICrendentials, NetworkCredential, and Cre-dentialCache are defined under the namespace System.Net, which provides a simple programming interface for many of the common network protocols.

To consume the Web service, our client application generates and uses a proxy class MyTest using wsdl.exe (Chapter 6). The client code creates an instance of the proxy class, calls the method WhoAmI, and displays the return value.

Recall from Chapter 6 that the generated proxy class is inherited from SoapHttpClientProtocol. This class defines a property, Credentials, that we will use to set the client's credentials.

Anonymous Access. In the case of anonymous access, any client can connect to the Web server. The IIS server does not expect any credentials from the client.

Here is the client code that accesses the Web service using anonymous IIS authentication:

```
// Project WebSecurity/MyClient

class MyApp {
    static private readonly String
        MYURL="http://localhost/Demo/MyTest.asmx";

    // IIS is set for anonymous access
    public static void UseAnonymousIdentity() {
        MyTest t = new MyTest();
        t.Url = MYURL;
        String s = t.WhoAmI();
        Console.WriteLine(s);
    }
    ...
}
```

Note that the client need not specify any credentials to the server.

When you run this program, WhoAmI returns an empty string because ASP.NET does not associate any security context to the managed thread.

Integrated Windows Authentication. Integrated Windows authentication uses a cryptographic exchange with the client to confirm the client's identity. Currently, this communication mechanism is available to only two types of clients—Internet Explorer and .NET applications.

For .NET applications, the class CredentialCache defines a static property, DefaultCredentials, that can be used to pass the client's identity to the server. This is highlighted in the following code excerpt:

```
// IIS is set for Integrated Windows Authentication
public static void UseDefaultWindowsIdentity() {
    MyTest t = new MyTest();
    t.Url = MYURL;
    t.Credentials = CredentialCache.DefaultCredentials;
    String s = t.WhoAmI();
    Console.WriteLine(s);
}
```

The property DefaultCredentials represents the system credentials for the security context of the user running the client application. However, if the underlying OS thread is impersonating a user, DefaultCredentials represents the credentials of the user being impersonated.

Basic Authentication.   Basic authentication is used for nonsecure identification of clients. The user name and the password are sent to the server as base-64 encoded text. Note that the user name and the password are encoded, not encrypted, in this type of authentication.

A client can deal with this mode of authentication by using the class `NetworkCredential`, as illustrated in the following code excerpt:

```
public static void UseSpecificWindowsUserIdentity(
      String user, String password, String domain) {
   MyTest t = new MyTest();
   t.Url = MYURL;
   t.Credentials = new NetworkCredential(user, password,
     domain);
   String s = t.WhoAmI();
   Console.WriteLine(s);
}
```

The constructor of `NetworkCredential` takes as parameters the user name, password, and the domain to which the user belongs. This information is passed to the server as base-64 encoded text.

An overloaded constructor of `NetworkCredential` takes just the user name and the password as parameters. This is useful if basic authentication for the virtual directory is already configured with a default domain name.

There is yet another way to specify the credentials in the case of basic authentication: Use the class `CredentialCache` and add one or more credentials to it, as illustrated in the following code excerpt:

```
public static void UseSpecificWindowsUserIdentity2(
      String user, String password, String domain) {
   CredentialCache c = new CredentialCache();
   c.Add(new Uri("http://localhost/"), "Basic",
     new NetworkCredential(MYUSR, MYPSWRD, MYDOMAIN));
   MyTest t = new MyTest();
   t.Url = MYURL;
   t.Credentials =c;
   String s = t.WhoAmI();
   Console.WriteLine(s);
}
```

The `Add` method on `CredentialCache` takes three parameters. The first parameter is the URI prefix of the Web site. The second parameter represents the authentication method used by the URI. Possible options are `basic` and `digest`. The third parameter is the `NetworkCredential` object that should be used for the specified URI. The idea is to store a collection of credentials for various Web resources as a single unit. When the GetCredential method is called, CredentialCache returns the proper set of credentials, as determined by the URI of the Web resource and the requested authentication scheme. Applications that use a variety of Internet resources with different authentication schemes benefit from using the CredentialCache class, because it stores all the credentials and provides them as requested.

Digest Authentication.   Digest authentication sends a hash value over the network rather than the password. This mode was introduced in IIS 5.1 and is not widely supported on other platforms.

It is left as an exercise for you to take the previous implementation and modify it for digest authentication.

Now that we understand the various authentication methods available under IIS, here is a pop quiz for you: Let's say you set the IIS virtual directory to use anonymous access as well as integrated Windows authentication (Figure 9.8). What is the authentication method that you think will be used?

It turns out that if anonymous authentication is enabled along with any other authentication mode, IIS does not, by default, bother to authenticate any user. That is, all users are treated as anonymous users.

This default behavior can be overridden by sending to IIS an HTTP 401 status code (Unauthorized) from the code handling the request. On receiving this status code, IIS will go ahead and authenticate the user.

The following code is the revised implementation of our Web service method. This code returns the 401 status code to IIS if it finds that the identity of the caller is blank:

```
[WebMethod]
public String WhoAmIEx() {
    String s = Thread.CurrentPrincipal.Identity.Name;
    if (s.Length == 0) {
      Context.Trace.Write("Sending 401 status code");
      this.Context.Response.StatusCode = 401;
    }
    return s;
}
```

As the code shows, the status code is set on the response object. This object, which is of type HttpResponse, encapsulates all the HTTP response operations for the current HTTP request. Complete information about the current request itself is encapsulated in an object of type HttpContext and can be accessed as the Context property on WebService.

Instead of setting the 401 status code in each of the methods, there is a way to set it at the application level, by means of an HTTP module. HTTP modules are managed classes that implement `IHttpModule` and reside in the ASP.NET worker process. They get to intercept each request before it reaches your ASP.NET application. For a sample implementation, see [Bro-02].

This concludes our discussion of IIS authentication schemes. A final note on IIS authentication: It is also possible to configure IIS with SSL and use client certificates for authenticating the user. Check the SDK documentation under the topic "Securing XML Web Services Created Using ASP.NET" for a code sample on using client certificates.

ASP.NET Authentication

ASP.NET implements authentication using *authentication providers*, which are code modules that verify credentials and implement other security functionality, such as cookie generation.

At present, ASP.NET supports three authentication providers—Windows, Forms, and Passport. An ASP.NET application enables a specific authentication provider by means of `<authentication>` XML tag in the application's `Web.config` file. A sample configuration that corresponds to Windows provider is shown here:

```
<configuration>
  <system.web>
    <authentication mode="Windows" />
  </system.web>
</configuration>
```

Other possible options for the authentication mode are `Forms`, `Passport`, and `None`. The authentication mode `None` is used when you are not authenticating users at all. In this case, ASP.NET does not associate any security context with the managed threads.

Windows Authentication. This provider relies on the authentication capabilities of IIS. After IIS completes its authentication, ASP.NET associates the security context of the user with the managed thread where the user call is being processed.

Not all IIS authentication modes can be combined with all ASP.NET authentication modes. In the case of ASP.NET Windows authentication, for example, IIS cannot be set to anonymous access.

An excellent article that describes in detail the various authentication modes of IIS and ASP.NET, and their possible combinations, is [Ker-01]. The article also guides you in selecting the right authentication mode for your ASP.NET application.

Forms Authentication. Using this provider causes unauthenticated requests to be redirected to a specified HTML form using client-side redirection. The client can then supply logon credentials and post the form back to the server. If the application authenticates the request (using application-specific logic), ASP.NET issues a cookie that contains the credentials or a key for reacquiring the client identity. Subsequent requests are issued with the cookie in the request headers, which means that subsequent authentications are unnecessary.

Passport Authentication. This is a centralized authentication service provided by Microsoft that offers a single logon facility and membership services for participating sites.

ASP.NET, in conjunction with the Microsoft Passport SDK, provides similar functionality as Forms authentication to Passport users. Unfortunately, the client-side authentication module for Passport has not been released as of this writing.

Custom Authentication. Web services uses SOAP messages for communication and SOAP headers provide a great way of passing out-of-band information that is not related to the semantics of the Web service. Unlike the `Body` element of a SOAP message, which is processed by the Web service method, the `Header` element is optional and thus can be processed by the underlying infrastructure.

Interested readers may wish to check the section "Securing XML Web Services Created Using ASP.NET" in the SDK documentation for extending SOAP messages. The article also includes an HTTP module example that provides a custom authentication mechanism using SOAP headers.

Role-Based Security

The ASP.NET authentication mechanism, when appropriately configured, associates a security context of the client principal with the managed thread servicing the client's call. This principal can be accessed by calling `Thread.CurrentPrincipal`. Essentially, what this means is the same role-based security mechanism that is available to .NET client applications is also available to ASP.NET applications. The following code excerpt for a Web service method illustrates the use of `IPrincipal` method `IsInRole` to check if the caller belongs to the local administrators group:

```
[WebMethod]
public String SensitiveOperation() {
    IPrincipal pr = Thread.CurrentPrincipal;
    bool b = pr.IsInRole(@"BUILTIN\Administrators");
    if (!b) {
      throw new Exception("Only administrators allowed!");
    }
    return "Successful operation";
}
```

It is also possible to provide role-based checks for the entire ASP.NET application by means of the <authorization> XML element in the application's Web.config file. The following sample shows how to allow local administrators to use the application and deny the rest of the users:

```
<configuration>
  <system.web>
    <authentication mode="Windows" />
    <authorization>
        <allow roles="BUILTIN\Administrators" />
        <deny users="*" />
    </authorization>
  </system.web>
</configuration>
```

In this case, an HttpModule called UrlAuthorizationModule performs the role check and returns a 401 status code to IIS if the check fails, forcing IIS to authenticate an anonymous client or to simply fail the request.

Elements allow and deny can be applied on roles or users. The users list may contain specific names, as shown here:

```
<allow users="domain1\user1, domain2\user2, domain3\user3" />
```

Instead of specific names, you can also use wildcards. The configuration mechanism supports two wildcards—* to represent all users and ? to represent anonymous users.

Note the way the allow and the deny elements have been ordered in the configuration file. UrlAuthorizationModule concatenates authorizations, starting from the Web.config in the current directory (if any), back up to the parent directory, all the way to the virtual root. Finally, it adds the authorization information from Machine.config, which by default looks like this:

```
<authorization>
    <allow users="*" />
</authorization>
```

For our application, the resulting list would be:

```
<authorization>
    <allow roles="BUILTIN\Administrators" />
    <deny users="*" />
    <allow users="*" />
</authorization>
```

The `UrlAuthorizationModule` walks from the top of the list looking for a match. As soon as a match is found, it stops and either allows or denies the user based on the match. Had we not placed the `deny` element in the authorization list, access would have been granted to any user, making our role-based check worthless.

Code Access Security

The code access permissions that are available to a .NET client application are also available to an ASP.NET application.

ASP.NET Web applications can be further configured by assigning them trust levels. Trust levels are configured using the `<trust>` element within the configuration file, either at the machine level or at the application level:

```
<trust level="Full | High | Low | None" originUrl="url" />
```

The `originUrl` attribute specifies an application's URL of origin. If present, this can be used for some permissions such as connecting back to the host of origin over the Web. This is important for some ASP.NET applications that require connecting to the origin for proper functioning. Typically, `originUrl` points to an empty string.

Each level determines the application's permissions, the details of which are specified by an XML security policy file. Each level maps to a specific file that is present in the `<FrameworkRootDir>/CONFIG` subdirectory.

Full Trust

This level gives the ASP.NET application unrestricted permissions. There is no file associated with this trust.

High Trust

This level provides permissions that grant applications read and write access to the application directory (subject to OS permissions) and allows the application to replace the authentication principal object. It also restricts applications from calling into unmanaged code.

This trust level maps to the file `web_hightrust.config`.

Low Trust

This level allows applications to read from the application directory and provides limited network connectivity. Applications can connect back to their host site, assuming the `originUrl` attribute of the `<trust>` element is configured appropriately.

This trust level maps to the file `web_lowtrust.config`.

No Trust

This level provides basic execution permission and supports the application's use of isolated storage (a mechanism that allows code to be safely associated with saved data).

This trust level maps to `web_notrust.config`.

Impersonation

Recall from our earlier discussion that there are two security contexts under .NET, one associated with the managed thread processing the request and one used by the underlying physical thread when it tries to access a secured object such as an NTFS file. If the physical thread is not under impersonation, then the security context of the process is used to access the object.

Under ASP.NET, by default the security context of the user that IIS impersonates is available to `aspnet_isapi.dll` but is never passed to the ASP.NET worker process (refer to Figure 9.7). As a result, the underlying physical thread used to process the current request is not under impersonation. This means that the identity used to access a secured OS object is that of the ASP.NET worker process. Recall that this identity is ASPNET by default but can be configured via `Machine.config`.

You can enable impersonation for an ASP.NET application by means of the `<identity>` element in its `Web.config` file, as shown here:

```
<configuration>
  <system.web>
    <identity impersonate="true"/>
  </system.web>
</configuration>
```

When impersonation is enabled, the `aspnet_isapi.dll` hands over the impersonation token to the worker process. The physical thread on which your managed code is running will be impersonating the user represented by the token.

The user account being impersonated depends on how the IIS virtual directory has been set for authentication. If the IIS virtual directory is set for anonymous access, this user is IUSR_<SERVER> (by default, but this is configurable). For all other authentication schemes, it is the authenticated client.

ASP.NET provides yet another option for selecting the user to be impersonated. You can specify the user to be impersonated, along with the password, in the configuration file, as shown here:

```
<identity impersonate="true" userName="domain\usr"
    password="pwd"/>
```

This concludes our discussion on various security mechanisms under ASP.NET. Interested readers may wish to read [Pro-02] for building more secure sites with ASP.NET.

SUMMARY

.NET offers two types of security mechanisms—CAS and role-based security. These security mechanisms are defined on top of the security mechanism offered by the underlying OS.

CAS grants code access permissions to an assembly based on certain evidence about the origin or author of the assembly. The .NET Framework defines various code access permissions such as reading or writing files, changing environmental variables, displaying dialog boxes, and so on. The standard classes under .NET that deal with any security-sensitive operations are designed to perform the appropriate security check. If the assembly does not have the needed permissions, the security mechanism throws an exception of type SecurityException.

By default, the security access check is performed on all the callers in the call stack, which prevents luring security attacks.

Instead of relying on the standard classes to throw the SecurityException, a component can perform the security check by itself, or the code may deny itself certain permissions or assert certain permissions. When a permission is asserted, the common language runtime does not walk the stack to check if the permission has been granted to all the callers. Obviously, only those permissions that have been granted to the assembly can be asserted.

It is also possible to demand, assert, or deny code access permissions using attributes. The framework defines attributes corresponding to each of the code access permissions.

The common language runtime grants permissions to an assembly based on the information it obtains about the assembly. This information, called evidence, includes items such as the origin of the assembly or its author.

The exact permissions that are granted to an assembly are based on an entity on the local machine called the security policy. The security policy contains code groups and permission sets. A permission set is a named set of permissions and a code group maps a specific evidence to a specific permission set. The evidence is represented as a membership condition.

The security policy can be configured at four levels—enterprise, machine, user, and AppDomain. For the purpose of policy evaluation, the enterprise level gets the top priority, followed by machine, user, and AppDomain levels in that order. At each policy level, permissions from each matching code group are merged. In the final step, the granted permissions that are common to each policy level are selected and granted to the assembly.

You should be aware of a security issue with CAS: Although CAS is a good step toward preventing security attacks, it is still the first step. Hackers are still bound to find some holes in the security mechanism. Hopefully, the technology will mature with time.

Role-based security grants access to sensitive data based on the role a user belongs to. Under this mechanism, a user and his or her roles are encapsulated in an object referred to as the principal. Two types of principals come standard with .NET—generic and Windows-specific.

Each managed thread can be associated with a principal. The type of principal is dictated by a policy defined on the application domain.

There are three ways to perform a role check on the thread principal—explicit programming, imperative programming, and declarative programming.

.NET applications actually have two security contexts to deal with: one of the managed code and one of the underlying OS. .NET provides methods that the managed code can use to force the underlying physical thread to impersonate.

ASP.NET applications run in a separate worker process although the applications are hosted under IIS. By default, the worker process runs under an account ASPNET. However, the account to use can be configured from `Machine.config`.

ASP.NET applications have to deal with two levels of authentication. The first level of authentication is done by the IIS and the second level of authentication is handled by ASP.NET.

For IIS authentication, it is the responsibility of the client to provide credentials to the server. The .NET Framework provides some classes that the client code can use to provide the credentials.

ASP.NET authentication uses authentication providers to further authenticate the client.

The CAS and the role-based security mechanisms that are available to .NET applications are also available to ASP.NET applications. In addition, ASP.NET simplifies authorization by allowing you to define allowed and denied users in the application's `Web.config` file.

ASP.NET also provides a mechanism that allows you to force impersonation on the physical thread that is currently running the managed code.

In the next chapter, we will deal with another type of role-based security mechanism. This security mechanism is offered by COM+ but also is available to .NET applications.

REFERENCES

[Bro-01a]   Brown, Keith, "Enforce Code Access Rights with the Common Language Runtime," *MSDN Magazine*, February 2001.
             msdn.microsoft.com/msdnmag/issues/01/02/CAS/CAS.asp

[Bro-01b]   Brown, Keith, "Security Briefs: ASP.NET Security Issues," *MSDN Magazine*, November 2001.
             msdn.microsoft.com/msdnmag/issues/01/11/Security/Security0111.asp

[Bro-02]   Brown, Keith, "Security Briefs: Managed Security Context in ASP.NET," *MSDN Magazine*, January 2002.
             msdn.microsoft.com/msdnmag/issues/02/01/Security/Security0201.asp

[Ker-01]   Kercher, Jeff, "Authentication in ASP.NET: .NET Security Guidance," MSDN Online, Microsoft Corporation, August 2001.
             msdn.microsoft.com/library/en-us/dnbda/html/authaspdotnet.asp

[Pro-02]   Prosise, Jeff, "ASP.NET Security: An Introductory Guide to Building and Deploying More Secure Sites with ASP.NET and IIS," *MSDN Magazine*, April 2002.
             msdn.microsoft.com/msdnmag/issues/02/04/ASPSec/ASPSec.asp

bib. html
<html>
<title> ISBN Number </title>
<body>
<h1> ISBM Number </h1>
<ul>
    <li> 1-81100 -1773 </li>
    <li> .. - </li>
</ul>
</body>

Enterprise Services

Enterprise system development has historically been a very time- and resource-consuming process. The development complexity arises from the extra enterprise-level requirements such as scalability, robustness, security, automatic transaction processing, and so on.

The .NET Framework provides many infrastructural services to meet the needs of enterprise systems. This allows businesses to focus on their core competencies instead of building the plumbing themselves.

In this chapter, we examine in detail some important requirements for enterprise systems and the services provided by .NET to meet these requirements.

ENTERPRISE SYSTEMS: .NET AND COM+

An enterprise system typically consists of many programs running on different computers interacting with each other. It is a large application, at least when compared to a single desktop application, and typically integrates with databases and other services such as message queues. Enterprise systems are generally used in large organizations such as banks, airlines, insurance companies, and hospitals, and are accessed by hundreds of clients simultaneously.

Developing enterprise systems has historically been a long, expensive process. The development complexity arises from the extra enterprise-level requirements such as scalability, robustness, security, automatic transaction processing, and so on.

To meet these requirements, enterprise application designers tend to develop their own in-house software infrastructure. Thus, developing enterprise systems not only becomes a slow process, but it also consumes resources for development as well as for maintenance, for what is essentially a generic infrastructure problem.

To help developers build enterprise systems, Microsoft introduced a framework called COM+ [Tap-01]. COM+[1] is an advanced COM runtime environment that provides solutions to many generic infrastructure problems, including those just mentioned. It provides a set of services that makes building scalable distributed applications easier. COM+ is an integral part of Windows 2000 OS and later versions.

.NET carries on the trend by providing the necessary infrastructure to develop enterprise systems. However, as it turns out, the first release of the .NET Framework has provided a good replacement for COM, but not for COM+. This release depends on COM+ to provide the necessary enterprise services. Components that are built on .NET enterprise services are required to be hosted under COM+. Perhaps in a later release, this dependency will be completely eliminated. For now it forms a good mechanism to integrate .NET components with existing COM/COM+ components.

It is worth mentioning that .NET tries to isolate developers from knowing COM+ by providing the necessary classes and tools. I too will honor this tradition and will do my best to keep you isolated from knowing the internals of COM+. You will learn about enterprise services support only from .NET's perspective. Any COM+ concepts are introduced only on a need-to-know basis.

We start with developing a simple .NET component that needs COM+ enterprise services. Such components are referred to as serviced components.

DEVELOPING .NET SERVICED COMPONENTS

The component we will develop can be considered a part of the human resource management system. It provides salary information for an employee.

The .NET Framework provides many types to support building enterprise systems. These types are defined under the namespace `System.Enterprise-Services` and are implemented in an assembly named `System.Enterprise-Services`. If you are using Visual Studio .NET to develop your serviced component, you need to explicitly add a reference to this assembly in your project.

All the standard classes that we discuss in this chapter can be assumed to belong to the `System.EnterpriseServices` namespace unless otherwise explicitly stated.

The basic steps of developing a serviced component are as follows:

---

1. The origins of COM+ lie in a technology called Microsoft Transaction Server (MTS).

1. Create a serviced component class.
2. Use declarative attributes on the class to indicate one or more COM+ services that are needed by the class.
3. Configure the assembly by defining one or more assembly-level attributes.
4. Register the serviced component with COM+.

Serviced Component

The most important type defined in the `System.EnterpriseServices` namespace is the class `ServicedComponent`. Here is its partial definition:

```
public abstract class ServicedComponent : ContextBoundObject,
    IDisposable
{
    // ContextBoundObject methods
    ...

    // ServicedComponent methods
    ...

    // IDisposable methods (using Dispose pattern)
    public void Dispose();
    protected virtual void Dispose(bool disposing);
}
```

Any managed class that wishes to use .NET enterprise services must extend `ServicedComponent`, as highlighted in this code excerpt:

```
// Project SimpleExample/Employee

using System.EnterpriseServices; // ServicedComponent, etc.
namespace MyCompany {

    public class Employee : ServicedComponent {
        private String m_employeeName;
        public Employee(){
            m_employeeName = null;
        }

        public String Name {
            get {return m_employeeName; }
            set {m_employeeName = value; }
        }

        ...
    }
}
```

The presence of `ServicedComponent` in a class's hierarchy tells the common language runtime that this is a configured class and that the instances of this class need to live in COM+ contexts.

COM+ Contexts

COM+ contexts are conceptual regions within a Win32 process that hold objects requiring similar COM+ services (much like .NET contexts hold .NET objects having compatible context properties). If a class needs a COM+ service, as indicated by the COM+ attributes on the class, COM+ makes sure that the instances of that class always reside in contexts that provide that service. When a client from one context references an object in a different context, COM+ returns a proxy to the client. Any call made on the proxy is intercepted by COM+ so that the necessary services can be provided to the corresponding object.

Note that `ServicedComponent` inherits from `ContextBoundObject`, and from `MarshalByRefObject`, giving your serviced component the benefits of those two classes.

Also note that a serviced component must provide a public default constructor—it cannot have parameterized constructors. If you require such parameters, you need to design a workaround. In the preceding example, the employee name is set by exposing a public property `Name`.

Disposing Resources

It is interesting to note that the implementation of `IDisposable` that `ServicedComponent` provides is based on the `Dispose` pattern that we discussed at length in Chapter 4. Essentially, the base class exposes two `Dispose` methods, a public method that implements `IDisposable.Dispose` and a protected helper method. If you intend to implement `Dispose` in your `ServicedComponent`-derived class, for example, to dispose a resource that the class is holding, then you need to call one of the two `Dispose` methods of the base class from your implementation of `Dispose`. The following code excerpt shows an implementation of a serviced component that implements the `Dispose` pattern. We come across this class later in the chapter when we discuss transactions.

```
// Project Transactions/Banks

public class FidelityBank : ServicedComponent, IDisposable {
    private MyAccountsDB m_db;
    . . .

    //
```

```
// Standard Dispose pattern
//

~FidelityBank() {
  Dispose(false);
}

public void Close() {
  Dispose();
}

new public void Dispose() {
  Dispose(true);
  GC.SuppressFinalize(this);
}

// Always dispose unmanaged resources
// Disposing==true => dispose managed resource as well
protected override void Dispose(bool disposing) {
  if (disposing) {
    // dispose managed resources
    if (null != m_db) {
      m_db.Close();
      m_db = null;
    }
  }
  base.Dispose(disposing);
}
}
```

Note that the protected `Dispose` method on the serviced component properly invokes the base class's `Dispose` method.

Also note that, as this particular serviced component is not dealing with any unmanaged resource (at least directly), there is no real need to implement the destructor on the class. I have left it there for the sake of completeness.

After inheriting your class from `ServicedComponent` and implementing interface `IDisposable` if need be, the next step is to declare certain attributes on the class that dictate the required COM+ services on the class.

Enterprise Service Attributes

The `System.EnterpriseServices` namespace defines a set of attribute classes that can be used to define a serviced component's COM+ service requirements. Table 10.1 lists some important attributes that can be applied to a serviced component. We will be discussing these attributes in greater detail throughout the chapter as we learn more about configuring serviced components to take advantage of various COM+ services.

TABLE 10.1   Enterprise Service Attributes for Classes

Attribute Class	Description
AutoCompleteAttribute	Auto completion of transactions
ComponentAccessControlAttribute	Component, interface, and method-level access check
ConstructionEnabledAttribute	Object construction using externally specified construction strings
JustInTimeActivationAttribute	Enables JIT activation
ObjectPoolingAttribute	Enables object pooling
SecurityRoleAttribute	Role-based access check
TransactionAttribute	Enable transaction support

A serviced component is annotated with one or more attributes, as shown here:

```
[JustInTimeActivation]
public class Employee : ServicedComponent {
    ...
}
```

In this code, the presence of the JustInTimeActivation attribute indicates that the Employee class requires the use of COM+ JIT activation service.

.NET allows you to apply attributes to your serviced components with great flexibility. You can apply as many attributes as you like. You need not even apply any attribute and still can register the serviced component with the COM+ Catalog Manager, and configure it later using the Component Services Explorer, although it is not advised.

Based on the attributes specified on the serviced component, the instances of the serviced component are placed in a proper COM+ context.

It is interesting to note that none of the serviced attributes is inherited from ContextAttribute. This is because the common language runtime does not require a serviced component's objects to be placed in a .NET context. Instead, it relies on the interception provided by the COM+ to provide the necessary services.

So why does ServicedComponent inherit from ContextBoundObject? Well, this makes it possible for you to specify context attributes if need be (along with serviced attributes) on the serviced component.

COM+ Catalog

Classes that use COM+ runtime services and are annotated with COM+ attributes are called *configured classes*. COM+ stores the configuration information (attribute values) in a repository called the COM+ catalog.

The COM+ catalog is composed of COM+ applications. A COM+ application is a group of one or more associated configured classes. There are two types of COM+ applications—library applications and server applications. If a configured class belongs to a library application, new instances of the class are created in the client's process. If a configured class belongs to a server application, then COM+ creates a dedicated surrogate process (dllhost.exe) to house the instances of the configured class.

The OS comes with a GUI tool called the Component Services snap-in that one can use to view and modify the configuration information about a COM+ application.

Note that although .NET tries to isolate developers from knowing COM+, this isolation breaks down in a few places. For example, you need to use the COM+ Component Services snap-in to start or stop .NET-based COM+ server applications.

At this point, we are almost ready to compile the serviced component and register its configuration information in the COM+ catalog. However, let's first define a few useful assembly-level attributes on the serviced component.

Configuring the Assembly

To register a serviced component in the COM+ catalog, there are a few settings that you should specify on the assembly. These configuration settings include the name of the COM+ application for the serviced component, the mode of the COM+ application (library or server), and so on. These configuration settings are defined as assembly-level attributes in the System.EnterpriseServices namespace. Table 10.2 lists some routinely used assembly-level attributes.

TABLE 10.2 Attributes for COM+ Applications

Class	Description
ApplicationNameAttribute	Name of the application
ApplicationIDAttribute	Unique ID for the application
DescriptionAttribute	Application description (can also be used to describe classes, methods, and interfaces)
ApplicationActivationAttribute	Activation mode—either library or server
ApplicationAccessControlAttribute	Security settings
ApplicationQueuingAttribute	Enables the application for queued components

Note that the use of these attributes is optional. If not specified, the registration mechanism does a reasonable job of picking up a proper default value.

Application Name

The attribute `ApplicationName` is used to describe which COM+ application the configured classes in the assembly belong to. Its usage is shown here:

```
[assembly: ApplicationName("Employee Information System")]
```

If you do not provide an application name, .NET uses the name of the assembly as the COM+ application name.

Application Identity

The attribute `ApplicationID` is used to specify a globally unique identity for the COM+ application, as shown here:

```
[assembly: ApplicationID("5209F894-D801-44b7-BBBA-4706A2546467")].
```

The registration process installs the configured classes from the assembly into a COM+ application with the given ID (if specified) and name. If the COM+ application does not exist, the registration process creates a new COM+ application with the specified ID.

Application Description

Attribute `DescriptionAttribute` can be used to provide a description for the COM+ application. The usage is shown here:

```
[assembly: Description("My employee information system")]
```

Note that the `DescriptionAttribute` can also be applied to classes, class methods, and interfaces. When the assembly is registered in the COM+ catalog, the descriptions are also stored in the catalog and can be viewed at each level (application, class, method, interface) using the Component Services snap-in.

Activation Mode

The activation mode of the COM+ application can be specified by means of an attribute, `ApplicationActivation`. Possible options are `Activation-Option.Server` (for server application) and `ActivationOption.Library` for library application. The usage is shown here:

```
[assembly: ApplicationActivation(ActivationOption.Server)]
```

This attribute is used only during the creation of a new COM+ application. If not specified, the registration mechanism creates a library application.

Note that this attribute is ignored if the specified COM+ application already exists in the COM+ catalog.

It is important to understand the performance impact of server application versus library application from the .NET client's perspective. When a .NET serviced component that is hosted in a server application is instantiated, COM+ creates a client callable wrapper (CCW; see Chapter 7) for the serviced component. When a .NET client tries to access such a serviced component, the common language runtime creates a runtime callable wrapper (RCW) in the client's process. The client accesses the serviced component using the RCW through the CCW. This is illustrated in Figure 10.1.

However, in case of in-process activations (library application), the common language runtime does not use the COM interop layer (RCW/CCW) at all. Instead, it uses managed C++ calls to the COM+ API. This results in a significantly improved performance. This process is illustrated in Figure 10.2.

It is interesting to note that, although Figure 10.2 shows that the serviced component and the .NET client are in two different .NET contexts, it is entirely possible to have them in the same .NET context. Recall that the serviced attributes are not context attributes and hence do not require a newer compatible context.

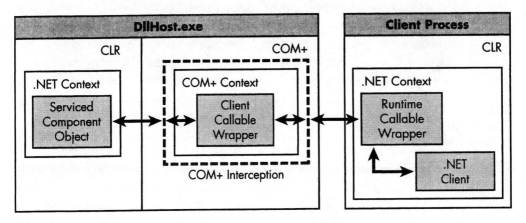

FIGURE 10.1 Out-of-process activation.

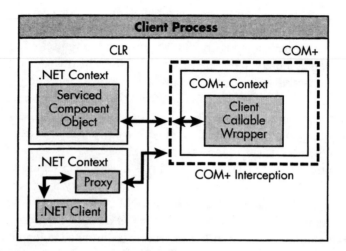

FIGURE 10.2 In-process activation.

Signing the Assembly

There is one assembly-level configuration that is a must (at least for now)—
the compiled assembly must be strong named. As the serviced component is
hosted by a COM+ application, the assembly should be accessible to the
common language runtime within the COM+ application. The common language runtime's assembly resolver can load the assembly only from known
locations. For example, for the library-type COM+ applications, the assembly
must be present in the directory where the client executable resides. Copying
an assembly to the client's directory is not always desirable (especially if
there are many clients for the same COM+ application). One location that the
assembly resolver can always use is the GAC. For this reason, the COM+
integration plumbing mandates that the compiled assembly be strong-named
(only strong-named assemblies can be installed in the GAC).

Recall from Chapter 3 that a strong-named assembly can be created by
defining an assembly-level attribute, `AssemblyKeyFile` (namespace `Sys-
tem.Reflection`), in the source code and specifying as the parameter the
name of the file containing the cryptographic public–private key pair. The
usage is shown here:

```
[assembly: AssemblyKeyFile("MyKey.snk")]
```

Note that although the assembly is required to be strong named, you
don't always have to install the assembly into the GAC. Evaluate your situa-

tion to see if this is the case. I prefer not to clutter the GAC unless absolutely required.

Compile your source code. At this point, the assembly is ready to be registered in the COM+ Catalog.

Registering the Serviced Components

The serviced components in your assembly can be registered in three ways:

- Manually, using a tool provided by .NET.
- Programmatically, using a utility class provided by .NET.
- Automatically, by running the client program.

Regardless of the technique you use, the registration process installs the configured classes from the assembly into a COM+ application and configures them using the specified attributes. For those attributes that are not specified, the default COM+ settings are used. Once registered, the serviced components are available for the clients to consume.

If the assembly contains incompatible attributes, the incompatibility is detected during registration and the registration is aborted.

It should be noted that registering the serviced components requires administrative privileges; that is, the user registering the serviced component must be a member of the local Administrators group.

Manual Registration

The .NET Framework provides a command-line tool called Services Installation Utility (regsvcs.exe) that can be used for this purpose. The usage is shown in the following command line:

```
regsvcs.exe MyServer.dll
```

When executed, this tool performs three operations:

1. It registers the assembly as a COM component (as if you had run regasm.exe).

2. It emits a COM type library (as if you had run tlbexp.exe).

3. Using the type library, it installs the serviced components from the assembly into the COM+ catalog.

By default, the tool tries to find and use the specified COM+ application. If the application does not exist, the tool creates a new one. The same behavior can be explicitly achieved by using the `-fc` command-line switch.

If the specified COM+ application is found, the tool also reconfigures the application based on the specified attributes.

If the default behavior is not acceptable, the tool provides many other command-line switches to customize the behavior. Check the SDK documentation or simply run `regsvcs.exe` from a command window for a list of available switches.

To uninstall an assembly from the COM+ catalog, the command-line switch `-u` can be specified, as shown here:

```
regsvcs.exe -u MyServer.dll
```

Programmatic Registration

The namespace `System.EnterpriseServices` provides a class, `RegistrationHelper`, that you can use to programmatically register or unregister an assembly containing serviced components. Even `regsvcs.exe` internally uses this class to perform the registration.

`RegistrationHelper` implements a method, `InstallAssembly`, that you can use to register an assembly in the COM+ catalog, as illustrated in the following code. This program registers our serviced component assembly `Employee.dll`:

```
// Project SimpleExample/MyInstaller

public static void Main() {
    RegistrationHelper helper = new RegistrationHelper();

    String appName = null;
    String tlbName = null;
    helper.InstallAssembly("Employee.Dll", ref appName,
        ref tlbName,
InstallationFlags.CreateTargetApplication);
    Console.WriteLine(
        "Registration succeeded. App={0}, Tlb={1}",
        appName, tlbName);
}
```

By passing in `null` for the application name (the second parameter) and the type library name (the third parameter), the call relies on `InstallAssembly` to appropriately generate the name of the application and the name of the type library. The final parameter defines the flags that control the installation process. In the preceding code, the passed value indicates that a new COM+ application will be created. If the application already exists in the catalog, the call will fail with a `RegistrationException`.

To uninstall an assembly from the COM+ catalog, `Registration-Helper` implements another method, `UninstallAssembly`. When calling this method, just supply the name of the assembly to uninstall.

Automatic Registration

When a .NET client instantiates a serviced component, the common language runtime checks whether the serviced component's assembly has already been registered with the COM+ catalog. If the assembly is not already registered, the runtime goes ahead and installs it (using the `RegistrationHelper` `.InstallAssembly` method).

In general, you should not rely on automatic registration. Installing an assembly in the COM+ catalog requires administrative privileges. If the .NET client that first uses the serviced component does not have the administrative privileges, the registration fails with a `Registration-Exception`.

Of course, anyone who runs `regsvcs.exe` must have administrative privileges as well. So, even if you choose one of the other methods of registration, the act of registration must still be done by an administrator.

Regardless of the registration mechanism used, the end result is that the serviced component is installed in the catalog under a COM+ application. Figure 10.3 shows a snapshot of the installed serviced component as seen from the Component Services snap-in.

A few things should be noted here. First, the COM interop mechanism generates a PROGID for the serviced component in the form `<namespace>.<class>` by default. In our case, this is `MyCompany.Employee`. However, you can override this default behavior by means of `ProgIdAttribute` (Chapter 7).

Second, the COM interface `_Employee` represents the .NET class `Employee`. Recall from Chapter 7 that by default any public method in the class `Employee` does not automatically appear in the interface `_Employee` (although you will still be able to invoke the method via `IDispatch` interface). You can change this behavior either by implementing interfaces on your serviced component or by annotating your class with the attribute `ClassInterfaceAttribute` (Chapter 7).

Finally, although you can modify configuration of your serviced component from the Component Services snap-in, you should never do so. In many

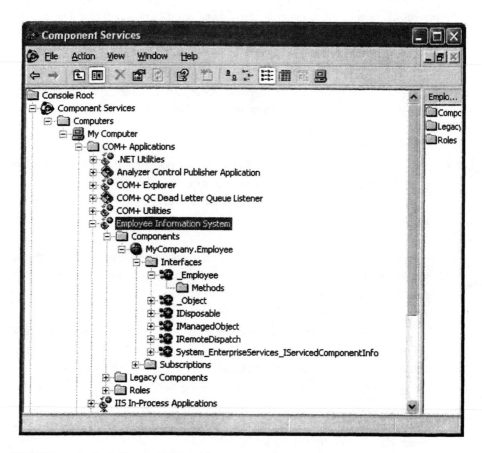

FIGURE 10.3   Installing a .NET serviced component.

cases, the underlying .NET to COM+ plumbing relies on the declarative attributes in your class's code and not on the COM+ catalog.

In general, you should view the COM+ catalog as a copy of your class's declarative attribute but not the real source. The only attributes you should be changing in the COM+ catalog are the ones that are deployment specific, such as security settings and construction strings (we cover these settings shortly). The COM+ catalog exists because COM did not have an extensible metadata model for binary components. The common language runtime does have one. You can expect to see a future version of the COM+ runtime that relies more and more on the declarative attribute of the common language runtime metadata model.

Implementing a Client

From the client's perspective, there is nothing special about a configured class; the fact that it uses COM+ runtime services is irrelevant. The following code shows a simple client that uses the Employee class defined earlier:

```
// Project SimpleExample/MyClient

class MyApp {
    static void Main(string[] args){
      Console.WriteLine(Thread.CurrentContext.ContextID);

      using (Employee emp = new Employee()) {
        emp.Name = "Jay";
        Console.WriteLine(emp.GetSalary());
      }
    }
}
```

Note that the Employee class is instantiated within the scope of a using statement. This is because the base class ServicedComponent implements the interface IDisposable. The ServicedComponent's implementation of the IDisposable method Dispose handles releasing expensive resources such as handles to database connections (if any).

Instead of calling Dispose on the object (which is what using does when the object goes out of scope), the client can also call a static method, ServicedComponent.DisposeObject, passing in the object to be disposed. However, using the Dispose design pattern is preferred over calling DisposeObject.

At this point, we know how to develop, deploy, and use a serviced component. Let's now start looking at some frequently used COM+ services.

JIT ACTIVATION

In an enterprise system, a user-driven client application often creates an object, makes a method call, and holds on to the object to use it later. The time between calls can vary from seconds to minutes or even hours. Meanwhile, on the server side, the object continues to stay alive, potentially tying up expensive resources. Imagine the resource-sharing problem that would arise if 100 or more clients locked access to the resources that they weren't even using.

JIT activation is a mechanism provided by COM+ to manage the lifetime of an object more efficiently. The idea is very simple: The actual object is activated just prior to the first call made on it and is deactivated immediately after finishing its work.

For now, assume object activation is the same as object creation and object deactivation is the same as object destruction. The distinction will become clear in the next section when we discuss object pooling.

Configuration and Working

A serviced component is marked for JIT activation using the class `JustIn-TimeActivationAttribute`, as shown in the following code excerpt:

```
// Project JITActivation/Employee

[JustInTimeActivation]
public class Employee : ServicedComponent {
    ...
}
```

When a client instantiates a serviced component that is marked for JIT activation, COM+ activates the actual object and returns a proxy to the client. Subsequently, the client makes method calls on the proxy as usual. When the object has finished doing its work, COM+ deactivates the object. However, the client continues to hold the reference to the object via its proxy (unaware that the underlying object has been deactivated). Later, when the client makes a call on the proxy, COM+ activates a new instance of the object and associates it with the proxy that the client is holding.

Now comes the million-dollar question: How does COM+ know that it is safe to deactivate the object?

COM+ could perhaps wait for a predefined timeout period to check if the client makes any call. If no call comes in within this timeout period, then COM+ can deactivate the object. However, such a timeout-based deactivation mechanism may result in an unexpected behavior.

Consider, for example, our `Employee` serviced component:

```
public class Employee : ServicedComponent {
    private String m_employeeName;

    public String Name {
      get {return m_employeeName; }
      set {m_employeeName = value; }
    }

    public long GetSalary() {
      ...
    }
  }
}
```

The idea is that the client first sets the employee Name property, and then calls GetSalary to obtain the salary of the employee. Let's say the client doesn't call GetSalary within the timeout period. As a result, COM+ deactivates the object. Later, when a GetSalary call comes in, a new instance is activated. However, the new instance has no idea who the employee is on which GetSalary is being called. In the best case, the call returns a failure condition. In the worst case, it returns an invalid value.

The real problem is that when the original object was being deactivated, it was in a state that contained the name of the employee. When the object got deactivated, this state got lost.

For JIT to work, the object should be deactivated when it is "stateless," meaning it either contains no data, or contains data that is not important and may be discarded. But COM+ doesn't have the foggiest idea about the statelessness or the statefulness of an object. As far as it is concerned, the object is nothing but an implementation of a bunch of methods. Unlike COM+, however, the object does know what state it is in. If it can inform COM+ that it is done with the work it is supposed to do, COM+ can go ahead and deactivate the object.

In our example case, it is not okay to deactivate the object after setting the Name property but it is fine to deactivate the object after the client calls the GetSalary method.

An object that has JIT enabled internally contains a property called the "done" bit or, more precisely, the deactivate-on-return bit. COM+ checks this bit after returning from each method call. If the bit is turned on, COM+ deactivates the object.

To allow the serviced component to interact with COM+, System .EnterpriseServices provides a static class, ContextUtil. This class implements many properties that the serviced component can access or modify. The property that we are interested in currently is DeactivateOnReturn. Let's revise our GetSalary method to set this property to true. This is highlighted in the following code excerpt:

```
public long GetSalary() {
    if (null == m_employeeName) {
      throw new Exception("Set the employee name first");
    }

    ContextUtil.DeactivateOnReturn = true;

    // Return a hard-coded value for our demo
    return 100000;
}
```

Setting `DeactivateOnReturn` to true within `GetSalary` causes the `Employee` object to be deactivated after the method call completes. If you make a subsequent call to `GetSalary`, for example, a new instance of the `ServicedObject` is created automatically. However, as the employee name has not been set on the new instance, the implementation `GetSalary` simply throws an exception.

Although JIT activation results in reclaiming the resource taken up by the object, it is often less than what you think. Moreover, keep in mind that repeated activation and deactivation of the object results in some performance degradation. Before enabling JIT activation, you should consider if the benefit of saving resources outweighs the performance degradation. JIT activation has more of an advantage when deactivating an object recovers a scarce, expensive resource, such as a database connection.

The real benefit of JIT is that it enforces transactional correctness, as we will see later.

If JIT activation is enabled on a component, it implies that its objects are created and destroyed frequently. The primary intention of destroying an object is to force the object to release its resources. If somehow we can force the object to release its resources without actually destroying the object, we could reuse the object without having to create it, thus saving some CPU cycles. This is what object pooling, a COM+ provided mechanism and our next topic of discussion, tries to achieve. By pooling JIT-activated objects, you can greatly speed up object reactivation for the client.

OBJECT POOLING

The concept of object pooling is simple. If an object is marked as pooled, and if the object is not currently being used by any client, then COM+ can reuse this object when a client requests a new object of the same type. This saves the cost of object creation.

Configuration and Working

A serviced component is marked as pooled using a serviced attribute, `ObjectPoolingAttribute`. When the COM+ application containing the component is first activated, COM+ creates a bunch of objects (the exact number is specified as the minimum pool size) and holds them in a pool. When a client creates an object of the serviced component, COM+ first checks the pool to see if the object of the specified type is available. If so, COM+ activates the object from the pool instead of creating a new one. If the object is not available, COM+ creates a new one, up to the maximum specified size of the pool. When the object is released, either because the client called `Dispose` on it or as a result of a JIT deactivate-on-return bit set, the object goes back to the pool for reuse.

If all the objects up to the maximum specified limit are already in use when a new object creation request comes in, COM+ waits for a specified timeout interval (configurable from `ObjectPoolingAttribute`) to see if any of the used objects become available for reuse. If not, the object creation fails.

Note that earlier in the chapter, we deliberately chose the words object activation and deactivation, as opposed to object creation and destruction. The semantic difference between the two should now become clear. When an object is activated, it either gets created or fetched from a pool of existing objects. When an object is deactivated, it either gets destroyed or placed back in the pool.

The `ObjectPooling` attribute lets you specify all possible settings for your serviced component's object pool. The following code excerpt, for example, enables object pooling for `Employee` component with a minimum pool size of 2, a maximum pool size of 5, and a creation timeout of 50 milliseconds:

```
// Project ObjectPooling/Employee

[ObjectPooling(MinPoolSize=2,MaxPoolSize=5,CreationTimeout=50)]
public class Employee : ServicedComponent {
    ...
}
```

There are times when a pooled object needs some information from COM+ during runtime. For example, a pooled object may need to know when it is getting deactivated so that it can release its resources. To address this, the base class `ServicedComponent` provides four virtual methods:

```
public abstract class ServicedComponent : ...
{
    ...

    protected internal virtual void Activate();
    protected internal virtual void Deactivate();
    protected internal virtual bool CanBePooled();
    protected internal virtual void Construct(String s);
}
```

It is worth noting the `ServicedComponent` class already provides a default implementation for all four methods. You can simply override the method that you are interested in.

When a serviced component object is being activated, COM+ calls its `Activate` method before handing the object over to the client. This gives the object a chance to do any necessary initialization.

When the object is being deactivated, COM+ calls the `Deactivate` method. This is the object's chance to perform whatever cleanup is necessary, such as releasing any held resources, before it is destroyed or recycled.

Immediately after calling `Deactivate`, COM+ calls the `CanBePooled` method on the object to check if the object is willing to be pooled for reuse. If the object returns `false`, COM+ destroys the object. Otherwise, COM+ places (or may place) the object back into the pool.

Note that returning `true` from `CanBePooled` does not guarantee that the object will be recycled; it only gives COM+ the permission to recycle it. Returning `false`, however, guarantees that the object will be destroyed.

Finally, it is possible to pass any extra information as a string to the object at the time of construction. An example where this is useful is to specify a database connection string for an object that needs to connect to a data-

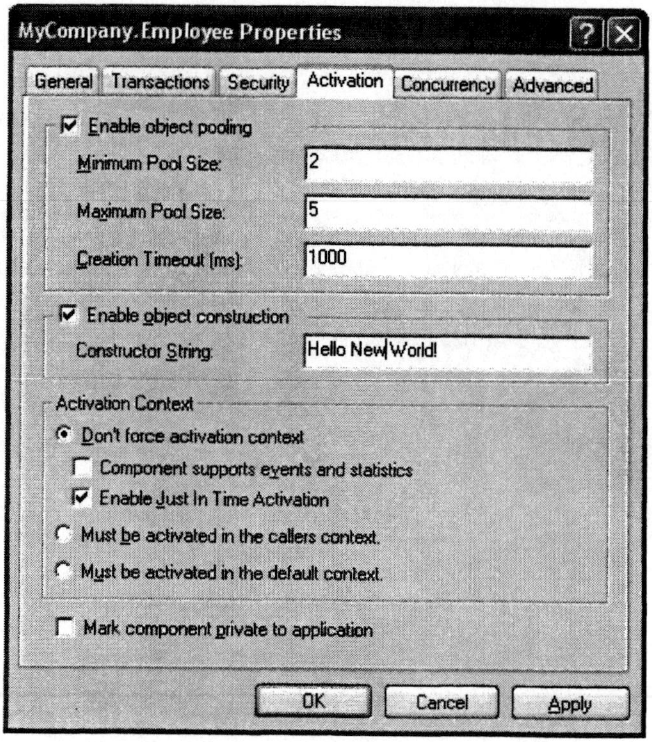

FIGURE 10.4 Activation properties configuration.

base. COM+ calls the method `Construct` just after the constructor is called, passing in the construction string.

You can enable construction string support from the Component Services snap-in. This option can be found on the Activation property page of the component properties dialog box. You can also specify the construction string on the same page. A snapshot of the Activation property page is shown in Figure 10.4.

The construction string support can also be enabled on a serviced component by marking it with an attribute, `ConstructionEnabledAttribute`. In addition, you can specify a default construction string using this attribute, as illustrated in the following code excerpt:

```
[ConstructionEnabled(Enabled = true,
    Default = "Hello Old World!")]
public class Employee : ServicedComponent {
    . . .
}
```

ROLE-BASED SECURITY

In Chapter 9, we looked at the role-based security mechanism offered by .NET. A similar role-based security service is offered by COM+. There are a few noteworthy differences:

1. The role-based security mechanism under COM+ works only for Windows principals. .NET offers a more generalized role-based security mechanism; the roles can be based either on Windows principals (`WindowsPrincipal`) or on generic principals (`GenericPrincipal`).

2. Under .NET, the roles defined by `WindowsPrincipal` are tied to the local Windows user groups. Under COM+, however, the roles can be arbitrarily defined. Each role can be assigned zero or more individual users or user groups.

Let's extend our employee salary program to deal with role-based security. We define an interface `ISalary` to obtain or to update an employee's salary. The interface is shown here:

```
// Project RoleBasedSecurity/Employee

public interface ISalary {
    long GetSalary();
    void SetSalary(long newSalary);
}
```

The roles that the serviced component will use can be defined declaratively at the assembly level using the attribute SecurityRoleAttribute. For our example, we define two roles, Manager and Employee, as illustrated in the following code excerpt:

```
[assembly: SecurityRole("Manager", Description="The big wigs")]
[assembly: SecurityRole("Employee")]
```

When the assembly is installed in the COM+ catalog, the specified roles are created at the COM+ application level. Optionally, the roles can be provided a descriptive text.

By default, the roles that are created at installation time do not have any users associated with them. However, the system administrator (or any privileged user) can then add or remove Windows users (or user groups) for each role using the Component Services snap-in.

It is possible to declaratively add the local user group Everyone to a role. This is done by setting a property, SetEveryoneAccess, on the class SecurityRoleAttribute to true, as illustrated in the following revised definition of the Employee role:

```
[assembly: SecurityRole("Employee", SetEveryoneAccess=true)]
```

This statement results in the Everyone local group being added to the Employee role when this assembly is installed in the COM+ catalog. However, opening an application to everyone may not always be a good idea (although it is convenient for debugging purposes). Evaluate your case to see if you need this feature for any of the roles your application defines.

Declarative Access Check

The first step in performing any access check is to configure your application to enforce access checks. This can be done using an assembly-level attribute, ApplicationAccessControlAttribute, in your code. The default constructor for this attribute causes the access checks to be enforced. However, you can also use an overloaded constructor to explicitly turn on the access check. Consequently, the following two statements behave identically:

```
[assembly: ApplicationAccessControl]
[assembly: ApplicationAccessControl(true)]
```

Access checks can be performed either at the process level or a finer level that includes components, interfaces, and interface methods. This behavior is controlled by a property, AccessChecksLevel, that ApplicationAccess-ControlAttribute defines. The options that can be set on this property are defined as an enumeration of type AccessCheckLevelOption. The possible options are Application (for a process-level check) and ApplicationComponent (for a finer level check).

The process-level access check makes sense only if the COM+ application is configured to run as a server (in a separate process dllhost.exe). The following code excerpt shows how to enforce the process-level access check:

```
[assembly: ApplicationActivation(ActivationOption.Server)]
[assembly: ApplicationAccessControl(AccessChecksLevel=
    AccessChecksLevelOption.Application)]
```

When an application is configured for a process-level access check, only those users present in the application-specific security roles can access the application. Recall that users can be added or removed from a role using the Component Services snap-in.

A process-level access check is a good first-level protection against unknown users. However, most applications desire a finer level of control on the component or interface method an individual user can access. This is where AccessChecksLevelOption.ApplicationComponent is useful:

```
[assembly: ApplicationActivation(ActivationOption.Server)]
[assembly: ApplicationAccessControl(AccessChecksLevel=
    AccessChecksLevelOption.ApplicationComponent)]
```

Applying the ApplicationComponent option for a server application enables the access check at the process level as well as the finer levels.

Note that the ApplicationComponent option can be applied to a library application as well. However, in this case there will not be any process-level access check; security checks occur only at the finer levels.

After applying the ApplicationComponent option, the next step is to identify each serviced component within the application on which the finer level access checks will be performed. This is done using an attribute ComponentAccessControlAttribute, as shown in the following code excerpt:

```
// Project RoleBasedSecurity/Employee

[ComponentAccessControl]
public class Employee : ServicedComponent, ISalary {
    ...
}
```

The default constructor for `ComponentAccessControlAttribute` turns on the access check for the serviced component. However, you can also turn the access on explicitly by using an overloaded constructor that takes a Boolean parameter. Consequently, the following two statements behave identically:

```
[ComponentAccessControl]
[ComponentAccessControl(true)]
```

Note that applying `ComponentAccessControlAttribute` is a must for each serviced component on which you intend to perform the finer level access checks. Without this attribute turned on, you will run into unpredictable behavior.

Now we are ready to declaratively define the security roles that can access the serviced component, any of the interfaces it supports, or the methods on the interface. This is done using our familiar `SecurityRoleAttribute` class. The following code excerpt shows how the `Employee`-serviced component can be set to be accessed only by users belonging to either the `Manager` or the `Employee` roles:

```
[SecurityRole("Manager")]
[SecurityRole("Employee")]
[ComponentAccessControl]
public class Employee : ServicedComponent, ISalary {
    ...
}
```

The security roles can be associated further at the interface or the interface method level. For example, it makes sense that only managers be set to change employee salaries. The following code excerpt shows how this can be done declaratively:

```
[SecurityRole("Manager")]
public void SetSalary(long newSalary) {
    ...
    m_Salary = newSalary;
}
```

Note that if you assign the role at the component, interface, or method level but not at the assembly level, the role is automatically added to the application during the assembly registration. However, it is a good practice to define all the possible roles at the assembly level.

Programmatic Access Check

A declarative access check is a great way to provide role-based security. However, declarative programming has its own limitations. For example, it cannot prevent any employee from accessing any other employee's salary information.

To provide programmatic access checks, the .NET/COM+ plumbing provides a class, `SecurityCallContext`. This class encapsulates security information about all the callers in the call chain. Table 10.3 lists some important properties and methods available on this class.

TABLE 10.3   SecurityCallContext Members

Member	Description
NumCallers	Number of callers in the call chain.
Callers	Collection of callers. Each caller is represented by a `Security-Identity` object.
DirectCaller	A `SecurityIdentity` object representing the direct caller of the method.
OriginalCaller	A `SecurityIdentity` object representing the original caller of the method.
IsSecurityEnabled	Checks if the security check is enabled in the current context.
IsCallerInRole	Checks if the direct caller is in the specified role.
IsUserInRole	Checks if the specified user is in the specified role.

The current security call context can be obtained by using a static property, `SecurityCallContext.CurrentCall`. Using this context, you can check, for example, whether or not the direct caller is in a specific role. You can also perform additional checks using the direct caller's account name. The following code excerpt checks the caller to ensure that only managers and the employee himself or herself can obtain the salary information:

```
// Project RoleBasedSecurity/Employee

public long GetSalary() {
    ...
    SecurityCallContext ctx = SecurityCallContext.CurrentCall;
    if (!ctx.IsSecurityEnabled) {
      throw new Exception(
        "Component not configured correctly");
    }

    if (ctx.IsCallerInRole("Manager")) {
        // managers always have access
        return m_Salary;
    }

    String caller = ctx.DirectCaller.AccountName;

    // Case-insensitive comparison
    if (0 == String.Compare(caller, m_employeeName)) {
      // only an employee can look up his/her salary
      throw new Exception("You are not authorized");
    }

    return m_Salary;
}
```

It is important to understand that for the programmatic access to work on a serviced component, you still need to set ApplicationAccessControl to ApplicationComponent as well as ComponentAccessControl to true for the component. Without these settings, the security call context may return incorrect results. To ensure that these settings are property enabled, you can check the property IsSecurityEnabled on the security call context, as shown in the preceding code.

QUEUED COMPONENTS

In Chapter 8, we learned that .NET provides a mechanism to invoke method calls on an object asynchronously. Using the BeginInvoke call on the delegate of a method, a client can invoke the method asynchronously, either on the same machine or on a remote machine.

Although the support provided by .NET in its current release is a good first step toward asynchronous programming, it still lacks a few useful features. For instance, there is no support for disconnected work; the client and the server have to be running at the same time. There is no built-in mechanism for auto-retry in case the server is down at the time the client is making a call. This gap is filled by the support provided by COM+ for queued components.

A queued component looks and feels like any other .NET component that you develop. When a client instantiates a queued component, the infrastructure returns a proxy object to the client. The real object is not yet created. The client makes method calls on a queued object much like any other .NET object, except that the proxy simply records the method calls (and its parameter values). When the client releases the object, the infrastructure stores the sequence of method calls as a message and sends it to an MSMQ queue that is associated with the COM+ application. The COM+ application is configured to listen on this queue. The infrastructure reads the message that arrives on the queue, creates an instance of the queued component (the real object), and plays back the method calls on the real object in the same sequence as the original caller.

If the COM+ application queue is not reachable at the time the proxy sends the message, then the message is stored in a local outgoing queue. The MSMQ infrastructure automatically forwards the message whenever the COM+ application queue becomes available.

Note that to use queued components, MSMQ has to be installed on both the client machine and the server machine.

Configuring a Queued Component

We will extend our Employee Information System COM+ application to avail COM+ queuing services. This is a three-step process.

The first step is to configure the COM+ application as a server application. Only server applications can avail COM+ queuing services.

```
[assembly: ApplicationActivation(ActivationOption.Server)]
```

The second step is to enable the application for queuing. This is done by means of an assembly-level attribute, ApplicationQueuingAttribute, as shown in the following code excerpt:

```
[assembly: ApplicationQueuing(Enabled=true,
    QueueListenerEnabled = true)]
```

Setting the property Enabled to true results in the creation of seven message queues on the local machine at the time of registering the application. Figure 10.5 shows a snapshot of the message queues created for our Employee Information System application. Note that this machine is set up in

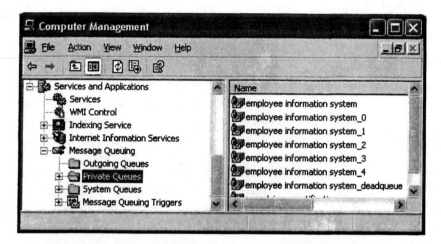

FIGURE 10.5 Message queues for queued components.

workgroup mode, so all the queues are created as private. If your machine is set up in the domain mode, you see one public queue and six private queues.

The queues that are created are called *transactional type queues*. This essentially ensures that the messages sent to the queue are never lost or duplicated.

Also note that uninstalling the COM+ application does not automatically remove the message queues. You will need to remove them explicitly.

Enabling the application for queuing simply allows request messages to be sent to the application queue. However, you also need to set the application to begin processing these queued requests. This is done by setting the `ApplicationQueuingAttribute` property `QueueListenerEnabled` to true, as shown in the preceding code. When the application is started, the infrastructure creates a listener thread for the application that processes the queued requests.

The final step in configuring the queued component is to encapsulate all the methods that the client will use in an interface, and enable the interface for queuing support. The latter part is done by marking the interface with an attribute `InterfaceQueuingAttribute`. The following code excerpt enables queuing on an interface `ISetSalary`. The client is expected to use this interface.

```
// Project QueuedComponent/Employee

[InterfaceQueuing(Enabled = true)]
public interface ISetSalary {
    String Name {set; }
    void SetSalary(long newSalary);
}
```

Note that the methods of a queuing interface cannot have `out` or `ref` type parameters, nor can they have a return value. As the methods will be invoked asynchronously, the return type parameters do not make any sense. Recall from Chapter 8 that similar restrictions were placed on methods based on the .NET asynchronous programming model.

The serviced component requires no further configuration, except, of course, to support the queuing interface. This is highlighted in the following code excerpt:

```
// Project QueuedComponent/Employee

public class Employee : ServicedComponent, ISetSalary {
    ...
    public String Name {
        get {return m_employeeName; }
        set {
            m_employeeName = value;
            m_Salary=100000; //hardcoded value is ok for our test
        }
    }
    public void SetSalary(long newSalary) {
        if (null == m_employeeName) {
            throw new Exception("Set the employee name first");
        }
        m_Salary = newSalary;
    }
}
```

Managed Clients

For a queued component's client, the identification of the queued component is represented as a textual string of the form:

```
"queue:ComputerName=MachineName/new:ProgId"
```

For example, our `Employee` serviced component running on a machine MYDEV can be represented as:

```
"queue:ComputerName=MYDEV/new:MyCompany.Employee"
```

If the queued component is running on the local machine, the Computer-Name field can be omitted and the component can simply be represented as:

```
"queue:/new:MyCompany.Employee"
```

The mechanism of resolving arbitrary object names, such as the preceding one, onto the object to which they refer is a standard part of COM. This mechanism is based on using locator objects (formally called *monikers*) to properly bind to the desired object.

The COM interoperability layer under .NET provides a static method, `Marshal.BindToMoniker` (the class `Marshal` can be found under the namespace `System.Runtime.InteropServices`) to bind to an object specified by its moniker name. The following code excerpt shows how a client for our `Employee` component can obtain an `ISetSalary` interface using `Marshal.BindToMoniker`:

```
// Project QueuedComponents/MyClient

static void Main(string[] args){
    String s = "queue:/new:MyCompany.Employee";
    ISetSalary sal = (ISetSalary) Marshal.BindToMoniker(s);
    sal.Name = "Jay";
    sal.SetSalary(110000);
    ...
}
```

Note that clients can also instantiate the serviced component directly (and not use `Marshal.BindToMoniker`). In this case, however, COM+ does not provide queuing services for the component. Any method call that the client makes on the object is invoked synchronously. You could use this to your advantage for testing the functionality of your component. Essentially, it is up to each client to decide if it wishes to use the serviced component synchronously or as a queued component.

Recall that the client has to release the proxy object for the queued component so that the recorded sequence of method calls can be dispatched to the queued component's queue. For a .NET client, this would happen when the proxy object is garbage collected. However, the .NET client can expedite releasing the proxy object by calling a static method, `Marshal.ReleaseComObject`. This is highlighted in the following code excerpt:

```
// Project QueuedComponents/MyClient

static void Main(string[] args){
    ...
    ISetSalary sal = (ISetSalary) Marshal.BindToMoniker(s);

    ... // use the object

    // Dispose the object after done with using it
    Marshal.ReleaseComObject(sal);
    Console.WriteLine("Done...");
}
```

This concludes our discussion on queued components. There are many other possibilities with queued components. For example, you can also set the client to get a response back from the queued component. An easy way to do this is for the client to create a message queue and pass the identity of the message queue as a method parameter to the queued component. Interested readers may wish to check [Tap-01] to learn more about MSMQ and to explore various possibilities with queued components.

TRANSACTIONS

In an enterprise system, maintaining the integrity of data across various applications and machines is critical. Regardless of the scope of the application, at least some aspects of transaction processing have to be implemented to guarantee the integrity of the data. However, developing code to handle data integrity can be very challenging. COM+ provides a service called *automatic transaction processing* that simplifies this development effort. In this section, we look at how to develop .NET serviced components that use COM+ transaction services.

A Simple Banking System

We need an example to explore the transaction support under COM+. In our example, a customer, Jay, has an account at two banks—Fidelity and Schwab. Jay wants to transfer some money from his account at Fidelity to his account at Schwab.

The Databases

Each bank stores customer balances in a database table `Accounts`. The table contains two columns, `Pin` to store the unique account number of the customer and `Balance` to store the current balance.

We will use Microsoft Desktop Engine (MSDE) as our database server. It is a Microsoft SQL Server-compatible database engine that ships with .NET Framework SDK (as well as some other products).

MSDE comes with a command-line program, `osql.exe`. We use this tool to create two databases, `FidelityDB` and `SchwabDB`. The `FidelityDB` database stores Jay's balance under the account number `FID-3456` and the `SchwabDB` stores the balance under the account number `SCH-4567`. The initial balance in both accounts is $100,000.

To simplify the creation of the databases, I have created an SQL batch file that contains the following SQL commands:

```
-- File Transactions/DBCreation/CreateAccounts.cmd
create database FidelityDB
go
use FidelityDB
create table Accounts ([Pin] varchar (15) NOT NULL,
    [Balance] int NOT NULL)
create unique index Pin on Accounts([Pin])
insert into Accounts Values ('FID-3456', '100000')
go
create database SchwabDB
go
use SchwabDB
create table Accounts ([Pin] varchar (15) NOT NULL,
    [Balance] int NOT NULL)
create unique index Pin on Accounts([Pin])
insert into Accounts Values ('SCH-4567', '100000')
go
quit
```

You can submit this batch file as input to OSQL as follows:

```
osql -S .\NetSDK -E -i CreateAccounts.sql
```

Here, `.\NetSDK` identifies the instance of MSDE on the local machine and switch `-E` informs OSQL to use Windows authentication to connect to the MSDE, eliminating the need for a separate user name and password.

The Coding Logic

Our banking system example consists of three serviced components:

1. Component `FidelityBank` represents the banking activity at Fidelity.

2. Component `SchwabBank` represents the banking activity at Schwab.

3. Component `TransferFund` is a utility component that provides a utility method, `FromFidelityToSchwab`, to transfer funds from a Fidelity account to a Schwab account.

Here is the relevant code excerpt for each of these components:

```
// Project Transactions/Banks

public class FidelityBank : ServicedComponent, IDisposable {
    private MyAccountsDB m_db;

    public void WithdrawMoney(String pin, int amount) {
      int balance = m_db.GetBalance(pin);
```

```
                    m_db.UpdateBalance(pin, balance - amount);
                }
                ...
        }

        public class SchwabBank : ServicedComponent, IDisposable {
            private MyAccountsDB m_db;

            public void AddMoney(String pin, int amount) {
                int balance = m_db.GetBalance(pin);
                m_db.UpdateBalance(pin, balance+amount);
            }
                ...
        }

        public class TransferFunds : ServicedComponent {

            public void FromFidelityToSchwab(String fidelityPin,
                int amount, String schwabPin) {
              using(FidelityBank fB = new FidelityBank()) {
                using (SchwabBank sB = new SchwabBank()) {
                    fB.WithdrawMoney(fidelityPin, amount);
                    sB.AddMoney(schwabPin, amount);
                }
              }
            }
        }
```

Class MyAccountsDB that is being used in this code isolates the use of the database and provides useful methods such as GetBalance (to obtain the balance for an account) and UpdateBalance (to update the balance for an account). It uses ADO.NET to access the database. Here is the code for the class in its entirety. Here I am giving you an opportunity to learn the basics of ADO.NET in two minutes or less:

```
public class MyAccountsDB : IDisposable {
    private SqlConnection m_Conn;
    public MyAccountsDB(String dbName) {
        String s = String.Format(
"server=(local)\\NetSDK;Trusted_Connection=yes;database={0}",
          dbName);
      m_Conn = new SqlConnection(s);
      m_Conn.Open();
    }

    public int GetBalance(String pin) {
```

```csharp
    String s = String.Format(
      "SELECT Balance FROM Accounts WHERE [Pin] = '{0}'",
        pin);
    using (SqlCommand cmd = new SqlCommand(s, m_Conn)) {
      using (SqlDataReader reader = cmd.ExecuteReader()) {

        if (!reader.Read()) {
          s = String.Format("Unknown pin: '{0}'", pin);
          throw new Exception(s);
        }
        int balance = (int) reader["Balance"];
        return balance;
      }
    }
  }

  public void UpdateBalance(String pin, int balance) {
    String s = String.Format(
    "UPDATE Accounts SET Balance = {0} WHERE [Pin] = '{1}'",
        balance, pin);
    using (SqlCommand cmd = new SqlCommand(s, m_Conn)) {
      int numRecords = cmd.ExecuteNonQuery();
      if (0 == numRecords) {
        s = String.Format("Unknown pin: '{0}'", pin);
        throw new Exception(s);
      }
    }
  }

  //
  // Standard Dispose pattern
  //

  ~MyAccountsDB() {
    Dispose(false);
  }

  public void Close() {
    Dispose();
  }

  public void Dispose() {
    Dispose(true);
    GC.SuppressFinalize(this);
  }

  // Always dispose unmanaged resources
  // Disposing==true => dispose managed resource as well
  protected virtual void Dispose(bool disposing) {
```

```
   if (disposing) {
     // dispose managed resources
     if (null != m_Conn) {
       // Must always close the connection
       m_Conn.Close();
       m_Conn = null;
     }
   }
  }
}
```

It is time for us to configure the serviced components to participate in a transaction. However, let's first examine the requirements for a transaction.

Theory of Transaction

For our banking example, a transfer transaction consists of two operations:

1. Reduce the balance for the account in the `FidelityDB` database.
2. Add to the balance for the account in the `SchwabDB` database.

A transaction must be such that it entirely succeeds or entirely fails. This implies that all of the operations involved in the transaction must be updated successfully or nothing should be updated at all. This all-or-nothing proposition of a transaction is called *atomicity*.

A transaction must be consistent. Any individual operation within a transaction may leave the data in such a state that it violates the system's integrity. In our case, after the completion of the first operation, some money has been taken out of the system. After the completion of the second operation, either the system should rollback to the original state (restore the money that was taken out), or, on success, go to a new state that still maintains the overall integrity of the system.

The system should isolate any uncommitted changes. A second transaction that happens concurrently should only be able to see the data in the state before the first transaction begins or in the state after the first transaction completes, but not in some half-done mode between the two states.

Finally, a transaction must be durable; that is, when a transaction is committed, the data sources involved must guarantee that the updates will persist, even if the computer crashes (or the power goes off) immediately after the commit. This requires specialized transaction logging that would allow the data source's restart procedure to complete any unfinished operations.

Atomicity, consistency, isolation, and durability: A transaction should support these properties. This is the ACID test for transactions.

Configuring the Serviced Components

Using the COM+ transaction support under .NET is a two-step process:

1. Each serviced component that intends to participate in a transaction needs to indicate its interest.

2. Each serviced component method that participates in a transaction should vote for either committing or aborting the transaction. There are three ways to vote in a transaction, and we will look at each of them next.

Enabling Transaction Support

A serviced component indicates its interest in participating in a transaction by means of an attribute, `TransactionAttribute`. A constructor for this attribute takes a parameter of enumeration type `TransactionOption`. Here is what each of the options means:

- `TransactionOption.Required`: This value implies that a component must have a transaction to do its work. If the component's object is activated within the context of an existing transaction, the transaction is propagated to the new object. If the activator's context has no transactional information, then COM+ creates a brand new context containing transactional information and attaches it to the object.

- `TransactionOption.RequiresNew`: Sometimes an object might wish to initiate a new transaction, regardless of the transactional status of its activator. When a `RequiresNew` value is specified, COM+ initiates a new transaction that is distinct from the activator's transaction. The outcome of the new transaction has no affect on the outcome of the activator's transaction.

- `TransactionOption.Supported`: A component with this value indicates that it does not care for the presence or absence of a transaction. If the activator is participating in a transaction, the object propagates the transaction to any new object that it activates. The object itself may or may not participate in the transaction. This value is generally used when the component doesn't really need a transaction of its own but wants to be able to work with other components.

- `TransactionOption.NotSupported`: The component has no interest in participating in a transaction, regardless of the transactional status of its activator. This guarantees that the component's object neither votes in its activator's transaction nor begins a transaction of its own; nor does it propagate the caller's transaction to any object that it activates. This value should be chosen if you wish to break the continuity of an existing transaction.

- `TransactionOption.Disabled`: If a component will never access a resource, setting the transaction attribute to disabled eliminates any transaction-related overhead for the component. This attribute simulates the transaction behavior of a nonconfigured component.

Each of the three serviced components in our example uses the `Required` transaction option, as illustrated in the following code excerpt:

```
[Transaction(TransactionOption.Required)]
public class FidelityBank : ServicedComponent, IDisposable {
    ...
}
```

COM+ automatically begins a transaction when it encounters either of the following conditions:

1. When a nontransactional client activates an object with a component that has a transaction option set to either `Required` or `RequiresNew`.
2. When a transactional client calls an object with a component that has a transaction option set to `RequiresNew`.

The object responsible for beginning a new transaction is referred to as the *root object* of that transaction. As we will see shortly, this root object has a special role in completing the transaction.

An object that subsequently gets activated within the boundary of this transaction, and is marked as either `Required` or `Supported`, shares the transaction.

If an object is participating in a transaction, it can obtain its transaction ID from its context, as highlighted in the following code fragment:

```
[Transaction(TransactionOption.Required)]
public class FidelityBank : ServicedComponent, IDisposable {
    ...
    public void WithdrawMoney(String pin, int amount) {
      Console.WriteLine("Transaction ID: {0}",
        ContextUtil.TransactionId);
      ...
    }
}
```

A transaction completes when the root object of the transaction is deactivated. At this point, COM+ checks if all the objects have individually given their consent to commit the transaction. If all the participants have committed, COM+ goes ahead and commits the transaction, in which case the databases are updated with the new values. If any participant disapproved of the transaction, the transaction is aborted and the databases are rolled back to their original state.

A transaction is completed only after the root object of the transaction is deactivated. Forcing the clients to release the root object and recreate it for each transaction not only requires some programming effort on the part of the client, but is also inefficient. Marking the root object transactional component as JIT-activated and setting the deactivate-on-return bit within an appropriate method implementation deactivates the root object. Not only does this enforce transaction completion, but it also leaves the setup (the proxy, the COM communication channel, etc.) intact. In fact, JIT activation is so crucial for transactional correctness that, if a component is marked to participate in a transaction, COM+ ensures that the component is also automatically enabled for JIT activation.

Voting Using MyTransactionVote

A serviced component can use a static property MyTransactionVote, to vote on the transaction's outcome. This property is of enumeration type TransactionVote with two possible options—Commit and Abort.

The following code excerpt demonstrates the use of MyTransaction-Vote:

```
// Class SchwabBank
public void AddMoney(String pin, int amount) {
    try {
      int balance = m_db.GetBalance(pin);
      m_db.UpdateBalance(pin, balance+amount);
      ContextUtil.MyTransactionVote =
        TransactionVote.Commit;
    }catch(Exception e) {
      ContextUtil.MyTransactionVote =
        TransactionVote.Abort;
      throw e; // propagate the error
    }finally {
      ContextUtil.DeactivateOnReturn = true;
    }
}
```

Note that, irrespective of the outcome of the transaction, the deactivate-on-return bit must always be set to true.

It is also possible to avoid the exception-handling code with a little programming trick. Start with setting the deactivate-on-return bit to true and the transaction vote to abort. All that is needed when returning from the method is to set the transaction vote to commit. Using this logic, the preceding implementation of AddMethod can be rewritten as follows:

```
public void AddMoneyEx(String pin, int amount) {
    ContextUtil.DeactivateOnReturn = true;
    ContextUtil.MyTransactionVote =
        TransactionVote.Abort;
    int balance = m_db.GetBalance(pin);
    m_db.UpdateBalance(pin, balance+amount);
    ContextUtil.MyTransactionVote =
        TransactionVote.Commit;
}
```

Voting Using SetComplete

It is possible to combine the two operations, voting for the transaction and setting the deactivate-on-return bit to true, into one. This is done by means of two static methods that are available on the class ContextUtil — SetComplete (to commit the transaction) and SetAbort (to abort the transaction). The following code excerpt illustrates the use of these methods:

```
// Class FidelityBank
public void WithdrawMoney(String pin, int amount) {
    try {
        int balance = m_db.GetBalance(pin);
        if (balance < amount) {
            String s = String.Format(
            "Client '{0}' does not have enough balance",pin);
            throw new Exception(s);
        }
        m_db.UpdateBalance(pin, balance - amount);
        ContextUtil.SetComplete();
    }catch(Exception e) {
        ContextUtil.SetAbort();
        throw e; // propagate the error
    }
}
```

Note that there is no need to explicitly set the deactivate-on-return bit. The implementation of SetComplete as well as SetAbort set this bit to true internally.

It is also possible to rearrange this code to avoid the exception-handling logic. The trick is to start with calling `SetAbort` first, as shown here:

```
public void WithdrawMoneyEx(String pin, int amount) {
    ContextUtil.SetAbort(); // to start with
    int balance = m_db.GetBalance(pin);
    if (balance < amount) {
      String s = String.Format(
         "Client '{0}' does not have enough balance",pin);
      throw new Exception(s);
    }
    m_db.UpdateBalance(pin, balance - amount);
    ContextUtil.SetComplete();
}
```

Declarative Voting

Finally, perhaps the easiest way to participate in a transaction is by marking a method with an attribute, `AutoCompleteAttribute`, and enabling it to true, as illustrated in the following code excerpt:

```
// Class TransferFunds
[AutoComplete(true)]
public void FromFidelityToSchwab(String fidelityPin,
       int amount, String schwabPin) {
    using(FidelityBank fB = new FidelityBank()) {
       using (SchwabBank sB = new SchwabBank()) {
          fB.WithdrawMoney(fidelityPin, amount);
          sB.AddMoney(schwabPin, amount);
       }
    }
}
```

When a method is marked with `AutoCompleteAttribute`, COM+ automatically calls `SetComplete` if the method call returns normally. If the method call throws an exception, then COM+ automatically aborts the transaction, as if `SetAbort` was called.

Finally, here is the code excerpt for the client application that wishes to transfer the money:

```
// Project Transactions/MyClient

public static void TransferFunds() {
    try {
      using (TransferFunds tf = new TransferFunds()) {
      // tf.FromFidelityToSchwab("FID-3456", 100, "SCH-4567");
        tf.FromFidelityToSchwab("FID-3456", 100, "SCH-4568");
```

```
  }
  Console.WriteLine("Transfer success");
}catch(Exception e) {
  Console.WriteLine("Transfer failed: {0}",e.Message);
  }
}
```

Using the account number SCH-4568 instead of SCH-4567 causes the transaction to fail. You can verify this by checking the tables in the databases.

At this point, you must have a fairly good understanding of how a serviced component can participate in a transaction. There is one thing that might have puzzled you. It makes sense to have FidelityBank and Schwab-Bank as two different serviced components. However, why do we need a third serviced component, TransferFunds? It seems the logic of transferring funds could have been implemented in the client application itself.

By using the TransferFunds object as the root of the transaction, and instantiating the two bank components in the context of the same transaction, we tie the operations from two banks together as a single transaction. Had the client application implemented the logic of instantiating the bank objects and transferring the funds between them, it would have resulted in two separate and independent transactions. The outcome of one transaction would not affect the outcome of the other. You can witness this behavior by temporarily removing the TransactionAttribute on TransferFunds and dumping the transaction ID from each of the methods involved in the transaction.

Essentially, the reason the client application had to rely on a serviced component was that the client itself could not initiate the transaction.

Extending Transactions to Clients

It is possible to set a nonserviced component to participate in a transaction. The COM+ library defines a class, TransactionContext, that the client can use for this purpose. When this class is instantiated, it automatically starts a transaction. Other objects can be instantiated in the same transaction context by means of a method, CreateInstance, on the TransactionContext object. The client itself must vote on the transaction by calling either Commit or Abort on the TransactionContext object. The following client-side code excerpt demonstrates the use of this class:

```
// Project Transactions/MyClient

public static void ParticipateInTransaction() {
    // Get the transaction object
    TransactionContext tc = new TransactionContext();
```

```
    // Create fidelity bank object and invoke
    // WithdrawMoney method on it using Reflection
    Object oF = tc.CreateInstance("Fidelity.Bank");
    Type tF = oF.GetType();
    MethodInfo mF = tF.GetMethod("WithdrawMoney");
    mF.Invoke(oF, new Object[]{"FID-3456", 100});

    // Create schwab bank object and invoke
    // AddMoney method on it using Reflection
    Object oS = tc.CreateInstance("Schwab.Bank");
    Type tS = oS.GetType();
    MethodInfo mS = tS.GetMethod("AddMoney");
    mS.Invoke(oS, new Object[]{"SCH-4568", 100});

    // Everything is OK. Commit
    tc.Commit();
    Console.WriteLine("Transfer success ...");
}
```

Note that the default behavior for the `TransactionContext` object is to abort the transaction. The client has to explicitly call `Commit` to indicate its positive intentions. Obviously, all the participating transactional objects also have to approve of the transaction for it to commit.

Also note that this specific code relies on `Reflection` to invoke the methods. This is because the proxy object that is returned by `CreateInstance` does not support the original type. Casting the object to its original type, as shown in the following code, causes the runtime to throw an exception:

```
Object oF = tc.CreateInstance("Fidelity.Bank");
FidelityBank fB = (FidelityBank) oF;
```

The only other way to avoid using Reflection is to encapsulate the functionality of the serviced component in an interface. The object returned by `CreateInstance` can then be cast to an appropriate interface and methods can be invoked from the interface.

Extending Transactions to Web Services

The .NET Framework makes it possible for a Web service method to participate in a transaction. Recall from Chapter 6 that a Web service method needs to be marked with an attribute, `WebMethodAttribute`. An overloaded constructor of this attribute takes a parameter of type `TransactionOption`. The following code excerpt for a Web service implements our logic of transferring funds from Fidelity to Schwab:

```
// File Transactions/TransferFunds.asmx

[WebService(Namespace="http://localhost/TransactionDemo/")]
public class TransferFunds : WebService {

    [WebMethod(TransactionOption =
TransactionOption.Required)]
    public void FromFidelityToSchwab(String fidelityPin,
        int amount, String schwabPin) {
      using(FidelityBank fB = new FidelityBank()) {
        using (SchwabBank sB = new SchwabBank()) {
          fB.WithdrawMoney(fidelityPin, amount);
            sB.AddMoney(schwabPin, amount);
        }
      }
    }
}
```

Note that Web service methods need not explicitly vote on a transaction. If an exception occurs within a Web service method, the transaction is automatically aborted (as if SetAbort was called). If the method returns successfully without throwing an exception, then the transaction is automatically committed (as if SetComplete was called). Of course, the Web service can still use ContextUtil to explicitly vote on the transaction.

Also note that for this particular example to work, you also need to turn client impersonation on via Web.Config and configure IIS virtual directly for Windows authentication. Otherwise, the call to open the database connection might fail.

SUMMARY

The .NET Framework provides many types to support building enterprise systems, defined under the namespace System.EnterpriseServices. The first release of .NET depends on COM+ to provide the needed enterprise services.

A .NET component that uses .NET/COM+ services is called a serviced component. Developing a serviced component is a four-step process:

1. Create a serviced component class that inherits from a standard class ServicedComponent.

2. Use declarative attributes on the class to indicate one or more COM+ services that are needed by the class.

3. Configure the COM+ application by defining one or more assembly-level attributes such as the name of the application, the unique GUID of the application, the services the COM+ application intends to use, and so on.

4. Register the assembly in the COM+ catalog. This can be done either manually by using the tool `regsvcs.exe`, programmatically by using the `RegistrationHelper` class, or automatically when the serviced component is used for the first time. Only strong-named assemblies can be registered in the COM+ catalog.

A client uses a serviced component object just as any other .NET object. The important thing to remember is to dispose the object after its use.

The .NET/COM+ plumbing provides many enterprise services. In this chapter we looked at some frequently used services such as JIT activation, object pooling, role-based security, queued components, and transaction support.

The COM+ infrastructure offers some other services such as synchronization, loosely coupled events, shared properties, and so on, that I haven't covered in this chapter. In particular, I haven't covered COM+ synchronization services, as .NET provides the same service natively. You should be able to use any other COM+ services using the .NET SDK documentation as a reference, combined with your knowledge of serviced components from this chapter. Interested readers may also wish to look at [EWA-01], [And-02], and [Mcc-02] to supplement their knowledge.

REFERENCES

[Tap-01]   Tapadiya, Pradeep, *COM+ Programming—A Practical Guide Using Visual C++ and ATL*, ISBN 0-13-088674-2, Prentice Hall PTR, 2001.

[Ewa-01]   Ewald, Tim, "COM+ Integration: How .NET Enterprise Services Can Help You Build Distributed Applications," *MSDN Magazine*, October 2001.
msdn.microsoft.com/msdnmag/issues/01/10/complus/complus.asp

[And-02]   Andera, Craig, and Ewald, Tim, "COM+ 1.5: Discover Powerful Low-Level Programming in Windows XP with New COM+ APIs," *MSDN Magazine*, April 2002.
msdn.microsoft.com/msdnmag/issues/02/04/COMXP/COMXP.asp

[Mcc-02]   McCarthy, Tim, "Using COM+ Services in .NET," MSDN Library, February 2002.
msdn.microsoft.com/library/en-us/dndotnet/html/comservnet.asp

Index

A

Abstract method/class, 53
`Activator`, 224–225
ADO.NET, 12, 114
"Anywhere computing" vision, 4–5
Application domains, 209–210, 210f, 277
    creation code example, 211
    domain-neutral assemblies, 213–214
    friendly name code example, 210–211
    global exception handler, 212–213
    listing, 211
    relationship with processes, 210, 214
    and threads, 214, 222–223
    unloading, 211–212, 214
ASP.NET, 12, 278
    contexts, 114
    hosting under, 240–242
        ASP.NET-hosted application configuration
            file, 80
        shadow copy mechanism, 242
    Web services, 247
        case example, 247–249
        customization/HTTP protocols, 255
        customization/SOAP message formatting,
            256
        ease of use, 250–253
        and MBV semantics, 248
        vs. NET remoting, 249–250
        state management, 253–254
        testing, 250, 251f
        tracing, 256–258
ASP.NET Web services security, 252, 391,
    405–406
    ASP.Net authentication, 399–400
    CAS, 402
        full trust, 402
        high trust, 402
        low trust, 403
        no trust, 403
    hosting ASP.NET under IIS, 391–395, 392f
        anonymous access, 395–396
        basic authentication, 397–398
        digest authentication, 398–399
        integrated Windows authentication, 396
    impersonation, 403–404
    role-based security, 400–402
Assemblies, 19, 22t, 61, 63–65, 88, 108, 116–117
    attributes for COM+ applications, 413–417,
        413t
    binding behavior, 86–88, 308
        Log Viewer, 88
        see also Configuration files
    code protection feature, 134
    deferred/lazy loading, 87, 93
    domain-neutral, 212, 213–214
    download cache, 117
    and dynamic linking, 43–44, 87
    evidence, 367
    identification, 65, 69–70
        culture, 66
        name, 65

free subscription

Want to know about new products, services and solutions from Hewlett-Packard Company — as soon as they're invented?

Need information about new HP services to help you implement new or existing products?

Looking for HP's newest solution to a specific challenge in your business?

inview features the latest from HP!

4 easy ways to subscribe, and it's FREE:

- **fax** complete and fax the form below to (651) 430-3388, or

- **online** sign up online at www.hp.com/go/inview, or

- **email** complete the information below and send to hporders@earthlink.net, or

- **mail** complete and mail the form below to:

Twin Cities Fulfillment Center
Hewlett-Packard Company
P.O. Box 408
Stillwater, MN 55082

reply now and don't miss an issue!

name _____ title _____

company _____ dept./mail stop _____

address _____

city _____ state _____ zip _____

email _____ signature _____ date _____

please indicate your industry below:

- [ ] accounting
- [ ] education
- [ ] financial services
- [ ] government
- [ ] healthcare/medical
- [ ] legal
- [ ] manufacturing
- [ ] publishing/printing
- [ ] online services
- [ ] real estate
- [ ] retail/wholesale distrib
- [ ] technical
- [ ] telecommunications
- [ ] transport and travel
- [ ] utilities
- [ ] other: _____

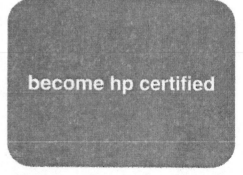
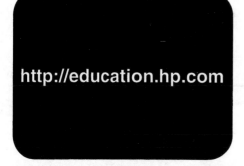